Three Centuries of
Children's Books in Europe

BETTINA HÜRLIMANN

Three Centuries of
Children's Books in Europe

Translated and edited by Brian W. Alderson

O. Speckter fec.

THE WORLD PUBLISHING COMPANY
CLEVELAND AND NEW YORK

Published by The World Publishing Company
2231 West 110th Street, Cleveland, Ohio 44102

First published 1959 under the title *Europäische Kinderbücher in drei Jahrhunderten*
by Atlantis Verlag, Zürich

© 1959 Atlantis Verlag AG, Zürich
English translation © Oxford University Press 1967. First published in this edition 1967

First United States Edition, 1968
Library of Congress Catalog Card Number 68–14703

The illustration on page 284 is from *A hole is to dig* by Ruth Kraus.
Harper and Brothers, New York, 1952. Line drawing by Maurice Sendak.

*Printed in Great Britain by Richard Clay (The Chaucer Press), Ltd.,
Bungay, Suffolk*

CONTENTS

Preface to the Second Edition   vii

Translator's Preface   ix

Introduction: A summary of development   xi

I   A MAGIC HORN FOR CHILDREN   I

2   ONCE UPON A TIME   21

3   THE UGLY DUCKLING   42

4   DR. HEINRICH HOFFMANN   53

5   JABBERWOCKY   64

6   FANTASY AND REALITY   76

7   THE LITTLE PRINCE FROM OUTER SPACE   93

8   ROBINSON   99

9   FROM DEERSLAYER TO OLD SHATTERHAND   113

10   EDUCATION THROUGH PICTURES   127

11   PHOTOGRAPHY   145

12   COLOUR PRINTS   152

13   WHAM! SOK! THINKS!   160

14   POLITICS IN CHILDREN'S BOOKS   173

15   JEAN DE BRUNHOFF   195

16   PICTURE-BOOKS IN THE TWENTIETH CENTURY   201

17   TOWARDS A HISTORY OF CHILDREN'S BOOKS IN SWITZERLAND   246

18   MEN OF LETTERS WRITE FOR CHILDREN   256

Life with children's books   267

Bibliography   272

Index   285

LIST OF PLATES

FACING PAGE

     I The Brothers Grimm   32

    II 'Die Viehmännin'   33

   III Hans Christian Andersen telling fairy stories   48

   IV EDGEWORTH, Maria. *Les enfans, ou les caractères*   49

    V Dr. Heinrich Hoffmann at about thirty years of age   54

   VI *Top:* Gavarni's *Les enfants terribles*   55
        Bottom: Hoffmann's *Struwwelpeter*

  VII HOFFMANN, Heinrich. *Der Velocipeter*   60

 VIII Lewis Carroll in 1863   66

   IX CARROLL, Lewis. *Alice's adventures under ground*   67

    X AYMÉ, Marcel. *Les contes du chat perché*   86

   XI BERTUCH, Friedrich Johann Justin. *Bilderbuch für Kinder*   87

  XII WYSS, J. D. *Charackteristick meiner Kinder in einer Robinsonade*   106

 XIII LONGFELLO, H. *Pyesne o Gayavate*   107

 XIV BÖER, Friedrich. *Klaus der Herr der Eisenbahnen*   148

  XV BERGMAN, A. *Micky the fox-cub*   149

 XVI AMICIS, Edmondo de. *Heart, a book for boys*   178

XVII ... *I never saw another butterfly*   179

XVIII Jean de Brunhoff   196

 XIX DEHMEL, Paula and Richard. *Fitzebutze*   206

  XX *Top:* BÄUMER, Eduard and Valerie. *Die Geschichte vom Fluss*   207
       Bottom: SCHNITTER, Rosie. *Der Leuchtturm*

 XXI SCHEPER-BERKENKAMP, Lou. *Die Geschichten von Jan und Jon und von*
       ihrem Lotsen-Fisch   220

XXII *Top:* SLADEK, Josef V. *Sladek detem*   221
       Bottom: CHUKOVSKY, Kornei. *Tarakanishche*

XXIII ALLINGHAM, W. *In fairyland*   224

XXIV HRUBIN, František. *Řikejte si se mnou*   225

 XXV LEWITT-HIM. *The football's revolt*   228

XXVI OLSEN, Ib Spang. *Det lille lokomotiv*   229

XXVII SAMIVEL. *Bon voyage, Monsieur Dumollet*   236

XXVIII Hans Fischer   237

Preface to the Second Edition

I would never have had the courage to prepare a second edition of this book had I not been convinced by innumerable kind letters and by the enthusiasm of the Press that there does exist a need for a book of this kind. It did not necessarily have to be a book like this, but, as one critic wrote to me, now that this one is here it has the duty to be here in a fuller and better edition.

But I must not conceal the chief reason for my hesitation, which stems from the enormous amount that has happened in recent years in the field of children's books. It has become quite impossible today for one person, however conscientious, to survey the whole field in just one country, let alone a continent or the world itself.

If, for this reason, this edition is found to have even more gaps in it than the first, I have, nevertheless, once again made it my principle to describe no books which I have not myself examined.

The main plan of the book remains the same. Here and there passages have been retouched, filled out, and, of course, corrected, and the following chapters in particular have been augmented: 'Politics in children's books', 'Photography in children's books', 'Fantasy and reality', and 'Men of letters write for children'. But the chapters on Cowboys and Indians and on factual books have also had fresh material added, and the bibliography has been considerably extended.

There was also a great temptation to include in the chapters on nursery and fairy stories much of what I have in the meantime learnt from many other countries. But the new edition ought not to differ more than is necessary from the first one in either price or scope and I therefore refrained from extending these self-contained chapters too greatly. The section on comics is new, as is the chapter on Swiss children's books.

Most of all, however, I received requests for the expansion of the chapter on picture-books. Already in the first edition this had caused me a lot of headaches, for even five years ago it was impossible to include everything of importance. I therefore kept to my own collection, assembled over twenty years, which is to say that I allowed myself the luxury of considerable subjectivity. Any other choice would have been just as incomplete.

Apart, therefore, from some small additions and some fresh comments this chapter has not been greatly altered. Instead I have decided, from my realization of the special position of picture-books today, to publish a supplementary volume[1] which will be devoted entirely to modern picture-books throughout the world, with examples of both their illustrations and their accompanying texts.

Finally, I should like once again to thank those colleagues and friends who have brought me material from all over the world, and those authors who took so much interest in my work.

My especial thanks this time, however, go to the critics, both the friendly and the less friendly. One among them—a teacher and a critic in Hamburg and an outstanding authority on modern children's books—should be particularly mentioned here, for during the last two years he has suggested many improvements and has given me much valuable material and much constant encouragement. He must excuse me if I have not been able to make use of all the suggestions which he has offered.

While I dedicated the first edition of this book to my husband and my children, around me as I write are two prancing granddaughters. To them likewise I owe a debt of gratitude, for they have seen to it that a book which was begun from a love of children has not turned into one of arid pedantry. To them, Bettina and Magdalena, as well as to my grandsons Thomas and Andreas in distant Venezuela, may this book be dedicated with my love.

BETTINA HÜRLIMANN

Uerikon: August 1963

---

[1] This volume, *Die Welt im Bilderbuch*, is now published and an English edition is in preparation.

Translator's Preface

Bettina Hürlimann intended her *Europäische Kinderbücher in drei Jahrhunderten* to be an informal introduction to a neglected field of study. In making this translation from the Second Edition (Zürich, 1963) I have carried out a number of alterations for which an explanation should be given.

The most obvious of these changes is in the order of the chapters, which I have here rearranged in the hope of emphasizing a little more clearly the comparative and historical aspects of the book. The same intention lies behind a number of silent alterations which have been made in the body of the text—certain passages being shortened or extended to give English readers a clearer picture of the events discussed.

Such tinkering about as this would, of course, be unwarrantable without the author's knowledge and I have to thank Mrs. Hürlimann very much for giving me a free hand to make these changes where I have thought necessary. She has also been most helpful in settling for me many questions of detail and in providing me with the framework for a substantially revised Introduction. Some of this I have rewritten myself, and I have added some paragraphs to replace Mrs. Hürlimann's chapter on American children's books, which has been omitted from this edition.

In the expression of my own opinions, and in the addition of one or two facts of interest mainly to English readers, I have resorted to the cumbersome measure of numbered footnotes and I have also supplied several chapters with tailpiece comments and book-lists. This has been done to show how certain European children's books have been received in this country and to provide references to English translations which are currently available. Purists will find a deplorable lack of balance and consistency in the way that this has been done, but to do it fully would have been to produce a supplementary volume within the work translated.

I have also attempted to check and to add to dates and other bibliographical facts given in the original book, supplying the titles of books in their original language where possible and adding translations where necessary. Only after beginning this task did I discover its inherent problems and the book makes no claim to being either more consistent or less fallible than many other surveys of this kind.

Among the many people who should be thanked for their help as this translation proceeded are: Miss Eva Berg, who assisted in the unravelling of several knotty bits of German prose; Mrs. Jella Lepman, who gave permission for me to translate the passage from *Die Kinderbuchbrücke* on p. 181; Miss Cecily Barker for information about picture-books and costume books at the turn of the century; and the editors of children's books for the following publishers: Messrs. Blackie, Bodley Head, Routledge and Kegan Paul, Frederick Warne, and Edmund Ward.

My colleagues, Miss Eleanor von Schweinitz and Mr. Edward Garrett, have given up much of their time to practical assistance on the bibliography and index, and my wife has laboured heroically in the preparation of the typescript. Not only did she decipher my appalling manuscript but she has also protected me for several months from the ravages of four small boys who, alas, could not be kept quiet on children's books all the time.

Finally, I do not know if it is in order for translators to dedicate their translations, but if it is, I should like to inscribe this to Mr. Don Gresswell who first aroused my interest in the fascinating cross-currents of influence among the writers and producers of children's books in Europe.

The opportunity has been taken in printing this edition to amend a few small errors and to give the names of American publishers in those bibliographical entries where there was an American publication.

B. W. A.

1968

Introduction
or A summary of the development of children's books in Europe

'Children's books are here to be pulled to pieces,' said Dr. Hoffmann, the author of *Struwwelpeter*, to his publisher during a discussion on the production of his now famous picture-book. This wholesome precept received all too welcome a recognition, with the result that it is now exceedingly difficult to write a history of children's books founded on a full knowledge of contemporary editions. The more beloved and successful a children's book was, the more complete has been its disappearance from the surface of its age, while those handsomely bound and decorated volumes of maxims, alphabets, and moral tales which survive on family bookshelves and in the shops of second-hand booksellers give a very one-sided impression of early children's books.

One of my chief aims in this book has been to revitalize our rather dusty image of this literature and to set it in some kind of relationship with present times. But unlike many of the admirable histories of children's books which also have this aim, I am here dealing not with one country alone but with publications throughout Europe. This has led me to modify the customary historical approach and to divide my survey first of all into subject groups and, as I have pursued the treatment of these subjects by different countries, so I have dwelt at length on matters which I found particularly attractive. The result of such indulgence is that a number of subjects have disappeared entirely from view and could easily form the material for a second volume. The most obvious omissions here are such matters as 'children's books and religion', 'the children's novel of the last few decades', 'the historical story', and that large body of 'ABC books' and books for the child who has not yet learned to read.

The initial impetus to this book was given by a request that I received to write an entry for an encyclopaedia under the heading: 'Children's books'. I soon found, however, that my inclinations carried me beyond the broad survey that this required and farther and farther into a detailed examination of the literary and sociological background to the books in question. Furthermore, this was taking place during the boom years for children's books after the Second World War, when new ideas and new dangers were appearing almost daily. So extensive has this output been in terms of number and variety that young literary historians, sociologists, and teachers will find much to occupy them in their researches for a long time to come.

Before launching into my own examination of the subjects I have chosen, the general reader may like to have a brief synopsis of the way that children's books have evolved in Europe during the last three hundred years. In a later chapter I have occasion to refer to Ellen Key's prescient and enthusiastic *The century of the child*, first published in Stockholm in 1900. Here she foresees the emphasis which was to be put on child-development in our century and makes it quite clear to us how late the child came into his rightful share of the life and literature of European society.

Almost exactly three hundred years ago, in the age of Franz Hals and Rembrandt, Velazquez and Murillo, a little book was published in Nuremberg entitled *Orbis sensualium pictus*. Its author was the Moravian bishop Jan Amos Komensky or Comenius and, like the great painters of his time, he was among the first to recognize the child as an individual. His book is considered in detail in a later chapter, but the importance of the man lies in the effort which he made to introduce a new humanity into the idea of education at a time when Europe was still suffering from the effects of the Thirty Years War.

The *Orbis pictus* long remained a unique achievement. The age once again forgot the child or saw him only as a damned soul who must be saved from perdition by a rigorous pietism. Children were not born to live happy but to die holy and true education lay in preparing the soul to meet its maker. The result of this was a crop of seventeenth-century books zealously depicting for children the holy lives and joyous deaths of their little contemporaries. Even the first half of the eighteenth century would have been a similar blank—or rather black—page in the history of children's books, had not Rousseau discovered *Robinson Crusoe* (first edition, London, 1719), and had not the fairy stories of Charles Perrault brought in a little sweetness and light from 1700 onward.

The books which children had apart from these were little more than cunningly wrapped instruction. A French educational fanatic, Madame de Genlis, carried things particularly far in this branch of literature and became a world success. Having herself grown up almost without schooling, she saw children's books as being nothing but a means for propagating education. Her chief work, *Adèle et Théodore, ou lettres sur l'éducation* (1782) is still worth looking at today, partly for laughs and partly as a reminder of the progress which has been made in educational theory.

Apart from instruction, however, the eighteenth century was a great time for morality and much good ink and paper was expended in persuading children of the profits of virtuous behaviour. Perhaps the culmination of this movement can be seen in Mrs. Sherwood's extraordinary work *The history of the Fairchild family*[1] (1818) with its famous afternoon outing to see the hanged man on the forest gallows.

That instruction and morality need not always be so obtrusively provided is apparent to an increasing extent in a number of books which were revolutionary for their time. Basedow's *Elementarwerk*, with Chodowiecki's masterly illustrations, and *Bertuchs Bilderbuch für Kinder*, which both appeared in the last quarter of the learned eighteenth century, are still, pictorially at any rate, handsome and enjoyable books. Campe's *Robinson der Jüngere* (1779) also appeared at this time—so the fruits of the Enlightenment were not entirely flavourless where children were concerned.

pag 209.

Traurige Folgen des Ungehorsams.

SCHERWOOD, Mstrs. *Die Familie Fairschild*. Düsselthal, 1839. Lithograph by W. Severin, showing as Hoffmann was to do a few years later 'the dire consequences of disobedience'.

Throughout the eighteenth century the appetite of children for books was difficult to satiate. We feel something of this hunger when we read in *Dichtung und Wahrheit* how Goethe would hurry down into the street to spend his pocket-money on a little book calling itself a *Volksschrift* or a *Volksbuch*, which 'since they were printed with battered type on the foulest blotting-paper were almost illegible. . . . We children therefore had the good fortune to

[1] The text of this passage is given in Darton's *Children's books in England* pp. 176–7. Comparison with a later German edition based on a French version, Mstrs. Scherwood: *Die Familie Fairschild; zum Heile der lieben Jugend. Nach der französischen Übersetzung deutsch bearbeitet* (Düsselthal, 1839), shows some modifications for Continental sensibilities. The corpse has gone, but the sermon remains. (B.A.)

JACK AND JILL,

AND

OLD DAME GILL.

Read it who will,
They'll laugh their fill

———

YORK :
Printed and Sold by J. Kendrew, Colliergate.

JACK AND JILL.

Jack and Jill
Went up the hill,
To fetch a pail of water
Jack fell down,
And broke his crown,
And Jill came tumbling after.

AND OLD DAME GILL.   3

A a   B b

Then up Jack got,
And home did trot,
As fast as he could caper ;
Dame Gill did the job,
To plaster his nob
With vinegar and brown paper.

4   JACK AND JILL.

C c   D d

Then Jill came in,
And she did grin,
To see Jack's paper plaster ;
Her mother whipt her,
Across her knee,
For laughing at Jack's disaster.

Four pages from an English chapbook, published c. 1820.
(Reproduced from *The Oxford dictionary of nursery rhymes*, p. 225.)

find daily on the little table in front of the second-hand bookseller's doorway these precious remnants of the Middle Ages: *Eulenspiegel, The four sons of Aymon, Fair Melusine, Kaiser Octavian, Fortunatus*—the whole bunch, right

It is not the purpose of this present edition to trace the history of American children's books, nor even their introduction to Europe, but it is important to recognize the cross-currents of influence which exist between the continents. Along with Fenimore Cooper and Harriet Beecher Stowe such writers as Mark Twain and Joel Chandler Harris produced books which were popular not only in English-speaking countries (most of whom had to have *Uncle Remus* translated anyway) but also throughout Europe. And unlike the children's books of Nathaniel Hawthorne or the pirated and widely imitated Peter Parley (Samuel Goodrich) they were popular for their specifically American character.

At the present time and at all levels, from Mickey Mouse to Laura Ingalls Wilder, the European market is permeated by American writing or by graphic work originating in the United States. There are those who find this regrettable and it is perhaps especially so for the smaller countries whose native productions may be at a disadvantage against the 'syndicated' books which can be imported so much more cheaply. But one can also point to the many translations of foreign books which achieve an often simultaneous publication in England and America; and one has only to look at the names of some of the greatest American picture-book artists—Rojankovsky and Provensen, Artzybasheff and Sendak, Duvoisin and D'Aulaire—to realize that the national barriers are down, the heritage a common one.

It is against this background, then, of uncertain beginnings, of the trials and errors of moralists and entertainers, that the details in the following chapters must be considered. Naturally, with the growing demands for books for enjoyment and with the great changes in nineteenth-century graphic techniques, there were important developments in the illustration of children's books as well as their writing. Many of my comments on this will be found in the extensive survey of picture-books which occurs later in the book.

I have, however, tried to see all these developments in the light of our present time, more than half-way through 'the century of the child'. For this in some ways is a time of crisis for children's books. The unhindered expansion of the years since 1945, the increasing internationalism and standardization of products is perhaps diverting our attention from the simple fact of what a book is to a child—what the *Orbis pictus* achieved in 1658, what Shockheaded Peter meant to a little boy in Frankfurt-am-Main nearly two hundred years later. For in this restless age of technology, when the emphasis is always on records of attainment and higher productivity, there is some danger of forgetting that a child does not require too much in the way of books. What he does need are the right books at the right time so that he may find in literature a true point of balance in an often disordered life. It is for us as parents or teachers, librarians or publishers, to recognize this need and to know how best, how most imaginatively, to fulfil it.

At the same time there were significant developments in the children's novel and the story of adventure—a category which in the past had relied on such adult books as *Don Quixote, Robinson Crusoe,* and *Gulliver's travels* for its most entertaining contributions. Once again books in the English language showed the way, and such authors as James Fenimore Cooper, Harriet Beecher Stowe, and Frederick Marryat became known throughout Europe.

DAY, Thomas. *Tommy och Harry.* Sweden, 1861. Illustrations from a Swedish adaptation of *The history of Sandford and Merton.* London, 1781–83. (Reproduced from EVA VON ZWEIG- BERGK, *Barnboken i Sverige 1750–1950.*)

Harry fattade ormen om nacken och kastade den långt bort. Sid 7.

Tommy var så ifrig och uppmärksam, att han första dagen lärde sig hela alfabetet. Sid. 22.

Leatherstocking and Uncle Tom brought with them a new range of experience for the European reader. Until the nineteenth century the traffic in popular literature across the Atlantic had been largely in a westerly direction, but as America explored her own character she began to return influence for influence. In the field of literature there was no place for the Monroe Doctrine.

B

for adults. But in 1804 when Ann and Jane Taylor (with some other 'young persons') published their *Original poems for infant minds* they brought back a natural tone of voice to children's poetry in England which had not been heard since Isaac Watts issued his *Divine songs attempted in easy language* in 1715.

> No, little worm, you need not slip
> Into your hole with such a skip;
> Drawing the gravel as you glide
> On to your smooth and slimy side.

This may not be great writing, but it combines a verbal and a graphic felicity in a way particularly attractive to children. Both in their nature poems and in their cautionary verses the Taylor sisters exploited the requirements of the didactic with a sure sense of what would amuse their readers:

> 'I think I want some pies this morning,'
> Said Dick, stretching himself and yawning;
> So down he threw his slate and books
> And sauntered to the pastry cooks.

What follows is a lesson in the virtue of charity, but it is a very readable one and, given the circumstances, it is not surprising that these poems not only found favour in England and America but were also translated into Dutch, German and Russian.

Three years after their first appearance another poem was published which made no concessions at all to the demands of moral instruction. *The butterfly's ball* (1807) was written by William Roscoe for the entertainment of his own family circle, but by its very artlessness it made an immediate appeal and was followed by what Harvey Darton has called 'a crop of sequels'.

Despite this, the moralists must have continued to hold their ground for when, in 1823, the first translation of Grimm appeared as *German popular stories* the translators saw fit to lament the neglect of popular tales in England: 'They are nearly discarded from the libraries of childhood. Philosophy is made the companion of the nursery; we have lisping chemists and leading-string mathematicians; this is the age of reason, not of imagination; and the loveliest dreams of fairy innocence are considered vain and frivolous.' And indeed it was only with the arrival of Edward Lear and Lewis Carroll that frivolity gained its head, but once it had done so it brought to the English child a treasure in books possessed by no other nation of the world.

Once the principle of children's books as entertainment began to be accepted, Europe saw the emergence of more and more of them. Germany had her *Struwwelpeter* and, later, the slapstick work of Wilhelm Busch and Franz Pocci. Even France, previously poor in literature expressly for children, produced a best-seller in *Les malheurs de Sophie* by La Comtesse de Ségur (1864).

down to *The wandering Jew*; everything was there for us so long as we desired such things, such masterpieces, instead of some alternative delicacy.'

Not only young Wolfgang Goethe was aware of this hunger for an imaginative complement to the all too serious reading-matter of that time, when even fairy stories had only become really respectable since the turn of the century. Just as Germany had her *Volksbücher*, so France had her *Librairie bleue* whose volumes were sold in the streets by travelling pedlars and contained the same sort of legends, fairy stories, and adventures. In England they were called chapbooks, and in England for the first time a bookseller was to draw far-reaching conclusions from the fact that a great many children belonged to the readership of these little books. This was John Newbery, who moved into London from Reading in 1743 and two years later set up his famous shop at the 'Bible and Sun' in St. Paul's Churchyard. Here once again, the man is important because he took a leading part in establishing children's books not just as manuals of behaviour but as reading that was to be enjoyed.

Towards the end of the eighteenth century, and especially in Germany, the fairy story was becoming more and more respectable. In the 1780s, well before the collections of the Brothers Grimm, Musäus published his *Volksmärchen der Deutschen*—stories which even today have not lost their attractiveness. Slightly later, but still with his roots in the eighteenth century, the writer Christoph von Schmid (1786–1854) published many tales and Bible stories for Catholic children which have continued in print down to the present time. Such was his fame in his own day that he was raised to the ranks of the nobility 'for his services to literature'.

A contemporary of Schmid's who sank his roots deep in the Allemannic province of south-west Germany was Johann Peter Hebel[1] (1760–1826). Although much of his work was written in the dialect of the area it has a poetry which has survived translation to High German. Along with such famous figures as Matthias Claudius, the Brothers Grimm, and the romantics Clemens Brentano and Achim von Arnim, Hebel saw the start of one of the great periods of German literature which was reflected in the children's books of the time by a new richness of imagination stemming directly from the revival of fairy tales and folk poetry. Even the chapbook stories were given a new literary dress in the work of Gustav Schwab (*Deutsche Volksbücher*, 1835) and Karl Simrock (*Die deutschen Volksbücher*, 1845–67).

In England, too, the foundations laid by Newbery were not being entirely neglected. While there was no reversion to folk literature comparable to that in Germany, books continued to be produced for children's enjoyment. The most notable contributions were to the small range of really successful poetry for children—an area all too often filled by the anthologized cast-offs of writers

---

[1] Hebel was much celebrated for his retelling of Bible stories and a translation of these, with a sympathetic introduction by Emily Anderson, was published in London by Barrie and Rockliff in 1961. Schmid's most celebrated book is, of course, *The basket of flowers* which has gone through some thirty different editions in English since its translation in 1851. (B.A.)

I A MAGIC HORN FOR CHILDREN
Nursery rhymes and songs then and now

True nursery rhymes belong to a time quite different from our own, and it is a remarkable fact that they still survive at all. When they came into being, day-time and night-time were still governed simply by the sun, the moon, and the stars, while fires and candles were the attendant sources of warmth and light. The darkness was peopled by ghosts, a man lived in the moon, and nightingales could still be heard singing in the forests. Fathers still rode on horses and mothers took 'butter from the barrel' and 'meal from the sack'. People used to address the sun as a lady and the moon as a gentleman—except when he was a shepherd looking after the flocks of stars.[1] Even the rain was personified and spoken to in an appropriate fashion, for he gave longevity —and the rains of May were good for growing children.

Regen, Regen Tröpfchen,	Don't fall over there
Fall mir auf mein Köpfchen!	Little drops of rain,
Fall mir nicht daneben,	Fall upon my head so bare
Dass ich lang soll leben!	And I shall live a long, long time.

But in nursery rhymes the sun is the person to take preference:

Lieber Regen, geh weg,	Go away, gentle rain,
Liebe Sonne, komm wieder	Gentle sun, come again,
Mit deinem Gefieder,	Come with your feathered wings,
Mit dem goldenen Strahl	Come with your golden beams,
Komm wieder herdal!	Come among us once again.
(From *Des Knaben Wunderhorn*)	

[1] This reversal of the traditional concept of the sun as a god and the moon as a goddess is mirrored in the gender of the two words in German: *die Sonne* (feminine) and *der Mond* (masculine). Most European countries prefer the accepted formula, but we have it on the authority of Professor Tolkien that elves and hobbits always refer to the sun as 'she'. (B.A.)

Nursery rhymes, as they have been handed down to us by oral and, for more than 150 years, by written tradition, and as they have been bestowed on us by poets, even down to the present time, are the purest and the most spontaneous way of putting words together (to avoid for the time being using the more high-flown word 'poetry'). If we do use it, then we can refer to it as a kind of everyday poetry—one of those comfortable customs which parents may establish in bringing up and playing with their children.

It is entirely by design that I begin this book with a subject as homely as nursery rhymes. Our language still consists of words rather than pictures and at a time before the child can be affected by, let alone understand, pictures (in our case, picture-books) he hears the voice of his mother or his father humming the first nursery songs. They are sung or spoken for many reasons: for sending him to sleep or helping him to wake, for comforting his injuries or giving him knee-rides, for punishment or praise; whatever it be, these songs and verses remain and live, perhaps quite unconsciously, in the child's inner ear. For all their comical twists, their startling rhymes, their simple, homely tunes, they represent his first and most elementary contact with his native tongue.

On the other hand, I find some difficulty in making a start with this subject, for in spite of their centuries-long usage, these verses have an infinite freshness about them. Too close an analysis can do nothing but harm to their delicate surface, spoiling half their attraction. I have therefore tried to move carefully among them—old and at the same time young as they are. I have selected but a few for my examples, and I have left the rest for their rightful owners, the children, or else for no one at all.

I think that the first songs which have come to the ears of children throughout the ages have been lullabies. There is a particular wealth of these in all languages and they contain the manifold qualities which are peculiar to different countries and the potentialities of their various languages. Protective, defensive, full of love—but occasionally also of jovial admonition—they bear kindly witness to the magic power of speech.

Sleep is the time of dreams and fairyland when the child more than ever feels himself merge into the world around him, with animals, stars, and flowers, while beside him is his mother, talking and singing to him. However little she may be conscious of it, a sensitive mother's ability to experience with her child such a return to the elementary world is a wonderful gift.

The Sandman of Northern Germany, scattering the sands of sleep, the 'slumber-aunt' or 'slumber-wife' in Eastern countries are figures from ancient pagan fairy lore related to Frau Holle.[1] But more than these it is the animals who are summoned up, standing, as they are said to do, a little nearer paradise.

[1] A figure from popular legend, best known in Central Germany, but figuring also in a tale in Grimm. When she shook the down from her bed out of the window, mortals below would think that snow was falling. (B.A.)

Consider what an important part the innocent sheep alone plays in countless lullabies, and then not just because it rhymes so neatly with 'sleep'.

KREDEL, Fritz. *Eia Popeia*. Berlin, 1936

Schlaf, Kindlein, schlaf!	Sleep, little one, sleep.
Der Vater hüt' die Schaf,	Thy father guards the sheep,
Die Mutter schüttelt's Bäumelein,	Thy mother shakes the little tree
Da fällt herab ein Träumelein.	That peaceful dreams may light on thee.

Then in the second verse the gentle warning of the two sheep:

. . . Ein schwarzes und ein weisses,	. . . A black one and a white one.
Und wenn das Kind nicht schlafen will,	And if you will not go to sleep
	The black one he will eat you up.
So kommt das schwarz' und beisst es.	

The early Christian origin of such a song is shown in the following verse:

Schlaf, Kindlein, schlaf!	Sleep, little one, sleep.
Christkindlein hat ein Schaf,	Lord Jesus had a sheep,
Ist selbst das liebe Gotteslamm,	He who is a lamb of God's
Das um uns all zu Tode kam.	And died for us upon the cross.
Schlaf, Kindlein, schlaf.	Sleep, little one, sleep.
(From *Des Knaben Wunderhorn*)	

The enduring strength of this traditional form of lullaby can be clearly seen in the way that it can be taken over and modified by a poet like Christian Morgenstern without any harm being done to its essential simplicity.

Schlaf, Kindlein, schlaf!	Sleep, little one, sleep.
Es war einmal ein Schaf.	Once there was a sheep.
Das Schaf, das ward geschoren,	The sheep was shorn, his fleece was sold;
Da hat das Schaf gefroren,	
Da zog ein guter Mann	He would have caught his death of cold
Ihm seinen Mantel an.	Had not a good man passing there
(From *Klein Irmchen*)	Given him his coat to wear.

3

But the loveliest lullabies are those which the Virgin Mary sings to the Child of all children:

Da oben auf dem Berge,	High on the mountain
Da rauscht der Wind,	The wind blows wild,
Da sitzet Maria	There sits Mary
Und wieget ihr Kind.	Rocking her child.
Sie wiegt es mit ihrer schneeweissen Hand,	She rocks him with her snow-white hand
Dazu braucht sie kein Wiegenband.	And does not need a cradle band.

(From *Des Knaben Wunderhorn*)

LINES, Kathleen. *Lavender's blue*. London, O.U.P., 1954
Line drawing by Harold Jones

How much of primitive man is woven into these rhymes one can only guess at from hints, for in their present linguistic form almost all of them stem from the end of the eighteenth century or the beginning of the nineteenth when people began to set them down in books. There is one from Iceland:

Schlafe, schlafe, Schätzchen mein,	Sleep, sleep, my love, my joy,
Draussen weint der Regen sacht.	The rain falls, the wind moans,
Alle deine Sächelein,	Your mother guards your little toys
Kästlein mit den Knöchelein	Your treasures and your knuckle-
Deine Mutter dir bewacht.	bones.
Schlafe in der dunklen Nacht.	Sleep through the dark night.

From the most ancient times, decorated or undecorated knuckle-bones are to be found among children's playthings.

Or else historical facts play a part in helping to place rhymes which would otherwise be dateless. Thus from Greece there comes a rhyme which bribes the child to sleep with a hyperbole of promises: an Alexandria of sugar, an Egypt of rice, and three years on the throne of Byzantium:

> *Schlaf ein, mein Kind, schlaf ein,*
> *Dann schenk ich dir mein Töchterlein,*
> *Alexandria aus Zucker weiss,*
>
> *Das grosse Nil-Land ganz aus Reis.*
> *Schlaf ein, mein Kind, mein Töchterlein,*
> *Sollst in Byzanz drei Jahre,*
> *Drei Jahre Kaiser sein.*

or from Spain a warning reference to a Moorish lady who creeps from house to house making sure the children are all asleep:

> *Schlafe, denn die Mohrin schleichet*
> *Schon von Tür zu Tür nicht weit.*
> *Schlafe, schlafe, denn sie lauschet,*
> *Welches Kind so spät noch schreit.*
> (The German versions of these foreign lullabies
> are from Faber du Faur: *Kinderreime der Welt*)

or from the time of the Thirty Years' War when parents adjured their children:

> *Bet' Kinder, bet',*
> *Morge kommt der Schwed'.*
> *Morge kommt der Oxestern,*
> *Der wird die Kinder bete lern.*
> (From *Des Knaben Wunderhorn*)

paralleled in England by:

> Baby, baby, naughty baby,
> Hush, you squalling thing, I say.
> Peace this moment, peace or maybe
> Bonaparte will pass this way.
> (From *The Oxford nursery rhyme book*)

But such clues as these are rare, and the origin of most nursery rhymes is quite impossible to date. In German-speaking countries, however, they cannot help bearing the stamp of the Romantic period, since two of the most important Romantics (two of the most lovable into the bargain) were responsible for settling the rhymes in printed form. In 1806 and 1808 Clemens Brentano and Achim von Arnim published the two parts of *Des Knaben Wunderhorn*[1] with a dedication to His Excellency the Privy Councillor of the Court of Weimar, Herr von Goethe. They knew full well the implications of such a dedication, for had not Goethe himself in his years at Strassburg drawn much of his inspiration from folk-poetry, together with his friend Herder, who even then was working on his famous *Stimmen der Völker*; and had he not allowed it to bring many fresh influences into his work? Goethe warmly commended the compilation by the two young enthusiasts—a fact which contributed much to its rapid and widespread success.

They took many songs and verses from Herder's work and many from the devotional books and almanacks of their own time or from writers of popular verse. But most came by oral transmission and in this they took the same steps as their famous contemporaries, the Brothers Grimm, were taking with fairy tales. In those years of helplessness, when the shadow of Napoleon lay over Germany, the investigation of the unsullied sources of the German language became itself an act of patriotism. With an intuitive feeling for what was genuine they made a selection and, where necessary, a reconstruction, which was not only a joy to their own time but has remained a source of enjoyment down to the present. What is more, this collection of poems was to have a tremendous influence on the later poets of the nineteenth century.

In every way *Des Knaben Wunderhorn* was a fertilizing influence. But for the subject in hand we are concerned chiefly with the last part of the book: *Der Kinder Wunderhorn*, from which the quotations which follow are taken.

Children in today's nurseries are as fond as those 150 years ago of such things as the pure word-play which springs from the earliest finger-games:

Patsche, patsche Kügelchen,	Pat-a-cake, pat-a-cake, baker's man,
Mir und dir ein Krügelchen. . . .	Bake me a cake as fast as you can.

or the lyrics, taken over by so many composers: *Guten Abend, gute Nacht, Mit Rosen bedacht . . .*' or the jokes:

Eio Popeio, was raschelt im Stroh?	Heigh ho! The poor little goose
Die Gänslein gehn barfuss	Down in the farmyard
Und haben keine Schuh. . . .	Without any shoes.

After this we get to the somewhat more elevated rhymes where a little seriousness, or even something of a moral, is introduced. One of the most

---

[1] *Des Knaben Wunderhorn* is literally 'The boy's magic horn', a title derived from the first poem in the collection.

famous of these is *Die Ammenuhr* (*The nursery clock*), in whose nine verses one hour of the night after another is conjured up:

Der Mond, der scheint,	The moon gleams,
Das Kindlein weint,	A child cries,
Die Glock' schlägt zwölf,	The clock strikes twelve:
Dass Gott doch allen Kranken helf!	God bring the sick to health again.
Die Schwalbe lacht,	Swallows rejoice,
Die Sonn' erwacht,	The sun comes up,
Die Glock' schlägt fünf,	The clock strikes five:
Der Wandrer macht sich auf die Strümpf.	The traveller pulls his breeches on.
Zum Bäcker lauf,	Run to the baker
Ein Wecklein kauf,	Buy some bread,
Die Glock' schlägt sieben,	The clock strikes seven:
Die Milch tu an das Feuer schieben!	The milk is boiling in the pan.

This robust aubade, which embodies in each of its nine verses a vignette of our pastoral ancestry, was later to inspire the group around Ludwig Richter to what were perhaps the finest illustrations in this genre in the whole of nineteenth-century Germany.

But the poem from *Des Knaben Wunderhorn* which most completely embodies a primitive mysteriousness, while at the same time perfectly catching the speech of children, is:

Das bucklige Männlein	The humpy man
Will ich in mein Gärtlein gehn,	When I go in my garden,
Will mein Zwiebeln giessen,	To water the onion bed,
Steht ein bucklicht Männlein da,	A little humpy man is there,
Fängt als an zu niesen.	Sneezing off his head.
Will ich in mein Stüblein gehn,	When I go in my little room,
Will mein Müslein essen,	To eat my cabbage soup,
Steht ein bucklicht Männlein da,	A little humpy man is there,
Hat's schon halber gessen.	Eating it all up.
Will ich auf mein Boden gehn,	When I go in my yard to fetch
Will mein Hölzlein holen,	My firewood for the day,
Steht ein bucklicht Männlein da,	A little humpy man is there,
Hat's mir halber gstohlen.	Stealing it away.

7

KREDEL, Fritz. *Eia Popeia*. Berlin, 1936.

So he goes on, verse after verse, like a goblin who brings with him nothing but confusion and ill-will and mockery. He represents all the annoyances that can befall us, this curious little humpy man. Yet generations of children have loved him and they love him still—such being the magnetism of the unpleasant (we meet him again in fairy tales as Rumpelstiltskin). But finally there is that magical ending, out-doing all the happy endings of the fairy tale and cancelling out in one line the accumulated malice of seven verses:

Wenn ich an mein Bänklein knie,	When I kneel beside my bed,
Will ein bisschen beten,	And I begin to pray,
Steht ein bucklicht Männlein da,	A little humpy man is there,
Fängt als an zu reden:	And I hear him say:
Liebes Kindlein, ach, ich bitt,	Little mortal, if you can,
Bet fürs bucklicht Männlein mit!	Pray for the little humpy man!

It is not far from this, the profoundest and the most warm-hearted of nursery rhymes, to Claudius who ends his famous poem to the moon:

So legt euch denn, ihr Brüder,	Then come good friends; away to rest,
In Gottes Namen nieder,	Cold is the evening air.
Kalt weht der Abendhauch.	May God withhold his wrath from us
Verschon uns Gott mit Strafen	And let us sleep in holy peace,
Und lass uns ruhig schlafen	And our sick fellows everywhere.
Und unsern kranken Nachbarn auch.	

In these two rhymes, the sensitive child would become aware of a world of feeling far more likely to inspire him to goodness than all the sanctimonious little prayers which he usually has to learn.

This kind of tender nursery rhyme is of relatively frequent occurrence in German and was to be taken much farther by the poets of the nineteenth century, as we shall later see. On the other hand, in the classic land for this sort of children's literature—in England—it is much less frequent. The British certainly have their sad and their tragi-comic characters (otherwise theirs would not have been the land of Shakespeare), but what they have to offer in the way of nursery rhymes is something which laughs and cries by turns.

Thus it is with Simple Simon, a figure as well known in English nursery rhymes as *Das bucklichte Männlein*, but scarcely related to him; for however much his clumsiness and stupidity may arouse our sympathy, part of it at least evaporates in laughter at his weird doings and at the artlessness of their versification. Here are the last three verses of this famous piece:

> Simple Simon went a-fishing
> For to catch a whale;
> All the water he had got
> Was in his mother's pail.
>
> Simple Simon went to look
> If plums grew on a thistle;
> He pricked his fingers very much,
> Which made poor Simon whistle.

> He went for water in a sieve,
> But soon it all fell through;
> And now poor Simple Simon
> Bids you all adieu.
>
> (From *The Oxford nursery rhyme book*)

This delightful poem, anonymous in authorship, provides us straight away with an example of the Englishman's love of so-called 'nonsense', a kind of versifying which later, in Edward Lear, found for itself a true poet.

Our preoccupation with the humpy man and poor Simple Simon, though, has led us well away from lullabies into the realm of conversational and narrative nursery rhymes. Here there is less of the lyrical element. Apart from the story, the chief enjoyment lies in the language, in the interplay of rhyme and rhythm, delighting children from their very earliest years. With these verses it is often difficult to tell if the writer has not started with the rhyme and allowed it to determine the action. This is particularly so in England and may well be the cause of that 'nonsense' which English children understand so much better than children on the Continent.

These verses, which at their own level often bring in ballad-like stories or quite complicated trains of thought, appeal to the child's feeling for poetry. They show him that there is something more to language than the words of daily life and they often result in children beginning to make up poetry for themselves. By such artless activity they learn to use their faculty for language, one of the most precious gifts they possess, and to prepare themselves for literary experiences which later can mean so much to the sensitive adult. Take, for example, the *Bi-ba-butzemann*:

Es tantzt ein Bi-ba-butzemann	A Bi-ba-butzeman goes dancing
In unserm Haus herum.	All around our house.
Er rüttelt sich,	Shivering
Er schüttelt sich,	And shaking
Er wirft sein Säckchen hinter sich.	And tossing his little bag over his
Es tantzt ein Bi-ba-butzemann	shoulder.
In unserm Haus herum.	A Bi-ba-butzeman goes dancing
	All around our house.

Like the Sandman, this Bi-ba-butzeman was an almost mythical figure for me in my earliest years and much later he seemed to reappear in the pages of Theodor Storm's *Buhlemanns Haus*, reinforcing the mysterious atmosphere of that story.

In the same way, the three pretty maidens who turn up in rhymes again and again can hold the keys to a great deal of later poetic enjoyment, provided that they make their first appearance at the right moment.

Sonne, Sonne, scheine!	Shine, sun, shine,
Wir fahren übern Rheine,	We sail across the Rhine.
Wir fahren übers Glockenhaus,	We sail above the belfry high;
Gucken drei schöne Mädchen raus:	Three maids peep out as we go by.
Die eine wickelt Seide,	One of them is spinning silk,
Die andre macht den Laden zu,	Another claps the shutter up,
Die dritte geht ans Brünnchen	The third goes down to the well
Und find't ein goldig Kindchen,	And finds there a golden girl.
Wie soll das heissen . . .?	What shall we call her? Anne Marie.
Anne Mariechen—Titschle Tatschle.	Tee tum tiddley tee.
Wer soll das Kindchen waschen?	Who is going to wash the brat?
Kätchen aus dem Guckelkasten.	Go and ask the peep-show cat.

This poem crops up in countless variations. It can be found in a shorter form in *Des Knaben Wunderhorn* and also in the entrancing lines of the Swiss-German dialect version, where the pretty maidens, now five in number, occupy themselves not only with spinning silk and gauze but with the more archaic tasks of grating chalk and spinning oat stalks. Our Lady is fifth in the group, sitting with an apple and then going to the Sun's house so that her Child may have his share of sunshine and shade.

> Die eint spinnt Side,
> Die ander Floride,
> Die dritt schnätzlet Chride,
> Die viert spinnt Haberstrau,
> Die feuft isch eusi liebi Frau,
> Sie sitzt ennet a der Wand,
> Hät en Öpfel i der Hand.
> Si goot durab zum Sunnehuus,
> Und loot die heilig Sunne uus,
> Und loot die Schatten ine
> Für iri liebe Chlyne.
> Und wenn mers ghört singe
> Chömmet alli Engel z springe.

The sensibility of children is greatly enriched by poems such as these, which augment the world of reality with figures from the imagination. The English have a particularly rich literature here as well and play clever games with rhymes and thoughts. To quote just one celebrated rhyme:

> How many miles to Babylon?
> Three-score and ten.
> Can I get there by candle-light?
> Yes, and back again.
> If your heels are nimble and light,
> You may get there by candle-light.
>
> (From *The Oxford nursery rhyme book*)

SCHEEL, Marianne. *Wiegenlieder*. Freiburg i.Br., 1938.

Walter de la Mare, who knew all about writing for children, has said of rhymes that 'they free the fancy, charm tongue and ear, delight the inward eye' and 'however fantastic or nonsensical they may be, they are a direct short cut into poetry itself'. How right he is, and what a challenge these words contain for the parents, teachers, and poets of today.

Kinderlieder

Wacht auf ihr schönen Vögelein, ihr Nachtigallen kleine, die ihr auf grünem Zweigelein, noch eh die Sonn recht scheine, anstimmt die tönend Schnäbelein, gedreht von Helfenbeine. Lobt Gott ihr süßen Schwätzerlein, ihr sämtlich keusch und reine, ihr Luft- und Wolkensängerlein, für ihn bestellt alleine. Mit euch zum besten Liedelein, zwei schöne Kindlein reine, Anblasen ihre Pfeifelein, es schallt zum Wald hineine, hier bei dem Heiligenbildelein in Einsamkeit alleine, da nicken blicken Blümelein und duften also feine, und Hirsch und Reh und Häselein, die horchen in dem Haine, wie eure süßen Stimmelein erklingen am Gesteine, auch fällt ein klares Brünnelein, die Blumen schaun hineine, da netzet eure Züngelein nach Ordnung ein und eine, da spület Hals und Gürgelein, dann singt ihr noch so reine; den Takt schlagt mit den Flügelein, so schickt sich's recht ihr Feine, schwingt freudig auch die Federlein, regt Aermelein und Beine, erstreckt zum Klang die Hälselein, ein Jedes thu das Seine. Habt ihr kein andres Liedelein, so lerner nur das meine, ist nur ein einzig Seufzerlein bei Sonn und Mondenscheine, singt nur allein, gelobt sey Gott, Gott Sabaoth alleine.

Wacht auf ihr kleinen Schülerlein bei hellem Sonnenscheine, zieht au die Festtags Röckelein und macht euch die Beine, Gregorius das Schulfest heut ist wieder angekommen, auch schlägt der Frühling auf der Haid' die helle Freudentrommen. Ein alter Brauch bei Christen war, daß man zu diesen Zeiten die Kinder all in froher Schaar zu Schul und Kirch thät leiten. Ein Kinderbischoff wählet man, und neben ihm zwei Pfaffen, ihm folgen König, Handwerksmann, Soldat, Hanswurst und Affen. So zieht einher ein jeder Stand, in Kleidern schön gezieret, und jedes Kind in seiner Hand sein Handwerkszeug auch führet. Dem Bischoff wird am Hirtenstab die Bretzel vorgetragen, was das für ein Bewandniß hab, merkt auf, ich wills euch sagen. Die Bretzel heißt Pretiolum, ein Preißlein für die Kinder, die in der Schule nit sind stumm und dumm gleichwie die Rinder. Sie hat in sich auch die Figur von den Buchstaben allen. Weiß hier, weiß dort auf rechter Spur, gelt das will dir gefallen. Die Bretzel ist ein liebes Buch, du wirst's bald ausstudieren, du kennst's von Weitem am Geruch, und wirst's drum nit verlieren. Du kannst es schon bis zu dem S, wird dirs nit abgenommen, du lerntest also ungemäß, daß du zum W thät'st kommen.

Heidelberg bey Mohr und Zimmer 1808.

ARNIM, Achim von and BRENTANO, Clemens. *Des Knaben Wunderhorn*. Volume 3. Heidelberg, 1808.
Title page and engraved frontispiece for the section devoted to nursery songs.

Pleasure in rhyme, which can lead to the pleasure of playing with language, is also known in Germany, even though it is not so completely free from the logic of action. Verses like the following are therefore infrequent:

Der Wind, der weht,	The wind blows,
Der Hahn, der kräht,	The cock crows,
Der Fuchs sass auf dem Zaune	The fox sits up on the fence so high
Und pflückt sich eine Pflaume.	Plucking fruit from the plum-tree.

Though it may not be entirely nonsensical, the idea of a fox sitting up on a fence picking plums is scarcely realistic. Real nonsense appears chiefly in counting-out rhymes where the rhyming may not be pure (a thing which does not trouble children very much) but where the motive is thoroughly realistic.

The fox poem is also very graphic in its expression, and in its second half it typifies a whole series of nursery rhymes, technically known as sequence rhymes, which are themselves important:

Ich sprach, er (der Fuchs) soll mir eine geben,	I said he should give me plums,
	He said he would give me stones.
Er sprach, er wollt mir Steine geben.	So I took my little staff
Da nahm ich meinen Stachelstock	And hit him on his Adam's apple.
Und schlug ihm auf den Kehlkopf.	This made him shout out, 'O forgive
Da rief er: 'Meister Jakob!	Me, Master James, and let me live!
Jakob, lass mich leben,	I'll give you all my plums today.'
Ich will dir alle meine Pflaumen geben.'	'No; what I want from you is hay,
	I want some hay for Clarabel.
'Nein, du sollst mir Stroh geben,	Then she will give me milk as well,
Stroh will ich Mutjen (der Kuh) geben,	And if I take the milk to Mummy
Mutchen soll mir Milch geben,	She will give me a silver penny,
Milch will ich der Mutter geben,	And if I take it to the baker
Mutter soll mir Pfennig geben,	He will give me bread and cake,
Pfennig will ich dem Bäcker geben,	And if I give some to my cat
Bäcker soll mir Semmel geben,	She'll go and catch me mice and rats
Semmel will ich der Katze geben,	To hang up on my chimney-pots.'
Katze soll mir Mäuse fangen,	
Die will ich an den Schornstein hangen.'	

I have intentionally quoted here a little-known rhyme of this kind; perhaps the most famous is:

Der Herr, der schickt den Jockel aus,	The farmer sends young Johnny out
Er soll den Haber schneiden.	To go and cut the oats.

with its magnificent Allemannic version which every child in German-speaking Switzerland knows:

Joggeli wott go Birli schüttle,	Johnny goes to shake the pear-tree,
D Birli wänd nöd falle,	The pears refuse to fall.
Da schickt de Meister s Hündli us,	The farmer calls his little dog
Es söll go Joggeli bysse.	To go and bite the boy.
Hündli wott nöd Joggeli bysse,	The little dog won't bite Johnny,
Joggeli wott nöd Birli schüttle,	Johnny won't shake the tree,
D Birli wänd nöd fale.	The pears refuse to fall.
etc.	

In England the most famous rhymes corresponding to these are, of course, *The house that Jack built*[1] and *The old woman and her pig*.

These lines can be found in every anthology, however, together with the linguistically impressive:

Wide wide wenne	Pick-pick-pen
Heisst meine Puthenne.	Is the name of my hen.
Wenn ich eine Henne habe,	If I've got a hen bird
Muss ich auch einen Hahn haben.	I've got to have a cock bird.
Kikeriki heisst mein Hahn,	Kikeriki is my cock,
Wide wide wenne heisst mein	Pick-pick-pen is my hen.
Puthenne.	
etc.	

A wonderful accumulation of picturesque names runs right through to the end of this naïvely artistic poem:

Silberwert heisst mein Pferd,	Silver-purse is my horse.
Halb und Halb heisst mein Kalb,	Half-and-half is my calf,
Tritazu heisst meine Kuh,	Come-on-now is my cow,
Treibein heisst mein Schwein.	Three-leg is my pig.
etc.	

One of the most perceptive authorities on nursery rhymes, Irmgard von

[1] Iona and Peter Opie refer to this in *The Oxford dictionary of nursery rhymes* (p. 231): 'It has often been presumed that the original of "The House that Jack Built" is a Hebrew chant, "Had Gadyo", which was first printed in 1590 in a Prague edition of the *Haggadah*. The chant, a fine early example of the accumulative story, bears comparison with an English folk-tale, "The Old Woman and her Pig" . . .' A Swiss picture-book version of *Joggel*, illustrated by Felix Hoffman, has recently been published in England: *A boy went out to gather pears*. O.U.P., 1966. (B.A.)

Faber du Faur, sees in the oldest sequence poem known to us, *Das Lied vom Zicklein* (*The song of the little goat*) a connexion with Jewish tradition. For this poem, quoted without a source by Arnim and Brentano, had earlier been sung by children in Hebrew at the Feast of the Passover.

Ein Zicklein, ein Zicklein,	A little goat, a little goat,
das hat gekauft mein Väterlein	my daddy bought a little goat
um zwei Schilling Pfennig,	for two shillings and a penny,
ein Zicklein.	one little goat.
Da kam das Kätzlein	Then came a little cat
und ass das Zicklein,	and ate up the little goat,
das hat gekauft mein Väterlein	which my daddy went and bought
um zwei Schilling Pfennig,	for two shillings and a penny,
ein Zicklein.	one little goat.

And so it proceeds through nine verses in which the destructive powers of a little ox, a butcher, an angel of death, and (as in *Joggel* and *The old woman and her pig*) water and fire are all employed, until at the end everything is neatly linked together in the approved manner:

Da kam unser lieber Herr Gott	Then came the good Lord God
und vertrieb den Engel des Todes,	and drove out the angel Death
der hat erschlagen den Schlächter,	who slew the butcher
der hat geschlachtet das Öchslein,	who killed the little ox
der hat getrunken das Wässerlein,	who drank the little stream
der hat verlöscht das Feuerlein,	who quenched the little fire
der hat verbrannt das Stöcklein,	who burnt the little stick
das hat geschlagen das Hündlein,	who beat the little dog
das hat gebissen das Kätzlein,	who bit the little cat
das hat gegessen das Zicklein,	who ate the little goat
das hat gekauft mein Väterlein	which my daddy went and bought
um zwei Schilling Pfennig,	for two shillings and a penny,
ein Zicklein, ein Zicklein.	one little goat, one little goat.

The directness of these verses, the constant repetition, and the surprising culmination in the sequence of events, all contribute towards an unsuspected potentiality in the poem. At one and the same time children are given an immediate impression of the power which words can assert, together with a hint of the almost tragic interrelation of events and circumstances.

I have quoted less well-known versions of these accumulative poems since the familiar ones can be found in many anthologies and children's books. All of them, however, show their ancient origins in the unsentimental way in which they call spades spades: Master James who hits the fox on his Adam's apple and hangs mice from the chimney; the angel of death who kills the butcher, and so on.

Among these ancient stories in verse which make no effort to avoid unhappy events, the loveliest is undoubtedly the *Erschreckliche Geschichte vom Hühnchen und vom Hähnchen (The dreadful tale of chicken and cockerel)* from *Des Knaben Wunderhorn*, which was later to find its way into pure literature in an adaptation by Clemens Brentano.

Hähnchen ist zum Born gelaufen,	Cockerel hastens to the well:
Born, du sollst mir Wasser geben,	'Well, well, give me water,
Hühnchen liegt an jenem Berg	Chicken lies on yonder hill
und schluckt an einem Nusskern.	Choking on a walnut stone.'
Und da hat der Born gesprochen:	But the well only answered:
Erst sollst du zur Braut hinspringen	'First be off to yonder maiden,
und mir klare Seide bringen.	Fetch me a skein of purest silk.'
Hähnchen ist zur Braut gesprungen,	Cockerel hastens to the maiden:
Braut, du sollst mir Seide geben,	'Maiden, maiden, give me silk,
Seide soll ich Brunnen bringen,	I must take it to the well,
Brunnen soll mir Wasser geben,	Then the well will give me water,
Wasser soll ich Hühnchen bringen	The water I must take to Chicken . . .'
etc.	

But after many a dialogue and many a successfully completed errand we reach the saddest end that a nursery rhyme can ever have:

Wasser bringt er zu dem Hühnchen,	He reached Chicken with the water
aber Hühnchen war erstickt,	But she had choked to death alone,
hat den Nusskern nicht verschlickt.	Choked upon the walnut stone.[1]

Dedicated collectors, of whom I have here named only the important pair of friends Clemens Brentano and Achim von Arnim, have rescued for us through their researches a great abundance of this ancient literature. But whether recorded as such or not, undoubtedly the earliest rhymes that have survived for us are the truly occasional verses: the knee-ride songs, the lullabies, the counting-out rhymes, the ring-dances, and the riddle-me-rees. They have all taken their place, richly illustrated, in the pages of modern children's books. Every country has its own collection and it would take us too far out of our way to cite examples here. For it is the job of parents to pass on these things to their children, even in an age when ladies no longer ride 'a nim, a nim a nim'.

Already much has been lost of this simpler side of human nature, and much that remains has become little more than a set of empty rhymes. Seldom has anything new been produced to replace these old traditional rhymes, and now,

[1] It is only fair to add, however, that the tragic tale concludes with a rather slapstick funeral cortège and some ironic comments in prose on the whole sad affair. (B.A.)

at a time when mothers have been known to play fairy stories to their children on a bedside gramophone, it would not be surprising if this literature were to die out completely, for it takes its life from its vital contact with the child. And I know very well that all this is not the child's fault. The child of today, to whom I read, sitting beside me, the child of twenty years ago to whom I read as a young mother, and the child of forty years ago, who was I myself, all these were and continue to be enchanted by the *Bucklichte Männlein*, or by a poem such as the *Vogelhochzeit* (*The bird's wedding*) with the incomparable lines:

Der schwarze Rab, der war der Koch,	The cock he was an old black crow
Man siehts an seinen Federn noch	His feathers still can prove it so
Der Wiedehopf, der Wiedehopf,	The hoopoe (who possessed a lot)
der bringt der Braut den Kaffeetopf	Gave the bride a coffee pot.

KREDEL, Fritz. *Eia Popeia*. Berlin, 1936

or, from *Ball der Tiere* (*The animals' ball*):

Mich dünkt, wir geben einen Ball!	'Let's give a ball,'
Sprach die Nachtigall.	Said the nightingale.
So, sprach der Floh.	'Ay,' said the fly.
Was werden wir essen? sprachen die Wespen.	'What have we got?' asked the wasp.
Nudeln, sprachen die Pudeln.	'Noodles,' said the poodles.
etc.	

RACKHAM, Arthur. *Wenn ich in mein Gärtchen geh.* Munich, *c.* 1914.
Old and new children's verses and songs with 13 colour illustrations and 80 black and white drawings.

All that is needed is a parent's voice to speak the words. It is by no means an overstatement when the editors of that excellent anthology of English nursery rhymes, *The Oxford nursery rhyme book,* say: 'A mother's own voice is worth more than four-and-twenty professional singers trilling on the radio.'

With the exception of the English, poets have scarcely made any additions at all to this ballad-like, half-comic kind of children's poetry. Only during the middle years of the nineteenth century, and later, has the thread again been taken up by such men as Dr. Hoffmann, Wilhelm Busch, Count Pocci and even Christian Morgenstern. Since the beginning of that century, most of the poets who knew and loved this literary heritage have turned rather to the lyric strain in children's poetry, setting the child on familiar terms with nature, with the world around him, and with religion.

This lyrical element, however, may by no means have been absent from ancient popular poetry, but it did not have any of the sentimentality which was to threaten children's literature in later times. When a Bulgarian nursery rhyme can say:

> The forest did not weave or spin.
> But lay in pain the winter long;
> And yet, when April came again,
> The forest clad itself in green;
> From head to toe in verdant gown,
> Vain as a girl in peacock green.

it blends into a charming whole a poetic imagery, which the eighteenth century would have understood, and a realistic personification (the wood), of the kind that children love.

But above all it is the sun and the other heavenly bodies that inspire the most impressive verses, especially in Germany and the northern lands, which are sunless for so long. Let this translation (via German) of a Finnish rhyme stand as the representative of many others:

> Turn your face towards me, sun,
> Open for me your two eyes.
> Are they yellow, are they black,
> Are they green or are they blue,
> Are they white or silver grey?

Let me end with the image of a giant tree, with which this form of children's and popular literature may be compared. If I have only looked at it from the outside, picking here and there a sweet or a bitter fruit, stripping off a leaf or observing a gnarled root, I have done so with a sense of diffidence, however interesting or puzzling the whole may be. In fact, I am not certain that the tree itself is truly alive, though it be older than all other children's literature, measuring itself only against the 'Fairy-Tale Tree of the World' and, like it, having its share of dead leaves and dry branches. Has its custody been forgotten? If so, then why? Has something new been planted in its place? If so, then let us search for it.

COMMENT

Although *Des Knaben Wunderhorn* may be known by name in England (possibly through the music of Gustav Mahler who used a number of the poems in orchestral settings and in his symphonies) no large-scale effort has been made to translate the collection into English. Nor are there any volumes of nursery rhymes in translation like Irmgard Faber du Faur's *Kinderreime der Welt* mentioned on p. 5. Rose Fyleman published a small collection: *Widdy-Widdy-Wurkey: nursery rhymes from many lands* (Blackwell, 1934) which was followed in 1949 by a second volume, *Over the tree-tops*. There are also some isolated translations in *The Faber book of nursery verse* (Faber, 1958). For a great feast of information on comparative versions (often with foreign texts quoted) there is, of course, the unsurpassable *Oxford dictionary of nursery rhymes* noted in the bibliography at the end of this book.

Leslie Daiken in *The lullaby book* (Edmund Ward, 1959) contributes some interesting notes on and translations of lullabies from other countries, printing thirty-eight different examples with music. Several of the German rhymes which I have translated above are also translated and discussed in the Countess Martinengo-Cesaresco's essay in the now out of print *Essays in the study of folk-songs* (1886).

2 ONCE UPON A TIME
Some notes on fairy stories and how they have come down to us

Fairy stories are something of a peculiarity. 'That's how the story goes' is what people used to say, and from this sentence, which suggests movement, follows the idea that we are not dealing here with something printed and stable, but with something passing along by word of mouth and changing as it goes. And that is just how it is. The emergence of the same elements in fairy tales the world over, from Japan to Norway, does not make the investigation of the origins of fairy stories any easier, and the European fairy stories which must occupy us here for a short while are not by any means purely European products.

The fairy story is the only form of children's entertainment which has long been the subject of distinguished research. The reason for this may well be found in the fact that it was not originally children's entertainment at all but that it is primarily a kind of great-grandparent of narrative literature and thus belongs to the field of literary history. Moreover, since information about age-old folk-customs and yet older relationships between peoples can be gathered from the fairy tale, it becomes thereby an important subject for the investigation of facts about the history of nations and peoples.

So far as we can take it in at a glance, probably the strongest roots lie in the Middle East. There is a perfection in the way the young and beautiful Scheherazade in *The thousand and one nights* tells the stories which purchase her her life. This is the high peak of an ancient oral tradition revealed to the European who can enrich his own world of fairy stories with those from this new and unfamiliar one. On the other hand, however, for all their adventurousness, how little these intricate and, in part, darkly tragic tales have to do with our own children's fairy stories. Similarly, with the complexity of a novel, we find the vigorous tales of Giambattista Basile which appeared in Naples in the sixteen-thirties. The *Cinderella* or indeed *The Sleeping Beauty* of the Italian writer (to select two well-known fairy stories) are tales of some intensity in which fearful murder, plain but strangely committed marital infidelity, and horrible—but ultimately thwarted—child murder all play a considerable part. (Cinderella is induced to kill her first stepmother by her second, and even more evil one; while the Sleeping Beauty is seduced in her sleep by a king who is already married. She gives birth to twins and is finally woken up through their hungry nuzzling for food.)

Even Charles Perrault, who was the first to tell fairy stories to children themselves, cannot quite shake off an inclination towards the courtly novel wrapped up with political ethics.

And yet *The thousand and one nights* and Charles Perrault are the most distinguished ancestors of the fairy story as it was created by the nineteenth century—and created then indeed for children. With the flowering of the novel in the nineteenth century it was natural that the fairy story should increasingly become reading-matter for children only, in spite of the great artistic impetus given by Romanticism to fairy-tale literature, which got so full of wit, satire, poetry, and fantasy that only very clever adults could fully grasp its merit. Indeed, with the growth of the children's book of today, where boys and girls are told stories of events which could actually happen to them, the fairy story has been relegated to those young children who have stories read to them or who battle their way painfully through the under-growth of the printed page. This age group is designated by teachers and librarians the 'fairy-story age' and by this means, especially in German-speaking areas, a limitation is imposed which has an impoverishing effect throughout the whole of children's literature. People forget that often older children, particularly girls, take a natural delight in fairy stories and that they only fully appreciate the richness of certain stories, for example those of Andersen, when they have outgrown the so-called 'fairy-story age'.

The chief point of difference between fairy stories and other tales is to be found in their apparatus of fantastic happenings such as marvels, spells, and strange transmogrifications, all of which give rise to boundless possibilities. Why should these be confined to the world of little children and cease to exist in that of the nine- or ten-year-old, giving way to the stories of everyday reality? *Heidi* was one of the first and most famous books of this latter kind, a combination of human and poetic insight which was written in so simple and homely a style that it conquered the hearts of children immediately. If only it had not found so many imitators! Once the way had been paved the German-speaking peoples could not get away from it, although in more northerly countries, particularly England and Scandinavia, the lore of fairy tale with its daring possibilities penetrated the whole of children's literature, even in those age groups for whom claims to higher stylistic and intellectual appreciation are made.

Now what are the characteristic features of the fairy tale? One of its funda-mental qualities is its narrative flow, which stems from its very origin in the spoken word.

'The teller of fairy tales': an engraving by Ludwig Richter.

A second quality is that these tales for telling must be both true and not true at the same time. They must contain an inner truth which keeps them viable even though the path of the story can be anything but true, which is to say that magic and mystery are midwives to the impossible. The difficulties of ordinary life can be overcome by extraordinary means and through improbable powers, such as seven-league boots, prophetic insight (or cunning), escape into invisibility, or else through the helpful support of such spirits as dwarfs, elves, and giants. That witches, man-eaters, and evil stepmothers also belong to the powerful forces who keep the action of fairy stories on the move has brought the genre into disrepute among the modern educationists and has tempted the psychologists into many curious speculations. But obviously the normal child needs this supernatural presentation of evil as the Church needs the Devil; how would it otherwise be possible that in Germany, for example,

23

Hänsel and Gretel should be among the most read and most loved fairy tales? For the brief span of this tale contains perfect specimens not only of an inhuman stepmother and a wicked witch but even, for fattened-up Hänsel, of a situation where he will be gobbled up whole. But at the same time it contains other elements which appeal deeply to the hearts of children: the feeble father's hidden love for his children, their own affection for each other, even in the extremities of starvation, the solitude of the wood at night, and the allurement of the gingerbread house.

Such verses as:

> *Knuper, Knuper, Knäuschen,*
> *wer knupert an mein Häuschen?*

and the answer:

> *Der Wind, der Wind,*
> *das himmlische Kind.*

reach out to the deepest feelings of which a child is capable.

This is not the place to investigate whether Little Red Riding Hood, Snow-White, the Sleeping Beauty, or Hop o' my Thumb are of German or French origin. The wonderful thing about them is that they express so perfectly every nation's feeling for fairy stories. Fairy stories truly embody an 'international' European literature such as is only possible in other branches of writing through the increased activities of translators. That this should be so may be accounted for by the great power of conviction which fairy-tale figures carry with them and by their ancient principles of action, which express the primitive and unconscious needs of the human heart.

As a rule it is the prospect of saving something from extinction which inspires the activity of collectors. This is the case with fairy stories to a high degree, for the spread of printing and the recession of illiteracy in Europe increasingly brought about the disappearance of story-tellers, who gained their living from the demands made upon their traditional function.

This was the situation which confronted Charles Perrault and, a hundred years later, the Brothers Grimm. Today, 150 years on from them, story-tellers still miraculously exist in lonely mountain valleys, in isolated villages of Yugoslavia, Greece, or Asia Minor, even though to a growing extent they mingle elements of modern life with their ancient traditional tales.

The great collections of folk-tales which are now being established in almost every country are mostly museums of fairy-lore. Not so the stories of the Brothers Grimm, however. For reasons which it is almost impossible to explain, they managed to find the precise combination of respect for tradition and free personal expression which was necessary to give their collection its freshness, redolent of neither the study nor the glass-case and timeless as only a few works of great literature.

The enormous importance of this collection, however, did not reside solely in the consequences which followed upon its rediscovery of an ancient national heritage. It also immeasurably furthered the influence which the common elements of the fairy tale would have on the whole of children's literature from this time forward.

At this stage it is probably worth while to describe briefly those few corner-stones which support the superstructure of the European fairy tale—a meeting-place where you will find witches, dwarfs and elves, princes and princesses, kings and magicians, woodcutters and ragged children, sympathetic doves and talking storks, good and even wicked fairies, all together in a peaceable assembly.

The thousand and one nights

The thousand and one nights or *The Arabian nights' entertainments* arrived in Europe at the end of the seventeenth century through a young French diplo-mat and scholar, Antoine Galland, who was born in Picardy in 1646. In this book we have to deal with a long series of fairy stories which, so far as we know, found their way into manuscript in Arabia round about 1545. The

From an early edition of *The thousand and one nights*

provenance of some stories, however, leads back to Persia and even to India. Furthermore, the theme of the princess saving herself by telling stories existed for so long in this form that *The thousand and one nights* takes its place within a long written tradition. Thus, so far as the older civilization of the East was concerned, the committing of these stories to writing was an act corresponding to our own in the nineteenth century, when writers settled the form of fairy-tale literature for those who should succeed them. In this way we received the ancient and mighty narrative traditions of the East, with all their overtones of oriental manners and contemplativeness.

Galland's first translation was followed by countless others in almost every country in Europe. In passing, we should note the strong supposition that the Italians knew of the stories beforehand, since Basile's fairy tales, whose basic material came from the common people, nevertheless show some astonishing similarities.

Often many of those who retold the stories sought to suppress the more racy passages, inseparable from descriptions of harem life, but deemed un-suitable for European sensibilities. On the other hand, some editions turned these into the big attraction. But none of them could eradicate entirely the scent of eastern musk, the unbridled passion, the delicate and intricate filigree of the stories' construction, and thereby many of their other oriental charms. Many great illustrators of the last two hundred years down to the immediate present have made their attempts on these stories and have served to formulate our ideas of the East more than any of the other volumes of travellers' tales.

Among the German writers of fairy stories it is quite impossible to think of, say, Hauff without this literary inheritance. One has only to think of *Die Geschichte von dem kleinen Muck* or *Kalif Storch* to realize this. But even Andersen, as a small boy in his father's cobbler's shop, had these stories read to him as part of a common inheritance. Later he was to follow the attraction which had been aroused by this childhood experience and take a journey to the Near East. Whoever reads his diaries of this journey, his fairy stories or his *Picture-book without pictures* will find in the work of this northern story-teller astonishing echoes of the oriental themes which he first heard in *The thousand and one nights*.

Italian fairy stories

Europe's earliest fairy stories to be set down on paper are without doubt the *Piacevoli notti* (1550) of Giovan Francesco Straparola, in which recogniz-able fairy-story themes appear for the first time. The Italian folk-story, how-ever, reveals itself in all its abundance in the book by Giambattista Basile—*Lo cunto de li cunti*—which first appeared in the Neapolitan dialect in five parts between 1634 and 1636.

Basile, who was born around 1575, was a soldier of fortune who occupied himself at the courts of various Italian princes in some very varied roles. He wrote odes, eclogues, and all kinds of courtly poetry in the affected manner of his times. He was a member of numerous academies, among which was one of the largest in his native Naples: the *Otiosi* or 'Lazybones' Academy, and he named himself 'Pigro'—the sloth. But he also possessed something rare among the courtiers of his time: a sense of justice, an integrity and a feeling for the needs and the dignity of the Neapolitan people. In order to give

BASILE, Giambattista. *The Pentamerone*, translated by J. E. Taylor. London, 1848. Etched illustration by George Cruikshank.

expression to this he recited and wrote down his fairy stories in his native dialect. As Grimm and Perrault were to do later, he used for his foundation the, in parts, very primitive and entirely oral traditional tales which the women of the district told to their children. These fairy stories were only printed after Basile's death in 1632, a good sixty years before Perrault's collection.

As with Perrault's tales, these also are in no way a collection of items of folk-lore copied down straight from the mouths of the story-tellers. They are rather an expression of the powerful Baroque Age, which still lives for us in its marvellous pictures and which cannot see the sun rise without personifying it and having it sweep out the morning sky with a golden broom. Basile's portrayals of nature are always full of this kind of personal life, even where they stand as allegories or as symbols, while the action is dramatic, often bloody or full of complicated intrigue, but always reaching its climax in the triumph of right. Unnecessary decorative details are rarely found, but on the other hand, the dialogue is witty, full of allusion, and without concessions to the prudish. This above all is Basile's instrument for conveying the truth to his age.

While it cannot be denied that Basile obtained the framework of his stories from the women of his immediate locality, just as Perrault and the Grimms were to do in their time, the audience for the humane and humorous 'Pigro' of the Lazybones' Academy was composed of intelligent men—'all fellows at the same club', as we might say today. Certainly, therefore, he did not tell them fairy stories, although he wove in many threads from these. Even so we already find noted down here such tales as *Cinderella* and *The Sleeping Beauty*, just as there are clues pointing to sources in the Near East. Especially notable among these is the way the stories are arranged within a story about a treacherous Moorish slave-girl, whose wickedness is finally revealed so that the virtuous and patient princess finally gains her rightful reward. This firm framework holding the book together is found neither in Perrault nor in Grimm, but Jakob Grimm saw in Basile over the gulf of two hundred years a comrade of similar aims and helped him to his delayed fame in Northern Europe, writing an introduction to the first edition of his works in German in 1846.

In Italy itself the finest translation of the book into modern Italian was by Benedetto Croce, who saw in it not just a collection of popular tales but 'the finest book of the Italian baroque'. It has, in common with the two most famous fairy-tale collections which followed it, a naturalness and freshness which have lasted to our own times. Where wit and effervescent imagination are concerned, Basile's tales are inexhaustible and contain some ingredients so bizarre as to be seldom found elsewhere. Perhaps the most felicitous of these occurs in the scene in the bedroom when the heart of a sea-dragon is brought to the boil and the steam spreads pregnancy throughout the room; not only for the cook but also for the utensils and the furniture, so that the bedstead acquires a baby bed, the big chairs little chairs, and the chamber-pot a baby chamber-pot. Such an ingenious animation of lifeless objects is only found again in Andersen.

Histories or tales of past times, told by Mother Goose, with morals
Written in French and Englished by
G. M. Gent
A woodcut by Victor Stuyvaert from photographs of the woodcuts used in the 1802 edition, which were probably the same as those used in the first English edition, 1729. These had been copied from the 1697 edition published in Paris.

PERRAULT, Charles. *Histoires ou contes du temps passé*. Amsterdam, 1742.
Engraving for *La petite chaperon rouge* based upon the earlier woodcut illustration.

Perrault and the French fairy story

Charles Perrault (1628–1703) may not have been the first to write down fairy tales but he was the first writer of consequence to recognize that they belonged to the world of children. The whole of the vivid, power-flaunting seventeenth century was not unsympathetic to simplicity and straightforwardness, which were precisely the qualities of fairy tales. Telling them, however, was the occupation of women. It is said of Le Roi Soleil that when he was a little boy in the forties of that century he could not go to sleep without the fairy tales which the ladies-in-waiting used to tell him. At the end of the century such tales, racily adapted by the ladies who told them, were paraded in the elegant salons of the Parisian aristocracy. Particular delight, however, was brought to these salons by Perrault's versification of *Peau d'âne*—one of the most popular and typically French fairy stories.

With the publication soon after of his *Histoires ou contes du temps passé avec des moralités* (1697), in a delectable prose and patently intended for children, this same Perrault seems to have caused himself some embarrassment. For in doing such a thing he was likely to have become very conspicuous. Retiringly, therefore, he had the book registered for privilege under the name of his son,

Pierre d'Armancour, a fact which the most recent research has converted into a suspicion that the seventeen-year-old boy could have been the actual author. This would provide an explanation for the extraordinarily youthful freshness of the book which conquered in a trice the world of children who had never before possessed anything so much their own.

Charles Perrault was a gifted member of the Académie Française, but no poet. A literary historian of our own times, Paul Hazard in *Les livres, les enfants et les hommes,* finds it completely natural that such a prominent member of the Académie should veil behind a youthful pseudonym the fact that he writes fairy stories. After all, were not the Grimms, with their passion for collecting such stories, regarded as very singular gentlemen a hundred years later still? Even so, the assertions of an English authority on this matter (Percy Muir in *English children's books, 1600–1900*) cannot be rejected. He establishes that no edition in the father's lifetime bore the name Charles Perrault and that at the time of their publication the son Pierre was generally thought to be the author, having had the opportunity of getting the stories straight from his nurse. In this case it is fascinating to think that the first book of fairy stories for children in Europe could itself have been written by a very young man.

This emphasis on children marks the decisive difference between Perrault and Basile, with whom he has a number of things in common. Like his Italian predecessor, Perrault is a member of learned societies and to some extent a moralist. Both seek in the unsullied fairy-lore of the people a curative for the luxury, corruption, and self-satisfaction rampant in their own stratum of society.

Basile proffers his prescription straight to the men around him, but Perrault has a premonition of the ascendancy of the younger generation. He offers his discovery to children, who are to be the future lords and ladies of the land, but he could not know that it was to become the intellectual sustenance of so many of their heirs. And a full-blooded and to some extent frightening fare it was to be too, a thing which one only realizes when one compares it with the wordy, moralizing tales of Perrault's contemporaries and successors, who were almost all of them women.

Perrault's language is concise but lucid. Next to beauty and wealth, the most important attributes of his heroines are courage and a healthy understanding of humanity. Blood flows plentifully while romantic charm does not even get started, as, for example, in such a story as *Little Red Riding Hood*, which, when told by the Brothers Grimm, possesses a sweetness (in spite of the fearful scene in the bedroom) which persuades even little children to swallow the whole thing as a wonderful joke. Here, however, Little Red Riding Hood pays the penalty for her disobedience; the wolf begs her to come to him at Grandmother's bedside, and after all too short a conversation, Little Red Riding Hood follows the old lady down his gullet, never to be seen again. There is no romantic huntsman, no paying out the wolf, no happy ending with cakes and ale.

In Germany readers are, as a rule, surprised when they meet stories like this, which they had believed to be typically German, in such an early version. But the children of those days did not demand a lot of consideration for their delicate nerves. The language was direct and forceful and had not yet learned to adopt that consciously condescending tone which goes out of date so rapidly. Perrault's fairy tales have therefore kept their youthfulness to this very day and they belong to the 'daily bread' of the French nursery.

The Brothers Grimm and their times

Throughout its first half, the eighteenth century was once again the province of the grown-ups. With the exception of Perrault, fairy stories remained, like the old folk-tales, at most an extensively popular form of oral entertainment, even though they could now to some extent be come by in print. Goethe, who as a boy knew scarcely any children's books except for the so-called 'Robinsonaden', discovered for himself the cheap *Volksbücher* which were as little suited to the salon and the nursery as most fairy stories, but which fascinated children and the common people alike.

They represented a truly popular formulation of the old legends, and when Goethe later encouraged the Grimms and Arnim and Brentano in their efforts to reach the natural sources of poetry, he was but keeping faith with the secret love of his own childhood. Furthermore, his childish experiences with these books may well have provided the first impetus for his reworking into High German hexameters of the allegorical Low German beast epic *Reineke Fuchs*.

The older the century grew, the less was children's inclination to this kind of reading matter concealed. Between the years 1782–86 the poverty-stricken schoolmaster I. K. A. Musäus (born Jena, 1735, died Weimar, 1787) was publishing the volumes of his collection *Die Volksmärchen der Deutschen*. He himself wrote of this: 'Fairies seem to be coming quite back into fashion; the very Reverend Voss and the very respectable Bürger are vying with each other in the modernizing of *The thousand and one nights* and even fairy stories have been published afresh this year in Jena and again at Nuremberg. I am going to jump on the band-wagon myself and turn out something in this line, with the title of *Volksmärchen; ein Lesebuch für grosse und kleine Kinder* ("Folk-tales, a story-book for children great and small"). I am collecting the most trivial old wives' tales, trimming them up and making them ten times more marvellous than they originally were. My wife hopes that the whole thing will turn out to be a most lucrative piece of work.'

The poor poet outlived his lucrative success by only one year. From this extremely interesting letter, from which I have quoted only a short extract, we can grasp almost everything that is worth knowing about our subject. At the same time, however, the jokingly modest reference to 'something in this line' betrays the fact that a preoccupation with fairy stories was not yet taken entirely seriously. Further, the observation that he was 'trimming up' the fairy stories and 'making them ten times more marvellous' indicates that we are not yet in the exclusive circle of the Brothers Grimm, pursuing the purity and plainness of folk-poetry. And yet it was Herder, the creator of the *Stimmen der Völker*, who delivered a memorial speech on Musäus in the Weimar Grammar School soon after his death. In this he portrayed the fairy-tale writer: 'agreeable and comradely, of great simplicity of character and goodness of heart—a man who bore the heavy burden of his days with cheerfulness and equanimity, merriment and robust good humour.' And his fairy stories are still alive today. In my own childhood they were the ones I loved the best. The legendary world of the Middle Ages comes alive in them and their plots are decked out in the brightest colours, such as were never seen in the stories of Perrault nor would be in the stories of Grimm. Their images already foreshadow Romanticism, but at the same time the stories are extraordinarily compelling. Such titles as *Stumme Liebe* (*Mute love*), *Der geraubte Schleier* (*The stolen veil*), *Richilde* (*Richilda*), *Dämon Amor* (*Demon love*), *Die Nymphe des Brunnens* (*The nymph of the well*) hold promise of whole novels. 'Rübezahl' is also to be found in this book—one of the most interesting characters on that border line between legend and fairy tale.

In style these tales stand closer to the *Volksbuch* in the respectable form given to it by Schwab and Simrock than to the folk-tale as the nineteenth century and we today understand it. But we are made to feel this difference only on the arrival of the Brothers Grimm and Ludwig Bechstein who drew the dividing line so sharply between these two worlds. Just how ripe the time was for this kind of thing shows, for example, in the fact that in 1786–88 Herder published *Die Palmblätter*, a selection of Eastern tales of great beauty.

Twenty-five years after Musäus' *Volksmärchen* had appeared, the inseparable Brothers Grimm brought out the first volume of their *Kinder-und Hausmärchen* (1812). The French literary historian, Paul Hazard, describes their activity at that time as that of butterfly-catching, an occupation where it is all important to capture the specimens alive. And in a later simile he likens the result to home-made bread. Perhaps only a sympathetic foreign critic can express himself so clearly and simply—but how right he is in both his opinions.

'To catch alive' indeed meant much to the Brothers. They brought in much of their 'living' harvest of fairy tales from the home of the busy farmer's wife of the village of Zwehr bei Kassel, who went by the charming name of 'Viehmännin' (literally 'cattle woman'). The precise words of her stories, and those of other story-tellers, they got to some extent by heart, although it would be a wrongful underestimation of these worthy brothers to regard their merit as residing only in their activity as collectors.

For adult readers the versions of the fairy tales given in the original edition are especially valuable, for they reproduce most strongly the verbal rendering of the original source. There is not a single superfluous word in this first edition; everything stands clearly delineated as in a woodcut with only the meagrest of necessary detail. Indeed, returning to Hazard, this is the toughest

The Brothers Grimm; from the portrait by E. Jerichau-Baumann formerly
the possession of the Staatliche Museum, Berlin-Dahlem.

Plate I

'Die Viehmännin'. The teller of fairy tales on whom the Grimms drew for so many of their tales.
An engraving by Ludwig Emil Grimm which appeared as frontispiece to the enlarged second edition of *Kinder- und Hausmärchen*, 1819.

Plate II

THE BROTHERS GRIMM. *German popular stories*, translated by Edgar Taylor. Volume I. London, 1823. Etched illustration by George Cruikshank from the first English edition of Grimm.

of home-baked bread, with all its aromatic flavour. But if they had continued to present their stories in this way the brothers would never have made their total conquest of the world of children. Only with the second compilation (1814) does one get the feeling that the narrators are really thinking of children as they write. Only now are those small, delightful details added which turn this home-baked bread into the most inviting of the world's delicacies without taking away any of its nutriment. The result is that Hänsel and Gretel, Brother and Sister, Little Red Riding Hood, Snow-White and Rose-Red, and so many others have all found their way into the family circle of countless generations of children. Indeed, we grown-ups can never entirely forget these characters who are for ever young. They cannot outgrow us like our own children. Scarcely have these last got on to their feet than we must start telling them about Little Red Riding Hood. The gingerbread house which hides the cage where Hänsel is to be fattened up becomes at the same time the centre-piece of an incomparable woodland idyll. While, in earlier fairy stories, the world still belonged to princes, princesses, and kings, and exceptional cunning or beauty were the least that was required to distinguish the heroes, we now find, in this Age of Revolution, that a poor miller's lad, a simple servant-girl, or a woodcutter can move the heart as much as the banished princesses and valiant

33

knights of old. 'Hans in luck' comes to value the poverty that enables him to travel light, a typically Romantic concept. On the other hand, in *Starsilver*, it is demonstrated with contrasting logic that gold and riches are a quite proper reward for those who are pure in heart.

This story of the poor naked little girl in the forest on whom the stardust falls moves us in just the same remarkable way as the story thirty years later of 'the little match-girl', whose soul soars to heaven in the warmth and brightness of a blazing bundle of matches.

The two brothers, to whom the children of their own and following generations are so much in debt, were neither of them family men at the time of the first publication of their *Household stories*. Born in 1785 (Jakob) and 1786 (Wilhelm) they spent much of their lives in the ducal library at Kassel, foraging into German antiquity, German philology, and German literature. Having grown up in an occupied Germany, they experienced in these years (the years of the War of Liberation from 1814 onward) the freeing of their country from the French. The patriotic fervour which reigned at that time was marvellously transmuted by the two brothers into an intellectual quest for the purest and freshest springs of their nation's linguistic heritage.

The wonderful fairy-story figures who were brought to life in this way have been for many of us companions throughout the years of childhood. More than all our other education they have opened our hearts, extended our sensibilities, and acquainted us even at first reading with a prose style of exemplary simplicity. And children have shown their gratitude for this gift with a century and a half of loyalty, so that today the stories are more popular than ever. But they are threatened. In this age of ours, with its return to visual communication, they, too, have been taken over by pictures. Extravagant, all too emphatic illustrations have strangled their delicate but so much more unpretentious language, while on film Snow-White and so many other figures have been turned into goggling Hollywood stars. But even this debasement finally bears witness to the continuing power and the profound inner life of the fairy stories.

Before and after the Brothers Grimm

To be completely just it must be said that copying out fairy stories, whether their own or foreign ones, was not a sole privilege of the Brothers Grimm at this time. The great and justifiable success of the *Kinder-und Hausmärchen*, which brought a quantity of fairy stories into the consciousness of whole sections of society, caused at the same time a certain impoverishment, in so far as the stories which were not included in even the later editions of the Grimms' collection disappeared into oblivion. And even down to the present day the predominant popularity of some, but not all, of Grimms' fairy tales has somewhat mitigated against the spread of other fairy stories.

The fairy stories which at the end of the eighteenth century were already circulating in Germany were little more than the simplest of popular fare.

They were not preserved in libraries or in middle-class homes and they underwent continual changes through their mode of oral transmission. Take, for example, the fairy story *Das Erdkühlein* which comes first in an excellent collection: *Deutsche Märchen vor Grimm*, edited by Albert Wesselsky and illustrated by Fritz Kredel (1938). This fairy story, of which the first printed version appeared around 1560, and at Strassburg be it noted, is interesting because it contains for the first time in print two entirely typical fairy-story themes: first, the child who has been sent out scattering pebbles to ensure his return (as it were the Ariadne's thread of fairy tales, later to reappear in *Hänsel and Gretel*); and second, the theme of the magic tree which reappears in an astonishingly similar guise in Basile's *Cinderella* story of 1634. Perrault, remarkably, leaves this theme out of his *Cendrillon*, but with the Grimm version it returns in incomparable manner:

Bäumchen rüttel dich und schüttel dich,	Wave tree, shake tree,
wirf Gold und Silber über mich.	Shed gold and silver over me.[1]

Goethe, who was a student at Strassburg, must have taken this captivating story to his heart, for he uses the name 'Erdkülin' with a tender connotation at the end of a letter to Frau von Stein. This example of the now almost completely vanished 'Erdkühlein' is but one among many to show that from 1800 onwards the recording of texts by true writers had become necessary in order to preserve the fairy stories for the reading public and not just for the students of folk-lore. In any event, the magical 'Erdkühlein' who puts in an appearance here disappeared entirely from the fairy tales of the nineteenth century. Her place in otherwise very similar stories is filled by fairies imported from France.

Among the successors to the Brothers Grimm our gratitude must go chiefly to Ludwig Bechstein. This writer, born in Weimar in 1801, published in 1845 and 1856 two volumes of fairy stories. Here to some extent the already well-known tales came creeping back in slightly altered guise, but Bechstein's chief merit lies in the way that he has noted down fairy tales from all parts of Germany with their special regional characteristics, while investigating in detail the rich territory of his particular locality, the Thuringian Forest. (*Deutsches Märchenbuch*, 1845, and *Neues deutsches Märchenbuch*, 1856.)

Like the Grimms, Bechstein belongs among those who used their gifts as writers to set down serviceable versions of the existing heritage of fairy tales. In contrast to him are those writers who use the fairy story as an art-form, without feeling themselves thereby committed to the old, traditional themes, even though they bring them in here and there, consciously or unconsciously. Foremost among these are Ludwig Tieck, Justinus Kerner, E. T. A. Hoffmann,

[1] The generally accepted pantomime version in Great Britain also leaves out the magic tree. For a useful discussion of the variants in the story, see Geoffrey Brereton's introduction to Perrault's *Fairy tales* (Penguin, 1957). (B.A.)

and W. Hauff. In yet another direction there is Clemens Brentano who, with his incredibly sure instinct for the genuine, combines in the most exquisite way his own imagination with ancient popular themes, some of which he has taken over from the Italian.

Among those named above, only Hauff has proved an outstanding success with children. Born in Stuttgart in 1802, he wrote his fairy tales in 1826 to aid him in his work as a family tutor. His stories combine in an extraordinary way the richness and intensity of the world of Eastern tales with a Romantic and peculiarly Swabian style of recounting them. Without doubt they will long survive his other writings such as his novel in the manner of Scott, *Lichtenstein*. *Zwerg Nase* (*Dwarf Long-nose*), *Kalif Storch* (*Caliph Stork*), *Das Wirtshaus im Spessart* (*The inn in Spessart*), and *Das kalte Herz* (*The frozen heart*) are titles which can match some of our present gaudy literature, but which nevertheless came from a world of true literary sensibility.

One book of fairy tales which did gain a legitimate success was the *Träumereien am Französischen Kamin* (*Dreams by French firesides*) (1871) which a German officer, Richard von Volkmann-Leander, set down during the siege of Paris, when he had to spend long evenings in one of the chambers of a deserted château.

Nor should we pass over here a famous collection of fairy stories from Scandinavia, which appeared within a generation of those of the Brothers Grimm and in a similar way. This has found its way into many countries, often under its English title *East of the sun and west of the moon*, and in England it gained an independent life through the adaptation by Sir George Webbe Dasent, himself an authority on fairy stories and a pupil of Jakob Grimm.

The two authors of this Norwegian classic were Peter Christian Asbjörnsen (1812–85) and Jörgen E. Moe (1803–82), and they proceeded in much the same way as the Brothers Grimm. Asbjörnsen was a zoologist and collected the stories on his scientific expeditions, and his friend Moe, a theologian and a poet, also spent much of his spare time in collecting. Like those of their famous German counterparts, these stories are pervaded by a toughness and an unspoilt freshness; magical happenings, trolls, giants, witches all play a more important part than such things as fairies, while the heroes are blessed with at least as much good humour as courage.

Later on, English fairy stories were collected by Joseph Jacobs (1854–1916), but he took them from forgotten books and not direct from the oral tradition.

The folk-tale today

The wave of fairy stories which broke over the heads of children with the Brothers Grimm, if not with Perrault, would surely have completely swamped their sensitivity and their capacity to read, did not the history of children's literature, just as that of adult literature, display a principle of natural selection which for ever ensures that only the fittest of the books of fairy stories survive. Decades of mawkish variations all beginning with the words 'Once upon a time . . .' usually have nothing else in common with genuine fairy tales but the fact that what is being told is not 'true'.

The most wholesome reaction to the degeneration of the fairy story was the emergence of the realistic children's story already mentioned. But our century has seen a return to the study of genuine folk-tales, which are being collected the world over. On the threshold of our age Tolstoy came to join the group of master story-tellers: Basile (300 years ago), Perrault (250 years ago), and the Brothers Grimm (150 years ago), bringing with him the new and distinctive features of the Russian fairy tale.

But this is not sufficient for our cosmopolitan age. The students of folk-lore have brought together such collections from all round the world that the child of today can be encouraged and stimulated to reach for any fruit from the world's great tree of fairy tales. And he may reach for it with pleasure. The most beautiful and exceptional of all such collections is surely Lisa Tetzner's *Die schönsten Märchen der Welt für 365 und einen Tag*, which has become known far beyond the German-speaking territories.

This outstanding teller of tales (for she has the story-telling tradition in her blood) is apparently as much at home among the fairy stories of India as those of Italy. Naturally her knowledge of German tales is thorough, but when she writes for German-speaking children she takes care to avoid the well-trodden paths. We find all the themes and all the folk-wisdom of the world in these books, which even adults have found illuminating. The strangest and most familiar things are set down in a uniformly plain German, which contains enough personal style to give confidence to the young German reader, but never so much that it makes the frequently exotic contents impossible to understand.

I do not like to close this chapter on fairy tales without some mention of the genuine story-tellers who, even today, still exist among the common people. We find them chiefly in mountain districts and usually, when instances come to light among the inhabitants of the more civilized regions, nothing is spared to enable us to record these last expressions of an age-old popular wisdom.

The last case of this kind known to me was the cobbler Barba Plasch from the Swiss Engadin who died in 1945. His father had been a celebrated story-teller before him and Barba Plasch continued his tradition, plying his cobbler's trade from house to house. He told fairy stories in accordance with all the rules of the art, full of the old, well-known themes, but laced with the special characteristics of his mountainous locality on the one hand, and characteristics of the modern world on the other. Leza Uffer, who recorded his fairy stories for us, had heard the cobbler's tales in his childhood and was later to hear them once again from the lips of the old man (Leza Uffer: *Die Märchen des Barba Plasch*, Zürich, 1956).

There are still such story-tellers to be found, especially in villages where the radio and the cinema have not yet penetrated. These two technical marvels are the murderers of all the primitive creative impulses of the people, which find expression in dancing, music, acting, and story-telling. The only comfort that remains to us is that by virtue of this same technical progress we are able to record on tape and preserve things of this kind which still exist. There are now gramophone records as well—vicarious story-tellers—producing with a flick of the switch the voice of well-known actresses reading a story from Grimm. It is even possible to dial a number on the telephone and get your fairy story for the day. Where is it all leading us? Away from real story-telling—the intimate contact between teller and hearer? Away from books themselves? It is impossible to know.

UFFER, Leza. *Die Märchen des Barba Plasch*. Zürich, 1956.
Line drawing by Corina Steinrisser.

COMMENT

The first appearance in English of *The Arabian nights' entertainments* (1704–17), Perrault (*Mother Goose's tales*, 1729), and Grimm (*German popular stories:* 2 vols, 1823 and 1826) are dealt with in detail in the books by Darton, Muir and Thwaite noted in the final bibliography. The nineteenth century also saw translations into English of all the German fairy-tale writers mentioned in this chapter, but few are available in separate volumes today.

There is also no current English edition for children of Giambattista Basile, although several of his tales appear in the Andrew Lang collections noted below. The first serious attempt to turn his difficult Neapolitan into English was made by John Edward Taylor, a relative of the Edgar Taylor who first translated Grimm. This book, *The Pentamerone*, was published in 1848 with illustrations by Cruikshank but the translator deprecated 'the gross license in which Basile allowed his humour to indulge'. The 'moral sense' of the Victorians was 'happily too refined and elevated to tolerate indelicacy' and

Taylor therefore gave only thirty of the fifty stories and some of these, too, had matter of offence removed from them.

It was the resulting volume that formed the basis for an edition by Helen Zimmern in *The children's library* (T. Fisher Unwin, 1893), but even then she was 'obliged to revise many pages, omitting offensive words and expressions and adapting the stories to juvenile ears'. All this watering-down was characteristically remedied by Sir Richard Burton in a complete translation issued in two volumes in 1893, itself used for a one-volume edition of the work in 1952 published by William Kimber. The definitive English translation, however, is that by Benedetto Croce, edited with a full introduction and comprehensive notes by N. M. Penzer (John Lane, London, 1932).

There are, of course, a great many children's editions of the well-known European fairy stories currently available and in the following book-list I have confined myself to carefully prepared versions and have noted any features of particular interest.

THE ARABIAN NIGHTS

The Arabian nights, edited by Amabel Williams-Ellis, illustrated by Pauline Baynes. Criterion Books, 1957.
> A translation based on the main English editions giving admirable versions of nineteen tales. Mrs. Williams-Ellis also copes cleverly with the framework of the book and adds some very useful notes for adults.

Arabian nights, collected and edited by Andrew Lang, illustrated by Vera Bock. Longmans, 1951.
> First published 1898. Translated by Mr. and Mrs. Lang from the French of Galland, shortened and with the omission 'of pieces suitable for Arabs and old gentlemen'. Contains nineteen tales in a rather sketchy framework.

Arabian nights, selected by Dr. Hedwig Smola, adapted by Charlotte Dixon, illustrated by Janusz Grabianski. Duell, 1964.

Fairy tales from the Arabian nights, edited and arranged by E. Dixon, illustrated by Joan Kiddell-Monroe. Dutton, 1952.

Tales from the Arabian nights, illustrated by Brian Wildsmith. Walck, 1962 (text, 1946).
> Introduction by E. O. Lorimer gives the framework of the stories. This and the two editions above are less satisfactory to read than the others, but have enjoyable illustrations.

CHARLES PERRAULT

The fairy tales of Charles Perrault, translated by Geoffrey Brereton. Penguin, 1957.
> Illustrated with cuts from the earliest English edition. Includes also prose paraphrases of three verse tales, including *Peau d'âne* and a valuable introduction by the translator.

Perrault's complete fairy tales, translated by A. E. Johnson and others, with illustrations by W. Heath Robinson. Dodd, 1961.

Originally published as *Old time stories*, Constable (London), 1921.

THE BROTHERS GRIMM

Grimms' fairy tales, translated and edited by Margaret Hunt, revised by James Stern, illustrated by Josef Scharl. Pantheon, 1944.

Based on the 'almost complete edition' in Bohn's Library (1884). Contains 210 tales and a folkloristic commentary by Joseph Campbell.

Tales from Grimm, translated and illustrated by Wanda Gág. Coward, 1936.

The seventeen tales in this volume represent the ideal presentation of the stories for young children. The short introduction on the principles of selection and the problems of adaptation is excellent. In 1947 Wanda Gág added thirty-two more tales in *More tales from Grimm* (also Coward).

Grimms' fairy tales, illustrated by Charles Folkard. Dutton, 1951.

Forty-seven tales based on a selection from the original translation revised by A. A. Dent.

Grimms' fairy tales, illustrated by Ulrik Schramm. Walck., 1962 (text 1946).

Grimms' fairy tales, illustrated by Jean O'Neill. World, 1946.

OTHER AUTHORS

AULNOY, Marie, Comtesse d'. *The hind in the forest and other tales*, retold by Hilda McGill. New edition. Roger Ingram (London), 1965.

SÉ GUR, Sophie, Comtesse de. *Blondine and Bear-cub*, translated by Roland Gant, illustrated by Roland Pym. Heinemann (London), 1957.

HAUFF, W. *Hauff's fairy tales*, translated by Jean Rosemary Edwards, illustrated by Jiři Trnka. Hamlyn (London), 1961.

HOFFMANN, E. T. A. *The fairy tales of Hoffmann*, retold by Marjorie R. Watson, illustrated by W. F. Phillipps. Dutton, 1964.

ASBJÖRNSEN, P. C., and MOE, J. *East of the sun and west of the moon*, translated by Sir George Webbe Dasent, illustrated by Hedvig Collin. Macmillan, 1963.

ASBJÖRNSEN, P. C., and MOE, J. *Norwegian folk-tales*, translated by Pat Shaw Iversen and Carl Norman, illustrated by Erik Werenskiold and Theodor Kittelsen. Viking, 1961.

Thirty-five tales in a new translation but illustrated with drawings used by Asbjörnsen in early Norwegian editions.

COLLECTIONS

There are a great many collections of fairy tales now available either in single volumes or in series. The following is only a small selection:

ELLIS, Amabel Williams–. *Round the world fairy tales*, edited by Amabel Williams-Ellis, illustrated by William Stobbs. Warne, 1963.

Thirty-six tales with notes on sources.

MCNEILL, James. *The sunken city and other tales from round the world*, illustrated by Theo Dimson. Walck, 1959.

The double knights: more tales from round the world, illustrated by Theo Dimson. Walck, 1965.

LANG, Andrew. *The colour fairy books*. Longmans.

With the publication in 1899 of *The blue fairy book*, Andrew Lang commenced his 'supervision' of this famous series. For the history of the series, which today numbers nine volumes, see *Andrew Lang* by Roger Lancelyn Green (Walck, 1962). Photo-lithographic reprints of the original volumes have recently been issued in paperback by Dover Books.

The Oxford myths and legends, illustrated by Joan Kiddell-Monroe. Walck.

A collection of the folk-lore from countries all round the world, at present numbering fifteen volumes.

The favorite fairy tales series, retold by Virginia Haviland.

Four volumes devoted to Italy, Poland, Scotland and Spain have so far appeared in the United States (Little, Brown, 1965).

3 THE UGLY DUCKLING
Hans Christian Andersen, teller of fairy tales

Hans Christian Andersen was born in 1805. Nothing in the circumstances of his birth indicated any kind of glorious future; indeed, it is difficult to imagine very much greater destitution. But, bearing in mind the Europe of his time, it is clear that Andersen chose a fortunate moment to make his entrance into the world. For, however pitiful his private circumstances may have been at the start, at least he was to have contemporaries who would understand and applaud his special genius.

At the time of the birth of this poor cobbler's son there was living in Heidelberg a group of young idealists, two of whom were already in the process of publishing *Des Knaben Wunderhorn*, whose powerful effects have been described earlier in this book. One of these effects was the encouragement which the young brothers Jakob and Wilhelm Grimm found to get on with their collection of fairy tales. Their first volume appeared in 1812 and proved to be one of the world's ageless and unforgettable masterpieces and one which would mean much even to Andersen.

The story is told that many years later Andersen, now a world-famous man, was travelling round Europe and, on reaching Berlin, summoned up the courage to knock on the door of the Brothers Grimm. As a teller of fairy stories he himself had brought tears and laughter to countless thousands of people from children and their parents to kings, generals, and cabinet ministers, while the Grimms in the meantime had become respected professors of German philology. The housekeeper asked Andersen which of the brothers he wished to speak to. 'The one who has written the most,' said the nervous man on the doorstep; so he was taken to Wilhelm. But alas! Wilhelm had never heard of this enthusiastic Scandinavian traveller who was calling on him in such comradely fashion (the situation is not difficult to imagine when we remember Andersen's lean and awkward bearing). Thus, after a short, embarrassed conversation, during which his enormous admiration for the

Brothers Grimm prevented him from advertising his own fame to the great professor, Andersen withdrew. As for Grimm, he rapidly discovered who it was that had escaped him and, very respectfully, he paid Andersen a return visit in Copenhagen a year later.

Andersen's shyness also held him back from visiting Goethe, who had paid some attention to this remarkable man from Denmark—a thing not surprising when one considers the encouragement which he had given to the young Brentanos, Arnims, and Grimms at Heidelberg. Goethe's grandson Walther loved Andersen's stories before all others and based plays for his puppet theatre upon them when he visited his grandfather's house, a fact which Andersen was to learn later on from Goethe's daughter-in-law. But Andersen's contacts abroad were not confined only to Germany and her great thinkers; they also spread to France and England where, right down to the present day, he has a tremendous popularity.

In 1812, seven years after his own birth, Charles Dickens was born, a man with whom he was to be linked in friendship and whom he was to meet twice on his visits to England. Some years later still, Charles Kingsley was born and his most popular book *The water babies* was to show the closest similarities in all contemporary literature to Andersen's fairy-tale world.

All three men were joined in the profoundest sympathy for the suffering and deprivation which many children had to endure. While the Englishmen were impelled to fight such misery from social and Christian motives, Andersen, who had a by no means theoretical interest in social questions, came to it through the memory of his own indescribably poor and difficult childhood.

It is itself like a fairy tale to read how in 1955, 150 years after Andersen's birth, the present King of Denmark sat in front of a microphone in the poet's little room at Odense to honour again the nation's greatest writer. He then called upon one of the profoundest living interpreters of Hamlet (that other famous Dane) and from that little room the voice of Michael Redgrave broadcast the stories to the world. He broadcast in English, the language most widely understood, so that *The little match-girl*, *The princess and the swineherd*, *The princess and the pea*, and many other immortal figures took their way from Odense across the invisible wavelengths of the globe. Is that not a phenomenon more wonderful than the flying trunk? And what would the poet himself have said about it, with all his belief in miracles? He would surely have said 'Yes' with the same kind of enthusiasm which, right from the start, led him to accept railways as a good means of travelling or would have led him to accept the aeroplane, whose arrival he anticipated with prophetic foresight.

But let us now turn back to Odense where the life of the greatest modern teller of fairy tales began and where it was always rooted.

Here, in this idyllic little town, 'the ugly duckling' was born, the son of a twenty-two-year-old cobbler Hans Andersen and his wife Marie Andersdatter who was ten to fifteen years his senior and had married him only two months previously. Very often Andersen's fairy tales are little more than autobiographical sketches in which he casts in poetic form the fearsome and wonderful events of his life. Without doubt the writing of fairy tales helped him to throw off the all too heavy burden of his memories and to turn them into something of enduring value.

His actual autobiography he called *The fairy tale of my life* (*Mit Livs Eventyr*, 1855, published earlier in German as *Das Märchen meines Lebens ohne Dichtung*, 1847) and we have every reason to regard it as such. Researches based upon contemporary sources show that the poet's life, and especially his childhood, was very much harder than he himself describes, dominated as he was by a passionate longing to find a harmony in everything. And in the second half of his life what fell to the writer in the way of fame and affluence and affection was paid for with sickness, loneliness, and with a certain sense that he was a man without a country.

Since this is a book devoted to children's literature I ought to deal chiefly with Andersen as a creator of fairy tales. But in doing this I should like to use as a central theme that fairy tale which symbolizes most clearly the story of his life.

In this tale, Andersen takes a strange incident from the world of nature and turns it into a story of profound significance—the story of a grey, clumsy cygnet who grows up all too big and ugly in a respectable family of ducks. Because he is so different he is understood by nobody; he is pushed around, teased, driven from door to door, until, in the following spring, he meets the lordly swans, is recognized by them as one of themselves and accepted into their community.

Applying the moral of this fable to its author, the poor boy who grew up to move among the 'swans' of his time—the greatest poets and scholars, and even the royal courts—there is one thing which does not properly fit, namely, the ugly duckling's despair over his future. For Hans Christian, the problem child from the provincial cobbler's shop, seems to have felt, if not known, very early in life that he was born from a swan's egg. His actual nursery, the duck-yard of the fairy tale, was in fact a single room where the whole family ate, slept, and worked. His bed was a bunk beside his parents' bed which the cobbler had knocked together from the old framework of a dead count's bier. A piece of black crape must still have been hanging there when he was older to remind him of its origin.

His mother seems to have been a pious, superstitious but thoroughly able woman in spite of having something of a past (she had already had a daughter out of wedlock, whom Hans Christian was later to meet again in Copenhagen living a somewhat dissolute life). Like the mother-duck in the fairy story, Hans Andersen's mother had faith in her son and fed him, clothed him, and helped him along for as long as she knew how. Later on, after a second marriage and after her son had become a writer, she was to end up as an alcoholic in an asylum, but she witnessed with pride the start of his fame.

His father, on the other hand, was neither pious nor very able. He was a free-thinker and, had circumstances allowed, he saw himself as someone more important than just a jobbing boot-maker. His own parents, however, despite better origins, had had to give up their small property on account of his father's mental instability, so Hans Christian's splendid grandmother had had to keep herself and her harmlessly wayward husband by the work of her own hands. She was an ever-loving guardian to her grandson, while his grandfather went singing through the streets, festooned with garlands, carving remarkable figurines which he would exchange for food and drink with the peasant women in the surrounding countryside. In *The fairy tale of my life* Hans Christian neither concealed nor embroidered the dread which he felt for the man and yet even this grandfather with his carvings of animals with the heads of men and men with the heads of animals seems to have had some qualities which in spite of his madness or simply in his madness itself, lived on in his highly intelligent grandson.

Hans Andersen, père, the cobbler, was also a singular man. If he had had the gifts of his son he might perhaps have become a second Hans Sachs, but at least he sowed valuable seeds in the mind of his child. On his shelf, next to the Bible, there were volumes of La Fontaine, of Holberg, and a copy of *The thousand and one nights*, and these were read aloud to the little boy on Sundays and every evening. The father even made a little puppet theatre for his son with all kinds of movable sets and it always gave him some happiness to see the child think up whole plays for himself from the playbills of the real theatre which he managed to get hold of.

When Hans Christian was nine years old his father went off to become a soldier, promising by this means to find some way out of their grinding poverty. But he soon came back—less ebullient than before—and at the age of thirty-two, when his son was eleven, Hans Andersen the cobbler died in the big bed with the remnant of funeral crape stuck to its frame. In *The fairy tale of my life* this is related as follows:

'His corpse was left lying on the bed, and I slept on the floor with my mother; and a cricket chirped throughout the night. "He is dead already," my mother called to it. "You need not call him; the Ice Maiden has taken him," and I understood what she meant. I remembered the previous winter when our windows were frozen over; my father had shown us a figure on one of the panes like that of a maiden stretching out both her arms. "She must have come to fetch me," he said in fun; and now as he lay dead on the bed, my mother remembered this, and his words occupied my thoughts.'[1]

This little extract which relates the saddest and most momentous experience in Andersen's childhood shows better than anything the way in which he can touch with poetry a scene which even for a child is truly macabre.

[1] From the translation of *The fairy tale of my life* by W. Glyn Jones. Maxsons, British Book Centre, N.Y. (1955).

The only legacy from his father was the little puppet theatre, and, in the lonely time that followed, the seed which the cobbler had sown began to grow. But he was to spend only a little time longer in the cramped house for which he was later to feel a profound nostalgia. This is clear from the lines of a poem which he published at the age of seventy to go with a woodcut of the house where he lived as a child:

> One little room, a scullery,
> Kindliness and quiet things;
> Never a Christmas Eve like that
> In all the palaces of kings.

These lines already point to his fabulous rise to fame which would take him from country to country and from the tumbledown cottage in Odense to the palaces of kings. But for the time being he struggled with school work and work in a cloth-mill, all without success. At the age of fourteen he could scarcely write properly, he was unable to stay in a job, and he found his chief contentment in singing or reciting for the entertainment of his neighbours, or at the festivities of well-to-do townspeople.

Then, however, the moment arrived when the ugly duckling grew too big and became objectionable to everyone around him. He had to leave the farmyard and suffer a winter of unprecedented bitterness. For Hans Christian the ugly duckling's winter corresponds to ten years of the hardest privation and poverty. Fourteen years old and totally alone, he travelled to Copenhagen. And here, after years of failure in the theatre, in the ballet and as a writer, he finally found a patron who would give him what he really felt he lacked—a proper education—even though at first this too seemed a suspect gift. For when Andersen at the age of seventeen once again went to school, the duckling was already beginning to show a few white feathers and to feel the power in his wings.

But only when he was twenty-four, with success in his examinations behind him, did his energetic patron give him his freedom and allow him to travel and to write, becoming in truth the magnanimous father-figure and protector to the stray bird, but even so without ever fully recognizing the swan beneath the down.

Jonas Collin and his family provided the poet with the only home that he knew and that he could return to throughout his life, even though the self-assurance and the rather refined atmosphere of this middle-class household never entirely ceased to remind him of the wretchedness of his early years. The full-grown swan felt at his best when he could spread his wings and take his flight to foreign lands. And even in this that extraordinary Maecenas Jonas Collin was able time and again to procure royal scholarships for him or to help him out of his own pocket, for the novels and essays of the young writer were scarcely an overwhelming success, even though they earned him a solid reputation in literary circles. At the age of thirty, however, he published his first fairy tales, *Eventyr fortalte for Børn* (1835), a volume which each year was to be joined by others; and slowly he began to find that recognition which, at first abroad and later in his own country, was to turn into a quite unparalleled fame.

ANDERSEN, Hans Christian. *Eventyr*. Copenhagen.
Illustrated editions of Andersen's tales were published from 1850 onwards. His chosen illustrator was Vilhelm Pedersen, two of whose wood-engravings are reproduced here.

It seems to me worth noting that throughout his life Andersen was a restless soul. No poet of that time travelled as much as Denmark's national poet. His whole life was taken up with travels throughout Germany, France, Switzerland, his Scandinavian neighbours, England, and again Germany, where his work had made a wide appeal from the start. He also visited Italy, Greece, the Near East, and finally Spain, a country he especially loved. In the course of these journeys he wrote novels, travel-books, and innumerable letters.

Wherever he went he had to recite his fairy tales—and how well he must have done it! For with Andersen the written word takes its origin directly from the spoken word. Conversations and exclamations abound and although the language may often be a little precious and without that down-to-earth toughness which characterizes so many popular fairy tales, one nevertheless senses the spoken word behind it. We are being spoken to; we are drawn into the circle. This would, in fact, be a dangerous method of writing, were it not carried out in such a masterly and vivid way, full of wit and irony, and again and again interrupted by descriptions of nature or of human experience which have a quintessential poetry about them. An example of this occurs in the last part of *The nightingale* when the bird, singing on a branch outside the dying Emperor's window, awakens him to renewed life:

'And Death gave up each of these treasures for a song, and the nightingale still went on singing: it sang of the quiet churchyard where white roses grow,

E

where the elderberry-tree smells sweet and the fresh grass is damp with the tears of those who are left behind. Then Death was filled with longing for his garden, and drifted out through the window like a cold white mist.'[1]

Now what is it that has made Andersen a teller of fairy tales whom our age has found comparable only to the Brothers Grimm with their *Kinder- und Hausmärchen*? Perhaps this is a question which should not be asked. Brentano's fairy stories, Hoffmann's ghost stories, Hauff's fairy stories are to some extent more exciting or profounder and often more gripping than these plain and delicate creations with their roots in the damp, green meadows of Denmark. All his journeyings in the mountains of Switzerland, on the shores of the Mediterranean, or in the mysterious East could not rob Andersen of the homeliness of the flat, uncomplicated Danish countryside. He is like the moon, the narrator of *The picture-book without pictures*, Andersen's finest account of his own travels. His beams have fallen on everything, but they are at their loveliest when they shine through drifting clouds on drenched fields, or steep-pitched roofs, or upon the sea.

Andersen never knew a real home of his own, apart from the room in the humble cobbler's shop where he spent his childhood and which reappears time and again in his fairy tales in one form or another. When he was in Copenhagen he lived in rented rooms and in hotels, or he was guest at the house of his benefactor or of other friends. In addition, he had little good fortune where women were concerned, although he had a lasting friendship with Jenny Lind, 'the Swedish nightingale', while the children of Jonas Collin remained true friends to him all through his life. At the age of seventy he died in the country house of a Jewish friend, exhausted, spent, but mourned by countless people throughout the world.

The enormous social as well as financial improvement in Andersen's circumstances meant that he was able to apply his spellbinding powers of persuasion equally to a portrayal of 'the little match-girl' as to that of the little girl who proved the truth of her claim to be a princess by suffering the discomfort of a pea beneath a whole mountain of mattresses. It is this huge range of sensitivity and experience which is probably one chief reason for his success, although it is necessary to add that his most affecting stories in whatever form have almost all grown out of the depths of his childhood memories. Similarly they have roots which go down into the folk-tales which he knew so well and into the superstitions of the simple people from the spinning-rooms of his native town. There are also clear traces of *The thousand and one nights*, harking back to his childish enjoyment of that book in the one room of the cobbler's house.

But how he has enriched everything and given it a relevance for our own time. He has brought to the plain black and white of the European fairy tale

[1] From the translation by L. W. Kingsland.

Hans Christian Andersen telling fairy stories. An anonymous photograph.

Plate III

EDGEWORTH, Maria. *Les enfans, ou les caractères.* Paris, 1823.
An engraving to illustrate *César et son petit cheval, ou ne maltraitez pas les animaux.*

Plate IV

an artistry typical of the poetic sensibility of the North, its irony and its psychological subtlety. What is new here and has hardly ever been employed before, is the manner in which dead things are invested with a soul, are brought to life in a quite unforgettable way, learning to speak and to become creatures in their own right. It is true that in Grimm we find the cudgel who jumps out of the bag to beat the evil-doers, and the singing bone who betrays a brother's murder; but these living objects are means to an end, instruments of justice, not people at all. But it is quite a different matter when Ole Lukøje (Willie Winky), a relation of the Sandman, sprays droplets of milk upon children's eyes until they sleep, for then he makes the flowers in the flower-pots in Hjalmar's bedroom grow into trees, he turns the slate and the slate-pencil from Hjalmar's drawer into a pair of hopping zanies and with one squirt of milk all the furniture in the room starts chattering (except, of course, for the poor spittoon).

Again, never before or since, has a miserable little one-legged soldier been the hero of such a beautiful and enthralling story as *The steadfast tin-soldier*. Andersen shows a splendidly developed artistry in the way he brings these things to life and in the children's literature of the following decades he was often imitated, usually in an unintelligent and condescendingly silly manner. One of the few exceptions is Collodi's *Pinocchio* (c. 1881), the wooden puppet who came to life and has now found himself translated into language after language capturing the imagination of children wherever he goes.

Everything in Andersen has a soul of its own and is correspondingly capable of appealing to the reader's imagination. Only seldom are children moved to tears over Grimm's fairy tales, and then only when something particularly sad or horrible is taking place. The fairy tales always remain to a certain extent independent of the reader's experience, tales simply of what goes on in fairyland and thus impossible for ourselves. But with Andersen it is completely different. It is true that he adopts elements from old tales, but what happens to them then? What happens to the little mermaid, for instance, who to begin with is an actual figure from Nordic legend? In order to be near her beloved prince she barters her tail for a pair of human legs, but after that a great change takes place. In spite of her goodness and her obvious faery characteristics, the little princess from the sea must suffer monstrous agonies. Her happiness is paid for with pain, human happiness with human pain. With her we must walk on a thousand knives and our buried feelings are stirred up from depths far removed from those of the folk-tale, whose world of feeling is unsophisticated, and follows accepted rules among which the so-called happy and just ending to stories is one.

For the first time in fairy stories Andersen admits the tragic ending. The little tin-soldier melts in the stove, the little match-girl freezes to death in the street, and the lovelorn little mermaid vanishes in foam at the end of her life as a mortal. Nor is the effect of these tragic conclusions, which stem from Andersen's own experience of life, in any way mitigated by the superb poetry of their telling. The effect they have on a sensitive child is enormous. Thus when people talk about the dangerous influence of fairy tales on children (and people, especially in the fields of education and psychology, often do, thinking mostly of the rather horrific witches and stepmothers that are found in Grimm) it is necessary to affirm that such plainly wicked characters are common to all folk-tales and never emerge triumphant anyway. They cause a much less profound emotional disturbance in a child than the 'pure tragedy' of *The little mermaid*, to take one of the most prominent examples. Basically, however, both forms of fairy tale serve the purpose of introducing children to literature, representing as they do all the elements which will be met with later on in life in novels, in poetry, and on the stage.

The third important aspect of Andersen's tales is the fantasy in their poetic association with nature and with the cosmos, above all the moon, which finds its most beautiful expression in *The picture-book without pictures*. Andersen here places himself in the tradition of the great Romantics, except that his attitude to nature is free from their brand of mysticism, being on the contrary full of intelligence and wit. (This, of course, applies less to the kind of story which has been prevalent since classical times and which, by allowing animals speech and free-will, more or less robs them of their real nature.)

Wood-engraving by Vilhelm Pedersen.

In Andersen animals remain animals and plants plants, each peculiar to itself. If he allows the storks to speak then they have to speak Egyptian and they remain storks living on roof-tops and spending eight months of the year beside the Nile. In fact, storks are his favourite animals, embodying as they do the poet's own wanderlust and being at the same time visitors from the East, figures from *The thousand and one nights*. Furthermore, for the people of the North they are birds with an important place in popular superstitions.

But Andersen could get the subject for a story from such everyday things as a drop of water, which he observed through the recently perfected microscope, or a family of snails, simply by revealing the marvel of their real nature. In *Five peas from one pod,* for instance, a pea lodges in the crack in some roof-tiles outside a little girl's bedroom window. It germinates, grows, and blossoms, and saves the life of a child whom everyone expected to die. In other words, a small, accepted process of nature is seen in the light of its own mystery and turned into a fairy tale.

Simply by looking at the openings of these tales one can see how the countryside, the seas, and the rivers are made to become backcloths or even performers. Winds and tempests, the sun, the moon and the stars, elves, water-sprites, and mermen all push the action along, and often Death will come too. For Andersen was no escapist taking refuge in nature. He stood centrally between the age of Romanticism and the age of Technology. The one gave him his profundity, bearing him forward and enriching him, the other he greeted with enthusiasm.

I have said that the poet's favourite animals were the storks, the experienced travellers, the fabulous animals of his stories. But his heart belonged finally to the wild swans flying with majestically beating wings towards the rising sun. One of his late stories, *The swans' nest,* is indeed more a patriotic account of his Danish homeland. It begins: 'Between the North Sea and the Baltic there is an old swans' nest which is called Denmark. There swans are born and swans will be born whose names shall never die.' That nest between the two wild seas has produced many an immortal swan, but the former 'ugly duckling' from Odense has flown the farthest and has brought endless happiness and comfort to all those countries where his books are read and loved.

COMMENT

Andersen took ten years to reach England, but when he arrived in 1846 he arrived plentifully: four volumes being published with that date by three different translators:[1]

Wonderful stories for children by Hans Christian Anderson [*sic*] translated from the Danish by Mary Howitt (Chapman and Hall, London).
Danish fairy-legends and tales (Pickering, London). No translator is given, but she was Caroline Peachey.
A Danish story-book and *The nightingale and other tales,* both translated by Charles Boner and illustrated by Count Pocci (Cundall, London). Translated from German versions.

Among them these four books give a total of twenty-four stories, the ten by Mary Howitt being the most felicitous. There are more recent translations in print now, of course. One of the many good American collections is listed:

Andersen's Fairy Tales, illustrated by Jean O'Neill. World (Rainbow Classic), 1946.

[1] The account of these given by Muir (op. cit., p. 52) is a little confusing. I have checked the above titles and publishers with the copies in the British Museum.

From 1846 onwards there have been countless editions, often taken from German versions, and it was not until that by M. R. James, cited below, that it became clear just how inaccurate and sentimental many of these were. Since that time there has been a revival in conscientious translation of Andersen, but it is interesting to note how often the translators attach a note to their work lamenting the problems and difficulties which they find in putting their author's very personal style into both accurate and natural English.

Fairy tales (4 vols), edited by Svend Larsen, translated by R. P. Keigwin, illustrated by Vilhelm Pedersen. Edmund Ward (London), from 1951.

This might be called the 'official' translation. It is issued from Odense by the Danish publisher Flensted and the illustrations are reproduced from the original drawings in the Andersen Museum. It is, however, too restrained and elegant an edition to appeal to children and the set is no longer available in its entirety from the English agent.

Hans Andersen's fairy tales, translated by L. W. Kingsland, illustrated by Ernest H. Shepard. Walck, 1961.

Contains thirty-two stories and is probably the best translation for children. L. W. Kingsland has also translated the selection in the O.U.P. *World Classics* edition of Andersen, where he provides a useful note on his work. This edition also reproduces the original illustrations by Pedersen and by Lorenz Frølich.

Hans Andersen: forty-two stories, translated by M. R. James, illustrated by Robin Jacques. Faber (London), 1953.

Includes James's important preface on translating Andersen first published in the edition of 1930 (*Forty Stories*).

Hans Andersen's fairy tales, translated by Reginald Spink, illustrated by Hans Baumhauer. Dutton, 1958.

Contains twenty-six stories and gives examples of translation problems.

Fairy tales and legends, illustrated by Rex Whistler. Bodley Head (London), 1935.

Contains forty-eight stories, including *What the moon saw*. The illustrations are of course superb, but the translation (adapted from Bohn and Everyman editions) is very stilted.

Hans Andersen's fairy tales, illustrated by Shirley Hughes. Blackie (London), 1961.

Hans Andersen's fairy tales, illustrated by Janusz Grabianski. Duell, 1963.

These two editions are mentioned for the sake of their colourful pictures and because their translations are both adapted from the very early translations made by Caroline Peachey (see above).

Much bibliographical information on Andersen can be found in the National Book League catalogue: *Hans Christian Andersen, 1805–1955. A Jubilee exhibition.* N.B.L. 1955, and in the *Catalog of the Jean Hersholt Collection.* Washington, The Library of Congress, 1954.

4 DR. HEINRICH HOFFMANN
the author of Struwwelpeter *but not that alone*

In all households where there are children and children's books certain ideas from these books pass into the private language of the family. In my own childhood, for instance, it was difficult to eat pickled cabbage without thinking of Widow Bolte in *Max und Moritz* '*die für ihn besonders schwärmt, wenn er wieder aufgewärmt*'. If somebody fidgeted at the table, however (and who didn't do such things?), then we all thought of Fidgety Phil, while many a bowl of soup would never have been eaten had not the match-stick ghost of little Augustus haunted our minds from the time that we were four years old. For all that, it is many years since poor old Augustus in his blue velveteen jacket first met his dreadful fate in the pages of a crudely drawn picture-book:

Am vierten Tage endlich gar   Look at him, now the fourth day's
Der Kaspar wie ein Fädchen war.   come!
Er wog vielleicht ein halbes Loth   He scarcely weighs a sugar-plum;
und war am fünften Tage todt.   He's like a little bit of thread;
                                And on the fifth day, he was—dead!

Just what a 'Loth'[1] was we didn't know, but that did not make the whole affair any the less alarming.

It was in 1844 that the young Dr. Heinrich Hoffmann (1809–94) went out to look for a picture-book to amuse his three-year-old son. He returned, however, with nothing more than a blank exercise-book in which, just before Christmas, he completed the writing and illustration of his own now famous picture-book. Alas, when he came to paint his outline drawings their ink ran

---

[1] 'Loth' is an old form of a word meaning 'a lead weight' (perhaps half an ounce) and, by extension, 'a plummet'. By using 'sugar-plum' the anonymous English translator has solved his problem in quite an ingenious way. (B.A.)

into the colours and the inexperienced artist had to start all over again. But this first manuscript has a wonderful narrative directness, enabling the same pen that weaves such awkward flourishes around the figures of the stories to write:

Wenn die Kinder artig sind,	At Christmas-time the Christmas Boy
Kommt zu ihnen das Christkind.	Comes to children who've been good,
Bringt es ihnen Gut's genug	Bringing stocking-loads of toys
und ein schönes Bilderbuch.	And a lovely picture-book.

The manuscript begins with 'The Story of Cruel Frederick' and 'Struwwelpeter', who was later to give the book its title, takes his place right at the end, his immense power of attraction not yet having been discovered. Among the doctor's younger patients, however, he was a kind of trademark, for his portrait had often been drawn for them to help them to forget their aches and pains or to quiet them so that Dr. Hoffmann could examine them with his stethoscope.

This manuscript edition also lacked some of the stories we now know. But as Dr. Hoffmann, not without some pride, circulated the book among his friends it reached the hands of a certain Dr. Löning who had just founded his firm: the *Literarische Anstalt*. Having quite recently brought out a small volume of poems, which Dr. Hoffmann had written and had printed at his own expense, he now paid out a fee and in 1845 produced an edition of 1,500 copies of this curious little children's book with its crude illustrations.

The lithographer who transferred the outline drawings on to the stone and the women who coloured them by hand were all strictly supervised by Dr. Hoffmann in order to prevent any hint of artificiality or sentimentality, whether in line or colour, from creeping into the pages. For he had created this book for the one reason that in all the Frankfurt bookshops he could find nothing except elegantly designed but high-minded children's books, which seemed to the young doctor, who wanted to give his son his first picture-book, quite unsuitable for children. He had therefore himself written and painted something in a school exercise-book and he was now going to make sure that every one of his clear and expressive lines was exactly reproduced and that his colouring was similarly retained with all its runny but pleasing combinations of colours.[1]

The 1,500 copies were sold out in four weeks and edition rapidly followed edition until, with the fifth, we have the complete book that we know today, with Struwwelpeter at the beginning and the author's full name on the title page. He had only found the courage to do this after it had become generally

[1] The attractiveness of the original and its enormous difference from most printed versions can be seen in the facsimile introduced by G. A. E. Bogeng: *Das Struwwelpeter-Manuskript.* Frankfurt a. M., Literarische Anstalt, 1925. (B.A.)

Dr. Heinrich Hoffmann at about thirty years of age; an anonymous
portrait.
(Photo W. Keim. Frankfurt a.m.)

Plate V

Top: Gavarni's *Les enfants terribles,* 1842—Struwwelpeter's precursor.
Bottom: HOFFMANN, Heinrich. *Struwwelpeter* (1) in the original manuscript, 1844; (2) in a second draft, 1858.

Plate VI

known, for to start with there simply appeared at the end of the versified list of contents:

Das alles fein malte und beschrieb   Written and drawn from end to end
Der lustige Reimerich Kinderlieb.   By Merry Rhymerick, children's friend.

In spite of many badly printed and debased imitations the book has spread throughout the world in thousands of editions and if, in this Age of the Child, it has become a source of contention this may well have its justification in the fact that there are now so many unstable children around burdened with psychological problems. It is, of course, the irony of fortune that this book, which has been attacked by the psychiatrists, was itself written by a doctor, who, in his later career as a mental specialist, established and ran one of the finest and most progressive mental hospitals of his time.

Yet, as I write, there lies in front of me an early edition of *Struwwelpeter*. Probably it is one of those which was prepared under the keen supervision of the author, for nobody since has ever given Little Suck-a-Thumb's mother such a rich blue cloak or the short-sighted huntsman such a fine forest-green jacket. When I turn the pages of this century-old book, which for generations has been looked after, cleaned up, glued together, freshly bound, I can scarcely understand why anyone should wish to belittle its fame. Struwwelpeter is himself a figure of great moral import who has made life a lot easier for generations of mothers when the time comes round for neck-scrubbing and nail-cutting. The story of cruel Frederick is a splendid plea against cruelty to animals:

Und der Herr Doktor steht dabei   The family doctor stands beside him
Und gibt ihm bittere Arzenei.   Doling out horrible medicine.

and there at the foot of the bed stands good Dr. Hoffmann with his top-hat in his hand. Then there is 'The Dreadful Story about Harriet and the Matches' —why on earth did the girl take them after such grave warnings from the pussy-cats?

Es brennt die Hand; es brennt das   It burns her hair, it burns her feet;
   Haar;   It burns the little child complete.
Es brennt das ganze Kind sogar.

This may be dreadful, but it is neither a very large nor a very realistically rendered portrait, while at the end the little grey heap of ashes with the un-harmed red slippers and the weeping pussy-cats achieves its effect through symbolism rather than realism.

There is a plea for tolerance in the story of the inky boys, and again in the incident where the hare steals the hunter's gun and manages to shoot his wife's coffee-cup out of her hand. But these are also enchantingly comic incidents presented in a way sure to appeal to children:

Doch bei dem Brünnchen heimlich
   sass
Des Häschens Kind, der kleine Has.
Der hockte da im grünen Gras;
Dem floss der Kaffee auf die Nas'.
Er schrie: Wer hat mich da
   verbrannt?
Und hielt den Löffel in der Hand.

Now by the well in hiding lay
The rabbit's child and saw the fray,
And glanced aloft with aspect gay
(Unwatchful of the coffee spray)
And would have laughed, but changed
   his mind,
When that hot coffee struck him blind.
He snatched the spoon and capered out
With many a baleful murderous shout
To club to death the clumsy lout
Who'd brought this accident about.
But when he saw it was his pa
He changed his mind again, aha!

(From the translation by Mark Twain)

Little Suck-a-Thumb is indeed truly horrific and still gives me the shivers when I think of the picture of the prancing tailor and his huge shears with the blood dripping down: '*Hei, da schreit der Konrad sehr.*' ('That made little Conrad yell.') As a child I always turned that page very quickly, but I did not skip it altogether. Now I have no idea if the modern psychologists have found a cure for thumb-sucking. So far as I can discover the struggle has been abandoned. The children continue to suck and the psychologists draw their conclusions. Heinrich Hoffmann, on the other hand, as a doctor stuck at nothing to break children of this unfortunate habit.

Augustus, who would not have any soup, is so far beyond reality that he makes his point without being nearly so frightening. Fidgety Phil, Johnny-Head-in-Air, and Flying Robert are for children entirely figures of fun. They only notice the moral or the frightening bits, if at all, after they have laughed at the comedy.

The completely unrealistic way in which the book is illustrated produces a kind of symbolic hyper-reality which is far less dangerous for children than many of the photographic representations of similar happenings which they see daily in newspapers and magazines, to say nothing of television horse operas. It is nevertheless necessary to have a look at one of the early editions of *Struwwelpeter* in order to recognize and understand today the true qualities of this book, by which its author conquered a whole world of children.

The original drawings for the book are still extant and can be seen to combine delicacy with their well-known directness of expression. Every page makes it clear that the author and illustrator of the book was a cultured and highly intelligent man who did not think it entirely a good thing that he was

"How I came to write Struwwelpeter."

Doctor HEINRICH HOFFMANN, the author of Struwwelpeter, relates its origin as follows:

Towards Christmas in the year 1844, when my eldest son was three years old, I went to town with the intention to buy as a present for him a picture-book, which should be adapted to the little fellow's powers of comprehension. But what did I find? Long tales, stupid collections of pictures, moralizing stories, beginning and ending with admonitions like: "the good child must be truthful", or: "children must keep clean", etc. But I lost all patience when I found a folio volume, where a bench, a chair, a jug, and many other things were drawn, and under each picture neatly written: "half, a third, or a tenth of the natural size". A child, for whose amusement you are painting a bench, will think that a real bench; it has not and need not have an idea of the full size of a real bench. The child does not reason abstractedly, and the old tale of the bridge (*vide:* Gellert's celebrated German fable "the farmer and his son") will certainly impress him more than hundreds of general warnings like: "you must not tell stories".

Dr. Heinrich Hoffmann.

That evening I nevertheless brought home a book, and handing it over to my wife, said: "there is what you wished for the little one". She took it, calling out rather amazed: "well that is a note-book with blank leaves". — "Just so, but we are going to make a book out of it". And it happened thus: I was then, although the medical man of the lunatic asylum, obliged to practise in town, where I was often brought into contact with children. Now, it certainly is a difficult thing for a Doctor to make little ones from 3 to 6 years old feel at their ease with him, because when they are in good health, the medical man and the chimney-sweep are very often made bugbears of. „My dear, if you are naughty the chimney-sweep will carry you off", or: "child, if you eat too much, the Doctor will come with his nasty medecine". The consequence is, that the little angel, when ill, begins to cry violently and to struggle as soon as the physician enters the room. An examination becomes utterly impossible, and the medical man cannot stay for hours vainly andeavouring to soothe the little patient. On such occasions a slip of paper and a pencil generally came to my assistance. A story, such as you find written here, invented on the spur of the moment, illustrated with a few touches of the pencil and humorously related, will calm the little antagonist, dry his tears and allow the medical man to do his duty.

In this manner most of the following absurd scenes originated. Some of them were later inventions, sketched in the same impulsive manner, without the least intention on my part of literary fame. The book was bound, put under the Christmas-tree, and the effect on the boy was just what I expected; not so, that produced upon some of my grown up friends who caught sight of the manuscript. From all sides I was asked to have it printed and published. I refused at first, as I had not the most distant idea of appearing before the public as author of juvenile story- and picture-books. But meeting one evening at a friend's house one of my present publishers, I was forced into it almost against my will, and thus the little home-bird flew into the wide, wide world, beginning, I may well say its voyage round the world. Shock-headed Peter, on his 31st. birthday, celebrated his hundredth edition.

HOFFMANN, Heinrich. *The English Struwwelpeter.* Frankfort (n.d.)
An introductory leaf to the fortieth English edition published by Rütten & Loening for the German Literary Society.

sacrificing his time on pranks like this. The result, however, has not only been something for children or for teachers seeking to demonstrate theories but also for historians and psychologists. Even Sigmund Freud has examined *Struwwelpeter*, but without interpreting the riddle of its success.

In an extremely interesting study[1] Professor Donald Brinkmann has attempted to explain the magnetism of this character by saying that Hoffmann, perhaps unconsciously, has put new life into a primitive mythical figure. After all, a hundred years earlier another famous Frankfurt man, the young Goethe, was nicknamed 'Der Frankfurter Strubelpeter' by Frau Stock, his landlady in Leipzig. Furthermore, Brinkmann reminds us, perhaps rightly, of Dr. Hoffmann's previous very brisk activity in intellectual affairs. With the Swiss composer Schnyder von Wartensee, among others, he was an active member of a group called '*Die Bäder im Ganges*', who occupied themselves with Indian mythology. Brinkmann holds that a certain formal relationship exists between the Indian God Shiva the Destroyer and the defiant hero of Hoffmann's book. What is more, he pursues the possible provenance of this extraordinary figure through German and Greek mythology, finally saying that one may well see in the figure of Struwwelpeter one of those prototypes of the human soul which Jung has designated Archetypes.

This book was already in the press when there came into my hands an etching by the famous French artist Gavarni which strikingly depicts a twin figure to Struwwelpeter. He appears in a book called *Les enfants terribles* (1842) and is thus two years senior to Hoffmann's creation, and he partakes of all the important features of the German hero, such as overgrown hair and fingernails. This is therefore likely to start a fresh hare running, for is it not feasible that the doctor from Frankfurt knew of this newly published book from Paris? Or did he?

That, however, is enough about *Struwwelpeter*. His enormous success in almost every language is its own justification. Now it is more important to attend to those books which are in danger of being quite forgotten. Dr. Hoffmann has recounted how in the years 1840–43, that is to say, before *Struwwelpeter*, he was greatly addicted to poeticizing and even if this was done with only modest success it nevertheless contributed to what were the happiest years of his life. For it was neither the highly respected specialist of later years nor the author of *Struwwelpeter* who was happiest, but Hoffmann the versifier.

He also emphasizes time and again in his rather drily written autobiography his activity as a philosophical and political writer. He found it embarrassing to be simply the Hoffmann of *Struwwelpeter*, but he could not give up writing books for children, and his later works in this genre belong among the most enjoyable in all German children's literature. They have been outstandingly successful right down to our own day, and many a German reader of this book on glancing at the following descriptions of individual books will remember them with pleasure and may well start hunting them down among the relics which accumulate in lofts and ancient cabin-trunks.

Soon after *Struwwelpeter*, and probably intended for the little sister of 'Struwwelpeter's' original recipient, there arrived *Der König Nussknacker—*

[1] Brinkmann, Donald: *Heinrich Hoffmanns 'Struwwelpeter'*, Verlag Huber, Frauenfeld.

Hoffmann's favourite among his picture-books. With an incomparable deftness he tells how all the most popular children's toys unite together to try to give a merry Christmas to poor, sick Reinhold, the child-hero of the book. Apart from its virtues as a fairy tale the story is invaluable to the modern student of popular culture, for poor Reinhold is cured by a collection of Christmas presents who demonstrate in all their brightly painted finery the sort of playthings which are now yielding place to the flood of stamped-metal, rubber, and plastic toys. Every Christmas in my own home we still keep a wooden King Nutcracker in the room, and even though his jaws have suffered and his rabbit's-wool beard has got very sparse he has nevertheless helped to preserve Dr. Hoffmann's book as a vital experience.

Should the children of today no longer be acquainted with poor Reinhold, then they may meet him in Basel where an adult collector of children's toys has built a Nutcracker house where Reinhold lives in miniature, surrounded by lovingly modelled replicas of all the pieces of furniture and all the toys which are shown in the book. Friends of the collector have presented Reinhold with handkerchiefs the size of a finger-nail, with sheets, and with crockery.

By 1854, when the doctor's children were now at school, there appeared *Bastian der Faulpelz* (*Sebastian the lazybones*), an enjoyable alphabet book which had been preceded by *Im Himmel wie auf Erden* (*In heaven so on earth*), a charming enough production, but less successful than his other books.

In 1870 there was published *Prinz Grünewald und Perlenfein mit ihrem lieben Eselein*. The dedication reads: 'To his dear grandchildren, Heiner and Carl, this book is dedicated by their grandfather' and underneath there is a picture of two fat children in the costume of the 1870s. In his introductory verses the author writes nostalgically of the books that he wrote for his own children, and then thanks these children of theirs for all the renewed pleasure he has found in making up *Prinz Grünewald* for them.

This book, which arose from recollections of things past and from love for his grandchildren, seems to me to be the loveliest of the Hoffmann books. It contains a medieval world of fairy tale mingled with all the old comic stunts and figures of fun (for instance, the dog Knotter who guzzles enough for three, four or five according to the degree of his misfortunes). For the first time there is also a completely delightful figure: the incomparable Princess Perlenfein; there is the orchestra of animals deep in the primeval forest and the juxtaposed sequences of pictures and songs based upon contemporary children's games. All this goes to make up a picture-book which even today retains much of its appeal.

This was the last book that Hoffmann himself published. But in 1924 his grandchildren Eduard and Walther Hessenberg compiled a volume from his unpublished remains. This consisted of sheets composed in pencil a generation earlier for the children of his youngest son, verses which he had made up and written down in front of the children themselves. The book is called *Besuch bei Frau Sonne* (*A visit to Madam Sun*), and among its pages are some of the most captivating and liveliest improvisations which were ever dreamed up for children to 'enjoy and pull to pieces'. (Hoffmann, by the way, was an advocate for children's books printed on soft paper and bound very loosely. It seemed to him that the right thing in children's literature was a kind of planned obsolescence: constant consumption and replacement.)

In these spontaneously produced verses an old man is apparently returning to the vigorous directness of his earliest stories. But this time they do not stem from the actuality of possible situations (as in parts of *Struwwelpeter*) but from marvellously nonsensical and crazy events:

Ein Mammut, das im Eise steckt,	Walter in a snow-bound pass
Hat unser Walther hier entdeckt;	Found a mammoth stuck in ice.
Da sass es wohl viel tausend Jahr,	Many and many a thousand year
Seit es dort eingefroren war.	The creature had been frozen there,
Jetzt aber plötzlich aufgewacht	But now, aroused so suddenly,
Hat es die Augen aufgemacht	He opens up his eyes and he
Und rief vergnügt trotz hohem	(Despite his age) cries out, 'Halloo!
Alter:	Now then, Walter, how d'y'do!'
'Ei, guten Morgen, lieber Walther!'	

Walther, addressed in this manner, was a grandchild to whom Hoffmann was drawn through no didactic intention but simply from an urge to entertain. In this way he wrote dozens of pages and illustrated them in pencil, just as the spirit moved him, creating a world that must have been sheer delight for his grandson. There is also a delicacy of tone which otherwise we only find in *Prinz Grünewald*:

Das Bienchen war von Honig satt,	The bee had had enough of honey,
Das Bienchen war schon alt und	The bee was feeling old and lazy.
matt.	In autumn in the soft sunshine
Zur Rose kam's zum letztenmal	He flew to the rose a final time—
Im Herbst bei hellem Sonnenstrahl.	Zum, zum, zum he buzzed at her
Das Bienchen macht' noch: Summ!	Then down he fell and buzzed no
Summ! Summ!	more.
Dann fiel es hin und war ganz	The rose bewailed him mournfully
stumm.	'Never again he'll come to me—
Die Rose aber jammert sehr:	But as my leaves fall to the ground
'Ach, jetzt hab' ich kein Bienchen	I'll heap for him a burial mound.'
mehr!	
Das Beste soll es haben,	
Mit Blättern will ich's begraben.'	

Such writing as this was only to reappear some decades later in the *Klein Irmchen* of Christian Morgenstern.

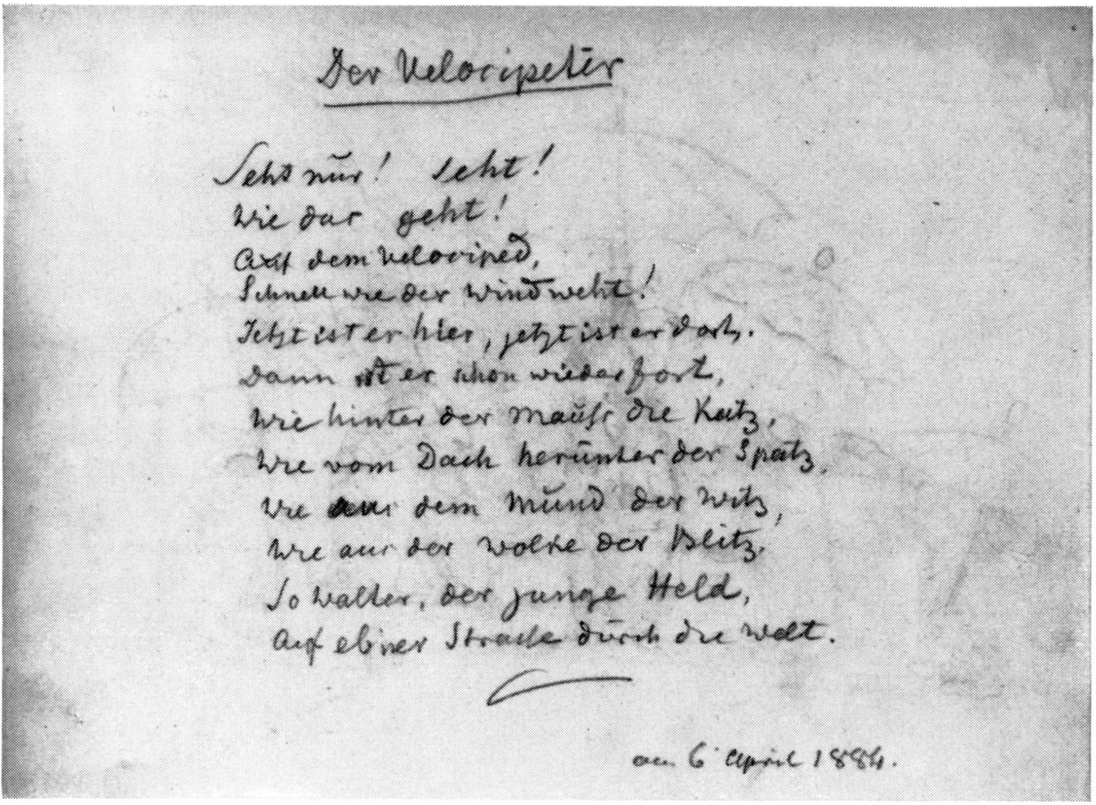

Der Velocipeter

Seht nur! seht!
Wie das geht!
Auf dem Velociped,
Schnell wie der Wind weht!
Jetzt ist er hier, jetzt ist er dort,
Dann ist er schon wieder fort,
Wie hinter der Maus die Katz,
Wie vom Dach herunter der Spatz,
Wie aus dem Mund der Witz,
Wie aus der Wolke der Blitz,
So wallet der junge Held,
Auf ebner Straße durch die Welt.

den 6 April 1884.

HOFFMANN, Heinrich. *Der Velocipeter.*
A drawing with its accompanying verse which Heinrich Hoffmann made for his grandchildren. From an unpublished sketch-book.

Plate VII

These comic, but none the less noteworthy, pages from Heinrich Hoffmann's papers have only been published in part, but they can surely only be compared to the nonsense of the English. Take, for example, the sheet on 'Karl der Bergspringer':

Der Karl, der ist ein Wanderer,	You've never really seen the like
Wie wohl nicht leicht ein anderer;	Of Charlie when he takes a hike.
Ja, staunt ihn an, ja seht ihn nur,	Just look at him as he sets out
Den Karl auf seiner ersten Tour!	As keen as any bright Boy Scout.
Hoch über Flüsse, Schlucht und Tal	Valleys deep and rivers wide
Hin schreitet er mit einem Mal;	He crosses with a single stride;
Von Bergesspitz zu Bergesspitz	From Langdale Pike to Wrynose Pass
Das ist für ihn ein leichter Witz.	Is just a joke for clever Charles.
Doch unten an dem Wirtshaus liegt	His supper at the close of day
Das, was der Karl zu essen kriegt:	Has even shocked the Y.H.A.:
Zehn Laibe frisches, schwarzes	Ten big loaves of good black bread
Brot,	And six York hams all lean and red,
Sechs Schinken, fein und rosenrot,	And liver sausages and marrow,
Und Leberwürste, Gelb- und	And chips brought on in a wheel-
Brat-,	barrow,
Ein Schubkarr'n voll Kartoffelsalat,	And butter heaped like Langdale
Ein Berg von süsser Butter und	Screes,
ein Schweizer Käs' von sechzig	And sixty pounds of Cheddar cheese.
Pfund!	

Or take the sheet about the person pouring water from a flask which doesn't stop until the whole room is under water.

Und es läuft und läuft und läuft,	And still the water falls and falls,
Bis darin die Stub' ersäuft.	and now it's half-way up the walls.
Sieh, der Stuhl steht tief darin,	Look, the chair is going down,
Hündchen schwimmet her und hin,	The little dog swims round and round.
und zwei Schiffe fahren auch	A pair of ships have got afloat,
Dort mit Segel und mit Rauch.	A steamer and a sailing-boat.
Von der Babett' an der Tür,	The little pig-tail showing yet
Sieht nur noch der Zopf herfür!	Is all that's left of poor Babett!

German children's books are accustomed to taking their subjects either direct from life or from popular tradition, as with the traditional fairy stories and nursery rhymes. In their whole history such an individual voice as that of Hoffmann in this book is most unusual and he has had few successors. For this reason alone it is worth saving it from oblivion. The verses and pictures which I have given here may give a brief impression of the glorious inconsequence proffered by an old grandfather to all little children. It is an inconsequence which will keep a child's imagination alive, surprising even the smallest by the way in which his accepted surroundings have suddenly become filled with all sorts of lively possibilities.

Apart from editions of *Struwwelpeter* which are either ugly or grossly sentimentalized, Hoffmann's work is surprisingly little known today and yet, next to Grimm's fairy tales, it is surely Germany's greatest contribution to children's literature. The year 1959 was the 150th anniversary of his birth and the town of Frankfurt paid a tribute to its former citizen with an exhibition of his manuscripts which shortly before (and for an enormous price) had passed over from private ownership to the possession of the town of his birth. I hope that this brief chapter will also contribute towards a fresh understanding of this abundant personality who for too long has been known only as the 'Struwwelpeter–Hoffmann'.

COMMENT

The English Struwwelpeter; or pretty stories and funny pictures was first printed in Leipzig in 1848 and was distributed in England for its German publishers, Rütten and Loening. Editions based on this anonymous translation continue to be published and those at present in print in England are:

The English Struwwelpeter; or, pretty stories and funny pictures (Routledge) and

Struwwelpeter; or, merry stories and funny pictures (Blackie).

Routledge quite early on took an interest in the book and their publication records for it go back to 1858, but Blackie do not seem to have taken it up until 1903. From information given me by these publishers they must, between them, have sold at least 200,000 copies of the book, and I am assured that it continues to justify its place in their catalogues. (Justification is harder to seek for the present colour printing. Up to a few years ago quite satisfactory editions were being produced either by direct litho or by line blocks. Now that offset litho is being used, however, there is a brashness in the colouring which makes Dr. Hoffmann's original anxiety about the printing entirely understandable.)

As in Germany, England has seen a fair crop of adaptations and parodies, the earliest perhaps being *The little minxes* (1857). Others include a *Political Struwwelpeter*, an *Egyptian Struwwelpeter*, and (in 1914) a *Swollen-headed William* by E. V. Lucas. In 1934 W. H. D. Rouse translated the book into Latin (giving us such things as *senticetum crinium* and *Junius contemplator nubium*), while in 1950 an interesting but not entirely successful attempt at re-illustration was made by Janet and Anne Grahame Johnstone.

The only other book by Hoffmann to have widespread popularity in England is *König Nussknacker*. This first appeared in 1853 as *King Nut-cracker, or the dream of poor Reinhold*, 'freely rendered' by J. R. Planché, and, like the early *Struwwelpeters*, printed in 'Leipsic'. The edition is interesting for a piece of concealed advertising which appears at that point in the story where the characters from *Struwwelpeter* are brought in: 'Henry Hoffmann's amusing Book for Children entitled "Struwwelpeter" is now generally and deservedly popular in England, and the character [*sic*] there mentioned are well known, we have no doubt, to hundreds of our little friends.'

This translation by Planché can still be obtained in the Everyman *A Book of Nonsense*, which also includes *Struwwelpeter*, but the monochrome illustrations to both of these are almost literally shadows of the originals.

Struwwelpeter is published in an authentic edition in America by Warne.

5 JABBERWOCKY
A typically English element in children's literature

The great contribution of the British to children's literature is 'nonsense'. It is true that fairy tales, as they are understood in Germany, are well enough known in England, for Perrault, Grimm, and Andersen have been published there in some splendid editions, illustrated by the finest artists. Fairy tales also gained a new lease of life through the now rather remotely relevant Christmas pantomimes.

But almost all these tales have their origin outside the British Isles and against this the English have produced a book entirely their own, which can stand comparison with all the best collections of fairy tales, a book which has been translated into many of the languages of the world from Welsh to Swahili and which English-speaking children have loved more than anything else. At the same time this 'fairy story' about little Alice and her adventures underground is the touchstone for that literature of nonsense which we must discuss in this chapter.

The scene is set in the year 1862, eighteen years after Dr. Hoffmann had paid his momentous visit to the stationers and bought the exercise-book which was later to become *Struwwelpeter*. One summer's day on the river at Oxford a thirty-year-old lecturer in mathematics at Christ Church was taking the three daughters of his Dean, Edith, Lorina, and Alice, out for a row. His name was Charles Lutwidge Dodgson. The day was hot and the children wanted to have a story told them, a thing they had come to expect from Mr. Dodgson. So the young lecturer complied, his mind relaxing in the drowsy heat and his thoughts, which did not tire so easily, following paths of their own making. Without doubt it was young Alice who saw to it that the story was told to the very end, for, of all the many little girls that he came to know during his lifetime, she was the one he loved best.

That the story was also written down shows that even at its first narration it must have been an unusual success. And it was doubtless with the one intention of pleasing this little girl that the learned story-teller himself got hold of a fine blank notebook and set down the story in his clear, almost Italianate, handwriting and decorated it with thirty-seven illustrations. The loving care with which it was composed shines through every page of the manuscript, which lies today in the British Museum alongside some of the most valuable literary manuscripts in the world. Its former owner had been Mrs. Alice Hargreaves, the original Alice, but in 1928 it was bought at auction by Dr. Rosenbach of Philadelphia, for £15,400. Twenty years later (and at a cost of $50,000) it was presented to the British Museum by a group of wealthy Americans 'to show their appreciation of the courage of these islands in protecting liberty during two great wars'.

In celebration of the centenary of Lewis Carroll's birth in 1932 the manuscript was exhibited at Columbia University, together with many documents relating to the history of the book. Its heroine, who by that time was eighty years old, was admitted Doctor of Letters 'honoris causa' by Carroll's old University. Concerning the problems and the meaning of this book we may well ask ourselves what was the reason for its unparalleled success. What is its peculiar quality and how did it come about?

Charles L. Dodgson, who wrote under the name of Lewis Carroll, thereby himself hinting at the cleavage in his remarkable personality, was born on 27 January 1832. He grew up in a happy family atmosphere with many brothers and sisters and, after all the unpleasantnesses of a public-school education, he moved on to Oxford where his studies met with fair success. He distinguished himself, above all, in mathematics, and spent the rest of his life as an Oxford don, undertaking various more or less important duties in the University or in his College. He was a devout man and was ordained a deacon of Christ Church in 1861. He died on 14 January 1898 and would have left little fame behind him if he had not written the story of *Alice's adventures in Wonderland*.

In all probability there has never been a children's book about whose textual and graphic origins so much material is available. Not only did Alice live on into our own times to give her evidence at first-hand but Dodgson himself kept a diary which has recently been published in book form. Furthermore, his sketches and his manuscripts have been preserved, and, above all, the fact that this story-teller was also one of the finest amateur photographers of his day has ensured that there is a pictorial record of all those who witnessed the genesis of the story and, first and foremost of course, of the bewitching young Alice herself.

We also possess a splendid photographic portrait of Lewis Carroll himself taken at about that time. With his pale, thoughtful face and high scholar's forehead, his gently waved hair and rather sad mouth he looks to be all in all an attractive personality. It therefore comes as no surprise when we learn that Dean Liddell's children spent whole days with him and admired him passionately. Carroll, who never married, had throughout his life a curious inclination to small girls, not only thinking up stories for them but also using them as the subjects of photographs, dressing them up and posing them as living pictures and ultimately building up a collection of photographs which ranks among the best from this early period of the art.

Not everyone regarded the curious affections of this amusing Oxford don as entirely harmless. Mrs. Liddell, Alice's mother, brought Alice's all too intimate association with Dodgson to an end while she was still a child, in spite of which Alice herself treasured his book into old age and preserved a faithful memory of the friend of her childhood years. In 1932, as an old lady, she wrote for a centenary issue of the *Cornhill Magazine*:

'Nearly all of *Alice's Adventures Underground* was told on that blazing summer afternoon with the heat haze shimmering over the meadows where the party landed to shelter for a while in the shadow cast by the haycocks near Godstow. I think the stories he told us that afternoon must have been better than usual, because I have such a distinct recollection of the expedition, and also, on the next day I started to pester him to write down the story for me, which I had never done before. It was due to my "going on, going on" and importunity that, after saying he would think about it, he eventually gave the hesitating promise which started him writing it down at all.'

Thus Alice wrote from her memory of an occasion which lay seventy years in the past.

On 4 July 1862 Carroll himself writes in his diary:

'Atkinson brought over to my rooms some friends of his . . . of whom I took photographs, and who afterwards looked over my album and stayed to lunch. They then went off to the Museum, and Duckworth and I made an expedition *up* the river to Godstow with the three Liddells: we had tea on the bank there, and did not reach Christ Church again till quarter past eight, when we took them on to my rooms to see my collection of microphotographs, and restored them to the Deanery just before nine.'

Then on 10 February 1863 he adds on this page:

'On which occasion I told them the fairy tale of *Alice's Adventures Underground*, which I undertook to write out for Alice, and which is now finished (as to the text) though the pictures are not yet nearly done.'

Later still, remembering the occasion, Carroll writes:

'I distinctly remember how, in a desperate attempt to strike out some new line in fairy-lore, I had sent my heroine straight down a rabbit-hole, to begin

Lewis Carroll in 1863.
Photo O. G. Rejlander (Sammlung Gernsheim, London).

Plate VIII

on their feet and hands, to make the arches.

The chief difficulty which Alice found at first was to manage her ostrich : she got its body tucked away, comfortably enough, under  her arm, with its legs hanging down, but generally, just as she had got its neck straightened out nicely, and was going to give a blow with its head, it would twist itself round, and look up into her face, with such a puzzled expression that she could not help bursting out laughing : and when she had got its head down, and was going to begin again, it was very confusing to find that the hedgehog had unrolled itself, and was in the act of crawling away : besides all this, there was generally a ridge or a furrow in her way, wherever she wanted to send the hedgehog to, and as the doubled-up soldiers were always getting up and walking off to other

CARROLL, Lewis. *Alice's adventures under ground* (1962–3).
A page from the Dover Press facsimile of Carroll's ms. with his own illustration.

Plate IX

with, without the least idea what was to happen afterwards.' (1887 in an essay in 'The Theatre' entitled 'Alice on the stage'.)

Nonsense thus gets going on the very first page of the book. There is neither plan nor plot, only a most improbable situation to start off with: a small, inquisitive girl following a white rabbit with pink eyes down into his hole and falling deeper and deeper into the earth, so that even the author has no idea how the fall will end. It is all like the impossible start of a nonsense rhyme whose progress depends upon finding a word to rhyme with the difficult last word of the line before.

Alice has fallen deep underground. What has to happen to her now, how shall she continue? This is Carroll's opportunity for his incomparable mischief with the poor girl's dimensions. She turns into a super-Gulliver. She does not only become small so as to resemble the animals under the earth, no, that would be quite conventional fairy-tale practice. Alice gets smaller one minute and larger the next. Several times she runs into danger of either shrinking to nothingness or growing huge enough to burst a house asunder. She loses herself completely in this performance and in the situations to which it gives rise. On the one hand, she remains the clear-headed, well-brought-up, spirited little girl that she is in the world above ground, but on the other hand, she enters so much into her new life that she forgets what her own size really is and thoughtlessly follows every passing fancy.

There can be no question that the course of the action with all its attendant dangers fascinates children. But what gives the book its wisdom and its charm, but at the same time makes it to a great extent incomprehensible to non-English children, is its many conversations and monologues. When Alice finds herself in one of the most impossible situations, growing bigger and bigger without being able to stop, she suddenly says: 'I do wonder what *can* have happened to me! When I used to read fairy tales, I fancied that kind of thing never happened, and now here I am in the middle of one! There ought to be a book written about me, that there ought!'

The suspension of accepted relationships where size and values and events are concerned has made the book a storehouse for psychologists, surrealists, and men of letters. But you have only to

CARROLL, Lewis. *Alice's adventures in Wonderland.* London, 1865.
Wood-engraving of the original pen drawing by John Tenniel.

look at the face of Lewis Carroll, you have only to consult his diaries or the letters he wrote to his young friends to realize that there is nothing more to this story than an attempt to think up an amusing tale for a child of whom he was very fond. Since the whole thing was improvised he perhaps followed more closely than is the case with other children's authors the suggestions of his sub-conscious, allowing every action to follow on from previous ones without a lot of careful thought. The conversations, too, are written entirely in the tone of voice which the little girl would use in talking to her friends. What makes the story so lively and so extraordinarily well-fitted for reading aloud is this naturalness of speech which has come from the author's fondness for children. But what has turned it into a part of world literature must surely be some-thing different from this.

Carroll was thirty years old and a bachelor when he dreamed up Alice. He did not adopt a paternal or an avuncular tone of voice. He spoke to children as his equals and did not shy away from any involved or even philosophical trains of thought, although the child that lurked in him made sure that the action was kept going at the same time. He was not a great poet in the same way as his elder contemporary Andersen, who preserved a similarly affection-ate relationship with children. All through his life Andersen was able to draw upon his power of poetic invention to create fairy tales, even if there were no children around to whom he could relate them. Carroll, however, wrote this one superlative story, for one child alone, even though she was at the same time the heroine of the book.

One of his child-friends said later in life that Carroll had told her 'that his most absurd ideas came to him on the borderland of dreams'. He suffered from insomnia, which in typical fashion he called his 'wakeful hours' and which he turned to productive ends by inventing an apparatus enabling him to write in bed; this he called a 'Nyctograph' from the Greek word for night. It was, however, his mathematical and logical problems which he mostly dreamed up in his 'wakeful hours' and he published several whole volumes of them. Alice is entirely a figure from this area of 'the borderland of dreams'. He probably knew very well what it is to dream and it is therefore not sur-prising that Alice's whole adventure turns out suddenly in the end to be not a fairy story but a dream.

Now it is by no means the case that Mr. Charles L. Dodgson, the plain Oxford don, told his tale of wonderland out of the blue and then once more disappeared into obscurity. Quite the opposite, for even as a boy he had brought out for the benefit of his ten brothers and sisters a series of family newspapers, the last of which, *Mischmash*, contained some remarkably crazy ideas, often quite incomprehensible, but very attractive to English children. From his student days he had been accustomed to sending comic verses of a satirical kind to journals which liked such humorous material, and some years after *Alice's adventures in Wonderland* he wrote *Through the looking-glass and what Alice found there*, a book which is, if possible, even richer than the first

CARROLL, Lewis. *Alicia en terra de meravelles*, translated by Josep Carner. Barcelona, 1928. Line drawing by Lola Anglada.

in comic nonsense, even though it does not possess quite the same narrative momentum. From the standpoint of the literature of nonsense it suggests all sorts of possibilities, showing as it does the inquisitive little girl this time leaving the real world of the drawing-room in order to enter the reversed world on the other side of the mirror. To get to where she wants to go she must always move in the opposite direction, a principle which provides opportunities for mischief similar to those arising from the variations in size in the first volume. Just as the underground queen in this book was taken from a pack of cards, so the queens in Looking-Glass Land are chess queens and Alice gets involved in the most extraordinary way in a game of looking-glass chess. Carroll was greatly interested in games and had even invented some himself. Also, throughout his life he used to write letters of the wittiest and most delightful kind to the little girls of his acquaintance. Finally, as author of *Alice's adventures in Wonderland*, as a first-class amateur photographer and as lecturer at one of Oxford's most famous colleges, he came into touch with some of the most important people of his time, many of whom he was able to capture in the eye of his camera.

Looked at closely, the world-wide success of *Alice*, as of Dr. Hoffmann's *Struwwelpeter*, can be seen to be due to more than chance. These books are the work of men who, though they were scarcely significant as poets, were none the less strong and radiant personalities. An intensity of thought and feeling found their expression in exactly the right form and gave to the resulting books a most remarkable power of penetration. They prove yet again that children's literature follows different rules from that of adults, even though it

... et les maillets des hérons vivants...

CARROLL, Lewis. *Alice au pays de merveilles*, translated by M. M. Fayet. Paris, 1930. Line drawing by Jean Hée.

is quite misleading to think that everyone who has the right attitude to children can necessarily write good children's books. This is the error which has led to the increasing production of so much mediocre work, which in its turn has been responsible for the general decline in the standard of children's literature.

For genuine success the craft of writing must be completely mastered. Before *Struwwelpeter* was thought of, Dr. Hoffmann was writing poems and political satires; before he began to write fairy tales Andersen wrote novels, poems, and dramas; and throughout his life Lewis Carroll produced satires, poems, and all kinds of mathematical and logical works. Each of these men was an experienced and capable writer, to whom a sudden stroke of fortune came against all the odds and gained them the hearts of the whole world—and especially the hearts of children.

The illustrations

Finally, something must still be said about the illustrations for this famous book.

The original manuscript was illustrated by the author himself and from our present view of the subject we may find it difficult to understand why these illustrations were not used as originals for the finished book (even though Carroll himself referred to them as rough drawings which sinned against every law of anatomy). Perhaps they do, in fact, express a feeling which is too close to that of the text, while John Tenniel, whom Carroll commissioned, brought a fresh approach to the book which served to enrich it even more. He worked exactly to the author's instructions, accepting the crazy story with an objective seriousness as though it were all very normal, and seeking out a little girl to act as his model for Alice just as Carroll had done. In this way he devoted all his sympathies not to building up the nonsensical or grotesque elements of the story but rather its immediately understandable ones. Carroll must have been a tyrannical taskmaster with some very wilful demands, but he seems to have paid some attention to Tenniel's wishes as well.

Lewis Carroll's book was published for him by Macmillan's but he paid for almost everything himself, including the illustrations, the printing, and the blockmaking—all of which gave him some right to be dictatorial. At the same time he jeopardized his own interests in so far as he withdrew the two thousand copies of the first edition from sale because they seemed both to himself and to Tenniel to be badly printed. The few copies that escaped into circulation are now among the most sought-after books of the nineteenth century. The edition (bibliographically the second) was finally completed to his satisfaction and issued towards the end of 1865 but dated 1866. In 1907 the text became free of copyright, and thus fell prey to the activities of all sorts of illustrators, although its success has continued unabated.

In Europe and America every style of illustration has been applied to the book from the most sentimental mush to the most frightful caricature. The only attempt, however, that has succeeded in creating from *Alice* an individual world which still conforms to Carroll's intentions is Arthur Rackham's. He has turned Alice into a charming sister for Peter Pan, that other remarkable and off-beat figure from the world of the English nursery. In 1930 Marie Laurencin attempted to illustrate the book, and the famous Swedish draughtsman Högfeld has provided some very unsatisfactory pictures for one of the most recent editions. The tale has been translated into over forty languages and has been adapted to the language of the cinema by Walt Disney. In this way it has circulated even more widely and has been brought among children for whom Carroll's way of talking might have been difficult to understand.

Peter Pan also came 'among the people' in this way, but before we deal with him we have still to make mention of Edward Lear, the man who raised nonsense to an art in itself and who has enjoyed in England a quite astonishing degree of fame among people of all ages. It must be admitted, however, that he is an artist who is unexportable.

Edward Lear: the poet of nonsense

Edward Lear's verses depend for their effect almost entirely upon the language in which they are written and they are therefore known on the Continent only to those people with a knowledge of English. Nevertheless, they have a place in the context of this book.

Edward Lear was born in 1812, twenty years before Lewis Carroll, and he was one of the youngest in a family of twenty-one. His father was the son of a Danish immigrant (the Scandinavians share with the English a gift for comedy and a strong sense of caricature) and had become a merchant of substance, so the children were well brought up. But Edward was a sickly child who suffered from a mild but frequently recurring form of epilepsy which prevented him from receiving a normal education. While he was still a boy, however, his father became bankrupt and, according to the law at that time, was thrust into gaol (like Dickens' father) until his wife could pay his debts. This left the numerous children to fend for themselves—a thing which few of them succeeded in doing very adequately.

The boy Edward went to live with his eldest sister, who was already grown up, and she brought him up, taught him, cared for him in his bouts of sickness, and behaved towards him as though she were his mother. As early as the age of fifteen he was in a position to earn his own living through his exceptional talent as a draughtsman, and as a young man he turned to preparing pathological drawings for doctors. At the age of eighteen, already with pupils of his own, he received a commission from the Zoological Society of London to make a complete set of drawings of all the species of parrot in the London Zoo. In its turn this led to other commissions from famous zoologists for drawings of apes, cats, turkey-cocks, turtles, and, again and again, birds of all kinds from all quarters of the globe.

Shortly afterwards, Lear was invited by the Earl of Derby to make some drawings of the animals which he kept at the private menagerie on his estate at Knowsley, near Liverpool and this led the young artist to a four-year residence there. All the drawings which he made, together with those of his earlier commissions in London, were published in large and expensive folios which today are rare collectors' items. This youthful activity is also important, however, because the animals which he studied and whose form he came to know in great detail were later to reappear in the words and pictures of his books of verse. There they took on an altered and less realistic character, but although the nonsense of the verse shunned all attachment to the facts of natural history the drawings never did.

During his stay on the huge Derby estate, which was at that time a meeting-place for the great people of the day, the somewhat retiring young man felt himself most nearly at home in the nursery along with the children from the various branches of the family who were all brought up together on the estate. For their delight he produced his first book, *A book of nonsense*—comic little rhymes with very striking illustrations—which immediately gained popularity among the upper-class coteries of the England of that day. It was published in 1846, one year after *Struwwelpeter*, and, springing from a similar impulse and approach, it embodied a feeling for the comic and the grotesque but tempered by a spirit of kindliness.

Lewis Carroll was fourteen years old when it appeared, and thus beyond the age for children's books. Since he himself had many younger brothers and sisters, however, it is probable that he had some acquaintance with this poetry, which was so akin in spirit to his own. Nevertheless, nothing has been discovered to show that there was ever a meeting between these two men whose combined influence was to pervade so strongly the whole of England's future literature for children. Their work and its effects are like that of a wide stream of clear water, carrying away with it everything tainted or stuffy. They brought a freshness to the moral and sentimental tone of the century's writing, which was as laden with these virtues in England as on the Continent. Finally, they raised the whole of English children's literature to an extremely high level of wit, fancy, and language, and because of this, English children's literature, more than that of any other country, has become a firm branch of the country's literature as a whole. One has only to think of Walter de la Mare, Graham Greene, Eric Linklater, and many other writers for adults who have not been too proud to put their art to the service of children.

But for the reader (and especially the Continental one) who possibly does not know Lear's verses, even though they can still be bought very cheaply in England, it is perhaps worth making an examination of this remarkable literary genre which calls itself 'nonsense'. Why does it do so, in fact? In the section on Carroll we decided it was a story which developed without relying on any principles taken over from the fairy-tale tradition or from straight reality. Instead it follows, if you like, a surrealist narrative logic, which is not logic at all but is plot and language cutting the wildest capers unfettered by any didactic or moralizing intentions.

Like Carroll, Lear lived in an age of particularly large families who were without doubt well acquainted with the customary nursery rhymes of the day. Deriving from popular oral tradition, these verses everywhere (but especially in England) contained a certain kind of nonsense which developed out of

73

comic rhymes and ancient folk-song traditions and captured alive for children all kinds of popular figures and customs. In most other countries the later development of children's verse from these pure sources moved in a more lyrical, even sentimental, direction as we know from the example of *Des Knaben Wunderhorn*. In England, however, it continues on the same regular course and finds in Lear's verses, above all, an extension into art.

He achieves his success to some extent from the crazy situations with which he begins his stories in verse: the owl and the pussy-cat setting out on their nuptial journey with a pot of honey, the strange tribe who go to sea in a sieve, and the kangaroo who goes three times round the world with a duck on his tail. These are only three of the sagas which he sets in verse and which today, after a hundred years, still ring as freshly as they did when he first captivated the world of children and adults.

A particular charm in these verse-stories lies in their illustrations. Here Lear shows himself to be that great connoisseur and portrayer of nature which he was from the beginning. (He was to spend almost all the later part of his life in travelling, since he could not endure the English climate, and he made his living as a landscape painter, drawing and painting in many different countries.) His owls, his ducks, his kangaroos are true representatives of their species however mad the situations may be in which each one finds himself. Thus these illustrations lead children along the right paths towards a full appreciation of nature.

All these attractions apart, however, Lear still adds something which raises him above all other writers in this field—even, in a certain context, above Lewis Carroll, despite the latter's greater wealth of ideas. This 'something' is the linguistic quality of his verse. His carillon world of words proves to be extraordinarily impressive, especially when read aloud, and it reveals a poet whose control of language is equivalent to that of a juggler whirling coloured balls around his head. Lear's greatest fame has come from his use of the traditional English limerick, but his great achievement probably lies in the virtuoso performances of his longer stories in verse. In this field of 'applied' poetry his nearest relation could well be Wilhelm Busch, despite the latter's own opinion that the chief part of his stories was the pictures.[1] It is also possible to see a relationship with the entrancing children's verse of Christian Morgenstern.

The nonsense literature of Lear has provided animals and things with a mad life of their own which in no way corresponds to the natural world. The child-reader is led away from reality into a world of fantasy. Ultimately, nonsense, even with Carroll, is not much more than a relaxation of the reins which guide and control our understanding and our thoughts. Fantasy takes over and children have always been only too glad to follow, and they remain so today as we shall see.

[1] Busch is discussed at greater length in Chapter 13.

I should now like to turn to a few examples of the way that 'nonsense' has cropped up again in modern literature, even though in an altered form. By now there should be no question of confusing it with the spirit behind fairy tales, even though borderline cases can be found from time to time.

COMMENT

Attempts to export Lear in translation have been far and few, but Alice has received the sort of treatment accorded to Shakespeare, Dickens, and Lenin. A checklist of editions of translations by Warren Weaver: *Alice in many tongues* has been published by the University of Wisconsin Press (1964). Forty-eight languages are represented, including Latin.

A number of references are made to Morgenstern in Chapters 1, 16, and 19, chiefly in connexion with his poetry for children. There is no English translation of this, but ninety-two of his nonsense poems from the *Galgenlieder* (a collection with superficial similarities to Edward Lear's) have recently been translated by Max Knight and published in England by Cambridge University Press. The book is mentioned in a front-page review in *The Times Literary Supplement* for 22 April 1965, which deals at length with an important new German book on nonsense: Alfred Liede: *Dichtung als Spiel*, 2 volumes. Berlin, 1964. Both Carroll and Lear are discussed in a section in Volume 1.

6 FANTASY AND REALITY
Nonsense from Peter Pan to Pippi Longstocking

The branch of literature which I have called 'nonsense', together with the types of story which have developed from it, do not draw their substance so much from the external world as from raids into the unreal and the impossible. These, then, gain their main effects from the capacity for thought and feeling of the child who reads them. If we attempt to follow their history further, we find that, apart from one or two exceptions, the most interesting work has been done in Northern Europe, that is to say, England and Scandinavia.

These tales which turn their backs on reality are in no way fairy stories. The time-honoured rules which govern the latter are frequently broken, for there are no rules in nonsense, which exists in the no-man's-land between the fairy-tale world and the real one. First of all, there is a clear distinction in the nature of the characters taking part, those in the nonsense books being individual conceptions and not stock types as in the fairy story. Secondly, there are the quite different modes of action employed by the two styles.

Peter Pan

Take Barrie's *Peter Pan* as an example. When the baby Peter meets the old raven in the park, having just flown out of his nursery, this is an encounter which is just as actual and exciting as the one between Heidi and Alm-Öhi, with the one difference that Heidi's experience stems from an entirely plausible sequence of events, while Peter's comes from the totally unreal world of the unconscious and of dreams—a world where there is a mysterious unity between the baby boy, who is hardly conscious of being alive, and the animals, especially the birds.

This marvellous idea by J. M. Barrie (1860–1937) took its first shape in a book for adults: *The little white bird*, published in 1902. The six chapters about Peter Pan were reissued in 1906 under the title *Peter Pan in Kensington*

Gardens, unsurpassably illustrated by Arthur Rackham.[1] It is the purest and most poetic example of fantasy for children, shot through with unreality but in no way a traditional fairy tale—for it takes place in a recognizable world with omnibuses and park-keepers in it and quite believable children with a quite believable mother. But these real people see only on the rarest occasions what goes on by night. That is the time when Peter Pan's life begins, the life of the eternal child who never grows up and who can converse with animals, listen to the fairies in the park, and experience to the full that secret world which lies beneath external appearances. And what a fascinating world it is! At the age of seven or eight, after I had come to know this book, I found that the old park which had been the scene of my own orderly childish walks, the little stream, the bridge, and the rocky vaults, all took on a new and secret delight. In spite of all beliefs in reality there was at least one schoolgirl who harboured longings to glimpse this elfin world by night, and even in the autumn twilight the lawns and shrubberies flickered with a secret light. For this park (in Weimar) was also the scene of one of Goethe's loveliest poems: *Füllest wieder Busch und Tal* and it has never ceased to revive for me the aura of that early mysteriousness.

Pinocchio

It would take too long to enumerate all the later books which occupy this border territory between reality and the world of the unconscious and of dreams. I should therefore like to follow the same principle which has guided me in other chapters of this book and only mention such books as I am familiar with and whose effect on children I have seen.

Collodi's *L'avventure di Pinocchio* which first appeared in book form at Florence *c.* 1883 and has been translated, adapted, and imitated innumerable times in our own century, can be classed in this branch of literature only with reservations, but it is perhaps the best South European variant of the nonsense theme. A wooden puppet comes to life in a world where poverty and riches, ugliness and beauty can all be found—briefly, in the real world. But this imaginary fellow has not been chosen in order to embody a world of poetic dreams, like Peter Pan, but rather as a symbol of sharpness and down-to-earth human understanding and he further provides the excuse for giving an exaggerated plot to a story which does not lie too far from the world of reality. It is, however, precisely this singular mixture of passionately conveyed reality, schoolboy cheekiness, and pure imagination (fairies and a little wooden boy with too much to say for himself) which has given the book its permanent attractiveness.

[1] The bibliography of *Peter Pan* is a complicated one. The play which grew out of the original story was first produced in December 1904, but not published until 1928. The fame which it immediately engendered, however, led to several story versions being published, the well-known one by Daniel O'Connor in 1914 and two by Mary Byron in 1929 and 1938. J. M. Barrie's own version, *Peter and Wendy*, appeared in 1911. (B.A.)

The author of the book was, in fact, called Carlo Lorenzini (1826–90). He was named Collodi after his mother's native village in Tuscany, and throughout Italy he has enjoyed enormous fame for the degree to which his hero reflects so many characteristic features of the Italian people.[1]

Children and animals in England

Three famous books were published in England before 1930, each of which made use of the sympathy which has existed between children and animals from time immemorial, and each giving its animal characters an intelligent command of language. These books are A. A. Milne's *Winnie-the-Pooh* (1926), Kenneth Grahame's *The wind in the willows* (1908), and Hugh Lofting's *The story of Doctor Dolittle* (first published in America in 1920).

In *Winnie-the-Pooh* the banal subject of 'child and teddy-bear' is handled with a new wit and delicacy, at the same time being set in the context of the natural world in a most unusual way. It has resulted in a book which for four decades has delighted the grown-ups as much as it has the children.

The wind in the willows tells of the adventures of a number of animals on or around the banks of a river, among others, Mole, Otter, Badger, Toad, and Water-rat. Despite the extraordinarily human flavour in the way the animals behave and talk, this is one of the loveliest nature books in English children's literature. After reading it no child with any imagination at all will be able to see a river-bank without wanting to meet Water-rat or Mole. In the style of a modern *Peter Pan* this classic of the English nursery seeks to draw back a veil from the visible world to reveal a glimpse of what lies behind.

The story of Doctor Dolittle and other books in this series are too well known for me to need to make more than the most important points about them in the few lines that I have. This story is perhaps the most striking proof that it is not always necessary to amuse children over the age of eight with stories which are founded entirely upon real life. Doctor Dolittle, for all his humaneness, his good sense, and his comical behaviour, undergoes adventures which are crazy and exciting at one and the same time. The books are thus enriched by the kind of exemplary morality which children enjoy. The doctor, always ready to help, always capable of doing what he ought, is a wonderful antidote to the death-defying heroes of the comics, to whom he is obviously superior himself, but with whom he shares the same ability to triumph over all the extraordinary things that happen to him.

I should now like to deal with one or two stories which are particularly remarkable for the way in which they introduce fantastic happenings into an otherwise realistic framework, thus opening up to children a whole new world of the imagination.

[1] A famous German translation of *Pinocchio* by Otto Julius Bierbaum was published in 1905 under the title *Zapfel Kerns Abenteuer*. The first English translation, *The story of a puppet*, appeared in 1891, but one suspects that much of its modern popularity stems from Walt Disney's Hollywood version of 1938. (B.A.)

Mary Poppins

The oldest of these books is the four-volume story *Mary Poppins* by P. L. Travers. The first book appeared in 1934 and its sequels are: *Mary Poppins comes back* (1935), *Mary Poppins opens the door* (1944), and *Mary Poppins in the park* (1952). They tell of the extraordinary adventures of a family of five children whose destinies are guided by their 'Nannie' Mary Poppins. Mary Poppins is one of the oddest figures in the whole of children's literature and quite an antiquated one to find in the age of modern technology. One is tempted to ask if, in her combined capacities as magician and strict children's nurse, she is a latter-day descendant of those curious characters in *Alice in Wonderland*, or if she symbolizes the natural relapse of modern man into a world of fantasy. Since the creator of the books is a woman with both her feet firmly in our own age it may well be surmised that a close familiarity with the English tradition is sending her in search of the modern equivalent for the fairy tale.

The four-volume story which has arisen in this way depicts a series of scenes from the daily life of an English family whose members are described entirely realistically. It contains, however, a large number of fantastic incidents, which are brought into the plot in a very remarkable way. There is no question here of the classic 'story-within-a-story', for the teller of fairy tales is a fairy-tale figure herself. But Mary Poppins possesses none of the customary attributes of a fairy-tale figure. She is neither a fairy nor a witch. She is a strict, severe, and completely unsentimental children's nannie who smells of boot-polish and goes around in stiffly starched dresses.

Nor are the stories told in a customary manner, but the children experience them as they go along. To some extent they are fairy stories in the traditional sense, such as the tale of the swineherd and the goosegirl, beautifully conceived variations on an old theme as seen through the eyes of a modern psychologist. Or else there are the typical nonsense stories, such as the marvellous tea-party at Mary Poppins' uncle's, where he and the children laugh so much that the whole party is finally filled up with laughing gas and everyone floats to the ceiling with the tea-table, the uncle, Mary Poppins, and all, and there the eating and drinking continue.

Loveliest and most original is the story where Mary Poppins spends her day out on a visit to her friend the match-seller and pavement-artist (a classic figure in the London street scene). She is so enchanted by his latest landscape chalked on the pavement that, thanks to Mary Poppins' magic powers, the two of them step into the picture and spend the day off in the beautiful green countryside far away from grey and mundane London. There are tones here akin to *Alice in Wonderland*, even though the style is quite the author's own and the events take place in and not beyond the modern world.

P. L. Travers is convinced that conscious recollection of the world of dreams and fairy tales and of those things which we see with our inward eye

G

can do nothing but good. She is as convinced as the French Père Castor that an understanding of nature will do much to soothe the restless spirit of the modern child. In her work we find the two concepts united in poetic garb. When she describes the morning mist in the park or the East or the West winds, then these are masterpieces of natural description for adult readers as well as children, so that her books may be placed in that rare category which used at one time to be labelled: 'For children from 7 to 70.' As it is, they have been translated into almost all the languages of Europe, together with a number outside Europe as well.

The Borrowers

Mary Norton is another English authoress whose books now have a permanent place in the modern English 'nursery'. Her most famous group of books about 'the Borrowers' have a fame comparable to that of Mary Poppins, even though they may lack some of the wealth of fantasy in the latter series. The fundamental idea behind these books is admittedly a marvellous one. Mrs. May, a wise old lady, is led by the circumstance that things are continually disappearing without trace to tell a child the story of the Borrowers, the little underground beings who live in a world of their own under the floor-boards and who improve their standard of living with all these vanished things. Mrs. May's story becomes imperceptibly the history of these subterranean folk with a great deal of traditional fairy-tale wisdom worked into it. Figures like the little humpy man of the nursery rhyme, Rumpel-Stiltskin, the dwarfs and hop-o'-my thumbs of fairy tales are again brought to life for the child. As a modern interpretation of ancient dwarf-lore coupled with the secrets of the underground life this has certainly helped to make these books into fascinating stories and they have enjoyed an enormous popularity among English children. A world where safety-pins become giant tools, where cotton-reels become stools, and chess-men classical statues has a glamour of its own, regardless of any profounder readings which can be made of this nether-nether land. As a modern story it has taken over elements mostly from fairy stories and especially from those of the dwarfs. It is most remarkable how the life of these people under the floor is brought into a relationship with that of human beings. There is something sinister and spooky, indeed occasionally malicious about it all. But to children reading the story it will come as a pleasure that a small boy is the only person to reach an understanding with these 'little people', as the author calls them, and to know them well. Here again we find a child who, like Peter Pan, understands the language of those who live beyond the boundaries of the visible, everyday world.

The Moomin books

'The little people' crop up again in the books of the young Finnish writer Tove Jansson. Scandinavian children are especially familiar with themes like this from their own fairy-tale literature. Nonsense is here given a new varia-

JANSSON, T. *Moominpappa at Sea*. London, Benn, 1966.
Line illustration by the author.

tion which is perhaps found at its best in the Moomin books of this author. The
Moomins are splendid little creatures from the world of her imagination and
they conquered children in a trice. But for all the crazy things they get up to,
these merry little fellows have an inner wholesomeness, and they have greatly
enriched the world of fantasy. They distinguish themselves from the traditional dwarfs of Scandinavian fairy stories, the trolls, by their origin, which
lies neither in reality nor in tradition but, if I mistake not, is solely the highly
successful product of a young poetess's imagination. Her books are somewhat
less intellectual and witty than English books in this category, but the Moomins
have an appeal to even the least sophisticated child. Apart from the Moomin
family the author has devoted a children's book to trolls as well.

Pippi Longstocking

Now we come to a special event in modern children's literature, which
raised a lot of dust among the grown-ups and brought a lot of pleasure to the
children. This is Astrid Lindgren's *Pippi Langstrump* (1945), a unique arrival
among the heroes of children's literature.

Many famous characters who have today become classics found their way
into the hearts of children straight from the books on the adult bookshelf.
Leatherstocking, Robinson Crusoe, David Copperfield, and many others have
done this, thereby avoiding the round-about route via the pundits. On the other
hand, others, like Heidi, Pinocchio, or Nils Holgersson, had all the textbook
qualities which the pundits require but nevertheless still found their way to a
long-lasting popularity. There can be no doubt that children fell in love with
Pippi Longstocking from the first moment, while the well-meaning adult
world just as violently repudiated her. It must, however, be said in favour of

those who abide by the textbook that in this case they have by and large allowed themselves to be converted.

Astrid Lindgren was born in Sweden in 1907 and she created this character at the bedside of her sick daughter, who was herself responsible for inventing Pippi's name. Gradually Pippi was furnished with such improbable attributes that the stories about her present no difficulty in being categorized with other fantasies for children. Astrid Lindgren has written over twenty books and has successfully turned her hand to writing such things as fairy stories, detective stories for boys, career stories, and stories for young girls, but she has never bettered her first book in spite of the exceptional merit which has distinguished her work in these other fields.

Pippi Longstocking probably had much the same appearance in the sick-room where she started life as in the books which came later—hair the colour of carrots, a nose the shape of a small potato, dotted with freckles, a large mouth, a home-made dress by no means long enough, one black stocking and one brown and two shoes like rowing-boats. This nine-year-old has a strength greater than anyone else in the town. She can pick up a couple of policemen or her own horse with one arm, and since she has no parents this comical creature can do as she likes. The necessary base for her operations is provided by her own cottage and a suitcase full of gold pieces.

Roughly speaking, that is the child's 'police-description'—a figure to strike terror to grown-ups in a way that the most exaggerated comics can scarcely surpass. Astrid Lindgren put it all into a book at the behest of her daughter in 1944, when she was herself confined to bed. With some difficulty she also found a publisher, although he considered that a wild little girl who does what she likes was hardly a good example to set before the public. Similarly, teachers found it impossible to accept Pippi's non-attendance at school, her preference instead to take ship for the South Seas or else wander around the town with her pet monkey Mr. Nilsson, looking for treasures. But police descriptions can deceive. Even though Pippi Longstocking fulfilled all the dreams suppressed in children's hearts, she also possessed other qualities which must have an almost therapeutic effect on the children of today. Her pranks are neither stupid nor damaging; she is full of a good-hearted willingness to help people weaker than herself; she is indescribably open-handed and, above all, never boring. And that is probably her finest quality, making her more invincible than all her superhuman powers and turning her into the best friend in the world for her companions Thomas and Annika.

It has now been generally accepted that the three books published in England as *Pippi Longstocking*, *Pippi goes aboard*, and *Pippi in the South Seas* are full of the most splendid and comical nonsense, which also fascinates those grown-ups who have not grown too old for it. In spite of their exciting plots the books are written extensively in a dialogue which packs plenty of punch (a feature which they share with the English nonsense stories) and even fifteen- or sixteen-year-olds, who are otherwise inclined to treat their children's books with scorn, cannot help chuckling when they inadvertently get hold of a Pippi Longstocking volume which eight or nine years previously may have set them free from Mickey Mouse or Noddy.

In contrast to Peter Pan, the first fantastic character in modern children's literature, and one who can be described as 'child eternal', Pippi Longstocking is a kind of 'superchild', setting free kindly impulses in the children who read about her, as respectable teachers throughout the world now admit. Pippi and her two friends find that, thanks to her extraordinary powers, being a child is a glorious experience and they therefore decide that they do not ever want to grow up. The 'superchild' has an excellent medicine which will deal with that little problem. In a situation like this one can see the connexion across the sea with that English 'superchild' Alice—a more civilized and perhaps somewhat more intellectual sister to the little Swedish girl.

In Sweden, Astrid Lindgren is a kind of children's idol. Such is the fame of her heroine that schoolchildren are allowed to call themselves 'Little Pippis' after doing some particularly good turn; moreover, Astrid Lindgren's other books, not mentioned in detail here, have also brought in some badly needed fresh air, particularly where fairy stories are concerned and in the rather difficult category of books for young adolescents.

Though she may be an idol in the children's pantheon, Astrid Lindgren is a very straightforward person who has not allowed her enormous success in almost every country of the world to go to her head. Like her English contemporary, P. L. Travers, she is a poetess. Humour, reverie, and sadness are reflected equally in her fine-featured nordic face—that restrained sadness which runs through the work of Andersen and which gives the true finish to the fantasy and humour of this genuinely poetic writer for children. No receptive child and no adult can read without emotion the closing pages about Pippi as she sits dreamily beside a candle in the middle of a children's paradise which has never been lost.

Some recent literature of the imagination

Since the first appearance of this book, Tove Jansson has given the children of many lands one or two amusing nonsense picture-books and Astrid

LINDGREN, Astrid. *Pippi Longstocking*
An illustration by Richard Kennedy for the English edition (London, O.U.P., 1954).

Lindgren continues her own inimitable way, although this is taking her more and more towards books which are completely grounded in the real world. But these two have not remained Scandinavia's only writers for children who have brought the fantastic and the unreal into their books.

The Norwegian Thorbjørn Egner has blazed new trails into this territory in all sorts of ways, including songs, poems, radio plays, stage plays, and stories. His poetry has even found its way into school-books, and in Norway and Denmark it has gained him high honours from the state. The children's book which has spread his fame most widely beyond these frontiers is about the robbers of Cardemon (Oslo, 1955). The English version is entitled *The singing town.*

Folk og rovere i Kardemomme. Oslo, 1955.
From a colour illustration by the author.

As with Egner, the children's poetry of the Swedish writer Britt Hallqvist was similarly composed for her country's school-books and it has gained for her the Nils-Holgersson medal, a high distinction in Scandinavian countries. Her children's poetry may well be said to be witty, but it is very difficult to translate. In one of her many books in prose, however—*The eldest in the class,* whose heroine is an old but greatly respected lady—there is an outstanding blend of humour and serious moral consideration, realism and nonsense. Britt Hallqvist, the mother of four children, is acknowledged in her own country as a fine scholar, a translator, and a poet. It is very likely that more will be heard of her soon.[1]

All these recently mentioned books have served to acquaint us with the manifold possibilities implicit in that genre which the English designate as

[1] It says much for the progressiveness of Scandinavian educationists that they have called upon authors like Egner and Hallqvist to give schoolchildren a creative introduction to their native language.

'nonsense'. In Scandinavian countries it seems to have got a firm foothold, and in Eastern Europe it also has an assured life, especially in books for small children, but for reasons of language I cannot give a more detailed description.

Germany

First of all, *Vevi* by Erika Lillegg (1955)—a book which signified a minor revolution in German children's books. It does not only dwell on the poetic implications in the relationships between children and animals but also highlights some of the rich potentialities which there are in children's lives. It is the work of a poetess at her most individual.

Another author, who has given a broader foundation to the possibilities of nonsense and unreality, is James Krüss, one of the most prolific of current German authors and one who, by his penchant for the fantastic and his witty conversation-pieces between children, makes considerable demands on his readers. The books of his which have brought a new and original voice to German children's books, cleaving a wide breach in its all too realistic world, are: *Der Leuchtturm auf den Hummer-Klippen* (1956), *Die glücklichen Inseln hinter dem Winde*, and *Mein Urgrossvater und ich* (1959). James Krüss is no children's author who, as it were, puts on a special literary hat when he talks to children. He talks his own language, often saying things which they cannot understand at once. He asks questions, he plays with words, and he lets children play with words until they understand what the craft of words actually is. What is more, he gets sea-gulls and clouds to make up poems and in *Mein Urgrossvater und ich* he even gets the old great-grandfather doing it as he teaches his great-grandson to use his native language properly. Towards the end of *Der Leuchtturm* there occurs the beautiful sentence: 'Jetzt brauchen wir nach einer Geschichte nicht mehr zu fragen, ob sie wahr ist, denn jetzt wissen wir, dass schöne Geschichten zugleich wahre Geschichten sind.' ('Now we need no longer ask if a story is true, for now we know that if a story is beautiful it must at the same time be true.') This is a revelation which is new in German children's books.

James Krüss has also set about writing some poems, which were finally collected in a book for young children: *Die kleinen Pferde heissen Pfohlen* (1962). But in spite of the wealth of ideas and images in these poems, Krüss seems to me to be more convincing when he gets the sea-gulls and the clouds to make up his poetry for him.

In his last book, *Timm Thaler* (1962), he reaches back to a theme which is now a classic in imaginative writing—the theme of a child who sells, not in this case his shadow, but his laughter. This profoundly sad and disturbing book reveals a fresh aspect of its author. He has suddenly become very serious and very adult before the eyes of his young readers of yesterday. It is much to be hoped, however, that from time to time he will return to the country of eternal childhood, so welcome has his bold attempt been to bring fantasy into these otherwise all too realistic children's books.

It may well be said that James Krüss was popularizing in Germany the idea behind English 'nonsense', but while he was attempting to write a modern *Peter Schlemihl*[1] for young people, a young German author was completing a two-volume work about Jim Knopf. This was Michael Ende, who neither had nor has the intention of becoming a professional writer for children, and *Jim Knopf* is the story of a little black foundling and his friend Lukas, the engine-driver, and of the engine as well, a mechanical marvel in its own right.

Now comic books about engines are strewn around almost as thickly as sand on the shore, for engines possess a symbolic value all their own within the world of technology. But with Michael Ende the value does not lie in this universal theme (as you might call it) but in the nature of the text. This is a most remarkable mixture of adventure and true poetry, fabulous and real worlds, witty dialogue and gay characterization. Although this is a first book, the imaginative content is handled with a confident mastery. The hackneyed themes of 'engines' and 'poor Negro children' and 'engine-drivers' are transformed in so fresh and original a manner and the story takes us into regions which, geographically, are so remote and, humanly, so many-sided, that it serves once again to prove that children's literature depends primarily not upon the subject matter but upon the way it is handled. The success of this book is also evidence that it is unwise to underrate the modern child's capability of accepting things which have to do with the imagination and the understanding.

Marcelino, Pan y Vino: a Spanish hero

Anyone who has given any attention to early children's literature will know that for a while all writing about conduct had no purpose beyond pointing out the easiest way to Heaven; for life did not count for very much, but Heaven counted for everything. An early death, however sad, meant a joyous entry into paradise—especially if the child were courageous in his dying. This idea prevailed in Puritan England, in most of the countries of Europe, and even more so in America. With the nineteenth century, however, the emphasis on holy dying was largely got rid of, even though the figure of the child destined for an early assumption of celestial glory persisted.

In *Marcelino* (1952) by Sanchez-Silva this subject of what we might call the glad acceptance of death is taken up in a way which is both modern and also rooted in popular tradition. Marcelino is a thoroughly normal orphan who possesses all the virtues and vices of a nine-year-old Spanish boy. He keeps small creatures and displays a love of blood and death in the elaborate way in which he kills them (an expression of the juvenile preliminaries to a passion for bull-fighting). He also tells lies and finally steals in order to bring bread

---

[1] *Peter Schlemihl* (1814) by Adelbert von Chamisso (1781–1838) is the book hinted at in the preceding paragraph. One of the most famous tales of German Romanticism, it concerns the tribulations of a man who sold his shadow to the Devil and it can be read as an allegory of its author's own sense of insecurity as an emigré from the French Revolution. (B.A.)

AYMÉ, Marcel. *Les contes du chat perché*. Paris, 1934.
Colour lithograph by Nathan Altmann for the first stories in this series. Nathalie Parain was among the illustrators for later books in the series, which typified the new approach to colour illustrations for children in pre-war France.

Plate X

BERTUCH, Friedrich Johann Justin. *Bilderbuch für Kinder*. Weimar, 1796.
A hand-coloured engraving on 'Air transport'.

Plate XI

and wine to a figure of Christ. This Christ figure is carved of wood and stands in a room which the child has been forbidden to enter. When he does so the figure comes alive before the child's eyes, holds a conversation with him, and finally takes him with Him into death, which is really the door to true life. The whole thing is very Spanish in conception and the Spaniards are probably affected more nearly than we are by the charming dialogue between Marcelino and Christ.

The most remarkable thing in the story is the character of the little urchin who, as an orphan, has been brought up by the monks. He combines in himself all the features of pulsing everyday life only to shine out suddenly with an inner greatness, a grace and a spirit of sacrifice, which has only been seen before in *The little prince*,[1] and then in a very different fashion.

The story of this boy and of his death in the forbidden attic in the arms of the wooden Christ can well be explained psychologically and thereby intellectually understood. But in doing such a thing we pass over the full meaning of the book which aims to present in real terms a quite supernatural experience. Its effect on the reader, and especially on the simple mind of a child, is deeper than something which is just apprehended by the understanding.

This celebrated story has been filmed and has thereby achieved an international fame. The book itself has become part of the Spanish heritage. Although its origins are entirely Spanish and Catholic, like all truly poetic utterances it breaks through the barriers of creed and has become after very few years a classic of world literature for children.

Sanchez-Silva has written numerous books, including some half-dozen for children. Of these it seems to me that the sadly beautiful *La Burrita Non* (1955) is well worth mentioning, the story of a donkey which, like *Marcelino*, brings a transcendental meaning to everyday life. Although the argument of the book is on the theme of kindness to animals, this is not to be understood simply at such a level. The cruelly treated little donkey Burrita dies without any consolation; there then follows a wonderfully conceived story of a paradise for animals, seen in the form of a dream. The world may not be changed by such things, but every child who reads this book will look with fresh eyes at the poor working-donkeys of Spain.

Les contes du chat perché

Marcel Aymé is a writer for adults and a man of typically French *esprit*, but he has written a series of children's books in which the subject of children and animals is wittily and warm-heartedly set out. It is not surprising that a poet from the country of La Fontaine has adapted the fable formula to suit his own purpose. His heroines are two little girls through whom the animals and their ways are reflected. As in *Peter Pan* the children and the animals speak the same language, and cats and wolves, dogs and birds, cows and donkeys

[1] *The little prince* is dealt with fully in the following chapter.

all unite together. Although the stories which go to make up the volumes of *Les contes du chat perché* move along with the speed and excitement of a fairy tale, they contain an astonishing amount of dialogue, which belongs with the cleverest and the most enjoyable that can be found in modern children's literature.

The two little girls in the story, Marinette and Delphine, are left alone in their parents' farmhouse during a cloud-burst and they decide to play at 'Noah's Ark'. They fetch one of each of the farmyard animals into the kitchen:

'The cow was very interested in the things she could see through the glass doors of the dresser. In particular she could scarcely take her eyes off a cheese and a bowl of milk and she murmured several times: "I see! . . . *Now* I understand!" '

It is necessary for a white hen to play the part of an elephant in this imaginative game, where the Great Flood recurs once more in a no-man's-land between play and fantasy and reality, for the rain and the animals and the kitchen are all quite real. The hen which has indeed become an imaginary elephant is so big that it cannot get out before the children's parents return and they hide it in the bedroom. But when their parents finally go to the bedroom and open the door the veil of childish magic dissolves and out flutters a terrified white hen.

Then there is the wise story of the wolf whom the children allow into the house, in spite of all their parents' prohibitions. Mind you, he promises always to be a well-behaved wolf and he plays with the children and talks to them like a little brother, although he does admit that in a weak moment he had gobbled up Little Red Riding Hood. They all play the wildest games together and all goes well until his return visit, when Delphine, who has grown too confident, calls out, 'Wolf, would you like to play "Wolf-where-are-you"?' (A game that the two girls had invented.) Then, alas, this reformed character of a wolf momentarily forgets himself and swallows his two little friends whole.[1] But they are, of course, saved and even the wolf with his sewn-up tummy renews his promise never more to eat up little girls.

This story and many another is told in a beautifully delicate but piquant manner. It brings the French child, with his thorough grounding in technical and intellectual matters, into a remarkable dialogue with nature—and indeed is conducted in such a plain, unadorned language that it has an appeal for all ages, delighting even grown-ups.

Les contes du chat perché are a mixture of fable, fairy tale, and straight story and they have a popularity in France similar to that of King Babar among younger children. Since the appearance of the first story in 1934 they have become some of the most-read books of France. Initially they appeared in

[1] English readers are spared this painful incident, for in the translation by Norman Denny the wolf swallows a flat-iron instead. (B.A.)

card covers, rather like the Père Castor books, and among their illustrators was Nathalie Parain. Since 1939, however, various collected volumes have appeared.

DRUON, Maurice. *Tistou, les pouces verts*. Paris, 1957.
Line drawing by Jacqueline Duhème.

Tistou and his green thumbs—a French philanthropist

Written by Maurice Druon and decorated by Jacqueline Duhème, *Tistou, les pouces verts* first appeared in 1957. It is a poetically conceived book, providing French children with a new neighbour for *Le petit prince*, *Peter Pan*, and *Pippi Longstocking*, all of which have a timeless wisdom and a sense of the permanence of childhood.

The introductory chapter says of Tistou:

'If we have been put into the world merely to become a grown-up, our

89

heads, as they grow bigger, very easily absorb ready-made ideas. And these ideas, which have been made for a long time, are to be found in books. So if we read, or listen attentively to people who have read a lot, we can very soon become a grown-up like all the others.

'It is also true that there are many ready-made ideas about almost everything, and this is very convenient because it means we can change our ideas quite often.

'But if we have been sent into the world on a special mission, if we have been charged with the accomplishment of some individual task, things are not quite so easy. The ready-made ideas, which other people find so useful, simply refuse to stay in our heads; they go in at one ear and go out at the other, fall on the floor and get broken.

'Thus we are liable to surprise our parents very much indeed, as well as all the other grown-ups who cling with such determination to their ready-made ideas.'[1]

And this is just what happened to the little boy called Tistou, without his own opinion even being asked.

Now what did the child do for traditional wisdom to end up in smithereens at his feet and for the accomplishment of a quite special task?

Quite early on he discovers that he has got green fingers, with the result that wherever he puts them long-dead seeds begin to germinate with the greatest rapidity, even without soil. What starts as a game becomes a serious statement as the child turns into a moralist, while still retaining his childishness. Finally, after many good deeds, he is able to prevent a war by filling up with all kinds of seeds the artillery which his father is supplying to two enemy forces. The result is that they arrive on the battlefield thickly tangled in an undergrowth of briars. This is the climax of his brief, innocent life and the book closes with him mounting as an angel to Heaven on a ladder of flowers.

This is a fairy tale which is close to present actualities, a fable which can be interpreted symbolically, almost a pacifist children's book. Nevertheless, it creates in the armaments manufacturer not a man of evil, as the accepted pattern demands, but an affectionate father; while the factory manager, a former officer and now Tistou's tutor, is no war criminal but a true human being whom the strange little boy loves.

This twentieth-century fable is also something rare in modern France: a nonsense story containing strong surrealist elements, which an adult reader will interpret differently from an eight-year-old child. In a few short years the little boy develops from a state of childish innocence to an understanding of the world and its unchanging deceptions and, indeed, to a knowledge of the inevitability of death. This done he disappears into the unknown, leaving behind in the figure of his horse a message of goodwill. The purpose of his life was to sow the seeds of kindness among neighbours and he has succeeded in awakening an awareness of it in the reader.

[1] From the translation by Humphrey Hare.

In contrast to the children previously mentioned in this chapter he may appear somewhat artificial, like one of those origami figures which Japanese children produce from folded paper. But even such creations carry their own justification between the covers of a book, provided that their actions are governed by a true sensibility. In my opinion Maurice Druon will soon take his own place by right in the children's pantheon.

BOOK LIST

Some recent translations of the Continental authors mentioned in this chapter are:

COLLODI, Carlo: *Pinocchio*, translated by JosephWalker, illustrated by Richard Floethe. World (Rainbow Classic), 1946.

JANSSON, Tove: *Finn family Moomintroll*, translated by Elizabeth Portch. Walck, 1965.

Also available as a Puffin story-book. The other titles in the Moomin series, all published by Walck, are: *Exploits of Moominpappa* (1966), *Moominsummer madness* (1961), *Moominland midwinter* (1962), *Tales from Moominvalley* (1964), and *Moominpappa at sea* (1967).

The picture-books, published by Benn (London), are *The book about Moomin, Mymble and Little My* (1953) and *Who will comfort Toffle?* (1960).

A volume of strip-cartoons, *Moomin*, was published in London by Alan Wingate in 1957.

LINDGREN, Astrid: *Pippi Longstocking*, translated by Florence Lamborn, illustrated by Louis Slanzman. Viking, 1954.

Also published by Viking are *Pippi goes on Board* (1957), *Pippi in the South Seas* (1957), *Mio my son* (1957), and *Mischievous Meg* (1962).

Rasmus and the Vagabond, for which Astrid Lindgren was awarded the Hans Christian Andersen Medal in 1958, has been translated by Gerry Bothmer (Viking, 1961). In England, Methuen has issued the stories about Bullerby. Astrid Lindgren's stories for adolescents about Kati are being published in translation in America by Grosset. Other books by this author are listed in the bibliographies on pp. 151 and 245.

EGNER, Thorbjørn: *The singing town*, translated by Evelyn Ramsden and Leila Berg. Macmillan, 1959.

Also available: *Karius and Baktus*, translated by Patricia Crampton. Nelson, 1963.

KRÜSS, James: *My great-grandfather and I*, translated by James Kirkup, illustrated by Jochen Bartsch. Atheneum, 1964.

Also available: *Happy islands behind the winds*, illustrated by E. Binder-Stassfurt. Atheneum, 1966. *Three by three*, translated by Geoffrey Strachan, pictures by Eva Johanna Rubin. Macmillan, 1965; and *The talking machine*, translated by Oliver Coburn, illustrated by Dietrich Lange. Ward (London), 1965.

ENDE, Michael: *Jim Button and Luke the engine driver*, translated by Renata Symonds, illustrated by Maurice Dodd. Harrap (London), 1963.

SANCHEZ-SILVA, José Maria: *Marcelino (a story from parents to children)*, translated by Angela Britton, illustrated by Goni. Newman Press, 1955.

Also available: *The boy and the whale*, translated by Michael Heron, illustrated by Margery Gill. McGraw-Hill, 1964.

AYMÉ, Marcel: *The wonderful farm*, translated by Norman Denny, illustrated by Charlotte Hough. Harper, 1951.

This is a translation of a selection of *Les contes du chat perché*. A second volume, *Return to the wonderful farm*, was published in 1954 by Lane.

DRUON, Maurice: *Tistou of the green thumbs*, translated by Humphrey Hare, illustrated by Jacqueline Duhème. Scribner, 1958.

7 THE LITTLE PRINCE FROM OUTER SPACE
An attempt to describe Antoine de Saint-Exupéry's Le petit prince

Saint-Exupéry's *Little prince* is the most fragile and delicate of all those child-figures in children's literature (even though they may be for children in only a limited sense) whom we may set against the violent and conceited figures of the 'Superman', 'Mickey Mouse', 'Knatterton', and 'Globi' tradition. He is indeed so delicate that it may seem perverse to mention him in the same breath as this little bunch of storm-troopers who seek to attack all that is most humane on behalf of a pulp literature, which ranges from the swashbuckling to the downright brutal. But the little prince is a figure of courage. He has left the asteroid which is his home, has flown down to earth and has given up his life to save his soul, and that should be courageous enough for us. He has a certain innocence, a purity of heart, which is common to all the men of goodwill in children's literature, however differently they may otherwise express themselves.

The little prince may count himself first in their ranks, born as he was from the brain of a courageous airman who lost his life in the last war and was mourned as few others by friend and foe alike. Let us examine his creation more closely. Is it rooted in fairy tale? Does the little prince represent one of those fairy-story characters that we know so well? To some extent he does, otherwise he would scarcely be a prince, for princes today are a dying race. But no prince in the fairy stories we know ever came down to us from outer space and none ever encountered before the figure that he met—an airman with his plane, forced down in the desert. This man is of the first importance, however, for it is up to him to tell the story; nobody except him, the airman with nine parched days in the desert behind him, has seen the prince or can say what happened. He talked to him every day and it is primarily their conversations which he has written down. With all the seriousness of an adult, but with the innocence of the child that he once was, Saint-Exupéry sets down these conversations and these events.

Since my main purpose is to write a book about children's literature it is necessary for me now to touch on some of the factors which make *Le petit prince* in spite of everything a book for children. If publishers' figures are correct, then hundreds of thousands, not to say millions, of people must have read this book, among them a great many children and young people, and it was, after all, for them that it was written.

SAINT-EXUPÉRY, Antoine de. *Le Petit Prince*. London, Heinemann, 1958.
The author's original colour drawing, redrawn for an English school edition of the French text by F. A. Shuffrey, M.C., M.A.

First of all there is the airman taking his engine to bits. For many children the story of the crashed airman, the final success of his repairs, the discovery of the well, and his return home, will be more interesting than the figure of the little prince, who is perhaps only some kind of Fata Morgana. He has to be accepted, because he leads the airman to the vital well.

But the more a child thinks about it, the more he will see the little prince as an important fellow actor. He will follow the dialogue between the two, without understanding all of it, and he will sense part of the great sadness which surrounds this eternally lonely little figure. But no child will understand the briefly recounted end of this little creature, which has every outward resemblance to a sacrifice. For if this were a proper fairy tale the prince would have to return to his asteroid and to his flower again, on whose account he got the airman to go through all that trouble of drawing a sheep with a muzzle on.

Saint-Exupéry the poet appends a comforting chapter to the end of his story. He says that he does believe that the little prince returned to his own planet. He himself loves to listen to the stars which are like five hundred million little bells and, 'full of wild surmise', he thinks of the desert as being the loveliest and saddest landscape in the world, where each of us may meet the little prince for ourselves. In this entrancing conclusion it is possible that he overestimates his audience of children in turning to them and only them in such an intimate way (*'Et aucune grande personne ne comprendra jamais que ça a tellement d'importance!'*).

There may be some rare 'corrupted' adults and perhaps some quite un-corrupted children who hear the music of the stars. And perhaps they will remark some change in the heavens when, on an invisible planet high in the firmament, inside the picture of a box, the picture of a sheep (the strap of whose muzzle the airman has forgotten to draw) eats up the red rose belonging to a little prince.

This mental flight into the firmament will fascinate many children. For here is a universe which is different from that in Grimm's *Sterntaler*, different from that with its paved Milky Way in the book *Peterchens Mondfahrt* (*Little Peter's journey to the moon*), which was the favourite of our own nurseries and is so still for many present-day children, different even from that of the bold adventurers in the books of Jules Verne. It is a universe which, despite the little golden-haired prince and his beloved flower, belongs to modern man with all the horrors and all the attractions of infinity—for some, nothing but fearful chaos, for others, an example of the most perfect order.

This is a book of pronounced individuality and the legacy of a writer tragically killed. Let us, nevertheless, try to place it in the context of great children's literature where, by reason of its conception and its unparalleled success, it truly belongs.

Saint-Exupéry, brought up in a kind and cultivated household, certainly knew the classic collections of fairy stories. He must surely have loved Ander-sen, for he has in common with him the rare courage to create a tragic ending. The little prince, bitten by the snake, 'fell as gently as a tree falls' and the little mermaid, whose destiny is fulfilled, dissolves into foam. Although a century separates them, they are both creations of the same temperament. They are even united in their courage and their final loneliness.

Is it possible that the author also knew the captivating nonsense of Carroll's *Alice in Wonderland*? Such a thing is easy to believe when you consider how the little prince put his planet in order, covering his flower with a glass globe, sweeping out his knee-high volcanoes, of which the two active ones were useful for cooking his breakfast on and the one extinct one served as a foot-stool. This little universe, so prosaic and yet so improbable, contains also the asteroid with the lamplighter on it, faced with a sun which rises and sets so quickly that he must be for ever lighting his lamp and putting it out again, with never a rest between; and the little prince need take only a couple of paces to enjoy the most beautiful sunset whenever he wishes to look at it. All such things belong to the realm which the English designate 'nonsense' and which, up to this time, was to be found chiefly in English children's books and most prominently of course in those of Lewis Carroll.

At one stage of his journey the little prince says to the businessman: '*Moi, je possède une fleur que j'arrose tous les jours. Je possède trois volcans que je ramone toutes les semaines. Car je ramone aussi celui qui est éteint. On ne sait jamais. C'est utile à mes volcans, et c'est utile à ma fleur, que je les possède.*' This is but one place among many where in a childishly simple but by no means primitive way the moralists are shown the arguments for kindness and usefulness in the running of a state, even if it is a state on the smallest planet in the universe.

Whoever knows his way round the world of children and children's books may also recall an older contemporary of the little prince, again French, but this time four-legged, emerging from the brush-strokes of a kindly painter. It is, of course, Babar, that philanthropic monarch who provided his people with happiness and the blessings of peace and culture. This remarkable king will be dealt with fully in a later chapter, but it is worth drawing attention here to the powerful support which he gives the little prince in today's peaceful battle over young children and their upbringing. Brunhoff's case indeed is simpler, in so far as he has already won the hearts of real children in many countries and in so far as his life is extensively the result of an optimism which still had faith in the progress of goodness. For Babar is a child of the thirties who has not experienced the Second World War. Brunhoff the painter, whose country was secure behind the invincible Maginot Line, could well portray a humorous war—a '*drôle de guerre*'.

Saint-Exupéry's story of the prince appeared in 1945, although its conception dates back to 1940, the year when France lost her freedom. The little prince was therefore born in a year of darkest sadness—the year when his creator's country was occupied (although, as has ironically been proved, countless numbers of the enemy themselves read the books of Saint-Exupéry). Where, therefore, could the little prince live except on a planet which had never been occupied, where could he go but to the desert?

From this we may understand the sadness which pervades this book and the feeling for humanity which radiates from this small, lonely child. The problems which the little prince argued with the airman are the problems of our own time—which the writer has now left for good.

The superficiality, the noise, and the harshness of our century, together with its cold reliance upon science and economics—all this is there. Its clearest symbol lies in the garden full of roses against which is set the one rose that is really treasured. It no longer has anything to do with children's books, or even with politics, and only to a limited extent with literature itself.

The lonely traveller in the skies, who passes hour upon hour alone with his wild machine, who has shut out all the voices of the outer world, has heard the voice within himself. The pilot, with death constantly before him, has listened to the voices of true life and from a keen love for just this life he has set down his 'little prince' on paper. The thing that moves us most is the extraordinarily delicate touch of this, the most masculine of modern writers; the tenderness which the big, coarse aviator feels for the small, charming creature who suddenly stands beside him and says: '*S'il vous plaît . . . dessine-moi un mouton.*' But there is a similar tenderness in the little prince's feelings for his one rose and also for his huge, thirsty friend.

At the end of the book, shortly before their parting, the little prince speaks comfortingly about his approaching death, building up a bit of courage to face the yellow snake. He says that from now on the stars, which for some people are only lights and for others only golden coins, will be for the airman a firmament ringing with five hundred million little bells. With these words there enters, in this book for children, a sense of the transcendental, of the things which last for ever. It is presented so strikingly that we are made to forget that such an ending to this fairy tale, such an act of self-destruction on the part of the little prince, has no place in the world of Christian ideas, which has always been for us identical with the transcendental. Instead it comes from the questing spirit of an unbeliever (in the Christian sense) who finds himself face to face with death and infinity. He takes no comfort from God or from eternal life; there are no angels in this modern, fairy-tale heaven; there is just a single, lonely child whose cares have gone out, deep into limitless space, to a little red flower and three small volcanoes, one of which is extinct.

This fairy tale contains a great deal of personal experience. For this reason I should like to add a brief biographical tailpiece.

Marie-Antoine-Roger de Saint-Exupéry was born in Lyons on 29 June 1900. Both of his parents were from solid, well-established families, but his father died early and his mother spent her life in alternating visits to the great houses of the grandparents of her children, all five of whom, therefore, grew up in the country under very favourable circumstances. Antoine was an unmanageable child who started to write very early on. Later he spent some time at a 'Collège' in Mans where his mother had taken up residence. His relationship with his mother was always very close and later led to a lifelong correspondence. At the beginning of the First World War she sent her two eldest sons to a school in Switzerland, where Antoine's brother was taken ill and died shortly afterwards at the age of fourteen. In *Pilote de guerre* Antoine was later to portray the very brave death of this young boy and the echoes of it linger on in *Le petit prince*.

After leaving school Saint-Exupéry hovered between several careers and for a time led a very miserable life. Only in 1926 did he finally turn to flying, and from 1933 onwards he was a commercial pilot in Argentina. In between whiles he found time to write his books, which were extensively based on his experiences as an aviator.

After his company in Argentina was dissolved he turned more to writing, married and settled down in Paris, which he did not like at all. Only with the coming of the second war in 1939 did he return to flying, and after France was occupied he went to America, where his fame as a writer was already established. But he could not stay there, and after a short while he joined the French forces in Morocco.

By this time he was forty-three years old—too old for war flying, said the Americans—and his responses had become so slow through various crash-landings that he was, for instance, no longer in a position to parachute from his aeroplane. In 1944, shortly before the end of the war, he failed to return from a reconnaissance flight over the Mediterranean. In spite of searches by both sides, no trace of him or his aircraft was ever found.

In 1938 a forced landing in the Sahara, during which he had to struggle hard for his life, was undoubtedly the first cause for the writing of *Le petit prince*. His determination not to let himself or his friends go under in the profound pessimism of his time, which he felt so profoundly, led him to put words into the mouth of a child which would tell of things no longer thought about by men—but things which Antoine de Saint-Exupéry hoped would offer some cure for the world.

BOOK LIST

SAINT-EXUPÉRY, Antoine de: *The little prince*, translated by Katherine Woods. Reynal and Hitchcock, 1943.
    Also available as a Puffin story-book.
    Airman's Odyssey, published by Harcourt in 1943, includes *Flight to Arras* (1942), a translation of *Pilote de guerre*, and *Wind, sand, and stars* (1939), a translation of *Terre des hommes*. Both translations are by Lewis Galantière.

8 ROBINSON
Dreams and educational methods

'Robinson Crusoe'—is there anyone whose heart is unmoved at the sound of that name? And when we consider that literate humanity has been moved by it for some 250 years we realize just how curious a phenomenon this is.

Defoe's *Robinson Crusoe* first appeared in 1719 as a serial publication and shortly afterwards as a book. It depicts in the form of a novel the life of a young man who is initially wicked, lazy, and disregardful of parental authority, but who is brought back to good fortune and godliness through enormous exertions, all very realistically described, and through twenty-eight years of loneliness. It is all too obviously a moral tale, but at the same time it is in its first part a lively portrayal of colonial trade in Africa and South America in the days when you could barter pocket-knives and coloured glass for gold, pearls, and slaves. The whole book bears the stamp of documentary exactitude, while remaining a novel of breathtaking tension. But is that sufficient to turn the book into one of the most popular of the eighteenth century and one of the greatest favourites among children's books of all time, even though one must bear in mind that Defoe was the first truly significant English novelist and, at the same time, was to become through *Robinson* the founder of an international literary genre—the so-called *Robinsonnades*—which were of importance not only to children?

No; all this is not sufficient to explain the magic of this book, nor the emotion that we feel when we see this creature standing in front of his cave with his furry breeches and his hide umbrella; this wicked fellow who has run away from home in the most unfeeling way and has now escaped as the sole survivor from a whole ship full of men.

And what does this fine gentleman do who has turned his back like this on the middle-class comforts of his parental home and has suddenly come into possession of nothing more than the tattered clothes he stands up in and the

DEFOE, Daniel. *Robinson Crusoe*. Paris, 1720.
An engraving by R. Picart for the first French edition. This same illustration, signed J. B. Brühle, Leipzig, also appeared in a German edition of 1720.

few bits and pieces left behind by the shipwreck? What does he do? In three decades he creates from all this nothingness a life which is morally unobjectionable and which emphasizes all the middle-class values such as tables and chairs and beds and cupboards—everything pedantically organized and bearing the stamp of good non-conformist piety.

Just at the right moment God sends him a companion, the magnificent Friday, 'the splendid savage', who will play an important part in literature

CAMPE, J. H. *Robinson den Yngre*. Copenhagen, 1784.
An engraving from the first Danish edition of Campe's 'adaptation'.

from now on. And, of course, with Friday the whole process repeats itself, but with even more attention paid to instruction. The 'good' savage who was no stranger to cannibalism and had himself almost become a victim of the practice, learns to put on trousers, to pray, and to go around with a gun.

Finally the reformed good-for-nothing returns to human society, but not without leaving behind on his island a model administration in the form which humane colonial governments usually take. And after a number of difficulties it is augmented by a jumbled population of English and Spanish mariners, adventurers of every kind and even a number of women.

Thus, in most exemplary manner, one human being, without goodness, piety or material possessions, portrays in half a lifetime the development of the human race. The simple man first discovers the mutual dependence of neighbours and is ultimately brought before the problems of human society, of justice, and of marriage, propagation and government. All this takes place in the unspoilt, untouched natural surroundings of a lonely island, far surpassing all other pastoral pieces and the 'back to nature' movements right down to our own day.

The man who created the figure of Robinson Crusoe did not get his story out of thin air. Daniel Defoe, born probably in 1659, was the son of a London chandler. He himself grew up to be an enterprising tradesman, who nevertheless several times landed in a debtors' prison—a fact which did not prevent him from writing. In spirit he was a man of passionate independence who managed to create enemies among his countrymen of all parties, with the result that political imprisonment, persecution, and the pillory were his rewards just as much as royal offices and honours of every kind.

Up to the age of sixty he confined his activity as a writer to fiery political journalism. The commencement of his career as a novelist coincided with a particularly bitter decline in his political and business aspirations so that from 1719 onwards—that is, from the date of the appearance of *Robinson*—he relied on his pen for the upkeep of himself and his family. Of the several novels which followed *Robinson, Moll Flanders* is the best known today. The last years of his life were again punctuated by spells in prison and in 1731 he died in obscurity and away from home, although by this time his fame as a writer was undisputed.

In 1711 the newspapers of the day had carried the personal accounts of a Scottish mariner, Alexander Selkirk, who had been marooned on an island off the Chilean coast after a disagreement with the captain of his ship. Here he had set up house for himself through four years of utter loneliness. He had then been discovered by an English captain and brought to London, where Defoe heard of his adventures and supposedly even met him. It is therefore possible to say that Selkirk gave the initial impetus to the novel and that the island of Juan Fernandez off the Chilean coast is Robinson's island. Defoe himself disavows such a geographical location, although the island now possesses a monument to the event and a cave, which is described as being Robinson's.

Thus far the facts take us and thus we now see this man for ever on his island: a permanent ideal for his own age and for countless generations, interpreted by men according to their own designs through two hundred years. Thus Jean-Jacques Rousseau, the founder of modern education, could make out of an exciting novel the Bible for his cause.

'This book will be the first to be read by my Émile; for a long time it will constitute his whole library and it will always be pre-eminent there . . .', such is the beginning of a long discussion by Rousseau in the second part of *Émile*, in which he portrays the exemplary behaviour and development of Robinson Crusoe, the man without technical resources, the man uninfluenced by corrupt civilization, the man who, thrown back entirely upon himself, experiences once again evolution in the highest sense. He receives as his companion the still unspoiled savage, who is a symbolic figure for his age which has started to believe in the natural goodness of mankind and which thinks to see corruption only in the influence of the surrounding world.

At this time Defoe had already been dead for thirty-one years, and it is very questionable whether he would have desired to be interpreted in this way. But the characters in books often grow up into a new world beyond the heads of their originators and the creator of Robinson who was in his own time so restless, independent and tormented in spirit, found for himself a deserved and worthy posthumous fame of a new kind.

It was in the years 1761–62 that Rousseau raised the firmly established fame of Robinson to new heights through his lines in *Émile*, something which, as we shall see, was to have a great many consequences. But at this time a twelve-year-old boy was living in Frankfurt-am-Main who was later to tell us in detail of his early experiences with books in *Dichtung und Wahrheit*. It is the *Robinson* of Defoe which provides the only common reading experience to link the young Goethe with the boys of future ages. The man who was later to write *Wilhelm Meister* here read the first novel of personal development and certainly the earliest of all to survive so well.

Joachim Heinrich Campe

Some twenty years later another book appeared with the title of *Robinson der Jüngere* (1779). It was a German adaptation of the Robinson story by a theologian and educationist born in 1746, Joachim Heinrich Campe. He was an enthusiastic devotee of *Émile* and tended in his own way to embody Rousseau's demands for a figure who would be a model and an example of natural education.

Campe was one of the great humane teachers of his century and attempted by school reforms, by the establishment of his own academy, and by the furtherance of the use of books, to put into practice the ideals of Rousseau (who was himself no practical teacher and whose own children finally ended up in a foundling institution). But everything about him would have been forgotten by this time had not Vater Campe (as he was called by his pupils) written his *Robinson*.

At this time Campe was tutor in the Humboldt household in Berlin and was indeed later to influence the studies of the two brothers Alexander and Wilhelm. Even though Georg Forster, the experienced traveller and travel writer of that time, is generally credited with inspiring Alexander von Humboldt to his famous journeys of discovery in the New World, it still seems to me entirely possible, indeed certain, that the first seed of this unbounded desire for travel and exploration was sown in the boy's heart by his first tutor.

Alexander was a boy when *Robinson der Jüngere* appeared. Without doubt he had read his teacher's now-forgotten book on Columbus and quite without doubt the same passion for unknown parts of the earth directed the course of instruction which Campe, the young teacher, gave to his two richly gifted and receptive pupils.

That is the way with the imagination once it has found a form and warmed it to life. It takes its incalculable journey from the England of 1720 to the revolutionary and visionary Rousseau, to Goethe and the Humboldts and to the practical mind of Joachim Heinrich Campe who turned the figure of Robinson into a hero of children's books and *Volksbücher*. Such was its unparalleled success that it was printed unchanged for decade after decade and was translated into all the languages of Europe, including English.

Campe's *Robinson* came just at the right time. The old Robinson of Defoe was burdened with too much antiquated material which no longer interested young people, while on the other hand, these same young people were beginning to demand a literature of their own. So if one excepts a few out-dated books such as Fénelon's *Télémaque*, it was through Campe that they received their first novel. His *Robinson* is a piece of work essentially different from Defoe's, which had not been conceived as a children's book at all, because in Defoe's time most people did not accept that children should have a literature of their own. Campe's book travelled in the opposite direction. Written for children, it was quickly stripped of its juvenile framework with all the necessary morals and turned into an anonymous chapbook, even though Campe's book has continued to be printed unchanged and accompanied by many illustrations almost to our own times.

Robinson der Jüngere matches Rousseau's intentions in so far as it portrays the 'natural life' which he demands but with an even more thoroughgoing Germanic fundamentalism and logic. The new Robinson is cast on his deserted beach absolutely destitute of any remnant of civilization. While his counterpart in Defoe provides himself to his heart's content with ship's biscuits, weapons, ammunition, tools, canvas, and hammocks from the wreck, the 'new' Robinson is totally alone in the wilderness of the island. Out of this nothingness he builds a new life. In his island fastness (and he too is there for twenty-eight years) we see him traverse once again animal fear and its subjugation, the return to God, the establishment of a life pleasing to God, together with all the sweat and toil of obtaining all the necessities of life. In contrast to Defoe's novel, the whole story is brought to a satisfactory end. On his return Robinson finds his aged father and, accompanied by Friday, he becomes a useful citizen of his home town; whereas the English Robinson, born in an age of realism and no illusions, turns once again to a life of rootless wandering and poor old Friday is shot by the followers of his own tribe.

In order to emphasize its educational tone, every chapter of *Robinson der*

Jüngere is accompanied by a discussion between Campe and his pupils. This seems to us today a primitive and old-fashioned device but it is a principle adopted by Wyss in his *Swiss family Robinson* which appeared some thirty years later. In Campe it has the advantage of freeing the movement of the actual story from moral observations, thus allowing it to flow more rapidly than in Defoe, whose original contained some passages which were found indescribably boring then as now.

In the main, however, Campe takes over the details of Robinson's story extensively from Defoe—except that Campe's absconding hero starts from Hamburg, while Defoe's, who indeed had his origins in Bremen and was originally called Kreutzer, actually boards his ship at Hull. For both of them the first port of call is London. The subsequent action, the sequence of events, has, except for the already mentioned differences, so many points of similarity that later abbreviated versions for children were often drawn from both books together but the pious superstructure of Campe's story, which is not without its old-world charm, was dismantled with growing rapidity.

The Academy which Campe directed not far from Hamburg came within the sphere of influence of Claudius who about this time may have written the poem *Der Schwarze in der Zuckerplantage* (*The Negro in the sugar plantation*). The following passage is quoted in order to give some idea of that humane star beneath which the second Robinson came into the world:

Weit von meinem Vaterlande
muss ich hier verschmachten und
  vergehn
Ohne Trost in Müh und Schande;
Oh die weissen Männer!! klug und
  schön!
Und ich hab' den Männern ohn'
  Erbarmen
nichts getan.
Du im Himmel! Hilf mir armen
schwarzen Mann.

Far from my own country I must perish here without comfort and in distress and weariness. Oh these white men! These fine, clever white men! These merciless men to whom I have done nothing at all. God in Heaven help me, poor black man that I am!

In Campe, as in Defoe, the action revolves round an individual by the name of Robinson—at that time nothing but a name, but later on to become a whole literary concept. This is seen most clearly by simply registering a few of the enormous number of similarly titled books which appeared at that time: *Emma, the female Robinson* (Stuttgart, 1837); Fouinet: *Le Robinson des glâces* (Paris, 1835); Lemaire: *Petit Robinson* (Paris, 1810); Mallès de Beaulieu: *Le Robinson de douze ans* (Paris, 1824); Vevenet: *Der Holländische Robinson* (Amsterdam around 1824). Over and above these there exist 'Robinson' titles for many countries: *The Austrian Robinson, The Upper Austrian Robinson, Robinson in the Pacific, Ivan, the Robinson of the North, The Hungarian Robinson,* which are just a few of the titles of these pretty worthless productions.

I have still said nothing here about the Robinson motif as such which spread into literature without actually using the name. Even before Defoe, Grimmelshausen had allowed his Simplicius to suffer shipwreck on a deserted island off Madagascar, and Bernardin de Saint-Pierre made very successful use of the desert-island motif in his sentimentally beautiful story *Paul et Virginie* (1788). Indeed, long before Campe, another German, the Saxon Johann Gottfried Schnabel (1692–1750), had written a *Volksbuch* called *Die Insel Felsenburg* (a translation of its exact title reading: 'Strange adventures of a number of mariners and particularly Albert Julius, a Saxon, and his colonies established on the Island of Felsenburg', appearing between 1731–42).

In this book, which likewise belonged among the early reading of the young Goethe, the author used the story of a shipwreck in order to freshen up the political ideals of the Enlightenment with a Robinson theme. Since a certain amount of feminine interest is also introduced, the romantic strain is stronger here than in other Robinson stories. Thus *Die Insel Felsenburg* rapidly became a true *Volksbuch*, but then disappeared only to enjoy resurrection at the time of the Romantics through a version by Tieck. The Danish poet Oehlenschläger gave the book a fresh lease of life in 1826 and the story seems to have disappeared from view less among the Scandinavians than among the Germans. Indeed, it plays an important part in *Ljos heimsins* (*The light of the world*, 1937), the novel by the Nobel prize-winning author Laxness, in which he portrays the career of the Icelandic folk poet Olafur Karason, who was indebted to the Felsenburg stories for the first profound impact which literature made upon him. In an isolated Icelandic farmstead we see the daughter of the house reading page after page of the book to the sick foster-child, especially the altogether very tame love scenes, and this harmlessly adventurous book accompanies the young man for a long time on his tormented journey in the world of letters. The longevity of these Robinson stories, which were bolted down by the young Goethe with the same voracious appetite that men have felt for them within our own lifetime, makes it possible to compare them to fairy stories in their capacity for staying alive.

The Wyss family Robinson

Now we come to a particularly important Robinson story, whose fame almost exceeds that of the previously mentioned ones, at least so far as children's books are concerned. And even though the affection in which it is held in Europe may be declining, it still today enjoys an amazing success in English-speaking countries, and above all in America. (In saying this it is perhaps worth recalling that the Americans do not take too pedantic a view of translations. The fact that this European book is still so much a favourite today on the other side of the Atlantic is probably connected to the fact that American editors, for the sake of liveliness, have treated their original, respected for almost 150 years, with considerably less reverence than we would have done.)

Falkenhorst nach feiner Volendung.

A. Der Haupteingang samt Vorhäffe oder Hausflur.
B. Hundeftall.
C. Hühner Stall.
D. Vieh Stall. N° zur Kuh-Schäfers: Ziegenftall unter
E. Terasse.　Holz Vorrath find auf der andern Seite

F. Thüre auf die Terasse.
G. Taglocher auf die Schneggenstiege.
H. Reben Colonier.
I. Die Wohnung auf dem Baum bei Nacht.
K. Fenster von Marienthal.

L. Gallerie mit der Ausficht in die Ferne.
M. Ausgang nach den großen Aesten des Baumes.
N. Die Tauben Nester von Calebaßen, und dreyfaches
O. Bienen Stöcke welche aus den Aesten fest gemacht.
P. Tagloch, u: Taubenschlag.

wyss, J. D. *Charackteristick meiner Kinder in einer Robinsonade.* 1792–1798.
A sepia illustration of Falkenhorst, the tree-house, by J. E. Wyss, the author's son, for Volume 4.

Plate XII

LONGFELLO, H. *Pyesne o Gayavate*. Moscow, 1956.
Paper-board cover, printed in 4 colours, for a recent Russian edition of *Hiawatha*.

Plate XIII

A delightful tale can itself be made from the way *Der Schweizerische Robinson* came into being. The English title which has become so famous—*The Swiss family Robinson*—already tells us something about it. The book does not only contain the story of a shipwreck, through which a whole family are turned into Crusoes; no, it was also itself the product of a highly gifted and imaginative family, whose head, Johann David Wyss (1743–1818)—originally a much-travelled army chaplain and later a pastor in Bern—devoted much time and care to the education of his talented sons. He undertook long walking tours with them through which he imbued them with his own love of nature. It is therefore no marvel that in this family Robinson Crusoe was a popular figure and it is no surprise that such a naturally imaginative family had the idea of transferring itself in a series of long discourses into the Robinson situation.

What boy and what man does not have something of the Robinson in him, even today? Whatever the answer, a great many Robinson ideals lodged in the breast of the enterprising and energetic pastor, who would otherwise scarcely have had the patience to write down the results of these family conversations and provide them with appropriate illustrations. This man of God wrote out 841 pages of the story for his children, and his very scientific drawings were supplemented by his adolescent son Johann Emanuel with some aquatints, which serve to augment the curious imagination of the narrator and demonstrate most delightfully how a father's tale can bring out the incipient creative powers of his child. But all this was only done for the family circle and for many years it remained in the family cupboard, doubtless next to the Bible and the hymn book; and the old pastor's manuscript, with its enchanting drawings by father and son, remains there down to the present time, carefully looked after by a great-great-grandson. Quite probably the story would never have come into contact with a printing press had not the pastor's second eldest son, Johann Rudolf Wyss (1781–1830),[1] retouched it a little and later on had it printed (1812, published by Orell-Füssli, Zürich). Unfortunately, the wonderful illustrations could only be employed to a limited extent, presumably on technical grounds connected with the printing; but even without them the book was an immediate success. The author used the name Robinson only in the title, for the sake of its symbolism which had long outstripped the simple tale of the man who first bore it.

The exceptional success of this new Robinson story for young people stems largely, on the one hand, from the fact that children predominate in it and experience some extraordinary adventures. On the other hand, weight must be given to the comic imagination of this energetic and learned army chaplain and his very Swiss kind of practicality. For these reasons the *Schweizerische Robinson* obtained a world-wide fame, immediately conquering the

[1] Johann Rudolf Wyss was later to become a Professor of Philosophy, but he also wrote a considerable quantity of popular poems, among them 'Rufst du mein Vaterland', the Swiss national anthem. (B.A.)

FRONTISPIECE.

Family Robinson Crusoe.

WYSS, J. D. *The Swiss family Robinson*. London, 1818.
Title page and engraved frontispiece of the earliest edition of the book to use this title.

THE
SWISS
𝕱amily 𝕽obinson:

OR,

ADVENTURES

OF A FATHER AND MOTHER AND FOUR
SONS IN A DESERT ISLAND:

BEING

A PRACTICAL ILLUSTRATION OF THE FIRST PRIN-
CIPLES OF MECHANICS, NATURAL PHILOSOPHY,
NATURAL HISTORY, AND ALL THOSE BRANCHES
OF SCIENCE WHICH MOST IMMEDIATELY APPLY
TO THE BUSINESS OF LIFE.

———

TRANSLATED FROM THE GERMAN OF
M. WISS.

———

IN TWO VOLUMES.
VOL. I.
SECOND EDITION.

══════

𝕷ondon:
PRINTED FOR M. J. GODWIN AND Co.,
At the JUVENILE LIBRARY, 41, Skinner-Street.

———

1818.

English-speaking world, who turned *The Swiss family Robinson* into one of the classics of their children's literature.

Its creator had never dreamed of such success and he survived the very late appearance of the printed version by only six years. The book had been written for his four sons and he delineated them clearly in it. He uses the story to portray the education of the four boys, who possess all the customary goodness and badness of normal children. And that their upbringing is at one and the same time wordly and fervently pious is hardly surprising coming from a contemporary of Lavater.[1] Every enterprise which the shipwrecked family undertakes is begun and ended with everybody down on his bended knees—yet another big contrast between the new Robinson and the prototype. As every connoisseur of the genre knows, old Crusoe started life as a good-for-nothing who only after bitter trials and long sickness found his way to God and the Bible (which, Lord be praised, he had saved from the wreck). Such a dramatic conversion was in no way necessary for the family of our Swiss parson.

This new Robinson was a typical product of the Romantic movement. Defoe, and even Campe, intended to be realistic, but Wyss turns his desert island into an unparalleled nature reserve. Plants and animals of all sizes and species serve him in his explanations of botany and zoology, in his obtaining the necessities of life and in providing suitable dangers. The topography unites the Alpine magnificence of his homeland with a tropical luxuriousness. The measureless Romantic imagination of the author was only fully brought home to me when I saw the original manuscript with its extraordinary illustrations. These were never needed after the first edition was published, for the text itself contained so much of their nostalgia and their ideals that the book became a 'best-seller' overnight without them. Incidentally, this not entirely realistic didacticism seems to have led Captain Marryat, one of England's finest writers about the sea, and a man to eschew all false romanticism, to write his *Masterman Ready* (1841–42). This book was published in Germany under the title of *Sigismund Rüstig* and it is one of the best-loved sea stories in the Robinson tradition.

With these, the last legitimate[2] offspring of good old Crusoe, let us take our leave of this splendid subject. Let us make our farewells to this remarkable man, who retained his humanity despite the animal-skin clothes that he wore. And, as a symbol of this humanity, he held high his mighty umbrella, an object from the antiquity of Egypt, Assyria, China, not only demonstrating usefulness but also a sign of human dignity. (For a long time I agreed with

---

[1] Johann Kaspar Lavater (1741–1801) was a Swiss pastor and the passionate advocate of a liberal and highly personalized Christianity. In his time it met with enthusiastic, if uncritical, support—as did his very curious ideas on phrenology. (B.A.)

[2] Evidence of the continued (if less legitimate) use of the Robinson formula is afforded by the titles of two films making the rounds of provincial circuits as this book was being translated: *The Space Family Robinson* and *Robinson Crusoe on Mars*. (B.A.)

Rousseau, who found such protection unnecessary for his *Émile*, but then I realized its symbolic importance. For was not Defoe an Englishman? And what Englishman can do without his umbrella?)

But, in spite of the umbrella, Robinson did not remain plain English. Like Odysseus he became the possession of humanity and his existence is un-exampled but at the same time exemplary. He has exercised an enormously fruitful and happy influence on mankind's periodic disillusionment with civilization and determination to return to nature. Even today things are not otherwise.

What a contentment there still is in sitting with Robinson and his book and shuddering at so much loneliness—and then after twenty years of desolation to see with bounding heart the footprint in the sand and to take the innocent Friday to be your closest friend in all the world. What a feast of the imagination there is between the two covers of that book! There is no later journey which can take us so far beyond ourselves and at the same time so deeply into ourselves.

COMMENT

Many of the foreign books mentioned in this chapter were at one time available in English, but for obvious reasons are no longer in print—even *Paul et Virginie*, which went through an enormous number of editions in the last century. The early proliferations of the Robinson Story have been charted to some extent by Hermann Ullrich in his book noted in the final bibliography (p. 273).

Robinson der Jüngere was first put into English by Campe himself, but the 'definitive' attempt was made by Stockdale in *The new Robinson Crusoe* (4 vols, 1788), illustrated with cuts by John Bewick. Up to 1870 there were over a dozen different editions of the book in English and translations also appeared of his *Discovery of America* (volumes on Columbus, Cortez, and Pizarro).

Two translations have recently appeared of Grimmelshausen's picaresque romance of the Thirty Years War: *The adventures of a simpleton*, translated and abridged by Walter Wallich, New English Library, 1962; and *Simplicius Simplicissimus*, translated by H. Weissenborn and L. Macdonald. Calder, 1964.

The Swiss family Robinson has, of course, a very complicated history. The first English edition was *The family Robinson Crusoe*, published by M. J. Godwin in 1814 and possibly translated by William Godwin. Its sixteen chapters emphasize the moral fervour of the book and this was even more prominent in the two-volume version which appeared in 1818—the first to be called *The Swiss family Robinson*.

Godwin's edition held the field till the late 1840s and from that time on close on three hundred different editions must have been published in England

and America. Many of these are based on the famous French edition of the book by the Baroness de Montolieu which expanded certain sections and provided a more satisfactory ending. Mrs. H. B. Paull (a translator of Andersen) was one of the first to use the French version (in Warne's Chandos Classics, 1868) and other notable nineteenth century editions are those by H. Frith, 1878, and W. H. G. Kingston, 1879.

Of the editions available today the following are probably the ones which children will most enjoy:

wyss, J. R.: *The Swiss family Robinson*, retranslated and abridged by Audrey Clark after the version by H. Frith, illustrated by Charles Folkard. Dent, 1949.

wyss, J. R.: *The Swiss family Robinson*, illustrated by C. Walter Hodges. O.U.P., 1949.

9 FROM DEERSLAYER TO OLD SHATTERHAND

Some thoughts on the attractiveness of Red Indians and on the literary sources which have given children their ideas about them

I belong to a generation for whom Cowboys and Indians was the game of all games. I associate it with glorious adventures in gardens and fields and woods —a game played according to clearly defined rules within whose framework one could identify oneself completely. I therefore hesitated a long time before turning to a subject so loaded with nostalgia, for to set down one's thoughts on a subject in writing requires one to put it in order, to investigate its sources and its true value and to free it from all its sentimental trimmings. This is not always an enjoyable task, but I must attempt it.

From the names which we took for ourselves in our childhood games it is obvious that it was from Cooper's *Leatherstocking* that we got our main ideas. By a lucky chance we also got hold of Eastman's *Ohijesa*, the true memoirs of a Sioux Indian who in his later years became a doctor among the whites, but as a child in the 1860s had experienced the life of a forest Indian, even down to the last bloody battles of the 'Redskins'. In addition to these we also gorged ourselves on Karl May and on cheap little books that we could get with our pocket-money.

Similarly, mixed up with various unconnected and inaccurate bits of knowledge which they have picked up later, most Europeans carry around with them a curiously rich, if inordinately confused, body of facts about these matters which is quite unique.

Why do we feel like this about the Indians and not about, say, the Chinese who had pigtails and invented gunpowder? Why did we never play 'Nigger-boys', even though they had existed for so long in our literature? Why did we never dress up as ancient Germans and play Romans and Germans instead of Redskins and Palefaces? Why does almost every twelve-year-old child today know at least as much about the Sioux Indians as he does about the original inhabitants of his own country? Even when such a twelve-year-old appears to have got his knowledge mainly from Karl May, it is nevertheless remarkably accurate, for May put himself to a deal of hard study in writing his books. And today, more than ever, children are flooded out with a stream of documentary or pseudo-documentary books about Red Indians. They swallow all this information about a vanished nation with an insatiable appetite—for all that it is not perhaps quite so ravenous as in my childhood, when we identified ourselves with single, opposing tribes to such an extent that I still feel myself to be, for instance, a 'Delaware'. All of which was the result of reading one book.

What other literature has had such an effect? As with most it started out from factual beginnings. In Goethe's childhood, for instance, nobody played Cowboys and Indians. Goethe, giving rein to his imagination on the stage of a puppet theatre, had his head full of fairy tales from the German chapbooks, even though something played a part in his childhood, which contained the first seed of the later craze for Indians. This something was the good uncorrupted savage—Man Friday from *Robinson Crusoe*, the noble savage who was to be followed in later generations by the pious and virtuous Negro slave in *Uncle Tom's cabin*. For the European discovers primeval innocence in the closeness to nature of the peoples whom at the same time he is overcoming and even obliterating. And among all these peoples it is the Red Indians of North America with their courage unto death and their unrestricted life, who have been most deeply injured, most hopelessly obliterated.

This was not because they did not defend themselves sufficiently bravely. They possessed a greater fearlessness in battle than almost any nation on earth. But precisely those qualities which turned them into unique heroes of literature—their pride, their simplicity, their animistic attachment to nature, and their independence—made them quite incapable after their suppression of adapting themselves to the new circumstances. They, the children of nature, were dedicated to destruction and, while they withdrew, battling ever farther westwards, they were already establishing for themselves a position in a new form of literature.

Here I would like to adduce some examples of this which are of special significance for children's literature. As with *Robinson*, the authors of the first books about the Indians in no way had their sights set on an audience of children. Even Karl May himself thought that he was writing a kind of entertaining *Volksbuch* with moral overtones rather than something for children.

But it was James Fenimore Cooper who was to immortalize the figure of the Indian as we understand it. His five-volume novel split the seams of the normal children's books with its extravagant richness in historical and imaginative happenings and in characters both white and red-skinned. It revealed a writer of considerable power of construction, honesty, and objectivity, especially concerning his own people.

It is understandable that America could possess no literature of her own so long as she had to fight for internal control over the land's original inhabitants and for external political independence. It is therefore the more surprising that three of the first significant writers of the independent country chose each in his own way to deal with the most troubled moments of her most recent past.

James Fenimore Cooper and his predecessors

In 1819 Washington Irving's *Sketch-Book of Geoffrey Crayon, Gent.* appeared, a book much read in Europe and containing a chapter on the character of the Indians in which the author put in a plea for the preservation of their natural conditions of life. At that time this was a bold demand, for the Indians were proving themselves to be a great danger to the settlers in their move Westwards.

More important was *The song of Hiawatha* by the Romantic Longfellow (1807–82), a poet whose many travels and literary contacts in Europe had given him a close knowledge of the German Romantics and the Scandinavian poets. In this long poem (1855) he created an Indian counterpart to the European hero-sagas, influenced above all by the Finnish *Kalevala*, and the effects the poem had were extraordinary. The poet, who by the way had also taken up a liberal stance on the question of slavery, pictures here in Romantic transfiguration the life of the Indian, the dangerous enemy of his own forefathers. But his nearness to these things in both space and time prevented him from giving a seriously falsified interpretation of actuality. From his portrayals we get a picture of the Red Indian similar in its attractiveness to the ones that emerge from later documentary studies.

But with a parallel intention it was Cooper who was the first to cause the Indian question to become a question of humanity.

Historically speaking, this Indian question was already decided when he began to write, even though the struggles were not completely finished. James Cooper himself, born in 1789 in New Jersey, came from English immigrant stock (his forebears were from Stratford-upon-Avon). Later on, as a writer, he was to call himself Fenimore Cooper to bring in his mother's maiden name. He grew up on the Western frontier in Cooperstown, a settlement founded by his father deep in the wilds on the shores of Lake Otsego. There on the doorstep was all the rough, untamed country which his Deerslayer inhabited, even though the Indians had already left the area for good. Cooper's father, however, had kept careful records and must have handed on to his son a lot of genuine knowledge. Furthermore, the son himself had met in his youth countless Indians and trappers and hunters from the forests, so that the prototypes for the characters appearing in his books still came from true observations.

Cooper had left his home town early in life in order to become a sailor, first on the ocean, then, later, on the lakes closer to home, which were themselves like seas and whose banks were still part of the wild lands inhabited by Indians and trappers. He had already reached the age of thirty when he began to write. He used to read English novels aloud to his wife and, on one occasion, when one of them particularly bored him, he decided that he could have a go himself. The upshot was that he set about writing a novel about English society (incidentally without much success). Only when he was struck with the idea of attempting a story based on the material of his own part of the world did his ability really show, and he began to pioneer for literature a whole new tract of uncultivated territory. His first American novel, *The spy* (1821), was a success.

The appearance of his five Leatherstocking novels, through which he became a figure in world literature and a king among authors for young people, spread itself over all the rest of his life. By marriage and by inheritance from his father he became well enough off to give up his sailor's life and he then devoted himself to writing, research, and travel. In 1851, at the age of sixty-two, he died in Cooperstown. His face shows powerfully masculine, well-proportioned features with beautifully expressive eyes. Immediately one can read from it that this man is related in spirit to the Romantic brotherhood of Europe, even though life in such different surroundings must naturally lead to writing on different subjects, not in the least like the work of, say, his German contemporaries who had turned to fairy tales (the Grimms, Tieck and Brentano) or ancient sagas (Simrock and Schwab) and the immortal treasury of verse (von Arnim and Brentano).

Cooper's subject was the mighty landscape of his homeland, unblemished by the ravages of civilization, and a land where the Indian belonged. His Romanticism shows itself in the great set-piece descriptions of this landscape, which often call the Austrian novelist Stifter to mind, just as the characterization of Deerslayer is not only the presentation of a particular man but is, like *Robinson Crusoe*, the embodiment of a whole vision of mankind.

Now what does this vision consist of and why did this story of a white trapper and hunter become the foundation for our ideas about Indians? As a text, most of my readers will be familiar with the single-volume edition of *Leatherstocking*—itself a very bulky volume, magnificently illustrated for the twentieth century by Slevogt.[1] (There are also, of course, innumerable popular editions which are so brutally abridged and rewritten that all that remains of the original are the taut outlines of the story and the names of the characters. But even these editions possess a certain fascination.) For the moment, however, it is worth recalling that the novels in question are: *The Deerslayer* (1841), *The last of the Mohicans* (1826), *The Pathfinder* (1840), *The pioneers* (1823), and *The prairie* (1827). It will be seen that the last two, dealing with the last years of Leatherstocking, were written before the volumes on his early life and they do, in fact, portray a period which Cooper actually knew from experience.

The character who holds these five novels together is, of course, just this Leatherstocking, so called on account of his dress, which has now assumed

---

[1] English readers are unlikely to be familiar with this volume, most editions currently available in this country being cramped to the point of illegibility. Leatherstocking's adventures were compounded into a single volume by Allan Nevins in 1955, illustrated by Reginald Marsh, and printed under the title *The Leatherstocking Saga*. (B.A.)

classic dignity. To the Indians he was known as Deerslayer largely because, if possible, he killed beasts rather than humans. His other names were Path-finder, gained through his service as a scout for the English, and Hawkeye, on account of his unsurpassed hunter's sight. This last name was given him by an enemy Indian, whom he had wounded in a fight; and Hawkeye became accepted as one of their own by the Indians whether they were friends or ene-mies. And Hawkeye saw in the Indians men like himself, and in their forest life and its harmony with nature he saw his own paradise—a paradise which in Cooper's time was in the process of disappearing, but which, like Long-fellow in his magnificent epic, he made immortal in the truly Romantic manner.

This vanishing paradise is symbolized in the retreat of the Indians, the de-cline and destruction of a noble and courageous hunting people, who must make way for the European demand for land. At the same time this decline is portrayed with respect to history. The rivalry between French and English, the partisanship of the Indians, who hope thereby to gain some advantage, even their occasional and generally unsuccessful attempts to persuade them-selves to Christianity, are facts from an immediate historical past and are exactly and correctly represented.

Chingachgook, the Great Serpent, is Deerslayer's unforgettable Indian comrade, an embodiment of all the noblest qualities of the Indian, without, however, being idealized out of all recognition (as happened to Karl May's later creation, Winnetou). While the young chieftain and his son Unkas are simply exemplary figures of uncorrupted power and members of a famous tribe, old Chingachgook in the novel *The pioneers* has become a Christian by the name of Indian John. His tribe has been destroyed, although he still re-mains the friend of Deerslayer. But he is a symbol of decline, of loneliness, and of sadness, a man who could not hold out against the trinkets and the fire-water of the whites, even though right to the end he never loses the dignity of his bearing.

Deerslayer, on the other hand, the white man with the heart of an Indian, flees from the rapidly spreading settlement of young America into the prairie, from which the last volume of the series takes its name. There, far from his compatriots, he dies among the Indians. Later generations in Cooperstown, however, have set up a sentimental monument to the old trapper, scarcely comparable with the true picture of him, which thousands of youthful readers carry in their hearts.

One of the most attractive themes, recurring throughout the whole story, is that of solitariness, of men thrust upon their own resources in an immense and savage realm of nature. This is shown at its most beautiful when the former sailor, James Cooper, describes the journeys by canoe of Deerslayer and his friend Chingachgook across lonely rivers and lakes. Even when the rifles of enemy Indians lie in wait in the undergrowth by the shore, waiting to attack Beaver Castle, the floating home of Deerslayer's paleface friend, the author cannot be prevented from lovingly drawing in the primeval solitude of the landscape, so that in the reading we become a part of it.

For the young reader these are almost the only pages of natural descriptions which he is not tempted to skip—a thing which otherwise he is rather fond of doing. For within them surprise is lurking, the danger from men in silent moccasins who may leap out at any moment from behind the long grass. Whereas in the contemporary literature of Europe, and especially Germany with such books as Stifter's *Hochwald* and Eichendorff's *Taugenichts*, there is the philosophy and the attitude of mind of an ancient culture, here we find ourselves transferred to a young country which is not yet able to boast of any abstract 'mental attitude' or any idyllic philosophy of nature. God's free world was conquered by the white men and defended with Indian blood. Of this huge struggle in the silent forests Cooper has given a magnificent poetic account, which is his contribution to the Age of Romanticism.

Historical truth in Fenimore Cooper

Whether or not his novels correspond to historical truth is another question. The magnitude of his widespread influence (in the middle of the nineteenth century the whole of the literate world seems to have read Cooper) makes him suspect, and the fact that young people were so totally overcome by his Leatherstocking makes him even more so. Furthermore, when one considers the effect which he must have had on later and much more popular writing it will clearly repay us to investigate this question more closely.

In an excellent book, *Von Cooper bis Karl May*, the Göttingen expert on folk-lore, Hans Plischke, demonstrates that the type of trapper friendly to the Indians, as Leatherstocking was, is an historical impossibility. All trappers were the natural enemies of Indians. And yet Leatherstocking was a product of the way of thinking prevalent in his time, when the world was still haunted by the ideals of the French Revolution and, even more, by the ghostly heirs of Jean-Jacques Rousseau. Thus the untypical trapper was perhaps more a symbol of the better feeling and the conscience of young America than a truly living figure. But the fact that he was accepted by the world means that he has none the less become a living figure, whose effect has been even greater than if he had simply been the exact portrait of a man of that time.

Our folk-lore expert also considers that the portrait of the Indian in *The last of the Mohicans* is vastly idealized. He produces as evidence the cruelty of the Indians and also their incapacity to come to any sort of positive terms with European civilization. And yet it cannot be denied that right down to the present day, anyone who studies the Indian problem and the Indians themselves is deeply fascinated by them and regards the extermination of this nation as one of the cardinal sins of white humanity. Even today projects are being undertaken by the Americans themselves to preserve at least some tribes from extinction. This never-failing attempt to make good had its beginning in the work of those writers at the beginning of the last century.

The latest research in religious and psychological studies is interesting itself once more to an increasing extent in the Indians and in the scanty remains of their myths and customs which it is still possible to hang on to.

This nation has none of the dullness of other primitive peoples, but is rather versatile, eloquent, steadfast, and often magnanimous. It wrecked itself against white civilization only because the settlers' need to control the wildness of nature signified the destruction of that which the Indian considered holy.

Another American from the time of the War of Independence, Benjamin Franklin, has said of them that because they have few artificial needs they have much time for the cultivation of their souls through conversation, and that to them the philosophy of work appeared knavish and base. Or again, a modern religious thinker, Frithjof Schuon, says in his epilogue to Schwarzer Hirsch's *Die heilige Pfeife*: 'To see things in this light is to see that the fate of the Redskins was tragic in the exact sense of the word: a situation from which there was no escape, which had been reached not by chance but as a result of the unavoidable confrontation of two principles. They succumbed not merely because they were weaker, these high-minded men from the stone age, but because they were the representatives of a spirit which could never reconcile itself to the quite un-Christian trader mentality of the opposing palefaces.'

It should be quite clear from these points of view that children, who are profoundly sympathetic to the affairs of nature and quite averse to the affairs of economists, must necessarily give their hearts to the Indians and adopt them completely into their literature.

The century in which Cooper lived believed in such ideals as these and did not bother itself too much as to whether his descriptions corresponded to actuality or not. It believed them and it loved this writer from the New World. Goethe himself read the first Leatherstocking novel *The pioneers* and found it of great interest, and we have already pointed out the obvious relationship which it bears to Stifter. His *Hochwald* appeared in 1842 after the Deerslayer sequence and Hauff's *Lichtenstein* also came out at this time. But much more germane to our subject are those authors who were influenced by him to turn to similar themes.

French literature on the subject of Indians had already found a poetic forerunner in the Romantic Chateaubriand (1768–1848). His beautiful and touching story *Atala* (1801), the tale of an Indian girl converted to Christianity, is an enduring work; but since the author was more concerned about following in Rousseau's footsteps than about setting down basic information on the problems of the Indians, his books have an interest more from the attitude which they display towards the creatures of a strange world than from their treatment of the Indians in any historical sense. And yet Chateaubriand's book contributed decisively to the very enthusiastic reception which Cooper's work received in France.

Among the most famous books in Germany as well as France were *Le coureur des bois* of Gabriel Ferry (1809–51) and the many Indian stories of

Gustave Aimard (1818–83). The former was also translated into English (as *The golden ranger*, 1886), but Aimard seems to have had the greater success. From 1860–64 twenty-six of his *Tales of Indian life* were issued and in the first of these, *The tiger slayer*, the editor speaks of the French regard for Aimard as their own Fenimore Cooper: a man who had lived among Indians as an Indian. Both of these authors drew a good part of their knowledge from travelling and from actual observation, but they were not so conscientious about their history as was their model, Cooper. But the contents of the books were as exciting as the titles suggest. True writers had called the novel of Indian life into being and it was now to enter the province of the better kind of light literature. The American Indians were all set to become the heroes of European popular novels and children's books.

The influence of Red Indian literature in Germany

The popularization of Fenimore Cooper and the influence of Red Indian literature were, however, strongest in Germany. As with Chateaubriand in France, so Heinrich Zschokke in Germany had written about the Indians in an idealistic vein before Cooper's books appeared. But he saw them only as guileless and friendly children of nature, and he had no influence on later children's books since his writings were quickly to be overshadowed by Cooper's books which appeared in the 1820s.

But America as a growing political entity was attracting more and more Europeans. Disgusted or driven out by abortive revolutions or campaigns for freedom in Germany and Austria, a swarm of emigrants set out for this unknown quarter of the globe, which was to foster so many literary talents and return them again to Europe.

The most interesting and important among these was the former Jesuit from Bohemia, Karl Postl, who, however, from the time of his flight to his death was known by the name of Charles Sealsfield.

He was the first realist among those who wrote about America and through him the Romanticism and Rousseau-ish idealism in books about America and the Indians was finally overcome. He spent a good part of his life in America, writing bitterly about his old homeland Austria, and even the things that he wrote about America were shots in the battle against political reaction aimed at an improvement in the education of the citizens of his own land. He was a journalist in the best sense of the word, making arduous journeys for the sake of the fullest information. It is a pity that we cannot examine more closely here his numerous novels and his books of history and description.

His first important Wild West story first appeared in English with the title *Tokeah, or the white rose* (1828).[1] In contrast to all his predecessors he paid attention to the limited abilities of the Indians, while his trappers and pioneers are hard-bitten characters who repel rather than attract. Yet every detail in the world revealed in his books is carefully observed and what is more, even

[1] The German edition, *Der Legitime und der Republikaner*, was published in 1833.

the rough accents of these adventurers are exactly imitated, one might almost say 'discovered for literature'. From now on such talk belongs to the Wild West novel, where previously even such heroes of the wilds as these had been accustomed to talking only the very best English.

If people devoured Sealsfield's books in spite of the fact that their tone was anything but idealistic it was largely for the sake of their truthfulness and on account of the interest that was being shown in emigration, especially after 1848. Also the books' markedly exaggerated plots and their colourful but genuine atmosphere were further reasons for their widespread success.

Sealsfield was a Bonapartist. He was active as a journalist in New York on behalf of the Bonaparte family and he spent a considerable time in their circle at Arenberg in Switzerland where at that time Queen Hortense was living with Louis Napoleon. When he once again returned to America he betook himself more to the deep South where the scene for most of his later books is set. He died in 1864 on his small estate at Solothurn in Switzerland. By his will a family named Postl in Bohemia were made the beneficiaries of his considerable fortune, thus bringing to light the secret of his origins.

The development away from Cooper can best be studied in the figures of the pioneer and the hunter, both of whom play an important part in all the books of this genre. From Leatherstocking, the lonely backwoodsman, there has grown Sealsfield's Nathan, a rough fellow struggling to win a place for himself and his family. We shall meet this realistically portrayed Wild West ruffian once again at second hand and much exaggerated in the characters in Karl May's work.

But Karl May's time, signifying both the climax in popularity and also the end of the Red Indian story, had not yet arrived. It is not possible to describe here all the writers who turned their attention to this subject. One of the most productive of them was Friedrich Gerstäcker, who was read with avidity into our own century. Born in Hamburg in 1816 he spent a great part of his life in America. He was equally influenced by Sealsfield the Realist and by Cooper the Romantic, and his *Flusspiraten des Mississippi* (1848) belonged among those favourites which were read to pieces in my childhood. But even Gerstäcker's books were not written intentionally as children's books.

Among the other authors from this period whose books have been (and are perhaps still being) read in our own time there can be singled out Balduin Möllhausen (born in 1825), a man from the circle around Alexander von Humboldt. He wandered through America as an explorer and surveyor and his gains were largely scientific. But it is obvious that the adventurous and romantic side of life on the prairie left him no peace, for in his old age he produced a series of novels which are to some extent intended for young people. *Das Mormonen-mädchen* (1864) and *Der Leuchtturm am Michigan* were the most famous of more than a hundred novels and tales.

The vaguely political, vaguely romantic interest which had given rise to the stories of the American adventurers and Red Indians was on the decline, only to be preserved for a few decades among the young, where it was at least borne up by a strong and stubborn affection, supported by the work of a no less powerful apostle among the writers. This apostle was Karl May, without whose appearance the literature of the Red Indian would have died a natural death a good fifty years earlier, at the end of the nineteenth century.

Karl May

Karl May is an oddity in the history of literature, provided, of course, that one is willing to accord him such an illustrious station. But since a great deal has crept into this book which strictly speaking is outside the literary pale we can scarcely neglect this peculiar but very successful phenomenon. (And even outside the pale he would still remain a peculiar phenomenon.)

In contrast to his predecessors in this branch of literature, who were either romantic and manly figures like Cooper, or footloose adventurers like Gerstäcker, Karl May in his prime has rather the appearance of a somewhat soft but well-meaning country parson—a high, almost aristocratic, forehead, dreamy eyes, and an aura of middle-class well-being. Naturally, he had not always looked like this, but in contrast to all his fellow writers on the subject of Red Indians he himself had undergone none of the hardships and dangers which his heroes had to endure. For one thing he arrived on the scene too late. All his hardships were the result of a poverty-stricken childhood from which he worked his way with a sure belief in his own destiny.

Karl May was born in 1842 in a poor village in the Erzgebirge. His father was a cottage worker, a weaver like those portrayed in Gerhart Hauptmann's play. This type of cottage industry was customary in the Erzgebirge down to our own times. It is a district poorly endowed by nature but rich in imagination (among other things it has produced Germany's finest wooden knick-knacks—complete living-rooms contained in match-boxes, dashing horsemen, nutcrackers, and whole villages sold in little hessian bags).

Perhaps the most decisive influence on Karl May's future was the fact that for four of his years as a child he was blind. This gave his imagination an early chance to develop and when he was once more able to see he learned to read and write faster than everyone else; he also had music lessons and even started to learn foreign languages. It is probable that quite early on he consumed all the popular adventure stories of his time, for who was there in a village like his to supervise the reading of a precocious child?

At the age of fourteen he moved into a proseminar (a kind of pre-teacher-training school) which he had to leave following a negligible act of stealing (the theft of some bits of wax in order to make Christmas candles). He finished his schooling at Plauen and at twenty he occupied an ill-paid position as a teacher. This did not last long since his pay was so small that he was led again to theft, discovered, and three times sent to gaol. Throughout his twenties he divided his time between frauds, thefts, forgeries, and spells in prison. These, however, he turned to good account to the extent that during his last and longest sentence he made active use of the prison library where he must have read and written an enormous amount. His parents arranged the printing of all this and on his final release they greeted him with a substantial sum of money. Shortly afterwards what might be called the pulp publishers of Dresden, the Münchmeyer Verlag, sought him out and offered him a permanent position. This led to the really grim period of his life in so far as he now perpetrated not only confidence tricks of a material nature as before but intellectual ones as well.

For his Dresden publisher he wrote, among other things, a series of works under the title of *Waldröschen*—undistinguished bits of work appearing under a pseudonym. At the same time, but for another publisher, Pustet, he wrote travel books and what appeared to be autobiographical books, both of which brought him much success.

At the beginning of the nineties he shook himself free from the pulp merchants in order to follow the dictates of his better self. This was not so easy to do, however, for Münchmeyer insisted upon his right to the trash which had been written for the sake of an outright fee. Meanwhile, Karl May had become so famous that he received much attention and publicity in the Press during the lawsuits which ensued. His opponents dug up his murky past and accused him afresh of being a swindler. They demonstrated that all his travel books written in the first person were purely imaginative, while he allowed his public to rest in the belief that he had experienced everything at first hand— indeed, that he allowed himself to be photographed as Old Shatterhand and sent the pictures of himself off as postcards with the legend 'Karl May: known as Old Shatterhand'.

It was at the start of the nineties that he wrote the three-volume novel *Winnetou* which is of most interest to us in connexion with this chapter. It appeared in 1892 and has become a classic in the literature about Red Indians, especially that for young people. The following is what we find, however, in his factual preface in a text which almost sounds like a history book and is signed 'Karl May; Radebeul (bei Dresden) 1892': 'Yes! I have come to know the Redskins through the passing of the years and one among them lives still in my heart and in my thoughts, high, wide and handsome . . . I loved him as I loved no other man and even today I love the dying nation whose noblest son he was. I would have laid down my life that he might have kept his, but that was not granted me . . . He shall live on here in these pages as he lives in my soul—he, Winnetou, the great chief of the Apaches, for him I will raise this well-deserved memorial. And if the reader—observing this with his inward eye—can form a true judgement of the nation whose paragon was this chieftain then I shall consider my work richly rewarded.'

Karl May—Old Shatterhand—the hero who wrote such affecting words and who had at the same time suffered such odd adventures of his own, must have greatly impressed his own age, which had a penchant for bombast anyway. He deserved well of it, even though it was not until 1908 that he first visited North America and those parts where his 'beloved friend' Winnetou had lived, ten years after his tour in the Near East, North Africa, and India.

Now how did it come about that a lawsuit was needed to show that these works so convincingly masquerading as autobiography were, in fact, the product of, on the one hand, an extraordinary fund of reading and, on the other, an almost inconceivable imaginative sympathy? The public was well accustomed to stories about Indians; they had been in fashion for a whole century. But Cooper's Deerslayer, the crack shot, and Sealsfield's Nathan, the rough pioneer, still do not have all the qualities of Old Shatterhand, the hero, although they do contribute many of his characteristics. Moreover, in contrast to Cooper's Leatherstocking, Old Shatterhand is placed in an environment of white men who are devoid of any redeeming feature and are simply caricatures—but caricatures such as children like best, encouraging them to open laughter. Old Shatterhand himself embodies a kind of childish superman who can do absolutely everything and who is not only, like Deerslayer, the Indians' equal in skill, but also excels them in everything else—a fact which he puts down to his German origins, which are emphasized again and again. In this way he makes use of the already familiar figure of the noble white man, friend of the Indians, and erects it into a credible experience for children and people of simple intelligence.

He proceeds in a similar way with the Indians. The young Winnetou bears most of the characteristics of Unkas, the Fleet Deer, one of Fenimore Cooper's Indian heroes. On the other hand, he has taken his information on the habits of Winnetou's tribesmen in the foothill country from a book about an Indian tribe in the South. His description of this river-girt village, and of all the day-to-day events within it is thoroughly convincing at a popular level, for the author based it on authentic sources. From time to time he will even call upon rather affected methods of showing his own knowledge. Old Shatterhand, for instance, espies a book in Winnetou's game-bag. It is that attempt at an Indian national epic by an American idealist, *The song of Hiawatha*, and by introducing it Winnetou is made out to be well-read along with everything else—or is it simply the author giving us proof that Karl May is well read? When one considers his frequently attacked position as a writer, which even had to be defended in a court of law, this becomes entirely possible. Nevertheless, it must be said that Karl May wrote *Winnetou* a good six years before the big case in 1898, in which the Press and indeed the whole literary world had to take sides either for him or against him.

Karl May's collected works number some sixty-five volumes which were later brought out in a 'uniform edition' by the Karl May Verlag. The number of copies printed is enormous and even before the First World War they had reached a total of almost two million in Germany alone. Serried ranks of them may still be seen on the shelves of popular bookshops, the editions varying from 'cheap' to 'imposing'—all got up in imitation calf.

Karl May died in 1912 at his home at Radebeul, near Dresden. After his death his sales scarcely declined and shortly before the Second World War they had reached the massive sum of seven and a half million simply in German-speaking parts of the world. In the forefront is *Winnetou*. The edition of the first volume which I have in front of me is dated 1952 and numbered 421–435 thousand.[1] When you pause to remember that each book sold is likely to be read by a fair number of people (and, in this case, children as well), then it is possible to gauge how great Karl May's influence has been, and indeed still is, on the whole of his youthful German-speaking audience.

After his death his house at Dresden was turned into a Karl May Museum, to which thousands made an annual pilgrimage. Most of his fortune he bequeathed to a Foundation devoted to the needs of young schoolteachers in order to prevent them in their penury from sliding down the slippery slope to disgrace as Karl May himself had done. Goodness thus triumphed all along the line, just as it had triumphed during the closing years of the author and in the pages of all his books.

The huge success of Karl May contradicts all the rules of art in the true sense of the word. It is said of young people that they at least know how to recognize what is genuine, therefore we must assume that there must be something genuine and powerfully magnetic in these books, a genuine vision and a genuine idealism. For an adult it is almost impossible to understand this properly, it is impossible for him to transfer himself to the position of a twelve-year-old reader and to recognize in the experience the true quality of the author. For young people, though, the most powerful attraction is undoubtedly the superhuman attributes of Karl May's heroes. Youngsters who lack strength or the opportunities to use it freely must find it almost intoxicating to be able to identify themselves with such men.

The noble Indian hero Winnetou surely exercises a completely elevating and in no way brutalizing influence with his ability to combine gentleness with strength, shrewdness with dignity, and cunning with bravery. A somewhat violent attitude is to be found in the trapper heroes, with Old Shatterhand at their head. They do not often kill their adversaries, preferring to lay them low with enormous knock-out punches and they are addicted to an all too Germanic cult of power, despite their concern for the triumph of the right cause. But the sense of power by which these fellows are possessed allows them to hit their targets from no matter what distance, to swim through swollen torrents, to look bears and buffaloes fearlessly in the eye, and to keep going without ever tiring. Such prodigies appear to engulf the young reader and to give him some special sense of happiness, especially the city child whose opportunities for running off his energy are somewhat limited.

Through all of this the astonishing phenomenon remains of the poor weaver's son from the Erzgebirge whose wishful thinking attained for him a

---

[1] The occasional Continental practice of numbering the print-run for each impression enables far more precise measurement of a book's popularity than the vaguer Anglo-Saxon '26th Impression' or Sir Victor Gollancz's famous '4th reprinting before publication'. (B.A.)

greater success than all the adventure-story writers of the nineteenth century.

Since this chapter has been devoted to Red Indians we have concentrated chiefly on Karl May's *Winnetou* trilogy. In fact, however, he opened up for children worlds of adventure which reached as far as China. But in his Indian stories, where he was working within a firm and time-hallowed tradition, his voice takes on its truest tone which even his opponents could not wholly stop their ears to.

In Italy Emilio Salgari exerted a similar influence with his books of adventure and stories of the Wild West. He was a contemporary of Karl May and shared with him many common characteristics.

By way of conscious or unconscious reaction to the improbable events which fill out Karl May's stories, a great many so-called documentary books about Red Indians have been filling the bookshelves for quite a long time. One of the finest and most worth while of these seems to me to be *Ohijesa* by Dr. Charles A. Eastman, to which I drew attention at the start of this chapter. It portrays in a fascinating way a Red Indian childhood in the 1860s and as with Eastman's other story, *Winona*, it has been reprinted again and again.

Among the many writers who, in contrast to Karl May, attacked Red Indian life from an historical standpoint, Fritz Steuben (born 1898) has the foremost place in the hearts of young readers. His many excellent stories which have appeared continuously since 1930, are set in the early years of the nineteenth century during the final struggles of the Redskins for independence.

Up and down the country today it is still a fairly frequent occurrence to see children playing in feathered head-dresses, waving their plastic tomahawks or their unsmokable pipes of peace. One feels that this remarkable transfiguration of the European child is something that will remain even after its political origins and its historical significance are quite forgotten.

10 EDUCATION THROUGH PICTURES

From Comenius to the picture-book of today

In the year 1656 a stranger entered the city of Amsterdam, a man with har-rowed, but kindly, features, who as a fugitive in those disturbed times had travelled a long way. His most recent abode had been at Leszno in Poland, where for the second or third time his total belongings, his books, his writings, had all been consigned to the flames, a disaster which occurred only a short time after he had lost his family in the plague.

This pious, tormented Job from the time of the Thirty Years War, this sixty-four-year-old man, exiled from all that was closest to his heart, was to become the father of books for children and of picture-books especially. His name was Jan Amos Komenský (Latinized as Johannes Amos Comenius) and he was born in 1592 in Bohemia, near the Hungarian border. From his youth upwards he was a member of the community of Bohemian Brethren, first as a teacher and then as priest and bishop. These Brothers in the Law of Christ, a community which had grown out of the Hussite Movement, had adopted an ethical system based upon the combined ideals of Christianity and humanism. After their complete extirpation in 1656 similar endeavours were only to re-emerge with the Moravian brethren and with Schleiermacher. Misery and poverty had opened the eyes of this hounded soul from the woods of Bohemia wider than those of most of his contemporaries, but they at least were to have the merit of recognizing his achievements.

The whole of this man's work must be understood in the light of his con-victions as one of the Unity of Brethren. Before their expulsion they had jogged their way from village to village through the woods and valleys of their homeland, each man a priest transmitting by word and by deeds of kindness Christ's teaching according to the words of the Bible. Even in exile in Swedish-occupied Leszno, Comenius remained as the last bishop of the Brethren until, eight years after the Peace of Westphalia, this last bulwark of the 'Brothers' fell (Bohemia itself having been ceded to the Catholic countries in 1648).

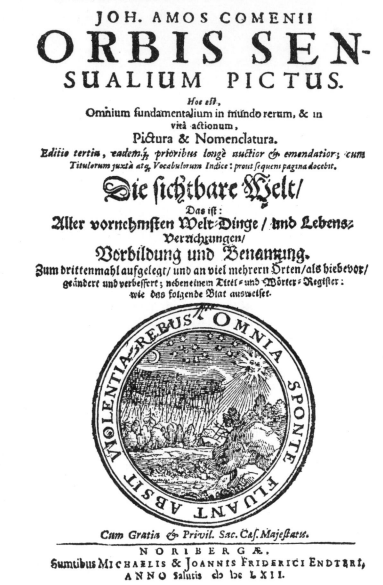

JOH. AMOS COMENII

ORBIS SEN-
SUALIUM PICTUS.

Hoc est,
Omnium fundamentalium in mundo rerum, & in
vitâ actionum,
Pictura & Nomenclatura.
*Editio tertia, eadem̄q̄, prioribus longè auctior & emendatior; cum
Titulorum juxtà atq̄ Vocabulorum Indice: prout sequens pagina docebit.*

Die sichtbare Welt/
Das ist:
Aller vornehmsten Welt-Dinge / und Lebens-
Verrichtungen/
Vorbildung und Benamung.
Zum drittenmahl aufgelegt/ und an viel mehrern Orten/als hiebevor/
geändert und verbessert; nebeneinem Titel-und Wörter-Register:
wie das folgende Blat ausweiset.

Cum Gratia & Privil. Sac. Cæs. Majestatis.

NORIBERGÆ,
Sumtibus MICHAELIS & JOANNIS FRIDERICI ENDTERI,
ANNO Salutis clɔ lɔc LXII.

COMENIUS, Johannes Amos. *Orbis sensualium pictus.* Nuremberg, 1662.
Title page of the third edition.

And when this brave man, who had held fast to his convictions through so
much adversity, arrived at the final halt in his journey, what did he do? He
published a book for children, more accurately perhaps a kind of school-book,
which was issued from Nuremberg in 1658 and which he called *Orbis sensualium pictus* or *Orbis pictus*. Under this title the book was to enter upon a
unique progress through the world and down the centuries.

What sort of book is it and from what kind of mind did it spring?

The Thirty Years War had made Comenius an unwilling wayfarer through many principalities and he must have seen on his journeying much childish suffering; what today we have called 'the refugee problem'. We know from contemporary sources what the schools were like at that time and Comenius was first and foremost an educational reformer, a campaigner for the schooling of children from all ranks of society, boys and girls alike. He produced a systematic curriculum which included an empirical method of language instruction, together with physical training, hygiene, and handicraft. Modern educationists should make him their patron saint, for he demanded three hundred years ago what is only now reaching fulfilment and he committed his ideas to the revolutionary manuals: the *Didactica magna*, 1657 (*The great system of teaching* or *The art of teaching everybody everything*) and the *Janua linguarum reserata*, 1631 (*The gate of languages unlocked*)—both of them books lively with new ideas.

But Comenius was also akin in spirit to the great Pestalozzi, as can be seen in his *School of infancy*. For in granting the same right to education for girls as for boys, he wished above all to bring up good mothers. Like Pestalozzi, he held that the influence of the mother in a child's education was decisive and that this influence began before the child had ever left the womb.

Comenius had already completed these books, and many more, when in the years 1650–54, working as master in a poor-school in Hungary, he conceived the *Orbis pictus*.

He had been brought to this through his interest in a direct method for teaching languages and this small book was little more than a kind of picture vocabulary of Latin. His method, which he got from the philosophers of his time (and especially Francis Bacon), was based upon the observation of the actual world—an idea which stood on its head the purely abstract method of teaching prevalent at that time.

For Comenius had not seen only the refugee children of war-torn Europe. He had also seen those children in better circumstances who were so stuffed up with abstract learning, who, before they were ten years old, were so tormented with ancient languages, theology, and mathematics that they became stricken with enigmatical mortal illnesses, which we would today diagnose as meningitis or as nervous diseases. This extraordinary passion to endow children with the languages of antiquity—not only Latin and Greek but also Hebrew—was an exaction of the Reformation, which demanded of every educated person that he could read the Bible in the original texts.

Now for those children who knew nothing of books nor of the world, and for those others who had got nothing by heart except the pointless abstractions of declensions, numbers, and maxims, Comenius's little book, with its abundance of crude but attractive woodcuts, was a sensation.

There were pictures crammed full of objects and events to be seen in the most immediate vicinity and in the farthest quarters of the globe; while next

XLII.

Anima hóminis Die Seele des Menschen.

Anima t. 1	Die Seele	Corpus, n.3. der Leib.
est *córporis vita,*	ist des Leibes Leben/	Vita, f.1. das Leben.
una in toto:	einig in dem gantzen:	Unus, a, um, einig.
		Totus, a, um, gantz.
tantùm vegetatíva,	Allein eine Wachstümliche/	Vegetativus, a, um, wachstümlich.
in *plantis;*	in den Pflantzen;	Planta, f.1. die Pflantze.
simul sensitíva,	zugleich eine Sinnliche/	Sensitivus, a, um, Sinnlich.
in *animálibus;*	in den Thieren;	Animal, n.3. das Thier.
etiam rationális,	auch eine Vernünftige/	Rationális, c.3. e, n.3. vernünfftig.
in *hómine.*	in dem Menschen.	Homo, m.3. der Mensch.
Hæc, consistit in *tribus:*	Diese/ bestehet in dreyen Dingen:	Tres, c.3. tria, n.3. pl. drey.
primò in *mente*	Erstlich in der Vernunft	Mens, f.3. die Vernunft sive

COMENIUS, Johannes Amos. *Orbis sensualium pictus.* Nuremberg, 1662.

to them were their descriptions in both Latin and the child's own mother-tongue. Take, for example, those pictures the size of a postage stamp which show a charming little bird, a wolf with open jaws, and a coiling snake. Beside each of them are the words '*Upupa dicit*' ('The hoopoe calls'), '*Lupus ululat*' ('The wolf howls'), and '*Serpens sibilat*' ('The snake hisses'). Who would not enjoy learning Latin in this way? And to have at the same time pictures of the known and the unknown world in front of you in a single, pocket-size volume was indeed a small marvel.

Naturally, the profundity of the subjects dealt with increased with the young reader's progress. For instance, one page is entitled 'The world', and neatly composed within a small round woodcut are presented its most elementary attributes, from stars to human beings. Underneath in free but nevertheless rhythmic prose there is the bilingual explanation using the simplest words. In this way the different manifestations of nature and human life are dealt with and related to the child's image of the world. Then, almost at the end, we find 'The soul', pictured as a seemingly transparent human body with something of the appearance of a naked ghost. Without doubt there is some problem in representing so invisible a thing as the soul in a crude woodcut. But Comenius, who is said to have designed the cuts himself, shrank from nothing. The question of how far he was actually associated with the illustrations is today very much in dispute, but the relationship between text and picture is so close that it is quite unthinkable that they were produced separately.

This particular woodcut has a text which waxes almost philosophical: 'The soul / is the life of the body, / one in the whole: / only vegetative / in plants. / Withal sensitive / in animals; / and also rational / in man.'[1]

I should like to show in a bilingual example the way in which he brought the Latin language to life for children and at the same time incorporated points of scientific knowledge. It is also worth noting the thoroughly typical short, memorable lines:

Ex aqua	A vapour
ascendit	ascendeth from the
vapor.	water.
Inde fit	From it
nubes	a cloud
et prope terram	is made, and
nebula.	a white mist
E nube	near the
stillat (defluit guttatim)	Earth.
pluvia	Rain
et imber	and a small shower
quae	distilled out of a
gelato	cloud,
grando	drop by drop
	which being frozen,
	is Hail

[1] This and the following translation have been taken from the first English edition of Comenius by Charles Hoole, 1659. The reader may like to admire the aid that this book must have been to the seventeenth-century schoolchild in working out case endings and acquiring a limpid English prose style. (B.A.)

When I call to mind that even down to today instruction in Latin starts at the age of ten in most of the countries of Europe, and when I remember the Latin books of my childhood or even those of my children (in which a word like 'pluvia' crops up chiefly to provide a hindrance for some Roman or Germanic advance, and even then is probably brought in with some ghastly gerundive or ablative absolute), then I find it possible almost to envy the schoolchildren of that time, who learned Latin as a living language and not just as the language of Caesar or Cicero.

Even Goethe, who was a child a hundred years after the first appearance of the *Orbis pictus*, mentions this little book with great gratitude as the first picture-book he was to treasure. Then for the following century and indeed down to our own time it was imitated in increasingly sumptuous productions. None of the great figures who have exerted a decisive influence on education or the formation of character, neither Rousseau nor Pestalozzi, has actually written a book for children. Froebel wrote some little lullabies, now forgotten and deservedly so. Campe, who wrote the German *Robinson*, is now forgotten as an educationist. But Comenius is remembered still as both a teacher and a great originator, and with his *Orbis pictus*, this popularization of contemporary philosophical ideas, he has given the starting signal for a development which seems to have reached its climax in our time, but which seems to be approaching an impasse the way out from which it is very difficult to see.

Besides the pure imitations of the *Orbis pictus* which even copied its title, there poured out in the course of time many related efforts sympathetically inclined towards children, a flood of enjoyably instructive and educational picture-books to sate their obviously permanent demand to better their own minds. Let us consider more closely one or two of the products of this surge, once the delight of a good child's Sunday afternoon, now the carefully guarded treasures of special collections.

The charming thing about these books was that each of them brought into the home a complete world for children, a well-ordered world, to which the Enlightenment had stood godparent for decades, and one which consisted of subjects and modes of life from both near and far—the celestial world as well as the visceral, skeletons, and lives of the soul. Possession of just one of these books was all that was required. Modest Comenius may have sufficed the young Goethe, but the next generation of children received much more luxurious presents, which, thanks to their smarter presentation and their exclusive prices, were no longer accessible to all sections of society like the *Orbis pictus*.

The weightiest of these works was Johann Bernhard Basedow's *Elementarwerk*, which appeared between the years 1770–74. It consisted of three volumes of text and three oblong slip-cases containing a series of magnificent copper engravings, mostly by Chodowiecki. Each sheet contained two to four pictures, somewhat smaller than postcards, presenting in variegated succession the things that might be of interest to older or younger children in 1770—

BASEDOW, Johann Bernhard. *Das Elementarwerk*. Altona, 1770–74.
An engraving by Daniel Chodowiecki.

anything from children's games, dramatic historical scenes, pictures of classical
or Christian times, through to mathematical formulae, astronomical charts,
and even information about such things as boatbuilding.

Even today Chodowiecki's engravings place the book among the most
attractive and entertaining picture-books which it is possible to imagine and
one may confidently say that it is among the first, if not the first itself, of those
picture-books produced for children and illustrated by real artists. Nevertheless it would not be fair simply to look at the pictures and to regard as a
dry-as-dust supplement the companion text by the amiable Herr Basedow,
who 'prepared' the whole affair.

Indeed, Basedow's volumes of text, which contain the essence of his whole
philanthropic attitude to education, do not make for easy reading today. But
this is for the most part because what they say has now become the common
property of educational theory, even though we have perhaps taken to ex-
pressing ourselves differently. The volumes of text also contain the descriptions
of the plates, however, and to read these is a pleasure. The little pictures,
charming even without a text, take on, through the words, a depth and significance in a way which is often droll, often touching, but always entertaining
and instructive. There is, for instance, a plate under the heading 'Tolerance'.
Four pictures portray the burning of a heretic, a virtuous galley-slave, a
captive dissenter being taught about baptism and a meeting of the clerical
hierarchy. One can imagine the learned Herr Basedow, with these pictures in

133

his hand, teaching his pupils about religious tolerance in his school which he called the 'Philanthropinum'. Several similar institutions based on his ideas were later founded in Germany and Switzerland. For a while one of the teachers in this school was Campe, who was to bring so much pleasure to the children of the times with his *Robinson der Jüngere*, and who had among his pupils two such important people as the brothers Humboldt. The whole of Basedow's book is, in fact, a document for the cultural historian, pulsing with a sympathetic humanity which we could not improve upon in our present 'Age of the Child'. For the child had at last begun to take over his place in the sun, and in the next decades he was to receive offerings from men of considerable intellect.

Just how much importance was attached at that time to education through pictures, though, and how much of a prepared viewpoint Basedow could get into a single sheet of pictures, is clearly shown by his advice to the reader to look at only one plate per day (and a fearsome self-denying ordinance that would be for our own picture-crazy age).

The *Elementarwerk* falls a little short in its treatment of natural, as opposed to human, affairs. This is a gap which is filled in a remarkable way by *Bertuchs Bilderbuch*, which commenced publication in 1796 and today belongs among the most prized treasures for a collector of illustrated books.

'A picture-book for children, containing a pleasing collection of animals, fruits, minerals, costumes and all kinds of other instructive objects from the realms of nature, the arts and the sciences'—so runs a translation of the long-winded title of this magnificent book, for whose twenty-four resplendent volumes the name of 'picture-book' is altogether too modest. But here, once again, the reader is expected to concentrate on only one page at a time. The large and exceptionally beautifully coloured engravings have great decorative beauty and are accompanied by a text in German, French, English, and Italian. The arrangement is entirely random. For instance, a plate on 'The wonders of Egypt', in which the ascent to the inner chambers of a pyramid is displayed, is followed by one on 'Remarkable fungi', and we find 'Waterfalls' next to 'German moths'. 'The midnight sun' adjoins a truly perfect page showing 'The house-fly' enormously magnified, with his legs as long as pencils. What a world of marvel this must have been for the children of those times, and what a delicate beauty resides in the pictures. No one has yet invented a method of printing which can reproduce them adequately, which can give to those portraits of the old-fashioned dog-rose all the subtleties of pink which the meticulous hand-colourists achieved. Here, indeed, the best does seem good enough for children.

Friedrich Justin Bertuch (1747–1822) was, like Campe, an almost exact contemporary of Pestalozzi (1746–1827). He was a bookseller and a writer—among other things a versifier for children—in Weimar, where, apart from Goethe, Herder was working at this time and Musäus was achieving the great success of his *Volksmärchen*. Thus this picture-book appeared just in the right setting and not only assuaged young people's thirst for knowledge but also imbued them with a feeling for beauty.

I have selected these two famous picture-books because they are volumes which I have been able to get hold of and examine carefully. But I would like to add here the titles of some other books of this kind whose writers or 'managing editors' were all the spiritual offspring of the great Bohemian Comenius, although the original *Orbis pictus* with its modest pretensions was gradually submerged under the voluminous splendour of its successors until it has become one of the great bibliographical rarities.

The followers of Comenius, as also his imitators, all had the praiseworthy aim of getting children to learn. Many did it eloquently, many added four more languages to the two of the *Orbis pictus*, but the increasing richness of the proffered goods began gradually to break up the compactness of that view of the world which was put forward in Comenius's book.

Already in the nineteenth century people were beginning to regard science and the humanities as quite separate studies. The chance of finding between the covers of one book both the simplest words and sounds, together with information on the heavens and the highest moral concepts, may have been feasible to someone in Comenius's century and with his inward perfection. But after Basedow's *Elementarwerk* at the end of the eighteenth century the chance got rapidly less. And yet most books of this kind, which go to make up a high proportion of children's literature, retain for quite a long time the illusion that they are offering a total view.

It is only in our own century that the factual book for children has begun to cultivate a specialized approach, sacrificing the broader relationships for the sake of the more detailed dissemination of knowledge. Dozens of sets of picture-books for children of all age-ranges are trying with their popular productions and their cheap series to pin down an image of the phenomena of the world, from the life of plants and animals to the motions of the stars. Perhaps the very latest tendency, which started in America, to create all-embracing encyclopaedias matched to the mental capacity of the child, points to a new attempt to restore an earlier unity of knowledge which had, however, been encumbered with much less factual material.

The following volumes may not all hold to the bilingual principle but it is scarcely possible to think of any of them without Comenius. The most significant still remain Basedow's *Elementarwerk* and *Bertuchs Bilderbuch*, but the eighteenth century also produced Stoy's popular *Bilder Akademie für die Jugend* (1784), while the nineteenth century saw an immense increase of similar titles throughout Europe.

But the most conscientious of all Comenius's imitators seems to me to have been a certain Magister Gailer of Tübingen. His book is entitled: *Neuer Orbis Pictus für die Jugend oder Schauplatz der Natur und des Menschenlebens* (1835), and it possesses 322 lithographic reproductions arranged according to the earlier plans of Comenius but suitably adapted to the current demands by I. E. Gailer.

C. F. Lauckhard also created a charming *Orbis pictus* which mirrors in its pictures a rather Victorian sweetness and sense of comfort which is totally absent from the kindly but strict Comenius, brought up in such a serious-minded and virile age. In all this I have only mentioned books which are more or less known to me—by no means a complete catalogue. Many, too, are lacking from other countries where the influence of Comenius can likewise be traced, but not perhaps with the same clarity as in German-speaking areas.

The factual book today

The leap in a single sentence from these earlier times to our own, in order to discover the links which connect the modern factual book to its predecessors, is not so great as it may seem. For we pass over a time which was not very favourable to books about facts. Even though frequent attempts were made right up to the middle of the nineteenth century to revive the *Orbis pictus*, it was fairy stories, religion, and literature which held sway far more impressively than children's books full of factual instruction. Telling people how to do things was more and more a job for school-books pure and simple, and here, in the accustomed manner, that movement was dissipated which was once more leading towards fundamental decisions on the nature of education and training, decisions which are still not finally settled.

The wonderful unity of the world as taught by Comenius had been broken up. Nobody could again close the circle, least of all the schools. The things that men know and have to know had become too manifold, with the result that one lot of books was set aside for instruction, thus becoming associated with the largely unpleasant business of school, while a second lot was produced for recreation.

That was roughly the position up to the beginning of the twenties of this century. But then, at the instigation of educationists who, not without reason, called up the shade of Comenius, a movement set in which took 'enjoyable education' for its slogan and thereby greatly advanced the possibilities of instructing people through pictures.

There is not sufficient space here to demonstrate all the activity in this field and I should like to confine myself to picture-books, which is to say, books planned for the younger age-groups.

Père Castor and developments since 1930

Père Castor and the works which followed him stand at the end of the development which I have outlined in the preceding pages. The principle of guiding and educating children through pictures which had passed through so many stages since Comenius, was now magnificently restated for our own age. The *Albums du Père Castor*, of which the first appeared in 1932, have had an inestimable influence on the development of the modern children's picture-book. At once in their educational and their pictorial qualities they make no gesture towards artistic snobbishness or any kind of playing for effects.

Now why should I take for my example this publisher of picture-books who calls himself 'Père'? Certain things can only be said with particularly clear examples in mind and although there are others, the example of this man is especially convincing since his ideas have come to fruition over a period of more than thirty years.

My own acquaintance with his work dates back a long way. It began with *Plouf, canard sauvage* in 1935: a bird story told in the language of a child and produced in small compass but with modern illustrative techniques. There is no anthropomorphism here—but the child's attention is held. He sees in closest proximity what he had otherwise only seen or suspected from afar. He is able to identify himself with it—drawn by completely fair means, without any false emphases, into the realms of animal life.

The following books appeared in the same series: *Froux, le lièvre* (1935), *Bourru, l'ours brun, Scaf, le phoque* (1936), and *Quipic, le hérisson* (1937). All of them, and many similar ones, were illustrated by F. Rojankovsky, whose sympathetic knowledge of animals was combined in a unique way with freedom of graphic expression. Moreover, he drew the pages direct on to the lithographic stone, thereby doing away with photographic or blockmaking processes, which falsify, and at the same time giving the finished pictures the freshness of an original lithograph. The texts for the books were the work of a colleague of Père Castor, signing herself Lida and writing with satisfying plainness and naturalness.

This series of animal books was later continued by a similar one lasting down to the present on the life of children in different lands. Since it is now all the rage to get children acquainted as early as possible with other countries, these books by no means stand alone. Nor are they such bold and individual productions as other series by Père Castor. Nevertheless, *Apoutsiak, le petit flocon de neige* (1948)—the tale of an Eskimo from his birth to his death (which is to say, his arrival in the paradise reserved for Eskimos)—belongs among the more daring of modern children's books. Although it moves us by its appeal to the sad, eternal verities of the heart, it remains so simple in both its text and its illustrations that it does no injury to the accepted structure of the children's picture-book.

On all these books, and on many more which I have no space to name, there stands like a trademark the phrase *Albums du Père Castor*. (In twenty-five years 250 books, often in soft card binding, were published under this series title. Their total print quantity in France adds up to twelve million, to which can be added several million impressions in foreign editions as well.) They are all aimed at those children who are either not yet able to read or who are just enjoying the first fruits of this newly acquired skill. They are at the age of greatest and most complete receptiveness, during which the foundations of later mental development are laid. '*Je crois que la lecture intelligente, celle qui éclaire et enrichit l'esprit, dépend non seulement de l'acquisition du mécanisme de la lecture, mais de toute une "éducation préalable". Cette éducation préalable, cette pré-lecture est précisément la raison d'être de certain de nos albums. Ils ont été réalisés en équipe, suivant un plan médité, voulu, dirigé.'* Thus the words of Père Castor.

One day I paid this Père Castor a visit, after his publishers, Flammarion, had given me without a moment's hesitation, his real name and address. The inquisitive lady interviewer was received with just such unpretentiousness in a small courtyard behind the long façade of the Boulevard St. Michel. All round this inner court, in a variety of jumbled buildings, were to be found exhibition rooms for children's books and children's drawings, a kindergarten, and a small experimental school using the latest methods of education and instruction. The director of the whole place, with his headquarters in a single, small, old-fashioned study, is Monsieur F. who gathers from here the obser-vations for his now famous work on children's books.

Since, next to all his idealistic activities, his profession was that of a book-seller, it is natural that he chose books to put his ideas into effect. At first they were books about his special concern: a series *Éducation* (Flammarion, 1927) and, in 1932, Paul Hazard's celebrated volume *Les livres, les enfants et les hommes*, which he was the first to publish. But after he had assimilated all the theoretical knowledge of the greatest names in his subject, he turned his attention to the child itself. He modelled himself most closely on the Czech, Frantisek Bakule, who died in 1957 and whom he describes as a 'genius of education'. He worked under him in Prague at the end of the twenties and got from him the final impetus to turn his ideas and theories into reality.

And there he now sits—this ageing man with the friendly eyes of a child and the refined features and intellect of the typical Frenchman. With French clarity, too, he summed up the principles which seemed to him important in the production of his children's books; such ideas as the following: *'la poésie du réel'*, *'l'activité créatrice'*, *'la nécessité du contact avec la terre, avec l'univers, avec le merveilleux'*.

There are many things which he places above the social, the technical, and even the ethical questions which have dominated children's books in the last 150 years. A child who can see himself intelligently as part of the unity of nature and the universe, who can at an early age learn to make use of his creative or his productive abilities is much more likely to become a con-structive member of society. For Père Castor nature is the chief law and those children who can recognize every make of car before they are out of the kindergarten impress him not at all. On the other hand, the miracle of a bird's life, the magnificence of the heavens, or the intimate contact of an Eskimo boy with his environment—these are important things for the city child to know and understand. They are among the means he has to learn to overcome the total urbanization of his life.

The previously mentioned *Albums* represent only a part of the work of this atelier, which also sets out to provide both teachers and parents with valuable educational apparatus in the form of games, work-books, and other material. This man, who calls himself 'Père', has drawn around him a great number of colleagues, all of whom are inspired by the love of *'cet être mystérieux en lequel bouillonnent tant de forces vives, qu'est l'enfant'*.

While the books on subjects connected with nature cater for the child's need for an awareness of the world around him, the painting-books and work-books make an approach to his creative potentialities. Also, by their extra-ordinary attractiveness and their satisfying production, they are able to help even clumsy children or children lacking creative ability to much wider horizons.

In order to reach the widest possible public all these developments have taken place at minimum price levels, but to an aesthetic standard which had previously only applied to the more expensive picture-books, and even then not often. Just as Rojankovsky, who is now a famous children's book illustrator in America, set the artistic tone for the large books, so Nathalie Parain, after him the finest illustrator of the group, established the unimpeachable quality of the smaller albums and work-books.

Although the Second World War scattered this team of artists to all the corners of the earth, the good work was continued, so that the atelier and all its various departments is today a flourishing institution. But even so the rest-less brain of its founder ticks on, and for years he has been working at the task of adding new groups of books to the existing range. The finest of these seem to me to be a new series of photographic books which will, however, be dealt with in the next chapter.

It has been my full intention to give Père Castor's work this degree of prominence, even though there are at present similar talents being exerted all over the world. Nowhere, however, is work being done with the same idealistic concentration on the child's own good. The *Albums du Père Castor* have only a modest influence today, since their founder declines to follow the present trend towards ever more sumptuous and more abstract picture-books, even for the youngest children. Just how right he is in this is not for me to decide.

In the present field of cheap, educational picture-books *Puffin Picture Books*[1] are undoubtedly the most carefully planned series. They embrace subjects from technology and architecture to trade, geography, and history. Nothing is safe from these little Penguin mutants, neither stamps and puppets nor the

---

[1] An article by Noel Carrington celebrating the publication of the 100th Puffin Picture Book, was printed in the *Penrose Annual*, vol. 51 (1957). Besides giving a good account of the way the series started, he also stresses the importance that was attached to producing really good factual books which children could buy and read for themselves. It is therefore the more regrettable that the series has to some extent defeated its own aims.

Its format, which, artistically, is such a success, has deterred booksellers from giving adequate display, while any attempt to give the books a more durable binding has priced them beyond children's resources.

Although the series is continuing (*Seashore life*, published in 1964, was a splendid addition) it seems more than likely that its survival will depend on its use in schools and not as a group of books for children to buy for themselves. (B.A.)

discovery of the Poles and the curiosities of nature. The venerable originator of the series, Noel Carrington, deserves praise in all the English-speaking territories for the service he has done in presenting the world in such modern terms to their young people. At the same time, these booklets form a very appropriate course of reading for the increasing number of readers in the developing countries who often do not have sufficient material at their own disposal.

It is perhaps also worth mentioning here a series called *Pleiades Books* which appeared in London during and just after the Second World War. While they were less catholic in their choice of subject, these volumes had the services of such fine graphic artists as Oliver Hill and Hans Tisdall (*A picture-book of building* and *Wheels*) and Eileen Mayo (*Little animals* and *Shells*). Another series which pursued similar aims to the *Albums du Père Castor* was the *Atlantis Kinderbücher*[1] (Zürich, 1935 onwards) with its large format picture-books, several of which broke completely new ground where the provision of information for young children was concerned. Work here was interrupted during the Second World War and has only recently been restarted.

HILL, Oliver and TISDALL, Hans. *Balbus, a picture book of building.* London, 1944.
From a colour lithograph by the authors.

The publisher Herbert Stuffer carried out some daring experiments with his play-books by Tom Seidmann-Freud, which aimed to awaken the creative powers of the child, and also with his educational books by Friedrich Böer, which are more fully considered in the chapter on the use of photography in children's books. Political events, however, condemned these developments to premature oblivion.

Yet another undertaking in the spirit of Comenius was the series *Länder und*

[1] Some of the titles in this series were *Die Geschichte vom Fluss* and *Den Berg hinauf* by Eduard and Valerie Bäumer, *Das Lied vom Brot* and *Im tiefen Wald* by Walter Bergmann, *Tiere in Haus und Hof* by Luise Rinser and Marianne Scheel, *Die Jahreszeiten* by Bettina Kiepenheuer and Marianne Scheel, and *Sonne, Mond und Sterne* by Inge Diederichs and Peter Thienhaus. Although many books mentioned in this section are now out of print, their fine production and their new educational approach are so important as to warrant a permanent record of their titles being retained. (B.A.)

Völker (Potsdam, 1930 onwards) which was drawn and written by Claire With in close co-operation with children themselves.

The publishing house of Otto Maier at Ravensburg is a further example of a firm which for decades pursued a similar goal with its activity games and educational picture-books, designed to set young children's minds working and to direct their interests and their play along rewarding paths. Today this company continues its traditions in a quite different way by marketing German editions of those large volumes with which the Americans introduce their children to all kinds of knowledge: the famous *Golden Books*.

A more modest project was inaugurated in the same firm by Roderich Thun, who produced a series of simple educational books, which sought to create an interest in subjects dealing with natural and human activity through a combination of words and drawings. This might well have led to some lively developments if only better illustrators had been called upon.

Throughout Europe efforts are now being made to render the whole of the visual world and its puzzles in pictorial terms. Factual books for older children are often adaptations of the popular science books produced for adults, often indeed they are identical to them. For this reason I am not considering them here. But with younger children and with children in the lowest forms of primary schools, whose sense of wonder and whose relentless curiosity and desire for information are still unabated, it is left entirely to chance whether the parent or the teacher is able to bring some order to the confusion of facts which have accumulated in their young heads. This is especially noticeable in German-speaking Europe.

Although the handing on of knowledge to these young children is best done by human rather than by literary means, there are few adults who are capable of doing it without a backing of suitable printed material. This is not due simply to lack of time among the adults, but also to the multiplicity of problems and questions which present themselves. The reason why factual books picturing things in a purely representational way largely fail or miscarry can be found in the graphic style of the younger illustrators who do not have much patience with the objective approach. But the example of America shows, of course, that even subjects closely connected with nature can be treated in a free manner.

When natural history is chosen as a subject for a picture-book in Germany— as, for instance, Gerhard Oberländer's exemplary *Märchen von den drei Apfel-bäumen* (*The tale of the three apple-trees*) (1958)—then a playful style is often adopted which, in this case, as we should expect, is perfectly handled so that a natural occurrence is clarified for the child. Klaus Winter and Helmut Bischoff are two active artists here and the factual simplicity of their book about the ways of a mole, *Mool, was der Maulwurf erlebt* (1962), impressively portrays the dangerous subterranean life of the little creature.

Something quite fresh is attempted in the recent book by the French author-ess Colette Portal, translated into English by Marcia Nardi as *The life of a queen* (Cape, 1965). Here the reader is shown the life of an ant-queen in a remarkable pot-pourri of information and story, factual tabulation, and poetry. Among recent picture-books this is perhaps the most successful attempt to present a subject taken from nature in a child-like manner.

Another remarkable attempt which is worth mentioning is the combination of factual information, predominantly in pictures, with an exciting story in *Die Geburtstagsreise* (1961) by the Basel author Walter Grieder. The subject is a birthday journey on the Rhine and the book contains pictures which strongly emphasize its theme of the factors which help to create unity among different countries. At the same time it shows more clearly than the previously mentioned books the tendency to turn the actual subject of the book, which is here a particularly powerful one, into a piece of harmless stage-property by introducing crude modifications. (Here, for instance, the travelling children make adventurous journeys with a friendly stork.)

Many gaps in information can, of course, be filled by children's dictionaries and other reference books, which will not be described in any greater detail here. A great deal of entirely factual information seems today to be more and more part of the province of photographic picture-books.

England possesses in the excellent *Parrish colour books* by Marie Neurath a collection of information books which exactly correspond to what the English and the Americans understand by such a phrase.

Similarly, Spain has produced a large collection of educational picture-books in the series *El globo de colores*, published by Aguilar. Such subjects as air, fire, sea, mountains, and cars are presented to the reader on a generous scale. And Italy also includes among its children's literature a great deal of educational material.

East European picture-books place a pronounced emphasis on the demand for education and for an explanation of the world in a material sense. The Russian child comes to understand quite early in life that he has little neighbours growing up on the edge of the tundra or leading curious lives as nomads in the Southern Steppes. Heroic moments from the past or biographies of youthful pioneers are drummed into even the smallest children, while information about technology or natural history fills up countless unimaginatively produced textbooks which are certainly not used only by the children.

In Czechoslovakia children are brought to an understanding of technical, natural, or historical facts through systematically prepared series which are to some extent quite excellent. The books will often be prepared in the cheapest possible form so that children can buy copies for themselves. Everything from the simplest facts to biographies, travel books, histories of the remotest and the most recent past, all influenced more or less by the socialist concept of the world, is at the Czechoslovakian child's disposal. This is only possible because book production is in the hands of official or semi-official institutions. In any case, the value of such literature would not be so great if it were not for the very fine teachers and artists who are at present working in that country.

Things are much the same in Poland—as also in many other East European countries whose work we are not able even to glance at. It is perhaps worth mentioning, however, the beautiful Polish picture-book *Doremi* (1955) by Jan Brzechwa and Jan Scancer, a brilliant introduction to music for children which has been translated into many languages.

From what has been said, it should be clear that those countries which are going through a period of rapid political and social development set about establishing series of factual books in a much more systematic way than countries such as our own which are saturated in a tradition of such educational books. And in this I am not referring just to Communist countries but also to the Mediterranean lands and particularly Spain with her huge market in the newly developing countries of South America.

All the efforts which I have talked about here, and many others, have one thing in common—an urge to close the circle. If they cannot do it in one volume, then they attempt to reach completeness through the multiplicity of a series. Series today shoot up like mushrooms and too often they have the brand of boom conditions upon them. When Père Castor said that it was more important to him that children should grow up in an awareness of their place in nature, rather than that they should be able to tell the makes of twenty different cars, he was speaking as a committed teacher. Such a truly conscientious attitude is not to be discovered in all the publishing ventures of our times.

Meanwhile, development becomes more precipitate and the world scene daily more confusing. The fantasies of Jules Verne are coming to pass in reality and never before was there so much need of careful priorities. *The world we live in*—the *Orbis pictus* of 1958—has a staggering complexity, while today's child, hungry for knowledge and knowing all about moon-rockets, atomic power, and supersonic speed, is taken in by nothing.

Yet where is it all leading? Are we not stuck in a blind alley which one day will come to an end? Will children always want to know everything? Is knowledge, in fact, all that is important? Rousseau preached a return to nature to an over-civilized world and ordered teachers to provide *Robinson* as the only reading for their charges.

When, some weeks ago, I held in my hand for the first time an original edition of the *Orbis pictus* I opened it at a page and saw 'The soul of man—Anima hominis—vegetative in plants . . . rational in man'. When we consider the problems of the factual book, do not let us forget this 'soul' which Comenius saw fit to put into his own book along with the water, the stars, and the birds of the air.

BOOK LIST

The animal books of Père Castor have been translated into English by Rose Fyleman and published by Allen and Unwin (London). The eight titles are: *Mischief the squirrel; Quipic the hedgehog; Ploof the wild duck; Frou the hare; Bourru the brown bear; Scaf the seal; Martin the kingfisher;* and *Cuckoo.*

A group of Père Castor Colour Picture-Books is being published by Harrap (London), with texts by Antonia Ridge. These are story-books, not factual books, and Harrap also publish identical editions in French.

A picture encyclopaedia which sees itself in the Comenius tradition is the *Picture book of knowledge: from home to outer space,* adapted from an edition published in Munich in 1961 by Olive Cook (Thames and Hudson, London, 1961).

The name of Friedrich Böer appears as editor of *Igloos and totem-poles,* an account of the life and customs of thirteen peoples around the globe, translated by Florence McHugh (Pantheon, 1959), first published in Freiburg as *So lebt man anderswo* (1955).

11 PHOTOGRAPHY
A new contribution to education and children's books

Travellers in picturesque regions of the world are today regarded as mildly eccentric if they suddenly set about posting up an easel and painting the more charming aspects of their surroundings. On the other hand, anyone can produce a camera and take as many photographs as he likes without exciting any comment at all. The whole skill is taken for granted and even children find little difficulty in mastering the complexities of lenses and light-meters and when to press the button and when not to. And in the hands of adults, of course, such wonders can be achieved which quite surpass the amateur achievements of the Sunday painter. However sensitive his eye, the eye of the camera is likely to be more accurate and its results more impressive. (And whatever the technologists say, any fool can press a button, but few people are keen to labour at the long schooling and arduous practice that painting involves.)

The advantages enjoyed by travellers or explorers who are armed with pen and paper lie in their consequent independence of technical or financial considerations and their complete freedom of action. For this reason many ethnological, zoological, botanical, and other expeditions even today include someone who knows how to handle a pencil, while many scientific institutions also find such a person's services invaluable.

On the other hand, anyone can become a photographer if he has got eyes in his head and money in his purse. Photography is one of those very tempting occupations which can produce impressive results without a lot of hard work. There is quite a thrill to be had from watching film that was exposed in the sunshine of the South developed in the damps of the North and thrown up in all its brilliancy on to a screen three feet across.

This apparent transitory activity has naturally brought forth its own heroes and artists. The heroes are mostly among the press photographers who may have spent their lives in danger, may even have lost them, in order to satisfy mankind's demand for a sight of what actually happened; the artists are those who have been able to combine the sensitive vision of the painter with the technical demands made by photography as a science.

Now, no matter what your attitude may be to this phenomenon of contemporary man, taking photographs everywhere yet still hungry for more, there is no doubt that the camera's eye has conquered the human eye and consequently the world of books, magazines, and newspapers as well. It has not only replaced earlier reproductive methods such as woodcuts or auto-lithography, it has also replaced (and this should be underlined) the very words themselves. It has become the medium of a new kind of picture language, far more extensive than we are perhaps aware.

How should it be that this new medium has not penetrated child-education? For it is worth noting that only now is this beginning to happen on a large scale, a scale so large, in fact, that I have thought it worth while to put down a number of thoughts on the subject.

I talked to Père Castor about this and asked him what he thought about the use of photography in books for children and young people. It happens that he has recently introduced photography into some of his productions for older children and he answered me: 'I do not think that photographs can pretend to replace paintings and drawings in children's picture-books, but they can still be extremely useful for certain age-groups, always presuming that they stimulate the activity of the reader. In other words, let them give him the opportunity to see things for himself and make comparisons between different pieces of evidence.'

I should like to make this spontaneous answer the foundation for my own brief observations, for it contains in a few summary phrases everything, both negative and positive, which need be said on the subject. And it is necessary to repeat it because the buyer of books today has suddenly been placed in front of a vast number of photographic books for children, some of which are superbly fine picture-books with an international reputation, even though they do not fit in with the conditions demanded above.

To clarify my meaning I should like to take two particularly fine examples —the negative one being so delightful a book that my criticism of it is scarcely likely to harm its reputation.

I have in front of me two animal books for children, both of them dealing with wild animals and with quite exemplary wild animals at that. On the wrapper of the first book an entrancing little lion is shown cuddling an arm-chair cushion. Inside the book he appears in all sorts of attractive and unusual situations, each one superbly photographed by Ylla, the young photographer who was later to be killed so tragically while working in India.

Seen at first in his cage, the little lion next turns up somewhat embarrassed on a lawn in the city park in the company of an equally embarrassed collection of dogs, cats, rabbits, and children. He then appears in a pullover, then in front of a mirror, and finally beside a writing-table. Unity is imposed on the whole sequence through an at times almost philosophical text by Jacques

Prévert, one of France's leading writers, who just about succeeds in making a story out of this string of magnificent picture-postcards.

This book belongs among the first of an exceptionally successful outcrop of photographic picture-books and today the genre may be found in all countries and with every variation in quality. Ylla's are among the best of these and were a world-wide success.

At first glance my other example—*Micky the fox-cub*[1]—is not very different from *The little lion*. From its wrapper this time a young fox gazes out on the world just as cheerfully as the lion-cub did. A Danish woman, Astrid Bergman, has photographed him in his own habitat, and by so doing has taken the child reader into the remotest tracts of forest to see with his own eyes one of the few living beasts of prey of northern latitudes in its natural state. In this book, too, towards the end, there is an encounter with human beings and their children—an event which is almost statutory in this kind of book; but the essential point is that the reader is here urged into a world which would be totally closed to him without the aid of this masterly photographer. In the darkness of this northern forest there are roe-deer and otters, owls, badgers, jackdaws, and hares, and even the fox lives a life quite different from his reputed one as a stealer of chickens. Thanks to the techniques of modern photography—the panchromatic films, the telescopic lens, and so on—and thanks to the endless patience of the photographer, a piece of life has been given visual form which will have a greater effect on the child of today (accustomed though he may be to photographic representation) than if he had received the same information in an artist's drawing.

Each of these two books is first class in its own way and at first sight they may even appear to be two of a kind. But it has been my intention to show that so far as educational demands are concerned they are worlds apart. Certainly there may be no harm in bringing together a lot of attractive photographs as Ylla has done (and, in her wake, many another photographer). Often her photographs are interesting for technical as well as for purely pictorial reasons. But really these books are little more than offshoots of those picture-books for adults which are so popular today—no matter how many distinguished writers may be persuaded to get up a text which will make the whole thing look like a spontaneously told story.

Books like this appeal little or not at all to a child's creative faculties, and among them must also be numbered those often superb picture-books which have been created from films. Among these some of the most beautiful are those by Albert Lamorisse: *Bim, le petit âne* (Paris, 1952), *Crin-blanc* (Paris, 1953), and *Le balon rouge* (Paris, 1956). However beautiful this kind of book may be (and *Le balon rouge* was quite seductively so) it would be a great pity if such productions were to overwhelm the nursery. Sensible parents, therefore, and intelligent teachers will probably ration them out in small doses, in

[1] The first edition of this book appeared in Denmark in 1953 under the title of *Micki Rävungen*. (B.A.)

the same way that they will hold a child off from the destructive dullness and passivity of the cinema screen for as long as possible.[1]

But let us now turn to those photographic books for children which demand their full participation in the way that Père Castor has suggested. The history of this type of book is still very short and in many cases cannot be distinguished from that of the other type, but it is important to isolate and try to foster its special qualities.

It seems to me that what history there is will well repay full investigation in a few years' time. The movement began without doubt with some experiments during the twenties, but the first really successful children's book of this kind in German did not appear until 1932. This was produced by the original young picture-editor Friedrich Böer, to whom, as a modern believer in visual communication, both drawings and photographs were fair means for illustration or clarification. For this reason he used both together. His first book was called *Klaus, der Herr der Eisenbahnen*[2] and it told of a small boy's dream to spend a day behind the scenes on a railway—for children the most fascinating of all methods of transport. Wherever in this book clear instructions had to be given, Böer used the draughtsman, whose work was technically more explicit. But for action, atmosphere, direct experience, he turned to photography. Such a plan may seem contrary to expectation, but it had many attractions for the young reader.

The boy in the story is no airy contrivance living in some imaginary house. No, he is a very real creature, living in an ugly city tenement whose bare sooty walls butt on to the tracks of a huge and very real railway station. The whole scene is photographed with a fine sense of atmosphere. You can see the dismal block where Klaus lives, and a circle of red marks out for you the window of his little room. Reality predominates.

But then, with the arrival of an imaginary government minister, the fairy tale begins. This man is the product of the boy's daydreams and as such he is drawn in by the artist. He is the agent who will take Klaus everywhere and show him the world-wide power of the railways—and as he does so, drawing mingles with photography. This means that the child who is reading the book is being asked to do more than passively look at a series of pictures. His eye and his brain are given something to consider in that active way whose importance I stressed earlier.

[1] Discussing the implications of this sentence with Mrs. Hürlimann, I suggested that some additional comments on television and children's books might be helpful. It would seem, however, that the problems and possibilities of the 'new' medium have not been investigated on the Continent to the same extent that has occurred in England and America and a fuller discussion of the subject must await a later edition. (B.A.)

[2] *Klaus, der Herr der Eisenbahnen* was published in 1933 by the Herbert Stuffer Verlag. Although it has long been out of print this mention of it serves to draw attention to the very creative work done by Stuffer before Hitler's rise to power. Further notes on some of the picture-books he published will be found on pp. 140 and 216. (B.A.)

Auf dem Bahnsteig ist viel los. Die Reisenden sehen aus dem Fenster oder stehen noch vor dem Zuge. Und alle sind ein wenig aufgeregt.

Ein Professor blättert hastig in einem Kursbuch.

Ein junges Mädchen mit Rucksack und Stock sieht sich ruhig nach einem schönen Platz um. Bald ist sie weit weg in den Bergen.

Eine dicke Dame mit Hund und Vogelbauer, mit vielen Koffern und einem kleinen Jungen hat noch immer nicht alles Gepäck beisammen. — Ein anderer Junge erkundigt sich bei dem Aufsichtsbeamten

BÖER, Friedrich. *Klaus der Herr der Eisenbahnen* Berlin, 1933.

Plate XIV

BERGMAN, A. *Micky the fox-cub*. London, Methuen, 1963.

Plate XV

The publisher issued one successor by the same author in which the same principle was applied: *Drei Jungen erforschen eine Stadt* (*Three boys discover a town*), a book which was also very good, but lacked the adventurous touch of the railway book. The author has remained faithful to his method of illustration and his present-day books, which are directed at both young people and adults, continue to give photography a prominent role without ever compromising a consistent aesthetic purpose. (*Alles über ein Schiff* [*All for a ship*], and *Der Hafen* [*The harbour*].)

It is worth remarking that this imaginative use of photography in children's books has found scarcely any imitators. Nevertheless, as we saw with Astrid Bergman's story of the little fox, there are books today which put photography to use in a very encouraging way. *Micky the fox-cub* is just one of a series of books for which our thanks are due to Swedish and Danish authors and photographers. There are, for instance, the books by that excellent Swedish photographer Anna Riwkin-Brick, some of which have texts by Astrid Lindgren—such titles as *Elle Kari*, which describes the life of a little girl from Lapland, and *Noriko-San*, which tells the story of a Swedish girl's visit to Japan. Every picture here yields up facts which are interesting, or even astonishing, and which are carefully explained in the text.

Astrid and Bjarne Henning-Jensen in their story *Mikisoq* portray some of the beauty and sadness in the life of a Greenland fisher-boy, and it is books like this which can enormously enrich the lives of children everywhere. Certainly such things were produced before the days of photography, and even today wonderful textbooks are appearing on similar themes accompanied only by drawn illustrations. But there are a great many children today who can more easily be lured into taking an intelligent interest in things by the indirect method of photography.

Much more dangerous is the use of the camera to illustrate stories, a point which I should like to make with one or two examples. In her children's book *Die Autojagd* (1953), Uta von Witzleben mingles modern technology and elements from fairy tales in an extraordinary way. The hero is a boy who understands the language of cars and can talk to old lorries and cars as he would to his friends. In other words, this is Red Riding Hood and the wolf, or Peter Pan and the ravens, with a fascinating new twist. It is problematic, though, how far she succeeds with this remarkable adventure, which is admittedly very exciting but is illustrated with photographs which give the whole thing the air of a 'true story'. They pin down the child's abundant imaginative faculties and do not permit him to see the characters in the book in any other way. Drawings, on the other hand, would have allowed a freer play to his imagination. Despite this, however, the photographs are themselves excellent and it may be that they point a way to fresh developments.

In any case, books like this, which are attempting to find a contemporary style, are much more welcome and valuable than a certain type of story where famous authors, squandering the credit of their good names, write texts to accompany more or less common or prearranged stories in photographs. Two examples will perhaps make this clear.

The first concerns Eric Linklater, the author of some extraordinarily exciting and witty novels, who has written, in addition, two splendid stories for children: *The wind on the moon* (1944) and *The pirates in the deep green sea* (1949) —the first of which gained him the distinction of the Carnegie Medal. But in *Karina with love* (1958) he set a text to a group of photographs by a Swedish photographer, telling the story of the adventures of a young girl from the northern forests. It is the weakest book that Linklater has ever written. Good though the pictures are, they have failed to awaken any response in this otherwise very imaginative writer.

The second book that comes to mind is by André Maurois and is at least the product of a basically original idea. A child is changed into a dog (thus giving the photographer the opportunity for some charming dog shots). When the mother finds the dog in the boy's bed, for instance, there is a very pretty photographic situation. But the author uses the story for unrestrained and humourless didactic purposes and it shows this famous writer far below his usual level.

To end with let us get back to our prudent French educationist—Père Castor, whose ideas I have considered at length in the last chapter. As publisher of one of the most beautifully illustrated series of picture-books, the *Albums du Père Castor*, he has clearly shown what he considers to be good for children, even though it may deal with subjects similar to those mentioned above.

Nevertheless, he has paid some attention in his production department to the use of photography and in his series *Collection le montreur d'images* he has started a new enterprise which, coming from his experienced hands, must be given every consideration. The first volumes were in a small format and of a clearly defined scope. They aim to bring children into the closest contact with the facts of natural history and with the wonders of growth in both plants and animals. Such books can no longer be described simply as children's books, but they do show in splendid fashion what educational possibilities there are in the alliance between words and photographs. Since the publication of the first books, the series has developed along just the right lines.

In recent years other attempts have been made to improve the photographic story-book and from the many titles that have appeared it is perhaps worth singling out Edmond Séchan's *Der kleine Elefant* and Astrid Bergman Sucksdorff's *Chendru, the boy and the tiger* (1960), while Hed Wimmer's *Drei Fischerjungen auf Sizilien* discloses something of the hardships suffered by children in other parts of the world. As with illustrated books for adults, however, many of these books are printed in enormous editions for separate publication in many countries and the demands entailed by this necessarily hinder any individual or original experiments. As I write, the latest sensation is the international edition of the book based on the film of Selma Lagerlof's *Adventures of Nils.* This abridged version has some beautiful pictures which perhaps justify sacrifice of parts of the text—or is that really an arguable case?

One thing remains certain, however, and that is the inadvisability of allowing photographic picture-books to spread too widely among the children of pre-reading ages or those just learning to read. It would be abortive to narrow down in this way all the possibilities which 'conventional' picture-books can offer to the simple perception and the magical imagination of little children. Up till now everything that has appeared in this field has been well-intentioned, if uncertain, or else the product of international co-operative publishing. Without wishing to be inhospitable to such new productions (which cannot be avoided anyway), we should not retreat before their apparently superior methods of illustration. We should rather seek to find the most appropriate use for them.

After all, despite many worthy attempts, no book has yet appeared which has really used the wonderful instrument of the camera in a way which is both new and applicable to the needs of children's reading.[1]

BOOK LIST

The photographic books by Ylla are published in Great Britain by Hamish Hamilton, but *The little lion* is now out of print. *Micki Rävungen*, however, is available from Methuen (London) under the title *Micky, the fox-cub*, 1963.

Two books by Albert Lamorisse were translated by Roger Lubbock and issued by Putnam (*The wild white stallion*, 1954, and *Bim*, 1956). These are now out of print, but a story adaptation of *The wild white stallion*, translated by Gwen Marsh and illustrated by Jean Reschofsky, is published by Harrap (London). *The red balloon*, translated by Malcolm Barnes, is published by Doubleday.

The photographic books by Anna Riwkin-Brick are part of a series entitled *Children Everywhere*, published by Macmillan. Those with a text by Astrid Lindgren are: *Circus child; Dirk lives in Holland; Gerda lives in Norway; Marko lives in Yugoslavia; My Swedish cousins;* and *Sia lives on Kilimanjaro.*

Other books in English are:

MAUROIS, André: *Nico.* Acorn Press, 1957.

SUCKSDORFF, Astrid Bergman: *Chendru, the boy and the tiger*, English version by William Sansom. Harcourt, 1960.

[1] It is perhaps possible now to dispute this statement, especially in Great Britain. Our present 'educational revolution' is driving publishers to devote more of their imagination to the production of lively 'textbook' material and in doing so they are employing the camera with increasing flexibility. This is perhaps best seen in some of the montage work now being done and in such an exciting historical experiment as the *Jackdaw Series* of documents from history published by Putnam's. (B.A.)

12 COLOUR PRINTS

The cheapest intellectual sustenance for children of every age

Colour prints or picture broadsides (there is no exact English equivalent for the German *Bilderbogen*) have a close relationship with children's books, acting as they did for such a long time as popular illustrated newspapers. They might be brought to lonely villages by poor hawkers, who would use them as payment for picking up rags and bones, or they might be shipped to the farthest quarters of the earth. At a time when pictures and writing were still the privilege of the book-owning well-to-do, these gaudy prints prepared many sections of the populace for books and especially for children's books.

Since many Continental readers may only have heard of the *Münchener Bilderbogen*, this chapter will be devoted to a summary of some other kinds of picture broadsides from Germany and from other countries. For the origins of these productions reach back a long way and are almost as old as printing itself. In those days they were small affairs, usually called '*corantos*' (or '*courantes*' or '*fliegende Blätter*'), and naturally before long they were ornamented with woodcuts, since these had a much wider public appeal than plain print. These picture-sheets brought people a bit of general knowledge and a great deal of news about disasters, marvels, portents, and all kinds of remarkable happenings in the world, along with current religious and political opinion.

These popular picture-sheets have an existence which has lasted down to our own times and the most famous Continental centres for their production were Epinal, with its *Imagerie populaire* (1657 onwards), and the Brandenburg town of Neu-Ruppin, where the publisher Gustav Kühn started a bold undertaking in 1825 and one which had perhaps the widest dissemination in the world. There were also the publishing houses of Campe and Renner at Nuremberg, a town with a noble tradition in book publishing for both adults and children, while at Stuttgart the house of Gustav Weise produced for a short period during the seventies an excellent series called *Die deutschen Bilderbogen*. The *Münchener Bilderbogen* seem to me, however, to demonstrate

Trampelthier.

Nilpferd.

Auerochse.

Elenthier.

Hyäne.

Lama.

Part of a *Nürnberger Bilderbogen*. Nuremberg. Campe, (n.d.)

Gaukel-Linchen.

„Bring den Leuchter mir geschwind,"
Sagt die Mutter zu dem Kind, —
„Aber mit dem Kerzenlicht,
Wenn ich fortgeh, gaukle nicht."

Und die Mutter geht hinaus,
Holt sich Etwas in dem Haus.
Carolinchen denkt sich: „Ei!
Was das Gaukeln Uebles sei?!

Stellt den Leuchter auf den Tisch,
Brennt das Flämmchen hell und frisch.
Linchen schaut gerad ins Licht:
Warum soll ich gaukeln nicht? —

Carolinchen lacht dazu
Läßt dem Lichte keine Ruh,
Tappt mit seinen Fingerlein
In den Docht sogleich hinein.

Doch die Lichtputz warnend spricht:
„Mit dem Lichte gaukle nicht,
Wenn Du gaukelst brennst Du Dich
Und ich beiß Dich fürchterlich!

Sieh, da fällt der Leuchter um,
Aber Mädel, das war dumm,
„Weh, o weh, wie's Feuer brennt!
Kommt die Mutter gleich gerennt."

Putzscheer sperrt den Rachen auf,
Klippt und klappt frisch los darauf,
Schnippt und schnappt und schluckt und frißt,
Bis das Kind verschwunden ist.

Drum ihr Kinder gaukelt nicht
Mit den Händen an dem Licht;
Denn die Putzscheer kommt herbei,
Beißt Euch schnell die Köpf' entzwei.

Münchener Bilderbogen.   **Nro. 4.**   Herausgegeben und verlegt von K. Braun und F. Schneider in München.

Schnellpressendruck vom J. P. Himmer in Augsburg.

*Gaukel-Linchen. Münchener Bilderbogen No. 4. Munich, Braun und Schneider, 1849.
Wood-engravings by Franz Pocci in a style later to be developed by Wilhelm Busch.*

154

the closest relationship to the children's books of their time, appearing uninterruptedly from 1849 to 1898 and still to be obtained today from the same publisher in Munich. They are no longer an *Imagerie populaire* like most of the earlier papers, which set out to replace picture-books and, indeed, books themselves. Instead, they run parallel to the illustrated *Volksbücher*, although rather than being produced anonymously they are written and illustrated by prominent artists of the time.

In the field of broadsides a quite separate tradition is evident in the southern countries, Italy and Spain, which today play an important part in the production of comics. The Italian picture-papers were confined to religious matters, while in Spain they were always the instruments for youthful exhortation, instruction, and entertainment. The papers there are called by such titles as *Santos* or *Aleluyas*, a fair enough proof of their origin in legends and portraits of the saints. They contain, however, secular subjects of all kinds, and their enormous popularity in the nineteenth century is doubtless responsible for the Spanish child's particular receptivity to picture stories today. In France many picture-sheets are simply called *Saints*, and in Switzerland those plain little pictures done in popular style are still called today by the dialect word for saints, *Helgen*, transformed in Alsatian Strassburg to *Heljen* and in Sweden to *Hilligen*.

The connexion with children is immediately perceptible. Like fairy tales and folk-songs, these papers were enjoyed by children as well as adults, and in the course of time they became more and more organs for children's entertainment. Almost all the series contained from the start what might be called cut-out sections for children. For example, there are famous English papers which began by publishing souvenir pictures of famous actors. As time went by these multiplied to several characters from a play on one sheet together with pictures of the stage-settings, all of which could be cut out and put together by children. This was called the 'Toy Theatre', and it led to the development at the same time of a whole literature of juvenile drama, which, during the nineteenth century in England, enjoyed an extraordinary popularity. In 1946 the book-collector George Speaight published a detailed study of this English hobby which is closely connected to the broadside industry. Robert Louis Stevenson also has provided some childhood recollections of these theatre-sheets, in his essay *A penny plain and twopence coloured*.[1]

Dating from the end of the eighteenth century there is a somewhat similar phenomenon in the *Strossburjer Papiersoldätle*, to which a large department of the Strassburg Historical Museum is devoted. Their basic components are coloured pictures of soldiers, cut from picture-sheets, glued to wooden blocks, and used to build up models of whole parades and battles. Their inventor was a cavalry officer who was also an engraver, and they were originally bought by

[1] The English tradition in toy theatres may still be seen at Pollock's Toy Theatres and Toy Museum, 44 Monmouth St., W.C.2. Besides continuing to retail English and Continental toy theatres, they also issue a sophisticated edition of Stevenson's famous essay. (B.A.)

the customer as black-and-white copper-engravings which were then painted, cut out, and set up. Everything could be got from Potsdam Grenadiers, ferocious Turks from the time of Prince Eugen, Napoleonic forces, right down to the parade-ground figures of the early years of this century. It finally took the First World War to bring this game of war to an end.

It is worth noting here that although some of the Strassburg and Nuremberg picture-papers were printed with all the sharp detail afforded by copper engravings, the favourite and traditional printing method was that of the boldly expressive woodcut, which only gradually gave way in the nineteenth century to the colour work of lithography.

Now what did the enormous popularity of these papers consist in and what did they offer their world-wide assembly of customers? They offered a popular form of symbolism. One picture-sheet is called *Wilhelms Leben* (*William's life*), and its sixteen little pictures, almost devoid of text, present with a touching simplicity the life of an exemplary citizen from the cradle to the grave. Just as symbolic, but produced in the form of a full-page picture, *Der Baum der Liebe* (*The tree of love*) represents another variety. (Both of these examples are from Neu-Ruppin, *c.* 1860.) That world-famous drama of frustrated love, *Paul et Virginie*, is summarized in four bold woodcuts and a brief text, rather as happens today in the American countries with their pretext of handing down the classics, again a representative type of picture-paper (Epinal, *c.* 1840).

Secondly, the joys to be had from life are dealt with time and again. There is, for instance, a lithographed sheet of cut-outs from Neu-Ruppin (1860) called *Winter*, providing a set of individual pictures of such things as a sleigh party, a Christmas-tree, a hot-sausage stall, a snowball fight, and many other seasonal subjects. Children's games, Christmas and popular customs are other favourite themes and 'history', of course, plays a very important part, chiefly in anecdotal form. The Epinal papers are particularly fond of the Napoleonic Wars and their detailed portrayal of contemporary events has a documentary value for us today. Far older events, however, are also portrayed, such as the Neu-Ruppin version of the William Tell story, whose attractively horrific pictures provided the children of the middle of the last century with an example of an heroic struggle for liberty. In addition to this there were naturally plenty of pictorial presentations of plants and animals, together with such things as well-known proverbs and so on.

The publishers at Epinal remained most constant to the woodcut and their collection of blocks may still be seen today. It was here that half-way through the last century the chief centre for the production of humorous picture-stories was established—the direct ancestors of present-day comics, even though the 'moral of the story' corresponded closely to the ideals of the age. Incidentally, some of these picture-stories were published oncommission by the Humoristic Publishing Co., Kansas City, in 1856, bearing the imprint *Imagerie d'Epinal*. They have a quite different style from the European editions of that date.

From such funny picture-stories as these it is not a long step to the *Münchener*

Der Flug des Ikarus

Geschichte in Bildern, gezeichnet von einem Knaben (13 Jahre).

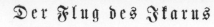

1. Ikarus sitzt hier am Meer
Und wünscht, daß er ein Vogel wär.

2. Er baut aus Federn sich zwei Flügel
Und schwebt bald über Dorf und Hügel.

3. Die Vogelschar ist nicht vergnügt,
Weil hier ein Mensch zum Himmel fliegt.

4. Es braust der Wind. Er hält nicht ein,
Hoch oben schon die Wolken bräun.

5. Es bricht ein Wetter los mit Krach!
Der Knabe fliegt mit festem Schlag.

6. Die Nacht ist weit, die Sterne groß,
Sie funkeln hell im Himmelsschoß.

7. Der Mond verblaßt im Morgenschein.
Der Flug geht hoch ins Licht hinein.

8. O Sonnenglut! Die Arme weit!
Es schmilzt das Wachs im Flügelkleid.

9. Der Flügel bricht, er trägt nicht mehr!
Und jäh stürzt Ikarus ins Meer.

10. Die Fluten ziehen ihn hinab.
Die Wogen schließen sich zum Grab.

11. Des Wassers Tiere schwimmen drein,
Sand und Algen hüllen ihn ein.

12. Fiel Ikarus? O nein! Er lebt!
Nun, wo der Mensch am Himmel schwebt.

Lübecker Bilderbogen Nr. 1

Der Flug des Ikarus. Lübecker Bilderbogen No. 1. Lübeck (n.d.)
The Fall of Icarus drawn by a thirteen-year-old boy.

Bilderbogen which began to appear five years after *Struwwelpeter*, the first comic picture-book for children. Apart from this, there were, of course, many contemporary picture-sheets in countries throughout Europe, but not always on the same scale as in France and Germany. Great Britain, for instance, had few pictorial broadsides for children, their place being taken by straight prints in the Rowlandson tradition, or by political cartoons, or such things as the famous Theatrical Prints of Benjamin Pollock. Mention has already been made of the Spanish editions which had a particularly wide dissemination because of the markets in South America.

The Dutch papers are oddly appealing to children with their portrayals of games, popular customs, or seafaring life. Among the English papers there was a series entitled *Scraps*, costing a penny plain or twopence coloured. They were on the whole less significant than, say, the papers of Epinal, but they covered themes somewhat similar to the 'Toy Theatre'. Even the Swiss *Neujahrsblätter*, which are dealt with more fully in Chapter 17, were nothing more than a kind of picture-broadsheet with text, folded once, and handed out to children on New Year's Day, a custom dating from the middle of the seventeenth century.

The lovely *Deutsche Bilderbogen* of Gustav Weise, which counted among its illustrators Theodor Hosemann and Adolf Menzel, eventually disappeared under the mass impact of the *Münchener Bilderbogen*. None of the series of the nineteenth century had anything like the versatility of this paper which from 1849 onwards was under the direction of Kaspar Braun and F. Schneider. Braun knew how to attract true artists to his firm, who were able to establish an individual style for its picture-stories. Wilhelm Busch, of course, was the most famous of these and his slapstick tales with their characteristic verses appear in many broadsheets from the sixties onwards, to the delight of old and young alike. Even today they can still be bought for very little money.

Another talented artist, perhaps even more at children's level than Busch, was L. Meggendorfer, to whom we also owe the famous movable picture-books. Otto Speckter did not set himself above contributing some delicately Romantic fairy-tale sheets, while Franz Pocci's broadsheets belong among the most amusing (and the most suitable for children) in the early series.

However, when I put myself into the position of a child of that time, thirsting for knowledge, I think I should be delighted most by those publications which bring into the confines of a single cheap sheet of paper all the colourful marvels from the other side of the world; or broadsheets showing the apparel of maharajas and emperors of China and similar mighty potentates; or maps depicting a river's course through tropical landscapes from its mouth, infested by crocodiles, along its banks where apes swing in the trees, to its source where, at the foot of snow-covered mountains, a donkey-boy lies prone with the vultures circling above his lonely final resting place. There is something here for all tastes, all temperaments, no matter what age, no matter what standard of education.

With the cessation of the *Münchener Bilderbogen* the age for this form of entertainment seemed to be at an end. But on a number of occasions people of taste and imagination have made efforts to bring about a return of the picture-broadside in a fresher style, at a time when paper was short and limitations were imposed upon the printed word. In the middle of the 1930s the *Lübecker Bilderbogen* was published by H. F. Geist, his first sheet being the Fall of Icarus drawn by a thirteen-year-old boy. We also find in this splendid series, whose brief life ended before the Second World War, some sheets by one of Germany's most gifted artists of that time, Alfred Mahlau, who illustrated such technical subjects as ships and railways and the Hanseatic trade routes.

At about the same time the Stuffer-Verlag brought out a series of beautiful broadsheets which seem to have been completely forgotten. Another attempt along such lines was the *Lindauer Bilderbogen* published by Friedrich Böer, who has other claims to merit for his work for children. These broadsheets probably owed their publication to the paper shortages and the tyrannous censorship of the Second World War; they blossomed for a short while and then disappeared, but, like the *Münchener Bilderbogen*, the original sheets can still be obtained today (Verlag Jan Thorbecke, Lindau). Some of Friedrich Böer's colleagues in this series were Albert Schäfer-Ast, with delightful picture-stories, Susanne Ehmcke, Josua Leander Gampp, Doris Böer-Puhonny, and many others. Wit, learning, and all kinds of innocuous items of popular culture such as proverbs and songs, followed each other in a colourful jumble. In the middle of the war, however, there appeared a sheet, beautifully illustrated in colour, on which the human virtues were depicted. It was based on an old saying which was nevertheless very relevant to the age of total war, the age of the final solution. Once again the traditional, ethical alignment of the picture-broadside was revealed, even though within the Third Reich it was only set out on the page of a cheap popular paper:

'*Redlichkeit ist aus der Welt gereiset und Aufrichtigkeit ist schlafen gegangen . . . die Gerechtigkeit kann den Weg nicht finden . . . die Wahrheit liegt schon lange begraben . . . das Gewissen hängt an der Wand.*'

('Integrity has vanished from the world and sincerity has fallen asleep . . . justice has lost her way . . . truth has long been buried . . . conscience rusts useless on the wall.')

Let us think of these broadsides, old and new, with a certain melancholy, while our children look at them with curiosity as the surviving witnesses of another age. They all belong to the past, having yielded their place to the picture-story-books or the comics, those products of an international industry which works towards a psychologically planned end.

13 WHAM! SOK! THINKS!

The development of comic strips from Wilhelm Busch to Walt Disney

Today a great deal, almost too much, is being said about the influences and the dangers of comics where young people are concerned. In the end almost all these earnest discussions reach the comforting conclusion that well-intentioned comics do exist (a whole series of such 'good' comics—*Eagle, Girl, Swift*—were, as we know, originally published by the Reverend Marcus Morris) and that both dangers and influences are on the wane, if only because the publication of particularly violent comics is forbidden. Such a ban has been imposed in many countries, such as England, while in others, most notably in the country of their origin, the U.S.A., a large number of publishers have joined in voluntary restrictions in order to eliminate at least horror and sex as far as possible. Such bannings and limitations, however, affect only the abuses of the system, not its root causes.

If we consider the matter from another point of view—what for adult literature would be called stylistic criticism—then the whole problem takes on a much deeper and more interesting aspect, for the straightforward story in pictures is of ancient origin. We have only to look at the mosaics in early Christian churches—for example, those at Ravenna—to realize that they are nothing other than picture-stories which tell the stories of the Bible to people unable to read. What are the frescoes of the Middle Ages and of the early Renaissance except the language of the Bible translated into magnificent pictures? The sculptures on the fronts of medieval cathedrals, the stained glass of Chartres are there as substitutes for the written word, which was accessible to only a few people in those days. But not long after, the printed word arrived and with it the spread of literacy so that the language of pictures gradually lost its original aim or became at most the illustration for a printed text.

Only in the education of children—that modern movement that began with Comenius—was fresh use made of picture-language, even though it was by no means the kind of high art that was known to the Middle Ages. Picture-books as they later developed, with their illustrative engravings, drawings, and etchings, do not have the dynamic quality of a row of pictures which one by one unfold the events of a single story rather like a slow-moving film. This was the effect of the early Christian mosaics and frescoes, but now the text has become paramount and the pictures simply illustrate it or fill it out.

Throughout the nineteenth century, however, the old ideas about picture-stories were once more in the air. Just take a look at *Struwwelpeter*: the words, however excellent, are supplementary. The pictures tell the stories almost without a gap and with unerring strokes. Then, twenty years later, in 1865, Wilhelm Busch published his *Max und Moritz* with which, both in form and content, we reach the essential elements from which comics were to develop.

BUSCH, Wilhelm. *Max und Moritz.*
A drawing from the earliest manuscript.

It is, of course, necessary to number among the forerunners of comics the picture-broadsides dealt with in the last chapter which, from the seventeenth century onwards, were designed to spread popular instruction and entertainment. As early as the middle of the nineteenth century the publishers of the Epinal 'images populaires' were exporting stories in pictures specially prepared for America, the American public even at that time apparently finding a strong attraction for such things. One can imagine these cheap picture-sheets being hawked around remote settlements, with all kinds of other necessities, and ending up finally on the walls of some log cabin, where they would form the only pictorial decoration and the only reading material. In this way they laid the foundation for a development in American taste which was to boomerang back upon Europe. These are, however, somewhat uncertain conjectures about a phenomenon which is as powerful as it is difficult to explain.

Returning now to *Max und Moritz*, we find what is really the first inspired story in pictures, but one which also has its own share of roughness and sensationalism. For this reason it is necessary to count Wilhelm Busch among the significant ancestors of the modern comic, noting also that he influenced and even took part in the production of contemporary picture-broadsides.

In *Max und Moritz* there was depicted for the first time a crazy series of pranks which children would find well worth copying, while the grown-ups who were included—such characters as '*Die Witwe Bolte*' and '*Der Lehrer Lämpel*'—have their absurdities unsparingly guyed. It was quite against the intentions of Wilhelm Busch, who as an artist was a sceptic and a pessimist, that the enormous success of his inspired drawings and rhymes should lie in the triumphs of his two good-for-nothings and not in their ignominious end in the mill, which is moreover unrealistic and therefore incredible.

In contrast to Dr. Hoffmann, whose success among children was numerically greater and not explicable through graphic excellence, Wilhelm Busch is both an inspired artist with his pencil and a singular juggler with words. While he controls the rhyme and rhythm of his language with a playfulness far more earnest than it looks, he can with a few strokes and flourishes of the pen depict a figure that one will remember to the end of one's days.

The full genius of Wilhelm Busch as an artist can only be gauged by looking at the originals or at accurate facsimiles of his picture-stories. Even quite early editions of his books show a sharp deterioration in standards of reproduction. It is indeed interesting to observe how the three most famous authors in the realm of children's entertainment, Lewis Carroll, Dr. Hoffmann, and Wilhelm Busch, were all most zealous concerning the technical presentation of their brain-children. Carroll pestered Tenniel a great deal and between them they withdrew the first edition of *Alice* because they were not satisfied with the quality of the printing; Hoffmann kept a strict eye on the work of the hand-colourists, in order to prevent any false or sentimental emphasis from creeping into the pictures for *Struwwelpeter*, and Wilhelm Busch transferred his drawings on to the wood of the printing block with his own hands. He also paid attention to new methods of printing which were being developed at that time. He himself stood by the press when the colours were being printed, but even then could not ensure completely that his books were produced with the transparent colours equivalent to his water-colours. Even the fine sepia tones of the writing and drawing inks which he mixed himself could not be accurately reproduced.

Busch's first little book, *Die Bilderpossen* (*Pranks in pictures*), was published by the Richter Verlag in Dresden in 1864. This publishing house had been formed through the group around Ludwig Richter (and was actually owned by his son) and, bearing in mind their leaning towards sentimentality, it is understandable that they rejected the artist's second work: *Max und Moritz*. Also the first publication had not sold very well, but nevertheless Richter's rejection of the second was to prove one of publishing's classic mistakes.

Since Busch had to earn a living and since his painting hardly sufficed for this, he became a colleague of his friend Kaspar Braun in Munich, who edited and published *Die fliegenden Blätter* and *Die Münchener Bilderbogen*. In this way,

Dem Karl ift fonderbar zu Muthe,
Die Here ſchwingt die Zauberruthe.

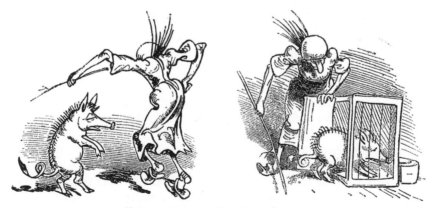

Und macht durch ihre Hexerei'n
Aus Karl ein kleines Quikeſchwein.

The transformation: a picture-story by Wilhelm Busch for a Bilderbogen.

almost by accident, he commenced a career which was to make him one of the great creators of the story told in pictures. Altogether he produced about sixty of these, which appeared either as books or as pictorial broadsides in black and white or in colour and which were all an immediate success. Nor has it ever been generally realized that the same man also left behind him some one thousand oil-paintings and two thousand serious drawings. Like many important artists he must have been a most industrious worker.

Let us, therefore, take a closer look at the personality of Busch, one of Germany's most popular artists and poets. He was born in 1832 at Wiedensahl near Hanover, the seventh child of a village shopkeeper, and after relatively few years of study in Düsseldorf, Holland, and Munich he retired once more to 'the provincial dream', assured of a regular income by the success of his first picture-stories. As a painter he was a willing disciple of German Romanticism, but as a poet he was both a cynic and a pessimist. This resulted in a sudden change in Continental children's books, which up till now had borne the stamp of their own variety of Victorianism or of the more idyllic tones of Romanticism (things, of course, being ordered somewhat differently in England). A cool spirit of caricature, not entirely free from malice, entered the pages of children's books greatly to the delight of the children themselves, who are unsentimental creatures, even though their parents may not like to admit the fact. It is by no means a coincidence that at the same time the crude, popularly based literature of the Punch and Judy shows, the sagas of the Devil and his Grandmother were celebrating a healthy renaissance in the work of Franz Pocci (1807–76).

Out of high regard, not to say affection, for Wilhelm Busch this soupçon of malice should not be concealed, for it was something which had never previously appeared in children's books. However much we may sneer at the strictly moral books of the eighteenth century or the piously sentimental ones of the nineteenth, we should not deny that today we have difficult educational problems of our own. Cheap books and comics have multiplied in such quantities and the caricaturing of humanity has been taken to such lengths that the truly human is far more deeply submerged and distorted here than in the cardboard heroics of times past. Not, of course, that we can hold the distinguished Mr. Busch responsible for the consequences of his own work. He knew the boundaries beyond which he might not pass and he was at heart a solidly moral person who gave rein to the idyllic and the poetic in many of his stories. In his *Sechs Geschichten für Nichten und Neffen* (*Six stories for nephews and nieces*), he seizes upon popular fairy-tale themes in an altogether deliciously sharp and unsentimental way. There is no lack of charm, even though the punishment of the wicked takes on some rather frightening forms.

Before he had ever begun his picture-stories he occupied himself by collecting Low German fairy tales and sayings. But from 1865 onwards he devoted all his energy to the picture-stories, which possessed the advantage that they ensured him a livelihood. *Max und Moritz* (1865) has had a success unsurpassed by any of his other books, but these, too, have become the fondest possessions of many generations and many age groups. *Die fromme Helene, Hans Huckebein, Pater Filucius, Herr und Frau Knopp, Maler Klecksel, Fipps der Affe* all appeared between 1871 and 1877 and occupy their tragicomic places in the heavily gilt Busch-Albums, which were the sacred family possessions, beloved by all, in countless German households.

Zu guter Letzt (1904) and *Schein und Sein* (1909) are profound collections of verse, the latter published posthumously, for in 1908 the poet had died, convinced to the end of his life equally of the imperfection and the beauty of the world. In 1905 he had written to a small boy:

Max und Moritz machten beide,	Max and Maurice, neither one,
Als sie lebten, keine Freude:	Brought much joy to anyone.
Bildlich siehst du jetzt die Possen,	The pranks you see in all these
die in Wirklichkeit verdrossen,	sketches
mit behaglichem Gekicher,	Were played by these two wicked
Weil du selbst vor ihnen sicher.	wretches,
Aber das bedenke stets:	And you can spare a laugh for them
wie man's treibt, mein Kind, so	Because you think you're safe from
geht's.	them.
	But, child, remember for your sake
	You have to sleep in the bed you
	make.

But none of these books leaves out wickedness. It is always there as it is in life and in great art. Does it have a place in children's books? An unanswerable question. Wickedness in the abstract world of art is always more bearable, even for children. In Shakespeare it takes on a purifying quality, whereas in the naturalistic thriller it has a debasing effect on the reader, more particularly on the youthful one. From the point of view of children, Wilhelm Busch is rather on the side of the angels. He stands opposed to the thrills of the comic, where the strong always win—often thanks only to their gift of the gab or, more violently, to their slickness with a gun. Only rarely, and then only in the best examples, does the comic have its origins in any kind of artistic inspiration and this, by its very success, leads down the slope to crude exploitation and mass-production—something which cannot be disguised by liberal intentions or originality in the central characters.

To be just, certain artistic forces cannot be disputed even in this new form of expression. Here and there in America gifted draughtsmen have created characters who are known to every adult and most children. Among them may be numbered Al Capp's Bald Iggle, Krazy Kat, Felix the Cat, and Albert Alligator who all serve to some extent as critics of the American scene.

A creator of stories almost equal to Busch, however, is Walt Disney who brought laughter to the whole world with his *Mickey Mouse* cartoons long before he ever turned to making books. Who knows indeed whether, if he were alive today, Busch himself would not have turned to cartoon films? The great distinguishing mark of these films, however, is the physical elasticity of the characters which enables them to move and alter shape in a quite delightful way. Furthermore, since the invention of the sound film they have been able to do this to a surprisingly sophisticated musical accompaniment.

These two elements of sound and movement, however, are impossible for static pictures. In their place we get the crude and banal ejaculations which rise from the speakers' mouths in balloons like blown-up American bubble-gum. That which possessed aesthetic charm and a liberating hilarity in the smooth sequences of a film becomes stilted and leering in a single drawing, thereby losing most of its satisfying effect.

In spite of its reliance on such bubble-talk, which neither Busch nor the broadsides found necessary, this new literature threatens to supplant its predecessors. In so far as it can be called literature it shares one effect with the films, for it has the same power, this time extending farther and lasting longer, of distracting people from books. Americans are inclined to take this literature very seriously, especially in its more presentable examples, and they ascribe a value to things which we can barely comprehend. John Steinbeck writes of Capp, one of the best-known writers in the medium: 'I think Capp may very possibly be the best writer in the world today.' And in another place he writes: 'I run into people who seem to feel that literature is all words and that those words should preferably be stuffy. The literature of Cro Magnon is painted on the walls of the caves of Altamira. . . .'[1]

Thus once again we return to the starting-point of this chapter. The walls of Altamira, the walls of the Ravenna churches presented stories in pictures for people who could not read. If John Steinbeck is right (and he is seconded by some weighty American names), then this bubble-talking 'literature' is in the process of becoming real literature, although its public is no longer quite illiterate. Our particular concern here is with these picture-stories in both books and newspapers as they affect young children. In America they have conquered the children's world and appear every year in their thousands. The so-called 'horror comics' have turned twelve-year-olds confessedly into murderers, while an American analysis of a hundred comic books and a thousand comic strips which was carried out some ten years ago produced the following figures for contents or representations: 218 major crimes, 313 minor crimes, 531 acts of bodily violence, 87 sadistic acts, and so forth. Under the heading of 'self defence' full advice was given on how to press someone's eye out with your thumb, kick someone in the kidneys and carry out other such pleasantries. Even in England some years ago it was possible to buy a horror-comic album (admittedly imported) in which six people were shot, five killed

[1] These quotations from Steinbeck appeared in *The Times Literary Supplement* for 29 May 1953. The reviewer adds: 'Mr. Steinbeck may be right. Literature began with comic strips; if we are not careful it may also end with them.' (B.A.)

by axe, spear or knife, three tortured, two trampled to death, and one embalmed alive.

In England today comics of this kind are banned, their publishers having desisted with what was to some extent a voluntary gesture. On the rest of the Continent they are still not nearly so widespread as in America, although some can be found in most places, especially in Italy.

From an Austrian comic with high intentions: *Bilderpost* (Kanka Comic).

In America, 95 per cent of all children read comic strips and, not so long ago, 75 per cent read nothing but comic books and strips. Accurate figures are not available for Europe, but in many countries, especially in the South, it is not likely to be much better. In America the publishers of the worst comics have imposed a certain amount of restraint upon themselves, and adults, so far as they have any concern for the upbringing of the young, are making great efforts both in America and Europe to halt this avalanche of print, cheap and horrible, but influential in all senses of the word. Perhaps in the ethical sense they will succeed. In America, above all, the counter-attack has been particularly strong, mounted by publishers and authors with ideals—among them many immigrants from Europe. Modern American picture-books are among the finest that there are and it is pertinent to ask if this counter-attack will succeed in halting the literature of the future, this picture and bubble language. For many Americans are coming to know the classic masterpieces of the world only through comic strips and balloon-talk or through the movies and the television.

The effect of this literature is already far too strong, not only in America. For in the most ingratiating way it offers to satisfy our express need for the pictorial or graphic delineation of facts, a technique which predominates in most educational books if not in education itself. The abstract letter, the representation of things through plain words, through well-constructed sentences, have all become devalued by the pleasure which pictures bring. When the adults of today were children they reached a certain age when they

167

rejected books with pictures in. They regarded them as aids to comprehension which one grew out of soon after one had passed the age of ten.

Today, however, we cannot have enough pictures. Made to correspond in all its design and presentation to the mental capacity of the semi-literates, the literature of the bubble-talkers has become for a great many people what those books previously were which confessed themselves on their title page to be written 'for children from 7 to 70'. However far our acceptance of the fact may lag behind the statistics of the evidence, however unpalatable it may be to educated people, it is nevertheless true that it is much easier for the eye to follow an enormous quantity of sensational picture-stories than for it to take in the more abstract matter of plain print. Even a semi-literate or a backward child can easily consume as many as a hundred comics in a week and according to the figures, two hundred a week is nothing unusual. The result is that those parents who from one year's end to the next buy their children nothing except Mickey Mouse comics or whatever the speciality of their particular family or country may be, those parents who only buy their children a real book at Christmas, if at all, suddenly become aware of the inconceivable fact that their children are no longer either capable or willing to read any book which makes a demand upon their intelligence.

From a Spanish comic.
The joke might well have been improved by leaving out the speech-balloons.

From the English comic *Girl*, founded by the Reverend Marcus Morris in an effort to 'prevent the Devil having the best tunes'.

The explosive punctuation marks in the balloons above Donald Duck's impudent beak have found their way into all quarters of the world. They are understood and laughed at everywhere: Mickey Mouse and similar characters (Mickey Mouse is by far the nicest) are in the course of becoming legendary figures like Robinson Crusoe and Heidi (in so far as these famous people have not been totally commandeered by the comics in the way that the Americans have translated such things as Shakespeare's plays, the classic novels of the nineteenth century, and even the Bible into the standard formula of the glib comic strip). Since many people in the U.S.A. only read those pages of the newspapers which have comic strips on them, the politicians and even the reformers have also taken to using them to get their messages across.

I do not see the danger simply in their somewhat violent, not to say gangsterly tendencies, for these have been proved to be ingredients which are not unconditionally necessary (for example, in the English comics *Eagle*, *Girl*, and *Swift*, and in a considerable quantity of American and other European comic strips). No, the danger lies in the way that language is reduced to becoming a crude accompaniment for pictures. Even in their best examples, these papers are still the result of a commercial mass-production which cannot bother itself with verbal subtleties. They have lost touch with their predecessor Wilhelm Busch whose drawings were themselves so expressive that he could do without words entirely, but who nevertheless provided accompanying verses which relied upon a fine understanding of and respect for language.

The supporters of the modern comic, psychologists among them, maintain that they can use these bubble-blowing comic strips to make difficult children read and maladjusted children laugh. And they add that they are a boon

169

to all those poor people who would otherwise never come to see a book at all.[1]

All this may be true, but in most countries there are today many good and responsibly edited books which are well worth the little that they cost. Furthermore, we should all have a care that, while the modern picture papers may never be stamped out, the children who look at them should also be educated to appreciate the printed word. Whether we are parents or teachers, booksellers or librarians, writers, artists or publishers, it is incumbent upon us that as many children as possible should be sufficiently educated in their native language that they may at some future date read with understanding the words of the great men, both past and present.

Those abrupt shorthand phrases, however, drifting about in their bulging balloons presage a new linguistic barbarism. They issue from the mouths of the most questionable characters and they represent a weakening of language and an oversimplification of human affairs which has never been known before in children's literature, regardless of any particular genre.

The great distinction between all this and the picture-language of earlier times is that in the prehistoric paintings of Altamira or the mosaics of Ravenna, or whatever else you care to think of, a grandly conceived, elemental language was translated into the medium of pictures because the written word was not understood sufficiently, if at all. Our picture-language today is indeed directed at the mentally illiterate, but this is happening with a civilization which prides itself on having reduced illiteracy to a minimum.

There are all too many people today who can only read in the most basic sense. For many there is no satisfaction to be had from the abstractions of print, whose marvellous power consists in its appeal to our imaginative faculties. Pictures have been brought in as a kind of visual aid with the result that pure print is in peril of being submerged under the age-old language of the artist. Already the vocabulary of American children is very much smaller than that of European children of the same age—although it is perhaps worth mentioning the one really positive aspect of balloon language: its property of universality, a kind of Esperanto, but one which has scarcely ever been used in a positive way.

It is quite possible that this form of entertainment, which may be regarded as a smaller and apparently less flamboyant brother of the cinema, will penetrate the Continent of Europe as it has done America. It behoves us, therefore, in my opinion, to be on our guard. In this context it is perhaps worth mentioning the use to which Hergé has put comic-strip techniques in his interminable *Tintin* stories. (Like Walt Disney in reverse these have now found their way on to film for television entertainment.) So far as they deploy ideas and

---

[1] This is, of course, reflected in the semantic changes in the word 'book'—no longer for many people just a printed volume complete in itself, but also a term applicable to any printed production not obviously a newspaper (e.g. the latest issues of *Beano* and *Woman's Realm* are equally with the *Hypnerotomachia Polyphili* books). (B.A.)

situations which are original and which truly catch-up the reader's attention they are worth careful investigation, but their impact fails all too rapidly from the sheer quantity of the production.

What example may we put before our children by way of an antidote, bearing in mind their love of absurd and comical and wildly knock-about goings on? What is the equivalent of the old Wild West sagas which gave my generation Cowboys and Indians? Alas, we possess little beyond our ancient and fine traditions which we carry about with us as a burden, an obligation, and a gift. We ought, however, to be able to draw some self-confidence from such riches. And even today figures still emerge from this fertile soil who can bear comparison in both word and image with those lively but frightening characters from the old Wild West.

Some of these characters are portrayed in this book as being European in the best sense of the word. They can hold their own completely against the American 'Superman', one of the most overwhelming figures of the American horror comic, possessed of limitless powers and a superiority over all natural elements and human contingencies. Others come from America herself and owe their creation perhaps to an internal revolt against the literature of violence. I am thinking here of Munro Leaf's bull Ferdinand, who contradicts all the rules of the comics by not fighting when he should have done, and there is also Roger Duvoisin's happy and peaceable little lion.

The subject of picture-stories, which has been so hotly contested on moral and artistic grounds, naturally has its positive aspects. The passion for pictures and for graphic representation is one of the characteristics of our times and it has given rise to many superb achievements, for example in the field of education or even of publicity. There ought to be many possibilities of using creatively this need which figures so prominently in the make-up of the modern child.

HERGÉ. *Tintin—The Secret of the Unicorn.* London, Methuen, 1959.

I know of one modern illustrator who has drawn countless picture-stories without any text at all. Their meaning is quite clear to children without the need for a lot of bubbles full of words disfiguring the drawings. Implicit in this there is the possibility which teachers might well adopt of supplying a fairly complicated story in pictures with a corresponding story in words, instead of the customary pictures illustrating a given written text.

On the other hand, I have myself tried the experiment of providing children of varying ages with a strip of paper four inches high and sixteen inches long and getting them to draw on it picture-stories of their own invention to illustrate stories which they have either had read to them or made up for themselves. The result was delightful and the children's participation was much more wholehearted than in other drawing exercises.

COMMENT

Wilhelm Busch appeared quite early on in Great Britain—*A bushel of merry thoughts* being published in 1868. In this, and in several other instances, only Busch's drawings were used with quite different verses. One edition, *The fools paradise*, 1883, even had prose captions added. *Max and Maurice* fared somewhat better and, in view of Mrs. Hürlimann's remarks about the American market, it may be noted that the first translation of this book, by C. T. Brookes, was published in Boston in 1871.

The only translations currently available also have an American imprint:

BUSCH, W.: *A bushel of merrythoughts*, translated by W. Harry Rogers. Dover Publications, 1968.

BUSCH, W.: *Hypocritical Helena plus plenty of other pleasures*, translated by H. A. and M. C. Klein. Dover Publications, 1962.
A bi-lingual edition.

BUSCH, W.: *Max and Moritz with many more mischief-makers more or less human or approximately animal*, translated by H. A. and M. C. Klein. Dover Publications, 1962.

BUSCH, W.: *Max and Maurice, the story of two rascals in seven pranks*, translated by Walter Roome. Montreal: Mansfield Book Mart, 1961.

14 POLITICS IN CHILDREN'S BOOKS

Political influence through classic children's books—modern children's books with political leanings—children's books and books for young people in the totalitarian states

Among all the occupations of this world, politics has been and is reckoned, rightly or wrongly, one of the questionable ones. Thus at first glance the notion of coupling politics with children and children's literature seems surprising. I found it so myself.

Then in the autumn of 1956, when the revolution broke out in Hungary, there came the enormous shock of reading how children aged anything from ten to sixteen themselves took part in the fighting. They hurled petrol bombs into tanks and risked not only their own lives but also sought cold-bloodedly to do away with others. Having learned this method of fighting in their youth groups they now turned it against their masters. It caused me to start asking myself just how far reading was responsible for this fact, which has seldom arisen in the past, that children are capable of killing. It is a question somewhat on the same lines as that which seeks to probe the responsibility of comic strips for the criminal deeds of the young.

I have found no answer to this question, but my preoccupation with it set me searching for the political elements in books for young people (that is to say, not just children's books but also those books for adults to which young people have laid a claim).

On the whole it must be said that, with a few exceptions which we will deal with soon, political influence through books is carried out with ethical intentions, even in the strongly biased political writing east of the Iron Curtain. It thereby distinguishes itself to a considerable degree from the commercially produced 'pop' and comic books which have had such a devastating influence on the youth of a good part of the world.

In the limited space of this book I can select only a few subjects and books from both past and present, and I would like to begin with a book which even after more than a hundred years still possesses a real value and which during this time has become a classic for young people.

Uncle Tom's cabin

This book is Harriet Beecher Stowe's novel *Uncle Tom's cabin*, which she herself adapted in a children's edition soon after its first appearance.

Elizabeth Harriet Beecher (Stowe was her married name) was born in Litchfield, Connecticut in 1811. Both of her parents came from long-established Colonial families and she grew up in a strongly intellectual and, of course, strictly religious community. She was brought up by her elder sister, who was a considerable woman on her own account and who ran a very forward-looking girls' school. Harriet started writing early in life and, living on the borders of a slave-owning state, she soon became acquainted with the slavery problem. The escape route to Canada led through her home town and many fleeing slaves were tended by the group which formed around Harriet Beecher Stowe; clothing was found for them, and money for the next stage of their journey.

Only some time later, in the backwater of a provincial town where her husband had been appointed professor in a seminary, did she recognize her religious-cum-political mission and she wrote her famous book, which was to have more importance in the fight over the Negro question than many other battles in the whole affair. *Uncle Tom's cabin* was first published in serial form, appearing as a book in 1852, when it had an immediate and an enormous success. The book was translated into at least twenty-four languages and delivered into the hands of its author an influence which she was to wield powerfully in her activities as a journalist. She also travelled to Europe in order to win support for her ideas from European, and especially English women.

Uncle Tom's cabin is the story of the Negro slave, Tom, who is happily placed with a kind master, but who has to be sold for financial reasons and thus enters the machinery of the slave trade. A whole set of interlocking destinies is introduced into the story and helps to make up a richly conceived book, tense and moving, learned, and full of abundant humanity. It appealed to children and adults alike, and when, at the end of the century, it had accomplished its task, it continued to live indestructibly as a book for children. Mrs. Beecher Stowe died at the age of eighty-five in 1896, and today Uncle Tom's base condition has been overcome by the Negroes themselves. Their powerlessness in the battle for equality has gone for good and although the struggle is still not finally over, a great deal of other literature for young people has come to take the place of *Uncle Tom's cabin*.

Red Indian books

Although they have been dealt with fully in Chapter 9, mention should be made of the strongly political background to the books on Red Indians, which right down to our own times have had the biggest appeal to European children. The ideas of Rousseau and the French Revolution between them

So ein kleines Kind ist der einzige echte Demokrat.

Tom hatte sich jetzt über seine äußere Stellung, wie es die Welt nennt, in Nichts zu beklagen.

STOWE, Harriet Beecher. *Onkel Toms Hütte.* Leipzig, 1853.
Anonymous wood-engraving for an early German edition.

N

awoke the conscience of humanity to the fact that in North America (as earlier in South America) the simple, indigenous peoples were being exterminated to make room for the overflowing population of Europe. The first idealistic tales about the Indians appeared in Europe round about 1800 (by Chateaubriand and Zschokke), but the loudest voices were raised in America herself by Longfellow and James Fenimore Cooper. The latter was a Romantic, but he had political interests and the life of his Leatherstocking contained a moving portrayal of the decline of certain Indian tribes. These hunting peoples, the children of nature, had to give way to the pioneering demands of young America in spite of all their bloody and, for their part anyway, heroic fighting.

At the time this struggle caught the attention of all thinking humanity, but especially the peoples of Europe. This led to a world-wide success and a far greater political influence for Cooper's books than he had ever bargained for. Everybody who could read, even the most unromantic, knew of Leatherstocking, the trapper who embodied the sore consciences of the whites and became the companion of the Indians in order to die among them. In his Indian hero, Chingachgook, the Old Serpent, he depicted the tragedy of the Indian downfall, a hunting nation sacrificed to fire-arms and fire-water.

It is a remarkable fact that the sufferings of a far distant and quite alien nation could become the emotional property of another continent and its children through a single author; it bears strong witness to the force and the potentialities which reside in books.

The social question

I should now like to turn to another partly political theme which runs like a red thread through the history of children's books, or books which young people have taken over. This is the social problem or, better, the appeal to feelings of social justice, which at least figure importantly in the hearts of children.

This new theme originated in England, where for the first time in history there were children whose daylight hours were spent in shoving carts down the galleries of coal-mines. And England produced the first literature to attack these conditions or to appeal to conscience through a moving portrayal of them.

One figure came to stand as a symbol for all this childish suffering, a symbol particularly likely to conquer the hearts of children—the figure of the chimney-sweep. Perhaps people saw in him some relationship with the Negro slaves, but in any case the little chimney-sweep very early on became an exceptionally successful symbol for those who wanted to fight against the social iniquities of child labour. It is possible that the poet and artist William Blake was the man responsible for the fact that this figure rather than a pit-boy should overcome the hearts of both children and adults. For at the end of the eigh-

176

teenth century Blake wrote movingly on this subject in his *Songs of innocence* (1789) and most bitterly in his *Songs of experience* (1794):

> When my mother died, I was very young,
> And my father sold me, while yet my tongue
> Could scarcely cry 'Weep! weep! weep! weep!'
> So your chimneys I sweep, and in soot I sleep.

This poem, which was not written simply for children, ends in the vision of a future in paradise. It thus offers a solution which is still beyond earthly attainment, a consolation that the Kingdom of Heaven shall be more easily attained by the poor.

In 1863 Charles Kingsley took up this theme again in the oddest fairy tale that there has ever been. This is *The water babies*—and its hero is just such another destitute little chimney-sweep, moving people to pity in the most unexpected way. Here also, however, the solution of the problem requires a transcendent consummation, but this has in no way hindered the fairy tale from becoming a classic which is still being brought out in new editions.

Lisa Tetzner, in one of the finest children's books of this century, *Die schwarzen Büder*, has also made use of the figure of the little sweep, forcing his way through narrow chimneys so that the fires may burn more brightly in the houses of the rich and the castles of the mighty. Her story, however, is set in Tessin, where the little boys hire themselves out to the Italians.

Yet another example of this symbolic character was met with a few years ago in Benjamin Britten's work for children, *Let's make an opera*, which was based on a true event in the sixties of the last century. On this occasion children themselves take steps to interrupt the fate of poor young Sam with the result that once again this old and apparently played-out subject was given a new intensity through the emotional power of Britten's music. (An adaptation of this as a children's book was made by Eric Crozier, the librettist, in 1962—*The story of Let's make an opera*, O.U.P. Music Dept.)

In Kingsley's time, of course, the subject was still a brutally actual one and the books on it were intended to have a political repercussion. The children who were made to work in this way were often sold or hired out by their parents or simply came from the workhouse. It was Dickens, before all other writers, who made it his duty to mount an attack on behalf of these defenceless children. His child characters are well known to everyone, with David Copperfield and Oliver Twist at their head. They confronted his adult readers (who were pretty soon joined by younger ones too) with the great social problems presented by the Industrial Revolution: the growth of cities and the status of children.

Literary fashion, which has alternately rated Dickens as a great author, or no author at all, has still not been able to prevent the fascination which his characters have exerted for generations of young people, forcing them to think for themselves. And Dickens himself wrote from close experience, for his father had spent years in a debtors' prison, and had doomed his son to a bitter childhood. In this context it is worth knowing that Dickens was a friend and comrade of the temperamentally entirely different Hans Christian Andersen. Andersen's perfect touch in portraying poverty is likewise the result of bitter experience as those who have wept over the fate of the little match-girl may witness. The problems of poverty and pity here transformed themselves into a pure poetry which no longer has anything at all to do with politics.

I should now like to deal with a book which was written for children with the intention of making them aware of political problems. This is the *Cuore* of de Amicis, next to *Pinocchio* the most famous Italian children's book there is. It appeared in 1886 and it portrays in a remarkable manner the experiences and the fate of a class of children in a government school in the Turin of that time. Italy was beginning to enjoy her new-won unity. A new boy from Calabria is put into a class in this Turin school. The teacher introduces him and says: 'Bear in mind what I am about to tell you. In order for it to be possible today for a child from Calabria to live in Turin, or a child from Turin to live in Calabria, our country has had to fight for fifty years and thirty thousand Italians have had to die. . . .'

The political concern of the book was first and foremost patriotic, although it also preached tolerance towards the differences within a nation. In this school class there are also poor children and cripples and in the course of all kinds of dramatic events the young reader learns without even realizing it a tolerance and a sense of sympathy and kindness towards others, especially the less fortunate. The whole thing is a rare example of how a book written with strongly moral, not to say political, intentions has retained a vital freshness and become a wonderfully warm-hearted classic in children's literature.

Among German-speaking peoples there are no books from that period which presented children with political ideals in this way, at least there are none which have survived. When I spoke of the Italian book as being a patriotic children's book I should also have added that in certain countries, especially France and Germany as a result of the Franco-Prussian War, the children's book could not escape from a narrow, chauvinistic nationalism. A true love of one's country does not have to express itself in an ugly narrowness, as *Cuore*, or such a delightful book as *The adventures of Nils*, demonstrate. But it is necessary to mention it, however briefly, in order to say that this kind of nationalism, allied to some extent with doctrines of militarism, seems to me to be wholly vanquished. Even its recent revival in Germany just before the Second World War now seems to belong to the distant past. The whole realm of children's books today is in the grip of a fanatical sense of world-wide goodwill. Children of almost every nation know through their reading at least as much of the good in other countries as they do of their own.

Cheap broadsheets have always been responsible for a certain amount of political indoctrination and enlightenment, especially in France (e.g. Epinal).

AMICIS, Edmondo de. *Heart, a book for boys*. London, 1903.
Cloth-board cover, blocked in colour and gilt, for the English translation by G. S. Godkin.

Plate XVI

. . . I never saw another butterfly. London, 1965.
One of the children's paintings made at Theresienstadt Concentration Camp, 1942–1944.

Plate XVII

But only today with writers like Erich Kästner, Lisa Tetzner, and Kurt Held has the political education of young people been made into an integral part of books. With Kästner, who set up a superb monument to city children in *Emil und die Detektive* (1929), the political element is only indirectly present, except in *Die Konferenz der Tiere*, which he wrote with Jella Lepman, where it is strongly marked.

Kästner says himself that children cannot be trained too early for their role as members of the state and of society. The stake which each individual has in the group and the group in each individual, a readiness to help, a spirit of enterprise, the war against injustice, such things as these form the themes of his stories for children. By their means he seeks both consciously and unconsciously to awaken a socio-political sense of responsibility. His books would not be his without their humour and their vivid plots, but they would never have penetrated into so many countries if they did not have this serious core which Kästner, like Dickens, discovered from his own youthful experiences.

Lisa Tetzner, on the other hand, sets out her political message without any camouflage. In her children's odyssey she portrays for the youth of today a whole chapter from the history of our times, a chapter which was and is, humanly speaking, the saddest ever. And she did this with great courage at a time when it was all burningly real and actually in the process of happening. In telling the story of the flight of a band of children, whom fate or race had deprived of their homeland, she does not take up a stance of direct accusation. With her superb pleasure in just telling the story she allows the fate of each one of her characters to pass before the reader, who has himself been spared their tribulations. It is scarcely conceivable that the children who came across this will ever, as adults, turn their hands to any similar deeds.

But Lisa Tetzner's series of books *Die Kinder aus Nr. 67* (nine volumes, 1933–49) is not just about persecution and homelessness; it is also about war. This she depicts as it is experienced by the defenceless, something which has perhaps never been done before in a book for children. Up till now war has largely been shown to them as a deceptively heroic affair. Now they learn of its horror. But at the end of the book the child-characters, Germans, French, Americans, Swiss, English, Swedish, together with three emigrant children, conclude an alliance among themselves in the firelight of the August festivals of Switzerland. It is an alliance without rules, headed only by the words of Pestalozzi: 'If we want the world to be a better place then we must ourselves do what we can to help.' You might say that it is a very unpolitical kind of political doctrine—but political it ultimately is. Lisa Tetzner has been and still is much berated, especially in Germany, her native land, but millions of children have read her books and have found in them things that most grown-ups would sooner keep quiet about because, understandably, they want to forget them. Today her books are influential politically, just as they will one day be valuable historically, and for this reason she finds herself in the same tradition as the courageous author of *Uncle Tom's cabin*.

Kurt Held plays a similar part in this branch of writing for young people, and since he was Lisa Tetzner's husband the unity of their outlook is scarcely surprising. But with him things are more dynamic, tougher, more masculine. Held, who was a product of the German youth movement, set his sights on youth and his two most exciting books, *Die rote Zora* (1941) and the four-volume children's novel *Giuseppe und Maria* (1955–6), show this most plainly.

While Lisa Tetzner portrays children from every social class and concerns herself with demolishing the barriers between these classes as well as between countries, Kurt Held creates his heroes from the refugee children. I see less in this of his politically destructive urge against the establishment, for which he has been much criticized, and more of his pleasure in laying bare the elements of good and evil, which are clearly to be seen here and from whose conflict he finally allows the good to triumph. Since the emphasis on kindness and reliability, on the demands of work and comradeship and readiness to help is so strongly marked in these books, embodied in such figures as Giuseppe and Ulisse, its effect on children who are in danger of never knowing these qualities is consequently very great. And even though these books are set in a politically tense atmosphere, they are not received by children as political tracts. Rather they are seen as thrilling accounts of a world of adventure where character, courage, and integrity win through in the end.

In this section I have mentioned only authors whose work I know in detail. Every reader will probably be able to augment this group with other books that he knows himself.[1] There is, however, one important feature which distinguishes the work of these authors from the hosts of other books for young people which deal with fairy tales, or nature, or everyday things and which are as necessary to us as our daily bread. This is their determination to tackle the problems which are imposed upon us by the order or disorder of our present-day world.

Politics in picture-books

Politics hardly play much part in picture-books, but I should like to indicate out of curiosity one or two books which, although intended for young children, can bear the weight of a profounder interpretation. For instance, who has never come across Munro Leaf's pacifist bull Ferdinand? A bull who conquered the hearts of everyone hungry for peace after the last murderous war. By his refusal as a prize bull to enter the bullring he became a symbol for the hatred of war. And now, since the idea of peace seems to have been adopted

---

[1] English readers may call to mind Ian Serraillier's *The silver sword* (Cape, 1956; Puffin Books, 1960) and the less well-known and less successful *Story of Peter Cronheim* by Kenneth Ambrose (Constable, 1962). (B.A.)

by the Communist countries too, Eastern Europe has been conquered by this delightful book, beautifully re-illustrated by the Pole Maria Orlowska.[1]

A second example, known to everyone, is that of King Babar, that typically French creation of the thirties, ruling his Welfare State for Elephants and beset at one stage by every kind of disaster. He (that is to say, his Kingdom personified) is pursued even in dreams by monsters with the names of: 'Lâcheté', 'Paresse', 'Ignorance', 'Mollesse', 'Bêtise', and 'Découragement'. But Babar's kingdom is not the France of 1933, the year when the first book appeared. Nor is it the France of today, but a never-never land where goodness triumphs and the king's nightmare ends with the entry of flying elephant-angels with such names as 'Courage', 'Travail', 'Éspoir', 'Bonté', 'Intelligence', 'Amour', and 'Savoir' driving the evil spirits away.

And is there any better parody of war than the battle between the elephants and the rhinoceroses when Babar, in a move to prevent unnecessary bloodshed, orders his hugest elephants forward, colours their tails red and paints huge eyes on their backsides, and caps the result with red and green wigs? In this get-up they bravely turn their backs to the enemy, who is at once terrified into retreat by the resultant ghoulish faces, and the scene ends with the terse comment: '*Le roi Babar est un grand général.*' Almost all the volumes of this picture-book series, which is perhaps the finest of our times, are full of such flashes of

---

[1] The emphasis that is laid on Ferdinand's peace mission can perhaps be better appreciated by recalling Jella Lepman's account of the distribution of the first German edition, given in her book *Die Kinderbuchbrücke* (Frankfurt-am-Main, 1964).

Soon after the end of the Second World War Mrs. Lepman entered Germany as 'Adviser for the cultural and educational rehabilitation of women and children in the American Zone'. With prodigious energy and perseverance she manoeuvred the authorities into accepting her contention that books were of paramount importance, and by July 1946 she had set up an International Exhibition of Children's Books which was to make a powerful impact on the morale of that shattered country.

For Christmas, 1946, the exhibition moved to Berlin. In the past organizers had frequently been worried by the constant demands from children to take away the exhibits and the Berlin visit only increased this problem. Then, pondering upon it one evening, Mrs. Lepman hit upon the plan of printing a special edition of *Ferdinand the bull*, which the children could have 'to put under their pillows'. With typical zeal she set about 'obtaining' paper (newsprint from the Berlin newspapers), organizing the printing and translating the text:

'The printers in Tempelhof churned out 30,000 copies for us in a single night and a few days before Christmas, with a sense of serenity rather like Ferdinand's, I stood at the entrance to the main exhibition hall with copies of his "book" under my arm. The children greeted it with rapture; they chortled over the pictures and almost in a daze they walked about staring at the pages.

'Ferdinand was a huge success—Robert Lawson and Munro Leaf should have been straight-away awarded the Nobel peace prize. The story soon got around the streets and squares of Berlin. We hardly had time to snap our fingers before the whole edition was gone and we were left without even a copy for the file. The result was that we had to go out and pay a lot of money to buy back a few copies on the black market, where *Ferdinand* had turned up as a highly desirable commodity.

' "And how did you get on over the copyright?" a publisher asked us later. The copyright? Yes, the copyright had been quite a simple matter—we had forgotten all about it.' (B.A.)

LEAF, M. *The Story of Ferdinand*. London, Hamilton, 1937.
Line illustration by Robert Lawson. Copyright 1936 by Munro Leaf and Robert Lawson, © 1964
by Munro Leaf and John W. Boyd.
By permission of The Viking Press, Inc.

wisdom which border upon political comment without imposing upon the
rules which govern successful picture-books.

I call to mind another political picture-book from the time of the Second
World War. It came from a Dutch refugee and was the story of two ducks,
Kwik and Kwak, who embodied the peaceful contentment of pre-war Holland
with her tulips, her cheeses, and her ships. But another tribe of ducks sweeping
down from the skies put them to flight. At the time of its publication it was a
political story that was all too real, but it was converted into a nursery tale
with so much good nature that the child who was looking at it, while he might
notice the touch of bitterness, would not find it hurtful.

Picture-books like these are the work of individual artists and West European picture-books are largely free from any general adoption of political

themes, apart that is from one or two attempts by the United Nations to influence picture-books. These carry all too obvious a political implication (such as the production, originally in America, of *A garden we planted together*). Even the fascists and the National Socialists avoided, with very few exceptions, any systematic political indoctrination at the picture-book level. Perhaps the foulest exception is the anti-semitic picture-book from the Stürmer-Verlag, the Nuremberg hell's kitchen of Julius Streicher: *Trau keinem Fuchs auf grüner Heid' und keinem Jud bei seinem Eid!* by Elvira Bauer (*Don't trust a fox or the promise of a Jew*). This book is the most horrifyingly sadistic document ever to be produced as a child's picture-book and the copy which I possess shows that its edition reached at least 70,000 copies. As a picture-book it is capable of making a profound impression and its poisonous seed could scarcely have failed to bear fruit. But in spite of its huge print number it has disappeared beneath the surface even more completely than Hitler's *Mein Kampf*. The children who once owned it, and some must ultimately have done so, are now adults of between twenty and thirty. When I think of my own childhood and how vivid my earliest memories of pictures remain then I tremble at the thought of these people for whom this picture-book may have been their first 'literary' experience.

This brings us on to Soviet children's books and to those books published east of the Iron Curtain under the influence of the Soviet Union.

Children's books in the Soviet Union

The Soviet Union was the first country to take over the control of book production by the state and one by one all the countries of the Eastern Bloc have followed suit. It should also be obvious that when the state pours enormous sums into a cultural project it is going to make the fullest use of the results which have cost so much.

Children's books take up some 14 per cent of the total book-production figures, but only a part of these are books of a socialist or political character or books of popular enlightenment. It is, however, worth noting that, for example in 1954 (a year for which I have exact figures), 177 titles were published in an average edition of 54,000 copies (not counting school editions and textbooks). The other 1,800-odd titles are so-called 'literary works' for children and young people, published in editions averaging 61,000 copies (giving a final total production of altogether nearly 100,000,000 books).[1] They are all, however, more or less direct expressions of the Soviet view of politics and we must therefore consider the Russian children's book as itself an important political weapon. Just how powerful the position of the State Publishing Company is in the education of children can easily be imagined when one takes into account the fact that a large percentage of the children's books of East Germany and the countries of the Eastern Bloc are connected with material of Russian origin.

[1] The print run for the first edition of a children's novel in Great Britain is rarely more than 5,000 copies. (B.A.)

In the dictatorships of the West—Germany and Italy and their subject countries—production matters were in no way systematically organized but tended to be controlled by censorship and by cutting paper supplies. In Russia, however, and in the course of time in almost all Communist states, this was something which was organized on rigid lines very early on. Right at the beginning of the development of the post-revolutionary children's book there stands the towering and, in his own way, ideally disposed personality of Maxim Gorky. He is the father of Soviet children's books and of their complete centralization under the state, even though his own very individualist approach, not to mention his curious exile from 1921–28, make him anything but a cog-wheel of bureaucracy. A description of the planning which preceded the founding of the State Publishing Company in 1933 will, however, take us too much out of our way.

I should nevertheless like to quote in chronological sequence some typical and very revealing passages from Maxim Gorky's seminal book *On children's literature*:[1]

1916 (from a letter to Romain Rolland):[2]

'Dear and honoured comrade Romain Rolland,

May I entreat you to write a biography of Beethoven for children . . . At the same time I am turning to H. G. Wells for a biography of Edison; Fridtjof Nansen is submitting a *Life of Christopher Columbus* and I am myself writing *The life of Garibaldi* . . . , etc. With the aid of the best writers of our time I should like to produce a number of children's books which shall contain accounts of the lives of great men the world over. I myself will undertake the publishing of all these books.

'You know that in this age of ours nobody needs our attention more than the children. We grown-ups have put by a grievous inheritance for them. Once we have gone we shall leave behind a dismal kind of life for them. This stupid war bears eloquent witness to our moral weakness and the collapse of

[1] This book was published in Berlin in 1953 by the Verlag Neues Leben under the title *Über Kinderliteratur*. It consists of a collection of essays, speeches, and letters by Gorky on the theme of children's books edited originally in Russian by N. Medwedjew with the title: О детской литературе. There is no equivalent collection in English and translations of Gorky's numerous essays, letters, and speeches must be sought in a number of scattered publications, the most useful for our purpose being *On literature* (translated by Julius Katzer and Ivy Litvinov, Moscow, 1960). In reading Gorky's later pronouncements here, though, it is as well to bear in mind the words of a recent writer (Richard Hare in *Maxim Gorky*, Oxford, 1962) that 'it seems that Gorky also signed many articles, drafted or rewritten for him by the Party editors'.
Because of the difficulties of discovering all the sources of the following passages and suitable English counterparts, the translations are from the German version and not direct from the Russian. (B.A.)
[2] A letter to Wells was sent at the same time in much the same terms (see *On Literature*), and Gorky mentions here that the children's publishing house has been organized by two of his friends, Alexander Tikhonov and Ivan Ladyzhnikov. He also asks Wells for the names of colleagues who might tackle biographies of Dickens, Byron, and Shelley. (B.A.)

our culture. Therefore we ought to remind our children at least that people were not always so wicked as alas! we are today. We ought to impress upon them that there have been and still are great men and noble hearts in every nation! This must be done now, straight away, in these times of bestiality and the triumph of brutishness. I entreat you passionately, dear Romain Rolland, to write this *Life of Beethoven*, for I am certain that none will write it better . . .

'The one thing you must tell a child so that he understands it before everything else is this: Humanity must be looked upon as a single, world-wide family, which must always be drawing towards a closer unity in the struggle for improvement which is common to all its members.

'I am convinced that it would be enormously useful to young people making a start in literature if they were to make themselves familiar with fairy stories and folk-tales. I am not the only one who has been struck by the way that most of our young people prostrate themselves before reality, copy it almost photographically in verse and prose, turn it into something frigid, when our age demands pathos and a passionate irony . . .'

From the essay 'On people without any sense of responsibility and on the children's books of our age', written round about 1932:
'The scientist who examines micro-organisms and thereby discovers the sources of disease in the human system is carrying out the same work as the writer who, by studying and observing reality, discovers the parasites, that is to say, the people who hinder or destroy in one way or another the normal development of the "social organism". . .

'I maintain that one must talk to children "jokingly". . .

'The first ideas about the solar system, about our planet and its lands and peoples should be implanted through play and playthings. These are some of the widely varying conceptions of the one matter of central importance: how to bring children up to be socialists in a state which is successfully seeking to organize itself according to socialist principles, but which has not yet achieved this aim completely. Today's children must one day complete this organization, these children who live a life of contradictory circumstances which require them to conduct uninterruptedly a series of little daily battles on behalf of socialism against the giant of individualism, a giant who has been fattened over hundreds and indeed thousands of years. This is something which we should always bear in mind. . .

'I maintain that children should be told about the fearful crimes of Krupp and Thyssen in a calm way so that we arouse in them scorn and repugnance against these crimes but not fear of them. To be sure class hatred should grow from an inner aversion to the enemy, in whom one should see the creature of a lower order. It should not spring from any fear of the power of his cold-heartedness and his brutality, such as a sentimental "children's literature" had, albeit unknowingly, created before the revolution. This was a literature which was quite incapable of introducing such a death-dealing weapon as mockery.

'The story of great discoveries and inventions should be set down for children with a light and jocular touch. As a truly human story it embraces very many tragedies, but it also contains many examples of the ridiculous, of crankishness and the repulsive stinginess of the ruling classes.

'Children should learn and know how human idiocy has sought for centuries to maintain its personal welfare and thereby delayed the progress of human culture as a whole; it has even hindered the cultural development of the ruling idiots themselves . . .

'Social vices must be shown up for the repugnant and ridiculous disfigurements which they are by the light touch of satire. If you preach to children in a didactic tone you will arouse in them boredom and opposition to the theme of your sermon . . .

'Children have a natural disposition for the brilliant and the unusual. But for us in the Soviet Union the new thing that is brightest and most extraordinary is that which has been created by the revolutionary power of the working-classes. This is the object on which we must focus the attention of our children, the object which must provide the chief material for their social education.'

1931 (from a critical article):
'We really know nothing about the life of the young pioneer workers. Four of them came to see me today and one was an Englishman.

'We got into conversation and indeed they are already perfectly mature people—they have been working and have built a dam on a collective, thus saving the state a few thousand roubles. Yes—it would be a most interesting exercise to get hold of some young lads like these and show them off a bit.

'I have just been to the Exhibition of Children's Books. What a lamentable affair! What you see there corresponds neither to what we are capable of nor to the demands which are made of books today. For instance, there is a total lack of literature aimed at younger schoolchildren. To some extent this is because we have no really clear or comprehensive critical standards for children's literature, but it is also because criticism in this field is putting fetters on imagination, not understanding how important the development of imagination is for children and how important it is to guide the course of this development correctly.'

1933:
'We teach our seven- and eight-year-olds how to read and write, but there is nothing there for them to read. Each year the literate population grows by hundreds of thousands, but there are no books for them.

'No matter what its value was, the bourgeois literature for children before the revolution at least gave them a certain idea of the world: fairy stories and picture-books for the younger ones, stories and tales for the older, either original or translated.

'It is important to write books—not just one, but several—in which it can be shown how much physics and chemistry have already done for people and how much they can do for us in the circumstances of socialist reconstruction.

. . . Now you would not think that all children's books without exception should be vehicles for conveying knowledge. Our books do not have to be instructional or baldly tendentious. They should use pictures, become works of art. Furthermore, we want books that say what they have to say in an enjoyable manner, so that children develop a sense of humour. We must create some new comic characters to be the heroes of a series of children's books.

'Pre-revolutionary Russian literature covers a period of about 150 years. The Soviet children's book is only a tenth as old. It is impossible for there to be a sufficient range of books yet to answer all the questions that are being asked, to interest the child as he gets to know the world.

'1. Such editions can only be prepared by a special publishing house for children's literature: Detgis.

'2. This publishing house must have control of a competent and dedicated staff and also of its own finance.

'3. A factory should be prepared for the publisher where the paper and boards necessary to handsomely produce children's books can be manufactured; what is more, the publisher should have a decently equipped printing office and a workshop for display materials.

'It is time that the question of children's literature was taken up as a serious and important one just as here in the country of the soviets, all big questions are taken up which demand a rapid solution.'

The ethos of work and achievement played a great part in Gorky's ideas about children's literature. Without work nothing was possible:

'When our children enter a new world, a world of work, liberated by technological improvements, in a classless society, then they shall know the enormous significance of physical labour.'

From this he passes on to religion and mysticism:

'The oldest myths did not recognize any gods who were not also masters of a craft. That which people designate the religious creation of primitive man, was basically an artistic creation, without any trace of mysticism. Mysticism only forced its way in when the individual for one reason or another parted company with society and began to realize the senselessness of his existence, his powerlessness compared with nature, or with the might of the collective— the collective, which demanded and had to demand from each individual his complete submission to the work in hand. It will scarcely be possible to grasp that the original tribe has suffered all sorts of slothful hangers-on to breed in its midst, rejecting their part in the work of defending or foraging for the community. Such people should probably have been extirpated. . . .

'In their anxiety for the interest on their capital the individualists hit on the idea (of religion), while they represented it to the workers as profound wisdom, as a supra-rational penetration into secrets, which were hidden from the light of ordinary comprehension. It is highly probable that the founders of mystical religion, the organizers of religious cults and the priests, were just such revolting crooks and perverted creatures.'

Maxim Gorky then proceeds with this purely negative interpretation of religious phenomena with some sharp words on Christianity. A further and more important duty for the State Publishing House he sees as being the production of history books which may explain the origin of private wealth, and such books as might condemn the remains of the property concept which was still present even in the Soviet state.

A famous educational theorist and politician following in Gorky's footsteps, Kalinin, has also set down some principles which count in the preparation of children's books. They are given in his book which appeared in Britain in 1950 under the title of *On Communist education*. They number among them love for one's people, love for the working-classes, honesty, courage, comradeship, and love of work itself.

That which was demanded by Gorky and his circle: a children's literature prepared according to a specific point of view, has taken shape. Regardless of one's opinion of their doctrines this represents an enormous achievement in a country where formerly only a minute proportion of young people were literate. Moreover, studying this Russian literature for young people in detail (a thing which I must admit I could only do through German editions) it is possible to establish that these postulates, enunciated in the early years of the Soviet state by one of the Communist movement's great idealists, have been extensively realized.

Religion has disappeared completely from children's books.

The only unrealistic element in children's literature is the folk and fairy tale, to which Gorky attached so much importance.

The creed of work, in the present and in the past, is propounded with great seriousness, taking the place of religion (although during the Second World War patriotism, courage, and a willingness to make great sacrifices were given a similar importance).

But Gorky was a man of great humanity who loved and understood children and the things which he deemed so important—humour, comedy, popular imagination—are disappearing more and more from view the farther that he is left behind. Gorky's great affection for the children of the workers, which gave a gloss of idealism to his purely materialistic philosophy, has necessarily become at times empty and dull in the hands, or through the pens, of creatures who are too much in bondage. Those books which portray the lives of exemplary young pioneers or youthful workers and war heroes, often have a suspicious likeness to the ponderous morality of nineteenth-century children's literature which Gorky so violently repudiated. But while our old children's books were steeped in a gently sentimental religious pietism, these present Marxist materialism in a get-up which is designed to appeal to the credulity of youth.

Russian stories

In order not to advance theories on paper alone, I have with a deal of effort examined a lot of these books for young people and taken a good look into the faces of the young pioneers who figure so largely in them. The stories by the best Russian children's authors show us an exciting and extremely vivid world in full spate. Good, bad, and downright wicked children are there, together with pranks, deceits, foolishness, prodigious industry and heroism, duty and the neglect of duty. Adventure and instruction are there, together with political education and wild fabrications of history. In these, the best of the books for young people, there can be found more of the ideals of Communism (which perhaps all of us have been fascinated by at one time or another) than one can otherwise find in the life of the Soviet countries. What separates it from the corresponding literature of the West proceeds straight from Gorky's principles and can be confirmed in reading. It is something difficult to summarize briefly. For the children's author is a part of the Soviet educational system and its principles and he has no aim beyond spurring on the individual in the service of the fuller development of the community. All the didacticism, all the action, even the most adventurous and exciting, contributes eventually to this main stream. The thirst for knowledge and the will to work are two further important factors influencing the youthful department of a youthful state, which has placed absolutely everything at its own disposal. In this sense, therefore, all Soviet books are political ones, with the exception of the books of fairy tales. Even the picture-books play their part.

To establish where the difference lies between these and the best and most famous of our own children's books, does not properly belong to this chapter, and to give a true explanation of it, it is necessary to touch upon matters of some profundity. The rich literary traditions of the West, which are chiefly religious where children's books are concerned, do not expend themselves entirely on a world of visible, materially ascertainable facts. Affairs of the imagination, dreams, fantasies, the elemental forces which are latent in every child, are also the motive power behind the heroes of our finest children's books—to say nothing of the instinct for play, which has no utilitarian value at all.

Although she caused a lot of argument when she first appeared, a modern children's heroine like little Swedish *Pippi Longstocking*, who is probably known to most children in the Western world, is undoubtedly a striking antithesis to those eminently reasonable pioneer boys and girls who people the Russian children's books. She has her apparently senseless world of fantasy, her natural good humour, her playfulness, and her suitcase full of gold, while they are good, anxious to learn, enterprising and loyal to their duty, but not on account of any inner compulsion or for the sake of an ideal, an almost religious. transcendental command, but rather in the struggle for a better world in a clearly defined and material sense. This political directive, which even includes books intended for amusement, shuts out almost all humour and if it once does get in, as with the Italian *Il romanzo di Cipollino* by Gianni Rodari, then it almost turns into satire.

Without doubt children need some education in the structure of politics and one or two books which propagate this (in the best Western sense) are fine and well worth having. But to lump all children's literature under this denominator is dangerous, for we do not finally want to breed little citizens, little comrades, little pioneers, in miniature, but just children. Not for nothing have we come to recognize over the centuries that childhood is a state all to itself and not simply the first stage of adulthood. Turning children's books into political tracts, however, as now occurs in the East, once more disturbs this individuality which had been won for children and leads ultimately to what happened in Hungary. But, before reciting the customary phrases on these matters, anyone who wishes to get a closer understanding of this material should read some of the books for young people which have originated in Russia, of which the best have also appeared in East Germany. He should also look into the faces of these serious, industrious children, who believe that they are building a new world. He will discover that the problem is not such a simple one as those who see it simply in black and white would have us believe.

I have intentionally confined myself here to the situation in Russia, for Russia is the source which feeds developments in other Communist countries. Even Chinese children's books seem to tone in to the same key. But despite their basic tenets, which are foreign and indeed inimical to us, all these books are subservient to what is at the bottom a purely materialistic ethical attitude.

Let us, therefore, be grateful for the many enjoyable children's authors and illustrators in the Western world who are and will remain individualists, even if 'the little child Socialism' tries to start fighting a fanatical war against the stupid giant 'Individualism', as Gorky so graphically asks it to do. If, but only if, these authors, these stupid 'giants', and their books are good then they will probably help to educate better future citizens than those who get nothing but books written consciously with a single political aim in mind, no matter how fine and noble the intention behind each one of them may be.

Latest developments in Germany; mastering the past; the conquest of anti-Semitism

A closer look at literary production for children in Germany reveals beyond dispute that a notable change has taken place since the first appearance of this

DOMJAN, J. *Ungarische Legende*. Zürich, 1958.
Children in the Hungarian Revolution of 1956, described in an illustrated book for children.

book in 1959. It is only a few years ago that a group of young people at a public discussion in Munich deplored that there were no literary sources which could enlighten them about the events of the recent past. They wanted to know the truth about their fathers and about the reasons for the ticklish position which they, the German youth of today, found themselves to be in. Since then they have been presented with books which give a great deal of the truth of the situation and they have even been supplied with an unvarnished account of Hitler's life (Klose: *Adolf Hitler, ein Bericht für junge Menschen*).

Serious attempts grow ever more frequent to square up to the past in a way which will answer the questions of young people like these. H. G. Noack's book *Stern über der Mauer* (1962) is such an attempt, just as other books of this author carry a message of tolerance for those of another nation or of another colour (*Hautfarbe Nebensache*, 1960 and *Das grosse Lager*, 1960).

But this kind of literature is still in its early days. Its didactic intentions, though good, are too obvious for it to be classified as real literature. But the mere presence of these explanations, for which the young people in Munich were waiting, is encouraging. Their place, however, lies in the history of books for adolescents which this book on children's books can only touch on in passing.

Unfortunately it cannot be denied that next door to these serious explanations of the past another kind of literature on the subject is asserting its place. These are the books stuffed full of jingoism and the tales of military heroism: crude soldier stories, thrilling exploits in the air, the vengeful sinking of ships. Whether they are cheap booklets or books got up to look important, these stories are devoured in improbably large quantities by children over the age of ten and they play an even greater part in their reading than the notorious comics. To some extent, perhaps, they take the place of the old Red Indian shockers and serve the same purpose of stimulating the pseudo-heroic feelings of youth.

This same youthful audience, however, stands aghast at the documentary evidence of a book like *The diary of Anne Frank* (first published as *Het Achterhuis*, Amsterdam, 1947). A document like this has achieved more than political re-education ever could. Its appearance has a significance similar to those books of the nineteenth century which introduced political motives: *Deerslayer* and *Uncle Tom's cabin*. Both in print and on the stage Anne Frank opened the ears of young people to what other books had to say and then made them listen. Those who were quite untouched by re-education were deeply affected by these records of actual events. Anne Frank's fairy story *Blurry* and her *Stories from the house behind* are evidence enough of the vitality of spirit which was shown in such a tragic light in the diary.

Other books which belong with documents of this kind are *Das Tagebuch des David Rubinowicz*, the notebooks of a young boy, and a book which appeared first in Czechoslovakia: *Theresienstadt 1942–44*. This is a collection of poems and drawings by children which were discovered in the concentration camp after the war and were published in Prague by the Jüdisches Staatsmuseum (1959). Hardly any of the authors of this book are alive today.

The last page of the book is a poem by an unknown child:

Dort der Arme steht vergeblich	The poor thing stands there vainly.
und vergeblich ist sein Schrein.	Vainly he strains his voice.
Vielleicht stirbt er. Und nun weisst du,	Perhaps he'll die. Then can you say, How beautiful is the world today?
wie die Welt so schön könnt' sein.	

(From *I never saw another butterfly*)

This is, of course, no book for children, but its sense of the irrevocable and its documentary truth—signed and sealed by death—contain the material for a host of books on the fate of children.

An authoress from Holland has used her own experience in setting down for children in an admirable book the tragedy of the children who were Jews (Clara Asscher Pinkhoff: *Sterrekinderen* or *Children of the yellow star*). The book appeared in German in 1961 and gained the German children's book award of that year—a remarkable sign of change. The very moving effect of the book is accentuated by its refusal to make any direct accusations or to give rein to any feeling of hatred. In *Tirtsa* the same writer portrays something of present-day Judaism and indicates at the same time a way out from the misery of the past.

Another book in this category is Leonard de Vries's *Chawerim* (1955) which is the story of a boy from Holland who succeeds in escaping to Israel and there takes part in the arduous task of building a homeland for his persecuted nation. In contrast to the previously mentioned documentary compilations, books like these can be read quite comfortably by older children.

Of course, the problems of Judaism in Germany and of the establishment of Socialism in Eastern Europe are not the only ones that find their way into children's stories. There is also the whole question of the German past and there are problems of a more general nature, such as the racial conflict between black and white, exemplified in Catherine Marshall's *Julie's heritage* (1960). Or there is the Far East, magnificently portrayed by Meindert de Jong in his story *The house of sixty fathers* (1956). De Jong, moreover, is a special case. He offers us a real children's book which lacks neither horror nor humour nor poetry. It is the odyssey of a little boy who saves both himself and his little pig from the dangers of the Japanese invasion. Political and didactic motives are concealed within the story alongside its strong feeling for humanity.

The Austrian Karl Bruckner has tried to do something similar in his beautiful book *Sadako will leben*, in which he tells of the life and death of a little girl in Hiroshima. Without any direct political motive he thereby drags the atomic question into the child's field of vision.

I have introduced these scattered examples in order to show that children's books which are 'committed', as they are throughout Eastern Europe, are beginning to play a part here, even though they betoken something quite different. The future will show us if a branch of literature in its own right can develop from this as it has done to some extent in America. But at the moment it is still too early to pass a fully considered judgement.

BOOK LIST

The important books by Lisa Tetzner and Clara Pinkhoff have not been translated into English, but translations of other books mentioned are:

BRUCKNER, Karl: *The day of the bomb*, translated by Frances Lobb. Hale, 1966.

DE VRIES, Leonard: *The land is bright*, translated by Lawrence Wolfe. Dobson (London), 1964.

FRANK, Anne: *The diary of a young girl*, translated from the Dutch by B. M. Mooyaart, Doubleday, 1954.

FRANK, Anne: *Tales from the house behind: fables, personal reminiscences and short stories*, with drawings by Peter Spier. Barntam, 1962.

HELD, Kurt: Giuseppe, translated by Ray Ockenden, illustrated by Audrey Smith. Constable (London), 1963.

. . . I never saw another butterfly . . . Children's drawings and poems from Theresienstadt Concentration Camp, 1942–44. McGraw-Hill, 1965.

KÄSTNER, Erich: *The animals' conference*, from an idea by Jella Lepman, translated by Zita de Schauensee, illustrated by Walter Trier. McKay, 1953.

15 JEAN DE BRUNHOFF
and the benevolent monarchy of King Babar

Before I deal with the painter Jean de Brunhoff it is most necessary for me to introduce those readers who have never met him to Babar, King of the Elephants, whose realm belongs not to this world but to that of the huge picture-books which are the delight of almost every child who knows them.[1]

Babar first saw the light of day in 1931, a time when it was regarded as progressive to show children animals as they actually are in real life. Cats wearing little pointed caps and hares in leather breeches were abhorred, however much unprincipled children might take delight in them in secret. And then, in the middle of all these admittedly well-meaning and most necessary efforts, there suddenly stomped in this elephant Babar. At first, indeed, he was only a poor, naked little orphan elephant, but before long he became a respectably clad citizen, walking around on two legs, occupying (with great dignity) an ordinary bed, travelling in ships, cars, and aeroplanes, and eventually, when fate brought him to the kingship of the land of the elephants, deciding to rule his realm 'according to human principles'.

This Babar, mad for civilization, is something of an anachronism in our world-weary time; at the same time, however, he is a wonderfully inspiring example. For as an elephant he approaches the achievements of civilization with all the innocence of an animal. Those children who take such delight in the adventures of an enterprising elephant partake without realizing it in the evolution of an ideal society.

As a young elephant, Babar is directed to a human city and is adopted by an old lady with a pointed nose, herself an uncommon enough figure in a

[1] 'Huge picture-books' is now a misnomer. The economics of modern book production do not allow the liberality in picture-books that the lavish, but delicately coloured, 'old' Babar books enjoyed. So, along with Orlando and Little Tim, Babar has been cut down to standard size. The delight he gives to children may not be lessened, but it is a loss for those with a taste for truly distinguished picture-books. (B.A.)

children's book. Throughout all the books she simply remains '*la vieille dame*' and she represents the positive aspect of humanity. After turning her great awkward visitor from the primeval forest into a well-dressed and upright future king, she assists him to return to the land of the elephants. Later on he brings her to his own country and it is she who gives fresh heart to him at a time when his state is taking on too much of the character of a self-satisfied welfare-state. This is the occasion, mentioned in the last chapter, when Babar is visited by nightmares. After they have finally been dispelled by the triumphant elephant angels it is the old lady who adjures the king: '*Travaillons avec gaieté et nous continuerons d'être heureux.*'

This is only a single incident in the story. People have not often made the attempt of sneaking political ideas into books for such young children. Erich Kästner and Jella Lepman tried it out with some success in their *Konferenz der Tiere* (1949), but without Brunhoff's air of wide-eyed innocence. Political didacticism is so neatly camouflaged in his books that it goes unnoticed in the welter of comic and exciting incidents which unfold themselves before the child's eyes in huge, expressive pictures.

The artistic value of these pictures is a high one. Turn, for instance, to pages 6 and 7 of *Le voyage de Babar*, where the balloon journey of the royal bride and her bridegroom is set out. The whole thing is reminiscent of a fine Japanese woodcut; and if one considers pages 16 to 19 in the same volume, preferably with a child beside one, then one can only marvel at the artistic daring with which such elementary things as water and isolation and the arrival of the rescuing ship are presented. An extreme directness of language, such as is usually only achieved by children, is here united with an artistic perfection which was and is rarely found not only in children's books but also in modern graphic art. In this Brunhoff has been a guiding and an animating influence and even if his early death has prevented his genius from creating other works in a similar vein, it is certain that many fine children's books of the present day would never have appeared if these books of his had not shown the way—even down to the excellence of their printing.

But it is now necessary to enter a word or two about Brunhoff's life and personality, after which I shall try to show what is for children the most wonderful thing about these books, a thing even more difficult to put into 'adult' words than what I have written above.

Jean de Brunhoff was born in 1899 and spent his childhood in Paris, where he went to the 'École Alsacienne'. He was called up in the last year of the First World War, but had scarcely reached the front when the war ended. '*Babar est un grand général. La guerre est finie! Ah! Quel bonheur!*'—that is how he described it later after that magnificently ironic battle-scene when the elephants painted fearful faces on their hindquarters and then, by walking backwards, routed the enemy rhinoceroses 'without a shot being fired'. There is the same '*bonheur*' about the end of this war as the young Brunhoff must earlier have experienced.

Jean de Brunhoff (Photo. Schall, Paris)

Plate XVIII

He changed his uniform for a painter's smock and his rifle for a paint-brush. His brother, Michel de Brunhoff, who later administered his artistic estate, said of his artistic activity at that time: '*Sa peinture était très classique, mais tous ses tableaux, natures mortes, paysages, etc., montraient un talent de coloriste raffiné, tout à fait personnel et très agréable.*' That all sounds very satisfactory, but it indicates nothing at all of the singular gifts which were to show themselves later in his books and turn him into a world-famous figure.

In 1924 the painter married a young pianist—one who, like himself, came from a cultured family. His wife, Cécile Sabourand, presented him within a couple of years with two sons, but the young father had soon to leave his family, compelled by a disease of the lungs to spend much of the rest of his life in a mountain resort in distant Switzerland.

His wife loved to tell the children stories which went on from evening to evening, especially when they were ill. King Babar was the hero of one such story, which had its origins in the close-knit family life of the Brunhoffs. Here was his true birthplace, within the circle of a warm-hearted family.

Babar probably took on a pictorial form for the first time in the drawings which Jean de Brunhoff made for his distant sons. There in the Swiss sani-torium the drawings were seen by his attentive brother Michel, who as chief editor for *Le jardin des modes*, had an eye for things out of the ordinary. He encouraged Jean, who suffered much from his enforced idleness, to make them into a book and in this way, a few weeks later, there arrived in Paris a complete first draft. This *L'histoire de Babar*, was published in 1931 by *Le jardin des modes* and, in spite of an extraordinarily high price, it was a great success. In 1932 there appeared *Le voyage de Babar* and in 1933 *Le roi Babar*.

The fourth volume saw a change of publisher. In 1934 Hachette issued *Les vacances de Zéphir*, one of the most enchanting books of the series. Then in 1938 there came *Babar en famille*, the most intimate and charming of the books, and although the draft of *Babar et le Père Noël* had been made in 1936, it was only to appear in 1941.

In 1935 Brunhoff's youngest son was born. These last two volumes, and especially *Babar en famille*, reflect a family life of such warm-heartedness, without becoming sentimental, that it is necessary to go back to Larsson's *Ett hem* to find a comparable intensity of feeling translated into form and colour.

The artist had died a year before the appearance of this, the most radiant of all the Babar books (and to prove it you have only to look at the big centre spread with Babar lying on his tummy balancing his smallest son Pom on his trunk, while '*la vieille dame*' plays the flute and Cornelius, the wise chief-minister, gives little Alexandre a swing on a seat suspended from his two great tusks). In 1937, at the age of thirty-eight, Jean de Brunhoff died, leaving his wife alone with three small sons of whom the eldest, Laurent, was to become a painter like his father and, akin to him, was to give French children the pleasure of seeing his work continued.

197

The second son, Mathieu, is today a children's doctor and the third, Thierry, is a budding young pianist. Despite the early loss of their father, these boys had a good upbringing and there always remained for them their picture-book father, Father Babar, who knew how to chase out the evil demons of laziness and greed, stupidity and anger, replacing them by the kindly winged spirits of goodness, knowledge, prudence, courage, and patience.

The reason for this brief biography of Jean de Brunhoff is that his life is inseparable from his books. For although these stories were mostly written in the mountains of Switzerland and although they deal with elephants living in the wastes of Africa, they are entirely French in the fullest and finest meaning of the word. They contain all the lovable aspects of the world of France, translated to a world of animals—a fact which doubles their success with children, who like humanized animals more than anything. You have only to walk with the elephants in their pleasure-grounds—the Versailles of this animal state—or visit their theatre with its bejewelled audience and its carya-tids in the form of sculptured elephants; you have only to listen while little Arthur, the king's nephew, and Zéphir the monkey play Mozart trios with the old lady at the piano, the royal couple watching them with wonderment and then afterwards sending them to the '*pâtissier*' to choose as many cakes as they like; or you have only to go fishing with Babar, or riding on a round-about, or taking the salute at a parade, in all these manifold aspects he remains a French *père de famille* whose company it is always a pleasure to share.

'*La vieille dame*' is a sublime and, as I have already said, a singular figure in children's literature. Her delicate and fragile appearance is enormously effective beside that of the huge, fat elephants and it is the climax of the series when she is almost killed by a snake-bite. It is the moment when the demons appear to Babar, as I have already described, and it is followed by one of the most moving pictures when the little white-haired lady in her dressing-gown comes from the 'hospital' to greet her king and his chief-minister Cornelius with open arms.

The other character to delight children so much is Zéphir the little monkey. He belongs to the old lady, but often appears separately. One volume, *Les vacances de Zéphir*, is devoted solely to him. No child is likely to forget quickly the monkey colony with its tree-houses. Or again the night scene at the bed-room window, although drawn with an economical and expressive poetry, might well lapse into sentimentality on the arrival of the nightingale. But the text ensures that this remains a children's picture-book, for when Zéphir hears the nightingale singing, we are told: '*Joyeux il se lève, court à la fenêtre et s'écrie: "Salut mon vieux!"*'

This book also contains the scene with the little mermaid Eléonore, whom he catches in his net and then lets go again. Both pictures and text are full of especially happy inspirations and there are moments (particularly this one) which have a genuine fairy-tale ring to them. The little mermaid Eléonore is only a tiny 'extra' among all the characters who people these books so abundantly, but she is a portent of the fresh imaginative powers that the artist Jean de Brunhoff might have been able to exercise if he had been spared to devote himself to the things of this world.

This he could not do, but it is perhaps timely to bear in mind here the phenomenon, unusual today, of a son continuing the work of his father.

Laurent de Brunhoff

We scarcely dared believe our eyes when, in 1946, from a hungry Paris there appeared a new Babar book: *Babar et ce coquin d'Arthur*—a story which right from the start has Arthur for its '*enfant terrible*'.

It was obvious that there would be indications of weakness in the work of the twenty-year-old son of the painter and naturally these weaknesses are present. Consider the boldness and the painterly freedom with which Brunhoff *père* represented nature in, say, the trees, or the waves of the sea, or the attitudes of the animals (as an example of which you need only study the pictures on the middle pages of *Babar en famille*, when little Alexandre falls into the squirrel's tree, and then compare them with the somewhat conventional trees and, above all, the general lack of landscape in *Babar et ce coquin d'Arthur*). The numerous weaknesses which such a comparison showed in the son were not eradicated when *Pique-Nique chez Babar* appeared three years later—a volume which still fell short of his father's perfection.

Nevertheless, *Babar et ce coquin d'Arthur* quickly became one of my own son's special favourites. If the young Parisian's trees had somewhat the appearance of stage-property, he still had a mastery over the world of vehicles and indeed invented some which are a particular delight to all children. The railway on pages 4 and 5 of *Babar et ce coquin d'Arthur* is unforgettable, with the children travelling in a special train on wires above the train with the adults in. All the scenes with aircraft and parachute jumps in them are marvellously observed and the little forest track is quite charming with the monkeys jumping down on to it from the trees. It is still almost a boy's heart here, letting itself go with boyish dreams, but the result still lacks a quality which gives the first five volumes an almost indescribable magic for us grown-ups. Perhaps it was the gaiety of the dying painter, who lived so close to sadness, coupled with the tenderness of the young husband who put all his best into a simple children's book.

Children are not worried about that. Laurent the son gave them much pleasure in continuing his father's work with so much of his own fancy. It is therefore the more regrettable that the books by the son have proliferated to such an extent that they threaten to overwhelm the so much more delicate and poetic work of the father. This inventive young man would surely do better to turn his talents to some new subject.

The sagas of Babar, king of the elephants, will belong to the daily fare of the nursery for many generations to come, even though perhaps not to the same degree everywhere. The heart of every child nurtures seeds of good and evil and certain barbaric books and magazines, however harmless their appearance, have the quality of fostering the evil seeds. But only the good shall grow under Babar's majestic rule.

BOOK LIST

BRUNHOFF, Jean de: *The story of Babar the little elephant*, with a preface by A. A. Milne. Random House, 1937.

The rest of the Babar books are also published by Random House: *The travels of Babar* (1937); *Babar the king* (1937); *Babar and Zephir* (1942); *Babar and his children* (1938). *Babar and Father Christmas* (1940) seems to have been published in England, by Methuen, a year earlier than in France. In 1941 Methuen issued *The Babar story-book*. Its six chapters by Enid Blyton were re-tellings of the six stories, and the line illustrations were 'redrawn' by Olive F. Openshaw. Presumably this edition had something to do with War Economy Production Standards.

BRUNHOFF, Laurent de: *Babar's picnic*. Random House, 1949.

Other titles published by Random House: *Babar's cousin; That Rascal Arthur* (1948); *Babar's visit to Bird Island* (1952); *Babar's castle* (1962).

Published by World are: *Serafina the giraffe* (1961); *Serafina's lucky find* (1962); and *Captain Serafina* (1963).

Babar's French lessons (1963) and *Babar's Spanish lessons* (1965) have dual-language texts and are both published by Random House.

16 PICTURE-BOOKS IN THE TWENTIETH CENTURY

It is impossible to cover the development of modern European picture-books in a single short chapter, for the very good reason that there are too many of them. There are hundreds upon hundreds of bad, indifferent, or sentimental ones, but even these may seem a marvellous enrichment to a child of little or no education. Similarly, there are droves of ordinary, decently produced, instructive picture-books which, if we were talking about clothes, we would describe as good off-the-peg material. Frequently they are handsome productions, tasteful, decorated with all the refinements of modern graphic techniques, and tailored more or less closely to the laws of supply and demand.

But there is also a third category, not always easily distinguished from the two mentioned above, a group of books which I should like to call the pioneers, the breakers of new ground for children, and it is with them that I primarily want to concern myself here. For these are the books where inspiration goes hand in hand with a genuine love for children. They are books which are not attractive for their outward form alone, but which are charged with warmth and imagination and a sense of good things to come.

Just as the first word-plays, the nursery rhymes, and the earliest stories, with their stilted sentences in big block letters, help to found a future taste for literature, so picture-books prepare a future feeling for art. It is true that children as a rule are somewhat indifferent to matters of taste or of art, even though there may be some who early on develop their preferences for such things. But what children do have from the very beginning is an unquenchable curiosity and desire for knowledge, to which may be added the need for warmth and happiness and for something to love. If a picture-book should meet this need, if it should also contain truly lovable characters, then it may similarly become a child's imaginary companion, more so even than a teddy-bear, or a doll, or a much loved pet. Just what such an imaginary companion actually counts for anyone should know who cares in his heart for the experiences of his own childhood.

Most people preserve in some closed drawer of the mind the memories which spring from such an experience of picture-books. For each they will be different and for each they will form an imperishable personal possession. But when we see the great wealth of picture-books with which present-day children are blessed, it becomes imperative to trace back the still very short history of the modern picture-book and pull open for a moment some of the drawers of memory.

Modern printing processes

The history of picture-books as we know them today begins with the introduction of new ideas in the technique of printing and especially colour-printing. Before this occurred, picture-books were coloured by hand, and, as a rule, had a somewhat touching modesty in their format and appearance. The few exceptions, such as Bertuch's magnificent *Bilderbuch für Kinder*, only serve to emphasize this rule.

But with the coming of mechanical colour-printing people began to realize the boundless possibilities of picture-books in colour at a price which would appeal to a mass market. Right through the second half of the nineteenth century much time and money were spent on the techniques of colour printing in order to eliminate the old manual processes which could no longer cope with the public demand for sumptuous colour and plenty of it.

It was the process of chromo-lithography, from which offset printing was later to develop, which was first applied to this end, not always satisfactorily. The first productions, which were printed in huge editions, had an oiliness of surface which compared very unfavourably with the hand-coloured picture-books of earlier times. At the same time, however, thanks to the enterprise and skill of a few individuals, a technique of wood-engraving was developed by which it was possible to transfer the artist's original to the surface of the wood block photographically. A separate wood block was then engraved for every colour needed—a process which was later to be extended to the preparation of metal blocks by chemical means. This technique was developed in England during the second half of the nineteenth century and it approaches very close in its effects to the fine printing that could be got from metal surfaces. The great engraver and printer Edmund Evans perfected this process and his name is to be found in the imprint of many of the finest English picture-books of this time. He was, in fact, the pupil of a pupil of Thomas Bewick and deeply imbued with the Bewick tradition. But in spite of this, his splendid technical abilities would have been quite useless if he had not succeeded in attracting outstanding artists to his undertaking.

Two of these who are known far beyond the borders of their own country are Walter Crane and Kate Greenaway. At the time of their publication, Crane's *The fairy ship* (1869), *The baby's opera* (1877), *The baby's bouquet* (1879), *The baby's own Aesop* (1886), and *Flora's feast* (1888) were marvels of decorative book production for children. From title-page, dedication, contents page, through all the pages of pictures and text, everything is conceived as a unity. There is not a square inch of paper without ornament or illustration or text matter. It is of course pure 'art nouveau', and for this reason of only limited appeal to modern children—but for book collectors, on the other hand, it has a constantly increasing value.

In England the fame of this devoted illustrator of childish subjects was exceeded by that of Kate Greenaway, whose style was gentler and more intimate than Crane's and who was less a victim of the excesses of 'art nouveau'. Her children's books, *Under the window* (1878), *A day in a child's life* (1881), *Mother Goose* (1881), and *Marigold garden* (1885), belong among the most charming examples of Victorian book production. The physical attractiveness of these books was not a little enhanced by the clean, transparent way in which the colours were laid down, as many as nine colour blocks often being used and editions of between ten and twenty thousand being printed. Crane's *Baby's opera* had already had an initial run of 10,000 copies, while Kate Greenaway's first book, *Under the window*, started with 20,000. Her most famous book, however, is *Mother Goose*, which appeared in 1881 and which displays the climax of her artistry and the technique of Edmund Evans. Even today this book enjoys a certain popularity with children, coupled with Crane's *Baby's opera* and with the books of that other gifted artist Randolph Caldecott. All these books were originally published by Routledge and they are still available, although they are now issued by Frederick Warne & Co., many still being printed from the original wood blocks. It is also worth noting that in *Mother Goose* we meet a collection of children depicted so free from constraint (except in the matter of their Kate Greenaway clothes) that we may reflect that 'the children's century' has already begun. As so often happens, the sensitivity of the artist is preparing the way for the educationists.

The picture-books of Ernst Kreidolf

Ellen Key's famous book *The century of the child* appeared in Sweden in 1900. In 1896 the man who was to have so much influence on the character of children's books in Germany, the arch prophet of the movement for education through art (especially where books for young people were concerned), Heinrich Wolgast, published his famous critique: *Das Elend unserer Jugendliteratur* (*The sad state of our children's literature*). At the same time as this, in Bavaria, an unassuming, sickly painter from Switzerland began to prepare his first picture-book: *Die Blumenmärchen* (*Flower fairy tales*), in which he was to fulfil the demands of the revolutionary German educationist without even knowing about them. Nor is there any trace in Ernst Kreidolf's revealing autobiography that he knew anything of the famous books by Walter Crane, with their beautifully transparent colouring.

This is no place to examine all the arts and crafts movements of this period, such as that proclaimed by the *Hamburger Lichtwark*, for instance: a movement which regarded good art as a means of education and therefore demanded of the illustrations to children's books that they be sound and seriously intended works of art. Now although such educational experiments could only partly influence the development of illustration as an art, they nevertheless smoothed the way for artistically satisfying children's books in many circles which were previously quite indifferent to such things.

Instead of examining all the weighty theories of that time, which finally established for children their place as individuals in the complex structure of human society, I should like to deal briefly with the life and works of this strange man Ernst Kreidolf. For he is a standing proof that artistic inspiration and indeed that the artist all on his own, with scarcely any idea of all these theories, is absolutely necessary to carry out the demands of the theorists or even to anticipate them.

Kreidolf came from a country which itself could be compared to a beautiful picture-book. Even today there is no town in Switzerland too big to prevent the children seeing at least the tip of a mountain or getting to know their local hills and meadows. For a long time they were almost as familiar with cows as with motor-cars and a cheese-dairy figured as largely in their view of the world as a filling-station. And even though the spread of technology is continually altering the perspective of the picture, there is still scarcely a single picture-book from Switzerland without its complement of animals and flowers.

It is quite likely that present-day children are first introduced to Kreidolf through their parents. Born at Berne in 1863, he belongs to a time which is too different from our own, but he is still capable of catching the attention of modern children and making a considerable impression on them. There are still generations of people who, around the turn of the century, were given and fell in love with such picture-books as *Die Blumenmärchen* and *Die Wiesenzwerge (Field-dwarfs)*. Later on, in the twenties, they were able to present their own children with *Die Alpenblumenmärchen (Alpine flower fairy tales)*, *Das Hundefest (The dogs' party)*, or *Ein Wintermärchen (A winter fairy tale)*. Above all, there are still many artists who saw in Kreidolf an inspiring example of the painter who could realize his best work in a picture-book— and how few were to succeed as he did.

Ernst Kreidolf started to paint and draw as a child. His family back to his great-grandparents were all country people from East Switzerland and he grew up with his strict but highly eccentric paternal grandfather who was the last true farmer in the family. The boy loved nature before all else, but, to the grief of his grandfather, he was quite unfitted to be a farmer and therefore after leaving school he was apprenticed to a lithographer. This was to be of the greatest significance to the future illustrator of picture-books, for in his first books he himself drew each colour direct on to the lithographic stone, and in this way created illustrations of the highest artistic quality and the highest craftsmanship, illustrations which in the context of his time represented a breakthrough, especially in the field of children's books.

At the end of his apprenticeship he moved to Munich, where he began to earn his living as a lithographer while he trained himself as a freelance artist. Almost immediately he was faced with a decision between the attractions of becoming a large-scale painter (which he was never to be) or turning his gifts to illustration, working within the limitations of the drawing and the water-colour. In addition to this, his delicate physique (three of his brothers and sisters died of consumption) at about this time drove him into creative activity, until a course of hydropathy under Pastor Kneipp effected so powerful a cure that he was able to go on working up to his ninetieth year.

In these early years, for the good of his health, he lived mostly at Parten-kirchen in Bavaria. His surroundings here took him back to the earliest experiences of his childhood and the impressions which plants and small animals had made on him then, and in a critical period for his life as an artist he began to paint the pictures for his *Blumenmärchen*. This was his first picture-book and the foundation of his fame, but it by no means fell straight into his lap, for no publisher would take on the risk of printing an edition of these strangely personified flowers. Finally, the Countess of Schaumburg-Lippe, a patron to whom every summer for a number of years he had given drawing and painting lessons, made it possible for him to print the book himself.

Each of the pictures demanded anything from eight to ten colour printings. He prepared the stones for these with his own hands, and during the printing he stood guard to ensure that the colours were laid on correctly. In short, he spent almost a year working on this one book. These technical questions are worth mentioning here because as a rule too little attention is paid to them and also because this is the first time that lithography produced an artistically outstanding work. For some decades from this time on the two techniques of letterpress (i.e. printing from a raised surface) and lithography (printing from a flat surface) were to decide the range and character of children's picture-books. Today, however, litho printing of one sort or another predominates, supplemented by colour gravure—a technique whose development is now going forward apace and which is likely to open up many possibilities for the future.[1]

At the time of its publication in 1898 the clear and beautiful printing of Kreidolf's first book was a sensation, reproducing so perfectly the colours of the original. Both Dr. Hoffmann, with *Struwwelpeter* and its successors, and Wilhelm Busch, with *Max und Moritz*, had to suffer falsification of their artistic intentions by blockmakers and lithographers, who re-drew the originals according to their own abilities, and also by hand-colourists who falsified the original colours if they were not closely watched. Hoffmann and Busch have often enough themselves borne witness to this problem. But here, with the *Blumenmärchen*, an artist was at work whose mastery of his craft was peculiarly perfect, for he united in himself the ability to create the raw material of a

---

[1] Readers anxious for a good general explanation of these printing processes are referred to: Séan Jennett: *The making of books*, 3rd edition, Faber, 1964. Children could hardly ask for a better pictorial introduction than that given in the Puffin Picture-Book: *Printing* by Harold Curwen, illustrated by Jack Brough (2nd edition, 1955). (B.A.)

picture-book and then to attend to the reproduction of its colours in print. The effect of this book by the quiet painter, Ernst Kreidolf, was electric—on his contemporaries, but especially on his fellow artists and on children. There would never again be any need for him to worry about publishers and commissions.

In 1900 a volume of verse appeared called *Fitzebutze* by Paula and Richard Dehmel. Every page from one end-paper to the other was covered with illustrations or decorations by Kreidolf. It was 'art nouveau' in a modified form and the relationship with Walter Crane is unmistakable.[1] But Kreidolf exercises more restraint over his ornamentation, and in spite of boundless arabesques the book has such perfection in its printing and its composition that it still evokes amazement today. It belongs among some of the early publications of the famous Insel-Verlag which had just been founded at Leipzig. Later on, however, *Fitzebutze* was taken over, along with Kreidolf's other books, by Schaffstein-Verlag at Cologne, who were at that time pioneers in the field of the artistic picture-book. The poetry in the book, by the famous pair of married writers, the Dehmels, was also something new attempting to approach children's understanding through the poetic imitation of a young child's way of speaking—an experiment which was not wholly successful.[2]

Schaffstein then produced the book which was to make Kreidolf the man of his day at the turn of the century: *Die Wiesenzwerge* (1902). Here human qualities are seen in the character of a dwarf, rooted though he is in the ways of the earth with the dumb beasts and the grasshoppers, living in a world of plants and earth, sky and moon drawn in a completely realistic manner. Nature is marvellously brought out in this book alongside all the humanized action of the story. There are wonderful details of leaves and grasses and roadside stones and the sense of sunrise and moonlight are transmitted superbly. The draughtsmanship and the colouring are alike masterly, quite free from the predominant sentimentality of the period. Even in the context of the rest of Kreidolf's work the book is an exception. Is there any child who does not have some affection for dwarfs, for their littleness and their hidden lives? And what indescribable drivel they usually bring out from those who write about them, or draw them, or manufacture garden statues of them.

As he did for most of his books, Kreidolf composed the text for *Die Wiesenzwerge* himself. It is a plainly human piece of writing, pervaded by a gentle poetry, a tranquil complement to the pictures which are his truest and clearest voice. In later life he was also to illustrate texts by the poet Adolf Frey and also passages from the Bible.

[1] In this section I have translated 'Jugendstil' as 'art nouveau'. In fact, English and Continental opinions differ over definitions and John Russell Taylor in *The art-nouveau book in Britain* (1966) argues that Crane is really 'arts and crafts' and not 'art nouveau'. (B.A.)

[2] A comparable example of this kind of verse in England is Marion St. John Webb's *The littlest one*. Published by Harrap's in 1919 (well before A. A. Milne) it is astonishingly still in print—even though it lacks the benefit of illustrations by Ernst Kreidolf. (B.A.)

Staatsereignis.

Hurra, zum ersten Mal:
Mutter, der Peter,
hurra, jetzt geht er!
Kuck, ganz alleinechen
setzt er die Beinechen,
ganz wie zur Reichstagswahl,
wie Onkel Wackelpfahl!
Aua, Geschrei:
bautz, vorbei!

17

DEHMEL, Paula and Richard. *Fitzebutze*. Munich, 1900.
Coloured illustration by Ernst Kreidolf.

Plate XIX

Top: BÄUMER, Eduard and Valerie. *Die Geschichte vom Fluss.* Zürich, 1937. Colour lithograph by the authors.
Bottom: SCHNITTER, Rosie. *Der Leuchtturm.* Zürich, 1936. Colour lithographs by Berta Tappolet.

Plate XX

Children and personified nature

Already by this time, however, educational theorists and even art critics were beginning to reject too obvious a personification of nature as it appeared, for instance, in Kreidolf's *Blumenmärchen*.[1] The new movement was towards a portrayal of nature as she actually is, something which Kreidolf was well aware of and himself attempted to do. In his own words: 'On the educational side it was questioned whether it was good for children to personify everything in the way that I do. First flowers, now trees—indeed I also found myself saying that it could finally go too far and I decided to leave off and show that I was not yet the victim of an *idée fixe* but could still see and represent undisguised reality. I therefore created a picture-book of simple *Scenes from childhood*—but the book had no success at all . . . people only wanted "Blumenmärchen" from me. I was branded with them.'

In another part of his autobiography he writes: 'What is there that children cannot imagine! They personify everything. If they have not got a doll, then a chunk of wood will do. It is therefore quite natural for flowers to have faces—and especially when nature comes to their assistance, as it does with the pansy.' Contrary to every educational theory he has been justified by the whole of successful children's literature down to the present.

At this time many famous artists and writers were taking up their brushes and their pens with an eye towards children, but for most it remained a single attempt and only a few of those who achieved print are still known today. One book, however, has remained almost as popular as Kreidolf's books—*Etwas von den Wurzelkindern* by Sibylle von Olfers. It is the same mixture of real nature and 'the little people' as in *Die Wiesenzwerge*, but everything is slightly more awkward, slightly more dainty in the drawing, even more approachable. The widespread success of the book is almost unthinkable without Kreidolf, although it appeared in 1906, four years after *Die Wiesenzwerge*.

The Swedish authoress Elsa Beskow also took a similar direction in her innumerable picture-books. Her best-loved work about the little boy in the bilberry wood, *Putte i blåbärsskogen* (1901), brings us back once more to the subject of the tiny human creature who is thereby enabled so much better

---

[1] Miss Cicely Barker, who wrote and drew the well-known *Flower Fairy Books* (Blackie), has commented in a letter to me on the great vogue there was at the turn of the century for the imposition of human characteristics upon flowers. Although she has never come across Kreidolf she drew my attention to the work of Charles Wilhelm who designed flower costumes and 'did very delicate book-illustrations; we used to see his work in the old "Little Folks" '. (It is perhaps significant that Charles Wilhelm was English [Charles William], but teutonized his name in response to the current fashion for German design.)

I have not investigated the illustrative origins of flower-fairies, but the developments of the nineties must surely owe a great deal to that masterpiece of children's book illustration: Richard Doyle's *In fairyland* (Longmans, 1870). The colour printing was from wood blocks engraved by Edmund Evans and surely surpasses all his later achievements. (B.A.)

to get under nature's skin. This is a theme to which we are well enough accustomed through *Alice in Wonderland, Nils Holgersson,* and countless fairy stories, but it is here varied in a way particularly enjoyable to young children. This writer's other books betray an even stronger relationship to Kreidolf and are less well known outside Sweden, although they possess great charm in their somewhat modified 'art nouveau' style. Her early books are all printed by that same transparent letterpress process which was being used in England, although the author/artist later turned to a style using pastel effects in offset lithography, work which generally lacked in the individuality of the earlier books.

The plushy middle-class world of those days was inclined to wear too many clothes which were often too tight-fitting. It was therefore a natural reaction to try to get away from it all and commune with nature. Where children were concerned this opened a way into the world of plants and animals in a quite new manner. The personification of this nature was something which gave rise to a struggle which continues to this day. Such a thing does correspond, though, to a primitive need of humanity itself, and not just of children. Fables, plays, jokes, cartoons, and fairy stories all make use of talking animals. Why do the educationists always want to abolish them? In the books we have mentioned by Kreidolf, Sibylle von Olfers, and Elsa Beskow, real nature is not distorted but takes its place quietly in the splendid faithfulness and naturalness of the drawing.

Unfortunately this has not been the case with all books of this kind. A questionable example was the extraordinarily successful *Häschenschule* by Fritz Koch-Gotha (1923). The intended comedy of the book consists in the exact imitation of human behaviour by disguised rabbits. There is no attempt at a comparison with the natural world as in the previously mentioned books, but rather a very gifted misuse of natural phenomena in order to show up some all-too-human foibles.

Peter Rabbit and Beatrix Potter

An authoress who was to achieve world fame with this kind of book was Beatrix Potter, who was born in 1866, three years after Kreidolf. She created for children all over the world a group of animal characters who behaved like animals but also provided a humorous reflection of the life of children.

Beatrix Potter grew up in the seclusion of a strictly conventional Victorian middle-class household and from a lack of playfellows she turned her rich imagination towards animals. In 1893 she wrote a letter to Noël Moore, the son of her former governess, and set down for him in words and pictures the story of Peter Rabbit. This letter, with its pages of freely integrated words and pictures and with its beautifully observed and executed drawings, already contains all the elements of the little book that was to become so famous. From its first successful reception among the children of her friends Beatrix Potter was encouraged to offer the story to a number of publishers, including

Eastwood Dunkeld
Sep 4 93

My dear Noel,
I don't know what to write to you, so I shall tell you a story about four little rabbits whose names were

Flopsy, Mopsy Cottontail

and Peter

They lived with their mother in a sand bank under the root of a big fir tree.

The first page of Beatrix Potter's historic letter to Noël Moore.

Frederick Warne's, with whom Edmund Evans was associated. Apparently they did not have much confidence in its potentialities for, like so many famous and so many more insignificant authors, she paid for the printing of her first little book from her own pocket. It was issued privately in 1901, each page illustrated with line drawings and only the frontispiece being given a wash of colour. As with Kreidolf, success was to follow this venture, for on seeing the finished copy, Warne's accepted the book for a commercial edition and from then on handled all 'the Beatrix Potter books'.

What is the reason for the winning charm of these tiny books? There are many people who can recount witty or thrilling tales when they sit across the room from us, but fail completely in putting them down on paper just because they miss their live audience. With Beatrix Potter, however, one has the feeling that with every stroke of the pen or the paint-brush, with every word she writes, she sees her audience in front of her and translates for it her affection for the world of small animals. This is something which we find again and again—with *Alice in Wonderland*, with Hoffmann's books and with many others—it is a factor which is decisive in the creation of books for children. Nevertheless, it is a mistake to believe that mere contact with an audience is an automatic recipe for success—this is an error which has led to the printing of a vast deal of mediocre products. Other factors must also play their part. With the creator of *Peter Rabbit, Samuel Whiskers, Tom Kitten, Johnny Town-Mouse, Mrs. Tiggy-Winkle*, and all the rest, the other factor was above all her intimate knowledge of small animals. Even though Peter Rabbit wears a blue jacket with silver buttons, and Mrs. Tiggy-Winkle, the hedgehog, a starched apron, Beatrix Potter still knows what they look like underneath. And even though these animals may behave in a human fashion the artist knows all about their real lives. At the end of almost every one of these classic stories the animals end up without their disguise—ducks, hedgehogs, mice, rabbits, all of them. Peter Rabbit lies tired out and naked on the floor of his burrow, while his little coat and shoes serve Mr. MacGregor as a scarecrow. He has become a small, helpless creature. And Mrs. Hedgehog, however human she may appear in her little underground kitchen busy with her flat-iron, is at the end of the book only a tiny, unclad, prickly beast disappearing from Lucy's sight up the hill.

In the final analysis it is the real animals which Beatrix Potter knows and loves and sets before children in a charming but very superficial disguise. There is nothing in this of the old symbolic animal fables. However old-fashioned she may be thought today, Beatrix Potter is very much of our own times and devoted to life in the real world. This is clearly shown in her own life. For a long time she remained unmarried, writing book after book, all in the same tiny format, to the great delight of English-speaking children on both sides of the Atlantic (although she suffered from pirates on the eastern side). But when she was almost forty she became engaged to the youngest son of her publisher, Norman Warne, with whom she had worked in close and fruitful harmony. In graphic and commercial affairs he had been an invaluable help to this independently minded woman and, despite the objections of her family, who 'had no opinion' of an alliance with a trading publisher, she remained constant to her decision. Before the marriage could take place, however, Norman Warne died. With never a thought of resigning herself to a respectable suburban life, Miss Potter gradually eased herself free from family restraints, bought herself a little farm in the Lake District and became a farmer.

What a paradise this new country life must have been for her! In the books that stem from this period the heroes—the cats, the frogs, the mice—are all taken from the surroundings of her farm and in the tales of Jemima Puddle-Duck and Tom Kitten and Samuel Whiskers, the place is actually portrayed.

Approaching the age of fifty, Beatrix Potter married. But although she continued her life as a countrywoman, and indeed took a very active part in running her growing estates, in the work of the National Trust and, at the end of her life, in helping towards the agricultural self-sufficiency of the country in the Second World War, she seemed to have lost the artistic impulse to give expression to her combined love of animals and children. She herself denied that there was any such artistic impulse at all. In a letter to Bertha Mahony she writes of the texts of her books which we find so impressive: 'I think I write carefully because I enjoy my writing and enjoy taking pains over it. I have always disliked writing to order; I write to please myself . . . My usual way of writing is to scribble, and cut out, and write it again and again. The shorter and plainer the better. And I read the Bible (unrevised version and Old Testament) if I feel my style wants chastening.'

Beatrix Potter's fame and her popularity with generations of children is immeasurable. This strong-willed, vigorous woman, whose effect on children was almost terrifying in its demands, was a phenomenon comparable to Johanna Spyri, and both share a somewhat similar fate today. Many an English town child in the Second World War was evacuated with a copy of *Peter Rabbit* or *Tom Kitten* in his suitcase, thereby carrying with him one of his most valuable possessions, but today the stars are waning on this treasured land.[1] The heroes of contemporary children have a different appearance and one that we must come to very shortly.

Other illustrators from the turn of the century

Another book from this extremely fruitful period was Carl Larsson's *At home* (*Ett Hem*, 1904), a book which for many European households became a family possession and one which cannot be unconditionally described as a

[1] 1966 was the centenary of Beatrix Potter's birth and, despite the unhappy deterioration in the quality of reproduction which her drawings have suffered, there is little evidence that her popularity has declined at all in Great Britain. Her publishers are also extending the range of titles available in foreign languages, which at present number at least nine, including Latin. Readers who are interested in a discussion of some of the more recondite aspects of these translations are referred to the essay 'Babel in the nursery' by Paul Jennings (in *Next to oddliness*, Max Reinhart, 1955; reprinted in *The Jenguin Pennings*, 1963). (B.A.)

LARSSON, Carl. *Ett hem*. Stockholm, 1904.
Line illustration by the author.

children's book. It is a picture-book of large format setting out in Scandinavian fashion a family idyll which is full of vigour and gaiety. It must still stand out for many older people as one of their choicest childhood memories. Even today its colour pictures keep their attractiveness with their clean and honest lines, while the drawings have a witty progression which is reminiscent of Wilhelm Busch, although they have none of his tendency to malice.

The turn of the century is also a period when artists prettified the child and his surroundings. Among the most popular of such illustrators before the First World War was Gertrud Caspari who put much of her best work into illustrating children's poetry.

One of the particular attractions about studying such artists as I have just been talking about is to notice how almost always they have their links with the world of great art and its stylistic developments. Walter Crane, for instance, who worked for a while with William Morris, has a position not too distant from William Blake; Carl Larsson cannot deny a more than regional affinity to Munch; and none of them, not even Kreidolf, is conceivable without the influence of the Japanese woodcuts which in the decades at the end of the century had had such an impact on the art schools of Europe, affecting so decisively, among others, Toulouse-Lautrec, Gauguin, and Van Gogh.

The most successful French illustrator of this period and this style was M. Boutet de Monvel (1850–1913) who reflects the whole temperament of French culture in his bold line-drawings with their delicate colouring. He has caught the world of French children unforgettably in his pictures for Anatole France's books *Nos enfants* and *Filles et garçons*. He produced illustrations for many other books and the gentle nuances of his style are perhaps seen at their best in his picture-book on the life of Joan of Arc.

A personal note

These are some of the fundamental elements in the world of picture-books which we have inherited today. As a rule people forget about foundations so long as they hold the building up that rests on them and if we liken children's books of the present day to a house, then we can see that although it rests on the achievements of the artists we have mentioned and although, in their turn, they have built upon the modest developments of the eighteenth and nine-teenth centuries, the whole structure is beginning to fall apart. Too much has been erected on too narrow a base, but in spite of everything the house con-tinues to stand up with all its richly adorned, magnificently decorated rooms.

Part of the reason for this enormous increase in the production of picture-books is the ease with which they can be converted into 'international edi-tions'. Pictures speak a universal language; they can be run off in large quantities in a single print run and the sheets sold to different countries for suitably translated texts to be attached. The great gain is a substantial reduction in price for the customer (for a small print run would be quite uneconomical), but the risk lies in a tendency towards uniformity—different national charac-teristics becoming submerged for the sake of 'the European market'.[1]

Because of the impossibility of making any kind of total assessment of modern picture-books I have decided to discuss only those books which I have found the most beautiful. Such a subjective approach is justified if I can make clear how important those early experiences are which children gain from picture-books and therefore how careful we should be in our selection of books for them.

To illustrate this, perhaps I may be excused if I follow my fairly factual review of the foundations of the modern picture-book with a description of two books which have remained with me through all the depredations of childhood and through all the circumstances of war and destruction of later years. These were without doubt the examples on which my own feeling for picture-books was based, however fortuitously they may have been brought together.

Die Sonne im alten Kinderlied (Weimar, 1915) was a collection of traditional rhymes about the sun, which at one time were well known to every child but which today are sinking into an ever deeper oblivion. The words were taken

[1] This problem is discussed at greater length in Mrs. Hürlimann's article in *Books* (The journal of the National Book League) No. 356: Nov./Dec. 1964. (B.A.)

for granted and were thus of less importance than the pictures, and the book contained more of these than any picture-book of our own day. Each one of its 120 pages was covered with them, and even the end-papers formed a kind of overture introducing all the themes of the book. A whole page, just as richly decorated, was set aside for the owner's mark of possession; this was followed by the title-page with every letter in a different colour; and then, before the book finally got under way, a charmingly sentimental introduction which everyone skipped. By today's standards the pictures are perhaps very modest affairs—clear outlines, light colours, everyone saying simply what it had to. For us hungry children of the First World War the favourite picture came on page 15:

Wenn alle Berge Butter wären	If all the hills were butter
Und alle Täler Grütze,	And all the valleys groats
Und käm ein warmer Sonnenschein	Out would come the boiling sun
Und die Butter lief in die Grütze	And make the heaps of butter run,
hinein	And we'd have pudding by the ton!
Das müsst aber mal 'ne Grütze	
sein.	

That was the short text. But above it the sun was shining on golden hills at whose feet a river rises the colour of some fabulous children's pudding. On its banks there are hoards of tiny children, each one precisely drawn, spooning up the feast. The sun is laughing; the cock on the church steeple is laughing, even the houses are given friendly faces and, above all, 'die Butter fliesst in die Grütze hinein'. This was paradise. The whole book was a children's paradise, chock-full of the common things of everyday life, but also of things beyond our normal surroundings: St. Nicholas, the Sandman, the Christ Child and 'the spacious firmament on high'.

In the course of time I lost the book, but so great was my nostalgia for it over the twenty intervening years that I could not bear my own children to be without some similar picture-book. Since these children grew up between the High German of their mother and the Swiss German of their father we had to create two such books for them. These were called *Eia Popeia: alte Kinderreimer und Lieder* (Berlin, 1936) and *Alti Versli und Liedli* (Zürich, 1936). Since we succeeded in getting superb illustrations from Fritz Kredel for the one, and O. and H. Baumberger for the other, the books fulfilled their purpose edition by edition over two decades. Even Queen Mary, the grandmother of the present Queen, had to read *Eia Popeia* aloud to her grandchildren and ordered copies for this purpose on a number of occasions. (It ought to be noted that I am considering the books mentioned here by reason of their illustrations alone. Such subjects as poetry for children are dealt with in other chapters.)

Another book from my own childhood was *Ein Kinderbuch von Andreas Thom* (Weimar, 1915). This splendid book lies in front of me now, imperfect and much battered, and I would give a great deal to have it in its former completeness. It contains stories by a Viennese '*Volksschule*' teacher, 'freely illustrated in line and colour' by the pupils of his fifth form. Such a method of book illustration was still something new at that time and we used to call the book 'the true picture-book', for it seemed to us to give a notable account of what life is really like without any imaginary inventions. For instance, there was a picture of a bearded tailor, lean, homeless, and weary, plodding along beside ploughed fields, begging for work. Even today every pedlar that I see reminds me of this skinny fellow, while the picture was shared by dramatically placed and exactly executed·drawings of zeppelins and balloons and telegraph-poles with wires and morse signals. There were also some touching pictures of the life of a little orphan child, their text now in a very fragmentary state but the desperate pathos of the verses still intact in my memory.

That was 'the true picture-book' and I found through it that there were a great many sad and stirring things going on in the world which I could not see from my nursery window. On the whole, people are inclined to think today that children do not set much store by books illustrated by other children, even though there have been plenty of them in the past. The whole question would be worth studying from a psychological point of view.

Picture-books and modern painting

Turning away now from my own picture-book world I should like to describe some enjoyable and interesting children's books of more recent date—but this should not be taken to signify that all children's books of the last four decades have been either of these things. On the contrary, although illustrators and publishers before and, most of all, after the First World War were the witnesses of fresh movements in painting, fresh ideas about art, the average picture-book yielded itself up to a somewhat vulgarized form of painting which consisted of a cheap imitation of naturalism mixed in with a dash of impressionism. But the books that come next do express the new directions which graphic art was taking and, with the exception of the first, they all appeared in the years between 1918 and 1936.

Rumpumpel by Paula Dehmel (1903) illustrated by Karl Hofer, proved to be a book of special significance. Both author and artist were in the thick of the artistic developments during the period before the First World War and one can see in this picture-book, which was not the only one of its kind, an expression of the times. The verses, which are not directly our concern at the moment, are similar to those in *Fitzebutze* (see p. 206). They are the expression of a clearly defined movement in taste, seeking to comprehend the child's most intimate world, but directed in this to mothers rather than to children. The big pages of pictures, on the other hand, bear witness to an artist who, like many others, has truly retained a feeling for childhood, and although not all of the pictures are of equal excellence there are among them some remarkable felicities. Their outlines and their flat colouring have a simplicity and clarity which is most expressive. Much feeling obviously lies behind their composition but not a jot of sentimentality, while the large-scale planning of the pictures betrays an artist confident in his own powers. All these factors join to make up a book which played an important part in the history of modern German picture-books.

Rumpumpel has long been out of print, but other artists have time and again confirmed for me the influence which it had on them. This can be directly seen in such an example as the captivating illustrations which Josua Leander Gampp created for Christian Morgenstern's incomparable book of verse *Klein Irmchen* (1921), dealt with in detail in a later chapter (p. 262). Hofer's contemporary, Freyhold, to whom we owe a considerable number of picture-books, shows in his rigid stylization some striking similarities to Hofer himself, especially in his *Osterbuch* which appeared in the twenties and also was accompanied by verses by Morgenstern. In the freedom of their design and colour and in the boldness of their composition all these books continue to exercise a decisive influence today when everything or anything is permissible. For all their simplification of detail, however, they do not lose that delicacy of feeling which is so important for children.

The impulse stemming from modern painting and graphic art continued to be influential until the mid-1930s. Only then did the cultural conservatism of the National Socialists deal a mortal blow to the development of artistic picture-books in Germany, putting her out of the running in this field of activity. Here, nevertheless, are one or two books whose titles I should like to see preserved, safe from the oblivion, if not annihilation, which followed those dreadful years.

The play-books of Tom Seidmann-Freud

Two of these books, all of which are now out of print, were *Das Wunderhaus* (*The house of wonders*) and *Das Zauberboot* (*The magic boot*) by the authoress Tom Seidmann-Freud, published at the end of the twenties by Stuffer Verlag, Baden-Baden, whose pioneering activities have already been mentioned. Although they are in the modern style of the previously mentioned books, they are comfortable books with a greater delicacy of line and colour and they are influenced by the discoveries of child-psychology which assign an active role to the child even when he is looking at pictures. Every page, therefore, gives the child something to twist or pull, something to think about, whether it be the race between the hare and the hedgehog, or the stage of a Punch and Judy show, or even the moving windows in a house. Each activity is backed up by a suitable text in which this artistically very sensitive painter and teacher keeps a sharp eye on the education of children through play, a concept to be taken up but used differently in book form by Père Castor (see Chapter 10). Tom Seidmann-Freud's books were very successful, but disappeared from bookshops in about 1937 owing to their author's non-Aryan descent.

SEIDMANN-FREUD, Tom. *Das Zauberboot*. Berlin, 1929.
From the colour lithograph by the author. A movable tab causes the scenes at the windows to change.
Reproduced by permission of the publishers, Herbert Stuffer Verlag.

'Das Männchen' by Conny Meissen

Some other picture-books which are worthy of a rescue operation are those about 'the little man' and his visit to the wizard: *Das Männchen* and *Das Männchen kommt zum Zauberer* by Conny Meissen. They are books which it is practically impossible to dig out nowadays since they were little books cheaply produced and without the artistic pretensions that would make them worth while to collectors of illustrated books. *Das Männchen* consisted simply of the basic elements of human form—a big oval for his body, a little one for his head and straight lines for his arms and legs. All the other characters and objects in the book were similarly drawn—without any relationship to the new graphic ideas described above, but rather precursors of certain comic strips which crop up in some daily papers of the present time. But what stories they were! Every line, every movement, was right. You would think a child could have drawn them and that was part of their attractiveness; but all their simplicity hid an enormous amount of care for exactness of expression and motion. In any other country this splendid 'little man' would have been a classic figure of the nursery and it is very sad that he has disappeared into obscurity.

Es war einmal ein Männchen,	Once there was a little man
Das kroch in alle Kännchen,	Who crept in every little can,
Das kroch in jedes Tintenfass	Into the ink-pot he did get,
und wurde schwarz und wurde nass.	Which made him black and made him wet.

The pictures had the same clear-cut quality as these lines, but to show that such a conscious over-simplification was not just an undeveloped talent, the same authoress later produced two lovely picture-books, sumptuously illustrated: *In die weite Welt* (Potsdam, 1929), the story of a Japanese and a Negro doll, and *Thomas schreibt aus Mexiko* (Berlin, 1936), a documentary children's book written in the country to which she emigrated.

MEISSEN, Conny. *Das Männchen* Baden-Baden, *c.* 1935. Line illustration by the author.

Vogelbart and others

One curious fact is beginning to emerge from this personal selection of books. While at the beginning of the century the names that appeared on the title-pages were (with one or two notable exceptions) nearly always those of men, we now find that they more often belong to women—in Germany, practically always. We have just had a look at two of these, forgotten though they may be. Now I should like to snatch from a quite unmerited oblivion two books by a third authoress who is still very much at work. The books belong among the most delightful that German-speaking children possess and their author's name is Susanne Ehmcke. She has the rare gift of being able to write verse just as well as she paints pictures. She has produced countless fine picture-books, games, and picture-broadsides, while today she illustrates dictionaries and reference books for children (e.g. *Kinder-Duden*, 1959). But twenty-four years ago she wrote a book that is a classic for little children: *Bill und Bällchen* (Baden-Baden, 1934):

Bill spricht zum Bällchen:	'I like to play with you,'
Du gefällst mir sehr,	said Bill to his ball;
mein Spielgesellchen,	'but I should like to know
wo kommst du her?	how you come to be here at all.'

This is a very neatly handled kind of writing for children, a delightful introduction to reading for the younger ones embedded in a similarly neat, but at the same time enjoyable, sequence of colour pages.

The second book that I have selected from her considerable output demonstrates that Susanne Ehmcke is truly a poet. It is called *Vogelbart* (Ravensburg, 1943) and it appeared in the middle of the war, printed on yellow paper, held together with wire staples and, in the presence of today's books in all their finery, it seems something of a Cinderella.[1] But Vogelbart is by no means a Cinderella in any manner of speaking. No, he is a remarkable old man who lives in a wood. The birds nest in his beard and he can tell the most splendid stories in rhyme, which every child straightway knows by heart:

Da wo der Wald am tiefsten ist,	There where the forest is deepest,
Wo man die Menschenwelt vergisst,	Far from the world of men,
Da wohnt ein Mann besondrer Art,	A curious person spends his days,
Das ist der alte Vogelbart.	And Bird-beard is his name.

These picture-stories are full of gaiety and odd fancies, but possess at the same time an individual charm and poetry. There are echoes of fairy tales and of a German '*Waldromantik*' which I have seldom met before in any book for children. Is this an echo which must disappear? Are there no longer any children left who are capable of falling under the spell of the forest noises and the magic of the birds chirruping in the old man's beard?

Susanne Ehmcke has recently illustrated a *Kinder-Duden*—a task which she carried out superbly, being an apt pupil of her father, who is himself a teacher and man of letters of considerable repute. It is to be hoped, however, that in such useful work as this she will not forget old Vogelbart, for he is one of the oddest and most kindly figures in modern picture-book literature. Even so, one gets the feeling that this book which children a few years ago loved so much is already becoming one of the landmarks of yesterday.

Among all Germany's feminine talent for creating picture-books, Susanne Ehmcke is perhaps the most gifted and the most industrious artist. The only person to compare with her in output is the admittedly older Else Wenz-Vietor who, since 1924, has been illustrating book upon book with enormous

[1] The book appeared in an (unfortunately) revised edition, Ravensburg, 1965. (B.A.)

skill. She has mastered the techniques for dealing with all sorts of subjects, from animals and flowers to poetry and fairy stories. Her artistry is reminiscent of that of the much older Englishman Arthur Rackham, with whom she shares a similar range of subject matter. Without doubt she will occupy a prominent place in the bibliography of German picture-books, but I ought not to dwell too much on her work in a chapter devoted to the pioneers of new territory. Her many books are all rooted in a solid tradition.

With Elsa Eisgruber, who is almost as well known, the position is somewhat different. In so far as her illustrative work is almost entirely confined to children's verse and legends of earlier centuries she ought by rights to be the more old-fashioned of the two, but she has, in fact, brought a quite new look to German picture-books, thereby reviving certain old stories and poems in a form suitable for the modern nursery. The fineness and precision of her drawing and the transparency of her colours are reminiscent of the drawings of the Romantics; her very individual presentation of the fabulous, which she sees with a wholly fresh vision, the boldness of her perspectives, and the way she has of combining the gentle and the sinister, all contribute towards providing the watching child with a surprising and an entirely new kind of fairy-story world. This can be seen at its best in her large-format editions of German fairy tales: *Tulifäntchen* and *Romantische Märchen* (Leipzig, 1945), and in her books of rhymes and rhyming games: *Sause, Kreisel, sause* and *Rosmarin und Thymian* (Baden-Baden, 1930). From this latter date it can be seen that she, too, served her apprenticeship as an artist in the extraordinarily fruitful years at the end of the 1920s.

Similarly, from this period onwards, Marianne Scheel has been working almost exclusively as an illustrator for children's books, devoting herself perhaps more than anyone else to delineations of the natural world. Among her picture-books are: *Die Jahreszeiten* (Berlin, 1935), *Tiere in Haus und Hof* (Berlin, 1938), and *Die Geschichte von der Wiese* (Zürich, 1945). She has also contributed illustrations to many other books and many of these have introduced even the youngest children to plants and animals, with a rare sensitivity, avoiding the traps of a too adult realism or a too childish over-simplification. She continues to be an active figure and two recent books show her making fresh departures (*Das Haus zum Regenbogen*, 1958 and *Schornebogs Wald*, 1961).

Beatrice Braun-Fock also belongs to this group of artists who were trying out modern methods of book illustration well before the last war. She, too, has blazed new trails after it. Her early style is adapted most successfully to the needs of the present in her illustrations for Ernst Heimeran's rollicking story *Der Schwarze Schimmel* (1956).

Before finally taking leave of this collection of German books which have been influenced by modern painting, I should like to mention one or two other special instances of picture-books which were ahead of their times.

Die Geschichte vom Fluss (Berlin, 1937), by Eduard and Valerie Bäumer,

Erleichtert fahren Jan und Jon auf den sanften Licht-Schein eines übergross·n Feuer-Fisches zu, der als Wasserweg-Weiser am Übergang vom schwarzen zum gelbe∩ Meer liegt. Wie glatt und ungefährlich scheint es zu sein – und doch

bringt es Jan und Jon das Ende ihres Schiffs und damit ihrer Reise!

Eine spitze Felsnadel zerbricht das Schiff in zwei Teile

und lässt es ver- sinken.

Schon vor ihm sind Jan und Jon auf den Boden des gelben Meeres herabgesunken. Der Fisch begleitet sie.

HEPER–BERKENKAMP, Lou. *Die Geschichten von Jan und Jon und von ihrem Lotsen-Fisch*. Leipzig, 1948. thograph by the author.

Plate XXI

Top: SLADEK, Josef V. *Sladek detem.* Prague, 1948.
From the colour lithograph by A. Zabransky.

Bottom: CHUKOVSKY, Kornei. *Tarakanishche.* Leningrad, 1935.
From the colour lithograph by V. Konashsvicha,

Plate XXII

tells the story of a river's journey from its source to its mouth, and it did this for an age group who had not previously been introduced to factual material of this sort. The book has now become a classic, but on its first appearance it was greeted with delight by both children and adults as something completely fresh which made full use of the enlarged possibilities for expression inherent in modern painting. In 1938, again in Berlin, the same artists produced a second book: *Den Berg hinauf*, but alas, a third has never followed. At that time books of this kind which were not 100 per cent realistic, and those which too obviously displayed connexions with modern art were frowned upon as 'degenerate'. It is probably difficult for young people today to realize that such an accusation of degeneracy was levelled at artists like Franz Marc, Paula Modersohn, and Karl Hofer (to name only 'moderate' modernists), and their work could neither be exhibited nor bought and sold in public.

All the books just described which appeared after 1933, or which were still obtainable then, do at least serve to demonstrate that even in Germany the development of the picture-book did not entirely come to an end during those evil years. Without this quiet development, which was continued by a few small publishers through even the most difficult times, Germany's present position as a producer of picture-books would scarcely be thinkable. You have only to look at the average run of material being produced in Germany at that time with official support to realize what I mean.

In the years which saw the start of the Second World War a young graphic artist, Walter Bergmann, who was also a newspaper man, published three books in Berlin: *Christinchen* (1937), *Das Lied vom Brot* (1938), and *In tiefem Wald* (1940). These must be singled out in the annals of the German picture-book for their outstanding artistic refinement, their poetry, and their human sympathy. They reveal a truly creative artist, whose exemplary work brings to the town child a closer understanding of the beauty of nature and the place of the child in the natural world.

I should like to conclude this section with a note on a book which, as far as I am aware, is completely unknown: *Die Geschichten von Jan und Jon und von ihrem Lotsen-Fisch* (*The story of Jan and Jon and their Guide-fish*), by Lou Scheper-Berkenkamp (Leipzig, 1948). This book was a product of the post-war years and appeared as a glittering portent on the still very gloomy horizon of German publishing for children. To my knowledge it is one of the few examples of a German picture-book which has successfully adapted itself to the influences of cubism and abstract art. At the same time, the artist, who was associated with the Bauhaus at Dessau, guards against the dangers of losing objectivity or being merely decorative. Every picture embodies action, to whose interpretation the text gives only a small amount of help. The book shows evidence, as do all the other little books by this artist, of having been produced in close contact with children themselves.

.   .   .   .

The modern manner

In present-day Germany a new style in picture-books is slowly evolving, one which it is still too early to define clearly. Some of the distinguishing features in the work of contemporary German illustrators seem to me to be a renunciation of firm outlines, previously a *sine qua non* for the educationists, a leaning towards caricature, a retreat from sentiment, a strong influence from poster art, and a certain intentional naïvety, reminiscent of the paintings of the modern primitives.

In the books of Marlene Reidel, for instance, aimed at the lowest age groups, a great deal of powerful expression is gained from the daring juxtaposition of patches of colour allied to the most economical use of line. This has resulted in a complete departure from realism, further emphasized by her spirited use of assertive and all too angular forms.

Reiner Zimnik spells out in line what most people have to spell out in letters. For this reason his first books, where text and illustration are a unity, were his best. He reels off incidents like a child prodigy (e.g. *Xaver der Ringelstecher*). But one cannot be a child prodigy for ever and Reiner Zimnik has today become one of the most productive creators of picture-books, having in the meantime come to a fuller understanding of colour work. His books all retain a sense of humour which conceals a profound seriousness, and they still have this very individual unity of text and picture. So far he is to be seen at his best when he is given generous scope to bring to life his most personal thoughts and imaginings.

Another master in line-drawing is Gerhard Oberländer, one of the most sought after and talented illustrators in Germany. He writes most of his stories himself, but he has also turned his attention to *Robinson Crusoe* and *Grimm's fairy tales*, and more recently to the *Bible* (Stuttgart, 1965). He is especially fond of peculiar small animals, and although he has never given up the use of line, which is so important to preserve a sense of movement, he is, like Zimnik, very successful in giving free rein to colour in his books.

Lilo Fromm has also been working in a similar direction and has an enormous range of expression in crayon and colour wash. From time to time her talents have led her to over-emphatic caricature, especially in her treatment of adults. *Das Mondgesicht* (1960) is an example of her success in the field of coloured picture-books.

From the world of art the influence of the modern primitives and Sunday painters has been strong in German picture-books as well as elsewhere. Georgy Stefula, with his *Das Paradies* (1955), is one of the first and best examples of this. Without doubt this is one of the few attempts at a contemporary presentation of Biblical matter which is worthy of consideration.

Die Pimpelmaus and *Das Hündchen Benjamin* are two delicious stories by Wiltrud Roser which show most impressively her more childish, more naïve manner of illustration. They are both books in which the authoress has caught exactly a child's way of seeing things and they are thus naïve in the genuine sense of the word. Even the smallest children take her modest little heroes to heart as though they were truly alive.

The charming picture-books by Janosch offer us a quite different kind of naïvety. He paints his shepherds, horses, foxes, little urchins as a child might paint them, the transparent colours lightly laid on in a way that appeals especially to the adult's sense of childish simplicity.

The East German Werner Klemke has just completed a sumptuous and richly coloured edition of *Grimm's fairy tales* for a West German publishing house (1963). He has produced very many picture-books for small children, all of which are characterized by powerful effects which he gains with chalk, a technique much favoured in Eastern Europe. Klemke is at his most striking in his combination of chalk with pen-and-ink drawing. Another artist coming from East Germany, Kurth Wendlandt, brought with him a high reputation as an illustrator, for instance, in his fine pictures for Anna Dobrinskaja's *Ano lebt in der Tundra*. At present he is attempting something entirely new in his remarkable and, one might say, painterly efforts to establish a unified relationship between drawing and photography.

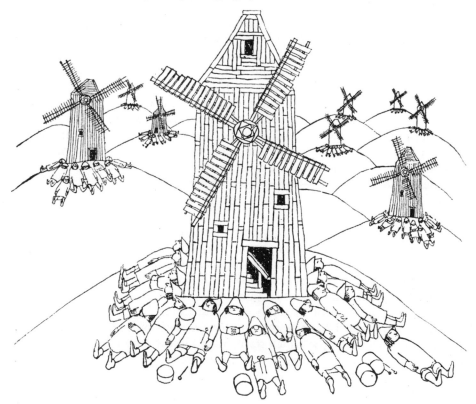

ZIMNIK, Reiner. *Die Trommler für eine bessere Zeit*, Zürich, 1958.
Line drawing by the author.

Q

Those qualities in picture-books which I mentioned earlier, especially the trend towards caricature and the use of advertising techniques, contribute an added strength when they come from a genuine spontaneity and a need to get something across to the child reader. When, however, they appear simply as imitation of externals or fashionable gimmickry then they are dangerous and far more degenerate than all the cheerful rubbish which we were often faced with as children.

Almost all modern picture-books have lost the way into what generations of children held to be their own paradise, namely, the warm seclusion of 'the nursery' or what Pestalozzi called '*die Wohnstube*' (not entirely the same thing). For all of us now it appears as a vanished illusion of security. Perhaps the artists that I have been talking about, and many others, all of them young, are questing for a new children's paradise. Perhaps the old one has gradually turned out to be dull and boring. We even come across the quest in adult literature about young people, say, in Ingrid Bacher's *Kinderinsel* (*The island of children*). For my part I think that the strange figure of Reiner Zimnik with the curious characters in his picture-fables is taking a definite way towards this sort of thing.

It is now necessary, however, to visit some other European countries to see what sort of a paradise their books hold for their children (and heaven knows most children need one). Naturally, it is not likely to be found any more in the dark forests of the fairy tale. In an age of technology and political uncertainty such a refuge in childish idylls will seem for many to be 'a receipt for deceit'. And yet even a picture-book about railways can radiate its own poetry and sense of humanity, as we shall shortly see, while subjects like nature or folk-lore can be so imbued with the character of our own time that they are by no means a flight from reality—they can lead children from the known world into the world of the imagination, of reflection, the world at the roots of their own being.

Eastern Europe

In order not to drift into international confusion, I propose to deal with the other picture-books that I know country by country, starting with Eastern Europe. As you will see, this is not intended politically since the political situation of books for young people east of the Iron Curtain was examined in the chapter on children's books and politics.

Now it is a question of methods of production. Up to this point all the picture-books which I have been considering, with only a few exceptions, have employed a technique which starts from a linear outline and then within this superimposes colours of greater or lesser strength or transparency. Now, suddenly, we come up against drawings and patches of colour done in bold chalk without any drawn outlines. Furthermore, this is carried out with a daring delight in colours which is a direct legacy of Slav folk-art. Such work as this was first seen at exhibitions which the youthful Soviet Republic organ-

ALLINGHAM, W. *In fairyland*. London, 1870.
An early example of a *Flower fairy book*. Illustrated by Richard Doyle and originally printed in nine colours from wood blocks by Edmund Evans.

Plate XXIII

HRUBIN, František. *Rikejte si se mnou*. Prague, 1946.
Colour lithograph by Jiři Trnka.

Plate XXIV

ized in western countries early in the 1920s. The books shown were cheap little affairs, but in their treatment of subjects for children they had a freshness and boldness of presentation whose 'new look' attracted a great deal of attention. As everyone knows, Russia had at this time a similar revelation to offer in the techniques of cinema.

For reasons which have not yet been satisfactorily explained, this movement, which was revolutionary in all the best senses, had to give way to a popular realism which took hold of picture-books as well. These early Russian productions, therefore, take on the attributes of pioneer work and such artists as X. A. Vasnetsov and V. Lebedev had an influence on the whole range of Russian book illustration, although the development of these ideas was left to other countries. When one considers the *Albums du Père Castor* (pp. 136–39), which are among the finest and most educative picture-books of the early thirties, it hardly comes as a surprise to learn that the two chief collaborators in the series, Nathalie Parain and Rojankovsky, were both of Eastern European extraction, creating their superb books for children under the direction of the French educational pioneer.

At the same time the Russian fairy stories, along with those of Tolstoy, found their way into the children's books of the West and they have maintained their place there ever since beside our own indigenous tales. Two such fairy-tale picture-books are in front of me as I write, occupying places of honour in my East European collection. The first is called *Histoires vraies, racontées par Tolstoi* and it is illustrated by Nathalie Parain (Paris, 1936). Here is Russia at its most attractive in both words and pictures. This is a book which is ethical in the best sense of the word and it has a clarity which will hold the attention of even the smallest child. The coloured pictures which surround every page complement the text perfectly, but at the same time they have an entirely modern freshness and enchantment.

My mother is the most beautiful woman in the world (Lothrop, 1945) was written by an Englishwoman, Becky Reyher, who got the story from her Russian-born mother. The whole world of the Russian countryside is set out here with all its colour and its emotional appeal, a gift from an unknown land for the child of Western Europe. Here too, pictures, and text combine in a rare unity, and the book is an example of all those delightful productions from the fruitful years after the Second World War which are now out of print. At the same time it is among the final representatives of the Russian art of story-telling and illustration, whose influence was once such a source of stimulation.[1] Much of this influence can still be traced today in the picture-books of East Germany.

[1] This version of an old Russian folk-tale achieved considerable fame in the United States in 1963, when a former trustee of the New City Library, New York was said to have burnt the library's copy because of its favourable attitude to Russia. In fact, he had only torn it in half. (B.A.)

Czechoslovakian picture-books

This style, deriving from Slav folk-art and running parallel to modern art in its development, was responsible for the production of some splendid books in the countries of Eastern Europe. For a time their pictorial daring was quite superior to anything appearing in the West. In Czechoslovakia, particularly, neither foreign occupation nor the miseries of the post-war years could suppress their artistic boldness. Their most influential artist in this field is Jiří Trnka who has done an enormous amount to bring happiness to the children of Czechoslovakia, even though his work is barely thinkable without the splendid popular tales and drawings produced by his predecessor Josef Lada. Lada is also a man of the people, speaking the language of simple folk and thus also of children. The pronounced outlines of his drawings and their flat, gay blocks of colour may seem somewhat out of fashion today, but his fresh and genuine vision is timeless. *Der Kater Mikesch* (*Purrkin the talking cat*), was first published in 1935 and yet in 1963 it was awarded the *Deutsche Kinderbuchpreis*.

Trnka's mother and grandmother were from a district near Pilsen and both worked in the local cottage-industry of carving country toys. This is an area which has always been the delight of students of folk-lore, but the son of this family turned it to true art. First of all he started a puppet theatre called 'Trnka's wooden theatre'. Here, surely, he established that richly populated fairy-story world which in the years of the Second World War and after was to find abundant expression in his picture-books. Today he also makes world-famous puppet films. As director of these, he says that puppets, for all their stylization and their unreality, are in fact much better suited than actual people for the transmission of thoughts and of atmosphere.

The situation in his picture-books is similar. The characters in them are creatures which he has invented, but they have been infused with a wonderful life of their own. Whether they are little chubby-cheeked children with mops of red hair, or whether they are chimney-sweeps, ravens, cats, clowns, or ancient grandmothers, every one of them is a living being from the child-like imagination of this one man. Nor is their liveliness in any way due to a realistic presentation. These curious and quite unrealistically portrayed creatures are full of a vitality which almost bursts the borders of the pictures, but it is the kind of life that is taken on by old and long-familiar toys like dolls and teddy-bears.

This can be seen at its clearest in his first illustrations to a book of verse, *Říkejte si se Mnou* (*Say it with me*) by František Hrubin (Prague, 1946). This little book, available in a German translation under the title *Sag auf*, was one of the first and finest representatives of a group of picture-books which were to take a completely new and unconventional direction.

Trnka's other books are largely based on fairy tales, but still using a very free treatment. Perhaps the most original are those in which he supplies folding puppets of a marvellous simplicity so that the book can be set up as a most impressive theatre. In their cubic construction the puppets resemble those painted wooden figures from Russia in the shape of spheres or eggs which, when opened, reveal ever smaller figures within. Many of Trnka's puppet films have also been turned into books possessing a real vitality of their own, but what is not realized from bibliographical details in, say, the German editions of these books, is that the best of them had already been published before 1946 when Czechoslovakia's incorporation into the Eastern Bloc took place. This was also a time when other countries had very few picture-books to match these freely constructed masterpieces.

One of the best illustrators in present-day Czechoslovakia seems to me to be Ota Janeček. His illustrations for the mysteriously poetic books of verse by František Halas are as delicate and transparent as a Chinese pen-drawing, but with a narrative freshness which is wholly European. His studies of animals are drawn with enormous precision, but only after they have been observed with an artist's eye. He has illustrated a great many books for children.

The Czechs are a nation extraordinarily rich in good illustrators. Of course, they have a lot of books which set out to mirror in a realistic way the changes in the State, its ethos and its new way of life. But one does not get the impression that Czechoslovakian children go short of truly pleasurable reading. The classics of the Western as well as of the Eastern powers are available together with a colourful collection of their own story-books and books of verse—everything illustrated by their own artists and obtainable in cheap editions.

Another among the best of contemporary illustrators is the Czech Adolf Zábransky, whose bold use of line is only comparable to the Swiss Hans Fischer. As early as 1946 I got hold of a copy of his book illustrating verses by Sladek (*Sladek detem*)—a book later to be translated into several languages. It contains pages of narrative cheekiness and freedom, as, for instance, in his drawings of cats or of the little goose-girl, but they are never merely impudent. There is a delicacy and warmth about them and a firm connexion with Czechoslovakian folk-art. A later book, published in Germany as *Kinderfreuden* (1958) with verses by J. Čarek, contains pages of a similar mastery, but here and there falls a prey to the same danger that has beset draughtsmen in Germany, namely, that of gaining visual effects at the expense of narrative accuracy.

Polish picture-books

Poland is the other Eastern country which is, graphically, really interesting. Since translations of Polish books are not so common in the West as those from Czechoslovakia, one is much more dependent on external appearances—but these are sufficient for much of what I have to say.

The show-piece here is a wonderful book published in Warsaw in 1938. It is called *Lokomotywa* and it has a text by Juljan Tuwim and illustrations by

Lewitt and Him. We meet here with a book of double significance. First, it is one of the boldest and most typically Polish of children's books and one which established a tradition which post-war picture-book producers could follow. Second, this was a picture-book based on a technical subject, the railway engine, and when I said at the beginning of this section that even technical matters can lead a child into fairyland, then it was this book and its successors that I was thinking about. Its two illustrators, Lewitt and Him, appear to have left Poland in 1939 and they crop up again in war-time England with their work printed on the dismal paper of those days.

Through work in advertising and newspaper cartoons they rapidly built up a name for themselves there, and a series of picture-books displays the two Poles as perfectly naturalized Englishmen in their choice of subjects. There was *The Little Red Engine gets a name*—one of the most poetic railway stories imaginable, and one which founded schools of such books in many countries. There was also *Blue Peter*, a magnificent dog story, *Five silly cats*, a crazy story about five cats going fishing, and finally, *The football's revolt*, a story full of the most delicious humour. Lewitt and Him prepared their texts to some extent themselves, and in their best books they show an artistic boldness similar to the Czech Trnka's. They, too, are capable of lifting children out of the everyday world into one of their own making where people talk with a stranger, freer language. Although their pictorial method is quite unrealistic, and indeed frequently approaches the abstract, they always maintain contact with what for children is the essential reality of their subjects and they never slip into being merely decorative. All their books were produced during the late thirties and early forties, for in later years they split up as an artistic team. Lewitt today works in London under the name of Jan le Witt, and his most recent picture-book, *The vegetabull* (Collins, 1956), is almost a piece of sur-realist art produced with a most refined craftsmanship. I am curious to find out if the children of today are willing to accept its style as a perfectly natural one. George Him has also returned to children's book illustration recently with more conventional but beautifully executed illustrations to Frank Herrmann's *The giant Alexander* (Methuen, 1964) and Leila Berg's *Folk-tales* (Brock-hampton, 1965).

Developments in Poland herself have not yet reached too far into modernity. Juljan Tuwim's *Lokomotywa* has twice been re-issued with fresh illustrations, the better of these being perhaps those by Jan Lenica in 1958. For all the bold-ness and freshness of its drawing there is no trace of any retreat into abstraction or stiltedness. This is also true of the other excellent illustrations for the book by Marcin Scancer and for two other books illustrated by him: the *Papa-geienbuch*, a book about parrots (published in Germany in 1953) and *Doremi* (Warsaw, 1955), an introduction to music for young children. The out-standing features of Poland's graphic tradition can be seen at their best in Maria Orlowska's illustrations for Munro Leaf's famous *Ferdinand*. It is arguable that she to some extent violates the text, which ought to be the most

LEWITT-HIM. *The football's revolt*. London, 1939.
From a colour lithograph by the authors.

Plate XXV

OLSEN, Ib Spang. *Det lille lokomotiv*. Copenhagen, 1963.
From a colour lithograph by the author.

Plate XXVI

important part of the book, but in such scenes as Ferdinand at pasture or Ferdinand in the bullring she achieves a superb pictorial design in the best tradition of picture-books. Like Czechoslovakia, Poland seems to maintain very high average standards, for almost every book that you open possesses this gay vitality coupled with modern forms of expression.

Finally, two newcomers to my collection: first, Olga Siemaszko, who as publisher of a children's magazine has always had the chance to keep close contact with young people's ideas. She has illustrated poetry, fairy stories, and fiction for children, and her occasionally somewhat febrile imagination is pre-eminent in the invention of fabulous creatures. Her work seems to typify the sort of thing which is enjoyed by Polish children and their parents as well. Adam Kilian, on the other hand, has come to children's books from other experience in graphic art. He is one of the few people who understand how to combine the demands of modern art with a sympathy for what children really like. As with so many East European artists he has also inherited the traditions of an ancient folk-art and, as with so many Polish artists, he is fortunate in having at his disposal the work of some outstanding children's authors.

Scandinavian picture-books

When we turn back from these exotic and truly stimulating picture-books, we may be excused for feeling that some of the contemporary publications from Western Europe are perhaps a little insipid. But they, nevertheless, are just as deeply rooted in their various national traditions and in the prevailing concepts of the nature of childhood.

Since, however, the whole of Western tradition is more familiar and more accessible to us, I only want to pick out a few really special achievements. If I were going to mention everything that is noteworthy I should need a whole book the size of this one, such is the wealth of book production these days in so many countries.

Among the Scandinavians it seems to me that while the Danes have produced the finest picture-books, the Swedes have given European children the most enjoyable stories. But almost all Scandinavian picture-books seem to possess a brightness, a clarity, a neatness—and most of them a cheerfulness as well—which is most infectious. What a discovery it is for us foreigners to see the icebergs melting in the sun, so that an Eskimo who has gone to sleep on one of them almost comes to grief (*Figge* by Victor Mall, Uppsala, 1945), or to meet the Greenlander among the polar-bears and seals of his marvellously depicted Northern landscape (*Gaba, den lille Groenländer* by Gitz-Johansen, Copenhagen, 1947), or to dream with the little boy that he is suddenly all by himself in the world and can do or not do whatever he pleases (*Palle alene i verden* by Jens Sigsgaard, illustrated by Arne Ungermann, Copenhagen, 1947). Then there is one of the most delightful children's books you could ever hope to find where a sea-lion and a tiger in a world gone crazy escape from their zoo and meet with the most impossible adventures in snow, ice, and tropical sunshine (*Jugga Jagga och Vagge Vugge*, by G. Ackerhielm, illustrated by Ingrid van Nyman).

Do not think that these picture-books, which all originated towards the end of the forties, are in any way lone examples. Even the average publications of the present time possess the same kind of liberating unselfconsciousness and plainness, as can be seen in such picture-books as *The little woman who forgot everything* by Janet Beattie, with pictures by Rita Rapp (Stockholm, 1958). This same decade which produced such an extraordinary number of fine picture-books also gave to children throughout the world such famous authors as Astrid Lindgren from Sweden and Tove Jansson from Finland.

Between whiles Astrid Lindgren has written the words for picture-books which bring alive the pastoral life of Sweden with a romantic naturalism (e.g. *Tomten*, 1960, illustrated by Harald Wiberg); and Inga Borg in her story of a reindeer (*Parrak, the white reindeer*, Stockholm, 1958) also manages to convey a sense of life in the far North in a most individual way.

The picture-books of the Dane, Spang Olsen, have a particularly cheerful and engaging style. An artist is at work here from the world of Hans Christian Andersen, with all his delicacy, his true sense of poetry and his feeling for colour. A greater success abroad, however, was gained by Egon Mathiesen whose plain and consciously primitive tale *Blue-eyed Mies* combined emotion and comedy in a way that appealed to an international audience.

Picture-books by the Swede, Poul Strøyer, similarly find their way across many frontiers, although his untranslatable *ABC* (with Lennart Hellsing) surely remains his most original piece of work. Another *ABC* by Britt Hallqvist, superbly illustrated by Stig Lindberg, is perhaps even more success-ful in its humour and its graphic effects, and in this connexion it is worth remarking that recent years have seen a transition from simple graphic work to more elaborate work in colour. Tones become brighter and harsher, but they are always used with elegance and with care for the transparency of shading. The Norwegian Reidar Berle has given life and colour to the riches of Norwegian fairy tales and poetry for children.

England, France, and Italy

Present-day English children are fond of meeting the same characters again and again in a whole series of picture-books. One such elemental character is Orlando the marmalade cat whose adventures have been depicted by Kathleen Hale in great big picture-books with very distinguished colour drawings. Another is Little Tim, a small boy whose adventures have found in Edward Ardizzone one of the most compelling artist-illustrators of our time. But perhaps the series which is most out of the ordinary is that which has the Little Red Engine for its subject. His soulful story is told by Diana Ross in eight volumes, illustrated with wit and poetry by Leslie Wood (except, of course, for the first volume, which was illustrated by Lewitt-Him).

As in Scandinavia, contemporary English picture-book publishing is taking its part in the international movement towards greater colour. In William Stobbs there is an illustrator who holds a careful balance between the techniques of graphic art (i.e. work prepared with a thorough knowledge of how it is to be printed) and an unrestrained use of colour. His pictures for the edition of Anton Chekhov's *Kashtanka* (1959) magnificently capture for children a sense of the Muscovite scene. Alan Howard, too, makes use of modern graphic techniques and is especially successful in his portrayal of the grey world of London, shot through with reds, in *Limping Ginger of London Town* (1962).

Gerald Rose, on the other hand, is a painter through and through. His book *Charlie on the run*, for instance, is a small masterpiece of painting in the modern manner transferred to the pages of a book. In 1962 Brian Wildsmith also turned his talents to creating picture-books, receiving the Kate Greenaway Medal for his *ABC*. Since then he has produced a number of brilliantly executed picture-books, including a *Mother Goose* (1964); a counting-book: *Brian Wildsmith's 1 2 3* (1965); and retellings of fables from La Fontaine: *The lion and the rat* (1963), *The north wind and the sun* (1964), and *The rich man and the shoemaker* (1965).

I have already devoted parts of this book to special studies of the work of Père Castor, Nathalie Parain, Rojankovsky and Jean de Brunhoff, but my French collection still contains three books which connoisseurs among the young ought to be told about. These are the picture-books by Samivel—an artist who knows, like Brunhoff, how to create a world of self-contained individuality within the covers of a book. His finest book is *Bon voyage, M. Dumollet* (1942). It tells of a hatter from St. Malo and his adventures on the high seas, among pirates of dreadful ferocity, sea-monsters of incredible grotesqueness and tempests with the formal splendour of those in a Japanese woodcut—everything ending happily, as all good fairy tales should. The whole book is a miracle of artistic and inventive imagination, and as a product of the berationed war years, with two-colour printing only, its achievement is unique. The figure of M. Dumollet from St. Malo whose only protection and whose most efficient weapon is his eternal umbrella is a typically French creation but one, nevertheless, capable of winning the hearts of children from other countries, as I know from my own experience.

Samivel's translation into pictures of the world of classical fable is also unforgettable (*Les malheurs d'Ysengrin*, 1939), while he has contributed exemplary illustrations for children of La Fontaine's *Fables* and such classic folktales as the *Pied Piper* in the *Albums du Père Castor*.

Samivel is by no means a folk-artist, however, and he makes demands on his reader's intelligence. There is an ingenious fantasy behind his portrayals of man, beast, and landscape, an element of the unusual or the surprising which gives his books a touch of magic. This is particularly true of *M. Dumollet* and *Les malheurs d'Ysengrin*, his two best books.

On the whole, the average French picture-books were not very distinguished, although the country has always been one to encourage experiment.

This gave rise in 1928 to a sumptuous private edition of an almost abstract picture-book by Joan Miró, with a text by Lisc Hirtz: *Il était une petite pie* (Edition Jean Bucher). This very witty and elegant book can hardly have moved the hearts of the children of 1928, but it was a nice plaything for their parents.

The enchanting picture-book *Ko et Ko, les deux esquimaux* by Viera da Silva and Pierre Gueguen is quite a different matter. This was a product of the same private press in 1933 and it brings the achievements of abstract painting into contact with the demands of objectivity in a way that was probably enjoyable to children. Cut-out figures which allowed the book itself to be used as a little stage added to the children's delight, while parents were at the same time presented with a little world of art which deserved a wider circulation than that allowed by a bibliophile's limited edition at a very high price.

This almost brings us to the end of our survey of European picture-books. All that remains for me to mention are one or two big Italian volumes dating from 1945 which were the delight of children soon after the war. There were about ten of them, originating from Bruno Munari, and they were what we might call high-class novelty books. Perhaps the best of them was *L'uomo del camion* (Verona, 1945), a book about a lorry driver with a present for his bambino. But he has an accident after going only a few miles along the road for home and this leads him to various changes in his mode of transport. As the vehicles change so this leads in the book to various alterations of page size. Making use of a car, a bicycle, a scooter, roller-skates, and Shanks's pony, finally shrunken and barefooted on a tiny page he reaches his son. This is followed on the next page by the opening of the present to show in full size again an abundance of good things. Fancy tricks, you may say, but they are full of playful ideas which were genuinely sympathetic to the needs of the deprived children of the Second World War.

Although Bruno Munari's books have only remained in print in America there are many signs today that great efforts are being made to bring Italian picture-books to the forefront again, and here, as in France, there has been a variety of very interesting picture-books produced in recent years. Artists like Vigo Fontana, illustrator of fairy tales and children's magazines, Emanuele Luzzati, creator of some wonderful modern picture-stories, and G. Carlois of more satirical books are especially worth mentioning.

From America back to Switzerland

No one can deny that since the war a number of American picture-book characters have got so well established in Europe that they seem to be entirely at home there. Now although it is not my aim to discuss American picture-books I would like to pick out one of these nursery heroes in particular: *The happy lion* by Louise Fatio and Roger Duvoisin. This is a really delightful piece of work, an exciting story in picture-book form carrying with it pro-

FATIO, Louise. *The happy lion.* McGraw-Hill, New York, 1954.
Lithograph by Roger Duvoisin.

found human implications. When I turned the pages of this book and saw the drawings of the little town through which the escaped lion trotted so peaceably, with no notion of the panic he was causing among the good townspeople, it struck me that to all outward appearances the book did not look American at all. Then I realized that the illustrator Roger Duvoisin and his wife, Louise Fatio, were respectively from Geneva and Lausanne, and that up to the age of thirty Duvoisin had been a graphic artist and stage-designer in Geneva. In this way, a splendid artist who has given us over the years an unparalleled group of picture-books has made a natural homecoming to a country, with whose most recent productions in this field I now want to end this chapter, namely, Switzerland.

It was from Switzerland that we started at the beginning of this chapter when I considered the work of Kreidolf. In those days Kreidolf had to turn from the inhospitality of a not very progressive country and address his first books to German readers. But with the Second World War this state of affairs has fundamentally altered. Switzerland's psychological dissociation from

Germany resulted in the development of her own native genius, which brought with it to some extent an international fame.

The first Swiss picture-book of our time to appeal to me so much that I immediately bought two copies of it (one for my children and one for my own collection, at that time only a very small one) had the appearance of a sketch-book in which someone had written and drawn all kinds of nonsense. It was called *Das lustige Männlein* and its creator was a young woman from Basle, Esther Hosch-Wackernagel. It was such an extraordinary book that she had had to establish her own company to publish it, but when it appeared in 1936 it found such favour with the children of Switzerland that it has continued in print to the present time. It is the story of a juvenile Don Quixote, a little man with a horse and a dog for whom everything is reduced to child-size proportions. The fifty-four pictures which recount the adventures of this company during a journey through the desert have a captivating originality. They are set down so simply and spontaneously that they appear as fresh today as they did on their first publication.

Recently, almost a quarter of a century after its appearance, I met the book's author for the first time and she told me how she came to write this classic of the Swiss nursery. It seems that she was staying at a holiday resort with her small son who was recuperating from a serious illness. Condemned to rest for most of the day, the boy could not and would not go to sleep at night. Finally, in a desperate effort to distract him, his mother began to draw pictures for him on the back of the hotel menu, promising him that if he would go to sleep she would add a sequel to the story which he would find beside his bed when he woke up in the morning. The trick succeeded and one of the most enchanting picture-books of her country was born. It is, moreover, the classic

für das Krokodilleder haben sie genug Geld bekommen, um ein Kamel und Sachen zu kaufen. Auch ein sehr feines Zelt, es ist aufgerollt auf dem Kamel. Das Rösslein trägt Essen und Wasser.

HOSCH-WACKERNAGEL, E. *Die Geschichte vom lustigen Männlein mit der langen Nase.* Basel, 1936. Line drawing by the author.

situation for a picture-book to arise: the urgency of the problem, the love of an anxious mother—and the result cannot be ascribed to the fads of any particular school of art.

The other Swiss children's books whose reputation has spread beyond the borders of the tiny country where they arose form an example of the high status enjoyed by graphic and advertising art in that country. At the same time they are an image of a relatively unspoiled world where nature and living things still have an appointed place in the order of things. But the life story of the artistic picture-book in Switzerland is still very short. A beginning was made before the Second World War with a book in large format by Rosie Schnitter, illustrated by Berta Tappolet, called *Der Leuchtturm* (Zürich, 1936). This portrayed on a generous scale a true incident in the life of a poor family in Tessin. The text was simple and unpretentious, the large pictures were full of feeling and, indeed, of genuine pathos, but it is only now that we realize that this was, above all, the foundation for the modern Swiss picture-book. Berta Tappolet continued to illustrate many Swiss fairy stories and sagas right up to her early death, which occurred not long after the appearance of her charming picture-book *Kinder im Garten* (Zürich, 1941). This was the kind of work where she stood supreme and she has not yet been surpassed.

In fact, fairy stories and their illustration play an important part in the work of Swiss artists. For instance, Herbert Leupin, an advertising artist, whose posters are seen all over Europe, produced a series of picture-books, each one devoted to a tale from Grimm. If the books had not been of an unwontedly fine production (appearing either during or immediately after the Second World War) it would have been necessary to refuse them consideration, just because of their impressiveness. This kind of illustration reduces too greatly the impact on the child's imagination of the written words themselves. But today it is the done thing to turn fairy stories into picture-books in this way and to argue against it now is to break lances with windmills.

It was just such a book as this which gained the pundits' award of the *Schweizer Jugendbuchpreis* in 1957 as the best Swiss picture-book of the year. The book was Grimm's *Der Wolf und die sieben Geisslein* (*The wolf and the seven little kids*) and it was illustrated by Felix Hoffmann with taste and sensibility, but with an overriding naturalism. He belongs among the best Swiss illustrators alive today and has won world-wide renown for the other fairy tales which he has subsequently illustrated in a similar manner.

One artist whose ideas for picture-books are quite independent of inspiration from fairy tales is Lili Roth-Streiff with *Wolkenbutzeli* (1943), *Das Rösslein Kilian* (1947) and *Der Dumme August und die Tiere* (1953) with a very successful text by Marguerite Paur-Ulrich.

To round off this long chapter I should like to describe in some detail the work of two other Swiss artists who are gaining international standing and whose works are possibly among the finest which the period after the Second World War created for the delectation of its children.

Alois Carigiet, Selina Chönz, and the 'Schellen-Ursli'

Among the host of lovely picture-books which are available today, I consider that the *Schellen-Ursli* books are singularly happy in their inspiration. This is not just because of their noteworthy artistic quality, it is much more because they have captured in their pages a young fellow who sprang to life as soon as he was drawn and became an immediate favourite with children, who avidly followed his adventures. During the last twenty years the picture-book characters who have impressed themselves on the deeper levels of children's consciousness have been almost entirely animals. Sometimes they have been hybrid creatures like Mickey Mouse, but by and large the pages of picture-books have been filled by a procession of ducks, cats, mice, royal elephants, and lions (who, if anything but royal, were at least *happy*). No other person has brought so much friendliness or so great a sense of wide horizons to the nursery as Babar, king of the elephants, as long ago as 1934.

Then suddenly Ursli, the Alpine farmer's boy, arrived (Zürich, 1946), and in no time at all he had become for the children of Switzerland, as now for many children all over the world, an equal, not to say a brother, to Heidi: a little boy who, for the sake of a dream, a childish longing, climbs into the high places, where he passes a night of loneliness under the glittering stars and gains his desire—the largest cowbell of the district to ring in the spring procession. And all this is done in the age of tarmac and of exact science, when children find the streets of cities as bright by night as they are by day, and when they know mountains either not at all or else through the picture-windows of hotels and children's homes, or from the nursery slopes 'with direct access to the ski-lift'.

Do you think that they tremble today as the night engulfs Ursli in his lonely shepherd's hut, as we used to tremble when for the first time we heard with Heidi the pine-trees whispering above the lonely pasture? We can never know precisely what really goes on in the heart of a child, but there must be profound reasons for Ursli's success. Let us examine more closely the way in which this remarkable children's book came into being—a good enough story on its own account.

A young schoolteacher and writer from the Engadine was anxious to write a story for her countless pupils which would be typical of their most immediate surroundings. Her name was Selina Chönz and her home was in one of the most beautiful villages of the Engadine, Guarda, which she chose for the starting-point of her story. The verses for *Schellen-Ursli* she wrote in the language of the district, Romansh, Switzerland's fourth native tongue. She also wrote a German transcription and found an artist who, himself living in the canton of Grisons, understood what she was trying to do. He came to Selina Chönz's village, lived in her old house, which became the model for Ursli's with its thick walls, its recessed windows, and its huge entrance hall. A small room was made over as a studio for him, his other studio was the sur-

SAMIVEL. *Bon voyage, Monsieur Dumollet*. Paris, 1942. Colour lithograph by the author.

Plate XXVII

Hans Fischer (Photo. F. Engesser, Zürich).

Plate XXVIII

rounding landscape, the mountains on three sides, climbing in steps to the eternal snow, and providing all the growing and living things which he needed to set down on his paper.

Three books came of this partnership and the value of Selina Chönz's contribution did not lie only in the texts which she wrote but also in the way that she encouraged a good artist to produce perhaps his most attractive work. Selina Chönz had long been noted for her Romansh poetry and she knew how to tell her story in plain unforced words and rhymes, even in its German version. Her description of Ursli, for instance, uses no unnecessary word, no opportunist rhymes, no verbal twisting and turning—a few lines and everything is there:

Da ist der Ursli, schaut ihn an,	Yes, here our mountain boy you see,
ein Bergbub wie ein kleiner Mann!	Quite like a man, you must agree.
Grad auf wie eine Bergesspitze	Upon his head a pointed hat,
steht auf dem Kopf die Zipfel-	(The mountain, too, is shaped like
mütze;	that.)
sie ist aus Wolle von den Schafen,	It's made from soft wool from the
die jetzt in Urslis Stalle schlafen.	sheep
Denn Urslis Mutter strickt und	That now in Ursli's stable sleep.
spinnt	For Ursli's mother spins, weaves,
und webt die Kleider für ihr Kind.	stitches,
Der Vater nagelt Urslis Schuhe	And knits his shirt and hat and
und schafft für ihn fast ohne Ruhe.	breeches,
	His father has the boots to make,
	And toils all day for Ursli's sake.

As a matter of interest, here are the first four lines in their original Romansh, an even more melodic version without any loss of simplicity:

Ed uossa vaina nos Uorsin,
chi'd ais ün mat scu ün homin
El ria, sguerschagiand adüna
suotour sieu clap chavlüra brüna.

It is a remarkable thought that three of the finest picture-books of our time have drawn their strength, their language, and their subject-matter from a district which makes up one of Europe's smallest linguistic groups.

The three books are called *Schellen-Ursli* (Zürich, 1946), *Flurina und das Wildvöglein* (1952), and *Der grosse Schnee* (1955), but as a children's picture-book the first is undoubtedly the one most to be treasured. Figures and objects in it are simply drawn, often just against the white ground of the paper, and they possess a force rarely present in picture-books since the appearance of *Struwwelpeter*. Such plainness in the delineation of detail lends an even greater

A sketch of Schellen-Ursli made by Alois Carigiet.

effectiveness to those scenes of pathos rather than drama such as the drawing of the Alpine hut by night, or the dark portrait in brown and turquoise of Ursli's worried parents calling him home. Occasionally, indeed, the effectiveness is positively awe-inspiring, as in the page showing the wooden bridge over the ravine, but showing it with a boldness of perspective that was quite foreign to picture-books at that time. Today such boldness has become fashionable—one of our picture gimmicks. It is encouraged on all sides; it receives prizes; and it has just about ceased to impress us any more.

In the second volume, *Flurina und das Wildvöglein*, Ursli's sister is the heroine, while in the third the two come together in an adventure in the Engadine in winter. The mountains in winter give plenty of scope for dramatic events and Flurina is carried away by an avalanche from which she is rescued by Ursli in a fashion half realistic, half fabulous, with the aid of a coloured cord which has been one of the elements of the story. These two volumes are less basic in their pictorial and in their linguistic approach than *Ursli* was. The text is beginning to have echoes of a lyrical feeling for nature. A fey little girl, who is on intimate terms with the animals of the wild, puts in an appearance.

Children, animals, and trees all blend more closely with the landscape. The forces of nature—storm, snow, avalanche—are portrayed on a grand scale, but without losing sight of the young reader's ability to understand them. Carigiet enriches his graphic performance with so much sensuousness, that the books themselves become works of art quite outside the frame of reference for mere picture-books.

But what is the special quality in these three books which has caused the image of a landscape and the story of a humble enough adventure to be carried across every frontier as far as Japan? Is it the artistry? Is it the simple story which appeals to human feelings everywhere? Is it the happy description of some of Switzerland's most popular customs? All of these things are part of the answer, and yet they would count for little if the books' creators had not succeeded in giving the central character a personality of his own. It is this which is most necessary if the figures of a children's book are really to live as Heidi and Nils Holgersson and Babar and the Little Prince all live. And Ursli, with his black curls and his round, shining eyes, this boy who feeds the cows and the calves, and milks the goats, and chases off into darkness and danger for the sake of a cowbell, he has got the something which we call 'soul', for which no recipe can be found.

The simple strokes with which he is depicted, nevertheless, enable his awkward farm-boy's limbs with their clumsy clothes to express both an intense and natural enjoyment of life and the most doleful care. At the same time we have a wonderful conspectus of his surroundings, the vastness and coldness of the landscape and the warm sense of security in the kindliness of grown-up folk and the cosiness of home and stable. Then, after all his adventures in the big world are over, there comes the final happiness of being alone with his parents at supper (for a good meal always makes for a happy ending):

Die Mutter bringt Kastanienribel	Mother brings chestnuts, piping hot,
und obendrauf geschwungnen Nidel.	With cream poured over—such a lot!
Der Ursli isst, so viel er kann.	And while they watch him happily,
Die Eltern sehn sich glücklich an.	Young Ursli eats enough for three.
(From *A bell for Ursli*)	

On the empty fourth chair sits the guest of honour, the huge bell, boldly painted like everything else in the book. For the whole thing could easily have been just another sentimental celebration of a particular locality had it not been set down with such a fresh eye for line and colour by a painter for whom this countryside was not merely a subject for a landscape but his own homeland, understood with closest sympathy.

Hans Fischer (1909–58)

Hans Fischer, illustrator and author of picture-books, is a difficult man to pin down. With a few quick, delicate movements of his pencil he is away; the

R

lines circle, wriggle, spiral, like a dancer; the joke is developed with wit and dexterity; and then he steps aside and the thing which grew so rapidly is finished. The few lines in the foreground have become a fairy-tale forest with gloomy depths or a robbers' house like the one in *The travelling musicians* with the night full of strange goings-on, or it is a cock likely at any moment to shout out 'cock-a-doodle-doo'. What animals he draws! Hens, cats, goats, fish, rabbits, ducks—he does not simply draw them but writes them on the paper like letters. Just as an ordinary person has mastered a fluent handwriting so Hans Fischer has mastered the forms of animals, and indeed their very essence itself expressed in these forms.

Whenever I saw him drawing I could not help thinking of that Chinese painter who was granted a period of years for study by his Emperor. At the end of the time the Emperor wanted to see what the painter had produced, so the painter asked for clean paper and on it he painted a rooster with exceeding skill. But all the Emperor said was: 'Is that all?' Now Fischer had no master to grant him years for study, so that he, too, might set down the portrait of a rooster to perfection. But uncountable sketches bear witness to his gigantic efforts to acquire for himself the forms of nature like a second kind of handwriting until he had completely mastered them and could dash them off on canvas or paper with either an exact realism or an almost abstract sketchiness.

That a considerable part of his work is directed at children doubtless ties in with the fact that after he had left his job in Berne as a successful advertising artist the first book that he read (and read so profoundly that it almost became part of him) was *Grimm's fairy tales*. He was never again to escape entirely from this world of fairy tale until his all too early death in the spring of 1958. But how he made that world his own, and how he changed it! As stage designer at the *Cornichon*, Zürich's once famous 'little theatre', he learned all about setting scenes and his picture-books are a kind of scenic setting so that the fabulous can take place in the intimate atmosphere of the nursery.

At his death Hans Fischer left behind a large and complete body of work, even though it had limitations due to its prevailingly graphic character. His total creative output included etchings, lithographs, numerous pictures, caricatures, advertising work, limited editions, and illustrations for textbooks and story-books as well as straightforward picture-books. In the summer of 1959, he was given the posthumous honour of a complete exhibition in Zürich for which a richly illustrated monograph was prepared.

His first picture-book was the version of the Brothers Grimm's tale of the travelling musicians: *Die Bremer Stadtmusikanten* (Zürich, 1944) and it is typical of Fischer that he was fascinated by this fairy tale of the four outcast creatures which reaches its climax in a spooky adventure in the forest in the middle of the night. The poor worked-out ass, the ancient hunting dog, the condemned cock, and the inevitable cat, who knows all about nocturnal serenades, were all perfect sitters for Hans Fischer the animal lover.

After they have all been introduced to us and, still somewhat downcast, have

FISCHER, Hans. An original sketch for the book *Die Bremer Stadtmusikanten.*

settled themselves to spend the night topsy-turvily in a tree, the page turns and straight away their night adventure begins. And what a magic night it is with the yellow stars and the gleaming eyes of the animals glinting through the black mass of the drawing. This is Hans Fischer the poet, who, a page later, makes fun of himself by letting his animals get up to ten times as much mischief as the Brothers Grimm give precedent for. Then, following an inner rhythm, nocturnal peace resumes with a study in blue and black of the quiet house with the silhouettes of the sleeping beasts. But turning the page once more, one meets with the final mad colourful joke with the house taken over by the four friends. It is all much more than just illustration. From his own ancestry (his family came from the mountains of the Bernese Oberland) Hans Fischer has brought an inner feeling for the popular superstitions that once resided in fairy tales.

Apart from many single illustrations and pictures based upon fairy-tale subjects, Hans Fischer has also produced the picture-books *Das Lumpengesindel* (1945) and his own adaptation of *Puss-in-Boots*: *Der gestiefelte Kater* (1957). In the latter he takes a completely new road and one in the direction of a somewhat higher age group. Taking the Perrault text as a basis, he has rewritten the story, putting in all sorts of comic remarks in which he completely identifies himself with the cat.

What a deal of pity he has for the poor creature who has to go around in boots! There are ten drawings of the cat getting used to this unfamiliar footwear, and it is said that Hans Fischer himself went around in a pair in order to make his drawings from actual experience. This late work of his carries the use of line to such a point of wit and subtlety that it is difficult to imagine any kind of continuation, any road forward, along which children could accompany him. This is something which he felt himself and he was on the look out for other new paths, other new subjects.

Still to be mentioned are the two picture-books *Der Geburtstag* (1947) and *Pitschi* (1948). These are stories which Hans Fischer wrote himself as presents for his own children, who used to watch him over his shoulder as he was working and made their own wishes clearly heard. Thus, added to the company of the animals already mentioned, we now get ducks, rabbits, a goat, and a wonderful old lady (a companion-piece to the old lady in *Babar*). As children's books these two volumes are perhaps the ones to be most treasured, for they contain everything to delight young people. They are full of the wit and kindliness, the colour and happiness, the great good humour of a man who turned into a child again among his own children.

The work of Hans Fischer is a standing example that a genuine artist of our time can turn his talents to children's illustration without sacrificing any of his true quality. For Fischer was an artist who was at home in a world not far from that of Paul Klee, whose student he was for a time, and I could wish that more artists of his integrity would realize what he has done and also turn their talents to picture-books.

These last two illustrators to whom I have devoted so much space in my survey have extended their influence on children in another way, for they have both performed commissions (in exemplary fashion) to illustrate reading-books for the schools of Zürich. Thus the primary school children of this city have since 1958 possessed some of the finest textbooks in the world and it is to be hoped that this will be an education for their visual powers as well as their reading abilities.

COMMENT

Bibliographies and book catalogues tend to treat illustrators with as little ceremony as they do translators, even when a picture-book artist has contributed more to a particular volume than its author may have done. The following list has therefore only been assembled after some searching and it can make no claim to being at all complete. It contains a selection of books in English by Continental illustrators mentioned in this chapter and a few out-of-print titles have been included where they seemed particularly worth noticing. Title lists of early editions (mostly American) of books by Elsa Beskow, Boutet de Monvel, Elsa Eisgruber, Carl Larsson, Sibylle von Olfers, and Samivel can be found in the bibliography to the Horn Book's *Illustrators of children's books 1744–1945* (op. cit., p. 273) and in Hill and Bondeli's *Children's books from foreign languages* (p. 273). I have not been able to discover any editions of Kreidolf's work published either in England or America.

BOOK LIST

BORG, Inga
> Borg, Inga: *Bru, the brown bear*. Warne, 1961.
> *Parrak, the white reindeer*. Warne, 1959.
> *Plupp builds a house*. Warne, 1960.
> *Redcoat the fox*. Warne, 1965.
> *Tramper, the elk*. Warne, 1962.
> *Whitewings the swan*. Warne, 1963.

BRAUN-FOCK, Beatrice
> Heimeran, Ernst: *Paint a black horse*, retold in English by Leila Berg. Methuen (London), 1958.

CARIGIET, Alois
> Chönz, Selina: *A bell for Ursli*. Walck, 1953.
> *Florina and the wild bird*, translated by Anne and Ian Serraillier. Walck, 1961.
> *The snowstorm*. Walck, 1961.

EHMCKE, Susanne
> Bibliographic Institute, Mannheim: *A first German pictorial dictionary*. Harrap (London), 1959.

FISCHER, Hans

  Fischer, Hans: *The birthday*. Harcourt, 1954.

  Chanticleer and Partlet. Cassell (London), 1947.

  Pitschi. Harcourt, 1953.

  Puss-in-boots, adapted from Perrault. Harcourt, 1959.

  Rum-pum-pum. Harcourt, 1964.

  Grimm, J. and W.: *The travelling musicians*. Cassell (London), 1948.

FROMM, Lilo

  Michels, Tilde: *Karline's duck*. O.U.P. (London), 1961.

  Pustau, Erna von: *The moonstruck bear*, translated by Marion Koenig. Nelson, 1964.

  Schirmann, Li: *Nosy Friday*, translated by Anthea Bell. Abelard-Schuman, 1964.

HOFFMANN, Felix

  Grimm, J. and W.: *Rapunzel*, translated by Katya Sheppard. O.U.P. (London), 1961.

  The seven ravens. Harcourt, 1963.

  The sleeping beauty, translated by Peter Collier. Harcourt, 1959.

  The wolf and the seven little kids, translated by Katya Sheppard. Harcourt, 1958.

JANEČEK, Ota

  Macleod, Ann, editor: *English fairy tales*. Hamlyn (London), 1966.

JANOSCH

  Janosch: *Just one apple*, translated by Refna Wilkin. Walck, 1966.

KLEMKE, Werner

  Rodrian, F., and Klemke, W.: *Hubert the deer*. Benn (London), 1963.

LADA, Josef

  Lada, Josef: *Purrkin the talking cat*, translated by R. Symonds. Harrap (London), 1966.

LEWITT–HIM

  Tuwim, Julian: *Locomotive; The turnip; The birds' broadcast*. Minerva, 1939.

LINDBERG, Stig

  Hellsing, L., and Strøyer, P.: *Billy's birthday lollipop*, translated by Marianne Hellweg. Burke (London), 1966.

MATHIESEN, Egon

  Mathiesen, Egon: *Oswald the monkey*. Macdowell, 1961.

MUNARI, Bruno

  Munari, Bruno: *Animals for sale; The birthday present; Bruno Munari's ABC; Bruno Munari's ZOO; The Elephant's Wish; Jimmy has lost his cap; Tic, tac, and toc;* and *Who's There? Open the door!* All published by World.

OBERLÄNDER, Gerhard

  Andres, Stefan: *The Bible story*, translated by Michael Bullock. McGraw-Hill, 1967.

  Baldner, Gaby: *Joba and the wild boar*. Constable (London), 1961.

  The penguins of penguin town. Heinemann (London), 1962.

Korschunow, Irina: *The piebald pup*, translated by Martha Murphy. Obolensky, 1959.

RAPP, Rita

Beattie, Janet: *The little woman who forgot everything*, adapted by Kay Ware and Lucille Sutherland. Webster, 1961.

REIDEL, Marlene

Stearns, Monroe: *Eric's journey*, based on a story by Marlene Reidel. Lippincott, 1960.

SCHEEL, Marianne

Bunn-Richards, Joan: *Secrets of the bees*. Ward-Lock (London), 1961.
Secrets of the marsh. Ward-Lock (London), 1961.

STRØYER, Poul

Hellsing, Lennart: *The cantankerous crow*. Obolensky, 1961.

TRNKA, Jiři

Andersen, Hans Christian: *Fairy tales*. Hamlyn (London), 1959.
Grimm, J. and W.: *Fairy tales*. Hamlyn (London), 1961.
Hauff, Wilhelm: *Fairy tales*. Hamlyn (London), 1961.
Hrubin, František: *Primrose and the winter witch*, adapted by James Reeves. Hamlyn (London), 1964.
La Fontaine, J. de: *Fables*. Hamlyn (London), 1962.
Prokofiev, Serge: *Peter and the wolf*. Hamlyn (London), 1965.
Trnka, Jiři: *Through the magic gate*. Hamlyn (London), 1962.

UNGERMANN, Arne

Sigsgaard, Jens: *Paul alone in the world*. O.U.P. (London), 1948.

WENDLANDT, Kurth

Dobrinskaja, Anna: *Ano lives in the tundra*, translated by Marion Koenig. Blond (London), 1964.

WIBERG, Harald

Lindgren, Astrid: *The tomten*, from a poem by Viktor Rydberg. Coward, 1961.
The fox and the tomten, after a poem by Karl-Erik Forsslund. Coward, 1962.
Christmas in the stable, translated by Anthea Bell. Coward, 1963.

ZABRANSKY, Adolf

Denk, Petr: *Ring-a-Ling*, translated by Monroe Stearns. Lippincott, 1959.

ZIMNIK, Reiner

Axmann, Hannah: *The little owl*, adapted by Leila Berg. Methuen (London), 1960.
De Regniers, Beatrice Schenk: *The snow party*. Pantheon, 1959.
Zimnik, Reiner: *The bear on the motor cycle*. Atheneum, 1963.
Drummers of dreams, translated by E. M. Hatt. Faber (London), 1960.
Jonah the fisherman, translated by R. and C. Winston. Pantheon, 1956.
The little roaring tiger, translated by E. M. Hatt. Pantheon, 1961.
The proud white circus horse, translated by E. M. Hatt. Pantheon, 1957.

17 TOWARDS A HISTORY OF CHILDREN'S BOOKS IN SWITZERLAND

With children's books as with books of adult literature it is equally impossible to say at what precise moment their history began. But people much prefer to see a starting-point which stands out clearly and where books written for children's pleasure in German-speaking Switzerland are concerned, such a starting-point can be found in the year 1645. The date has an added significance when we remember how close it stands to that crucial year for children's books as objects of pleasure: 1658, which saw the publication of Comenius's *Orbis pictus*. What is to be emphasized here, though, is the appearance of the so-called *Zürcherischen Neujahrsstücke* or *Neujahrsblätter*, which must certainly have delighted Comenius if he ever set eyes on them.

The story of their first publication is particularly amusing and has therefore remained in circulation down to the present day. An old Zürich custom demanded that the members of all kinds of scientific or public bodies should make a contribution towards the cost of heating their local drinking-places. This occurred at the New Year and the moneys were delivered by children, who were then treated to Veltliner wine and 'Tirggeli', a rock-hard pastry which is still a favourite in Zürich today if nowhere else. Now whether such sinful gluttony was forbidden during the serious events of the Thirty Years War, or whether mind triumphed over molars, one thing is certain: when, in 1645, the townschildren of Zürich arrived at the city library (founded in 1629) with the 'Stubenhitzen'—and the contributions are still called that to this day— and with the New Year's greetings from their parents, they received, instead of the expected sweetmeats, a beautiful copperplate engraving with a little bit of poetry underneath it. This was the first *Neujahrsstuck* and it seems to have been invented for economic reasons, for in a bound volume of these sheets I have found a manuscript note to the effect that the cost of the hospitality to the children was often in excess of the 'Stubenhitz' moneys received.

Today the custom still holds, but it takes place on 'Berchtoldstag', the 2nd

246

January, and the children who go to the city to get the *Neujahrsblätter* go in company of their fathers and receive chocolates and cakes. Our contemporary *Neujahrsblätter* are mostly learned dissertations on scientific or local matters which, from the point of view of the subject in hand, is a thoroughly unfortunate development.

Now this sheet which the city library first issued was indeed nothing more than a single page. But as the years passed and as many other Swiss communities began to follow Zürich's praiseworthy example, the thing soon grew into a whole literature. A Zürich painter, Conrad Meyer, was the first person to illustrate the publication, and in 1657 he even issued a complete little book: *Sechs und zwanzig nichtige Kinderspiel, zu wichtiger Erinnerung erhebt und in Kupfer gebracht durch C. M. Maalern in Zürich* ('Six and twenty harmless children's games seriously interpreted, with copper engravings by C.M.'). This is a pleasant quarto of fifty-two pages which he published himself and which brings him the distinction of being the first person to illustrate and publish a book for children in Switzerland. He was followed in this profession by his son, Johannes Meyer, who furthered the work in both fields of activity for several decades.

Conrad's little book provides us with two pictures on every opening showing both familiar and little-known games drawn in a simple but artistically very satisfying way. Among them we find whipping-tops, hobby-horses, bubble-blowing, skipping, windmills, stilts, headstands, and masquerades (this last being regarded with great suspicion). On the title-page there are the lines:

> *Was wir in der Jugend treiben,*
> *Hängt uns noch im Alter an,*
> *Ausgenommen, dass ein Alter*
> *Mehr die Jaare zälen kan*

And, beside a delightful picture showing Leap-frog, the words run:

> *Du springest hoch empor,*
> *Ein andrer kommt härfor,*
> *Und überspringt dich auch:*
> *Dier ist der Welt gebrauch.*

It is interesting to compare this verse with the rather similar description of Leap-frog in John Newbery's *A Little pretty pocket-book* (1767 edition):

> This stoops down his Head,
>   Whilst that springs up high;
> But then you will find,
>   He'll stoop by and by.

An die

lernbegierige Zürcherische Jugend

auf das Neujahr 1812.

Title page of a *Neujahrsblatt* for 1812 addressed to the young people of Zürich 'avid for knowledge'.

Moral
Just so 'tis at Court;
Today you're in Place;
Tomorrow, perhaps,
You're quite in Disgrace.

But in spite of such moralizing this is a book which also provided laughter for children, which was an uncommon enough thing in those days when print was thought to be the servant of nothing but instruction. Like the *Orbis pictus* which appeared a year later, the book still keeps some of its charm to this day, something which does not apply to the verses translated from the Dutch by Johann Heinrich Ammann of Schaffhausen, where all games are rejected as idle frivolity.

This was not the case with the first *Neujahrsblätter*. Established by the Zürich city library, they carried the words:

'. . . that it has often been represented to us that perhaps some pleasant stanzas, moral or divine, may be imprinted whereby we can do honour to those who come to us with greetings at the New Year.'

Now just what were these 'stanzas, moral or divine'?

They started with such things as table-manners and the first year's issue was quite taken up with instructive matter. But by 1659 we find a little song with pictures and printed notes, then, in 1663, a sheet showing the twelve months of the year. (With all its many details, this, to my mind, is the first issue which children would really enjoy completely.) In 1664 history appears for the first time. It is superscribed *A mirror of Turkish woe* and it depicts the plague raging among the Turks as a fulfilment of Biblical prophecies. It is altogether a remarkable piece of work, leading the child into the real world and into history. In 1666 we have a *Mirror of children*, which shows such Biblical children as Absalom and David, while in 1677 we have *The ages of man*, a subject which has been a favourite of children's books down to our own day. In between whiles editions were produced with stern but quite awful verses by Zuchtherr Simmler, matched with corresponding engravings.

From 1677 onwards there was an alternation of historical, Biblical, and symbolical editions. Splendid sheets such as *Freedom*, *Theology*, *The art of healing*, *The law*, *The art of reason*, *Physics*, and *Metaphysics* all attempt to introduce growing youngsters to their future mode of life. By this time the engraving is in the hands of Conrad Meyer's son Johannes and the subjects dealt with are becoming more multifarious, an important part being assigned to the history of Switzerland's heroic struggle for federal freedom.

Other artists who have engraved for the sheets are Herrliberger, Götz, Joh. R. Füssli, Bullinger, and Schellenberg, almost all of them famous illustrators of their time. As something originating from a custom of the more well-to-do citizens, the *Neujahrsblätter* naturally confined their appeal to the upper classes, in contrast to the broadsheets which began to appear in the eighteenth century in Spain, Italy, France, Holland, and Germany, which directed themselves to all levels of society.

In many respects it is a delight to follow these *Neujahrsblätter* further. Their development continues without pause to the middle of the nineteenth century. Under J. J. Bodmer's influence the history of Switzerland is set out in model fashion by such prominent Swiss writers as Salomon Hirzel (1727–1818). Plays are added and biographies of such great philanthropists as Pestalozzi, while 'The Society for Vocal and Instrumental Music' provided during almost all of the eighteenth century splendidly illustrated music-sheets for the use of young amateur musicians. Finally, in 1856, a series of broadsheets began to appear which were devoted to the history of the *Neujahrsblätter*. They had thus reached the stage where they were things of the past and from this time on their significance declined.

The subject of drama as a source of juvenile amusement is one that we can only hint at here but it is of very early origins. It had been encouraged by the Catholic Church who saw in the early plays a means of spreading Christian doctrine and rules of conduct. But this was something which the Protestants were also able to do. No less a person than Johann Jakob Bodmer (1698–1783), to whom the young writers of all the German-speaking nations made their pilgrimage, championed this form of literature. We possess two of his own plays 'dedicated to pure innocence', *Die Botschaft des Lebens* (1774) and *Der Fussfall vor dem Bruder* (1773), a particularly affecting tragedy in three acts.

Besides these, Bodmer was also responsible for some tales for young people about which it can be said that for the first time they gave more importance to narrative than to moral elements. The moral was usually an indirect one to be read between the lines of the very perceptive stories taken from the Bible, from history or from daily life and told in a very lucid manner.

Rousseau's influence on the most important educationists and writers for young people of the eighteenth century, men such as Campe, Basedow, and Wyss, is today uncontested. But at Yverdon at the beginning of the nineteenth century Pestalozzi's influence started to make itself felt. With Bodmer and Rousseau as a foundation he was to revolutionize the whole character of educational theory and practice. Many of the ideas of Johannes Fröbel also came extensively from Pestalozzi, whose colleague for a time he was. His theories on mother and child relationships and on pre-school education were to lead to the idea of the kindergarten, which in its turn lent an impetus to the production of picture-books. It is therefore not surprising that the first Swiss children's book that was to go out from this education-mad country to gain an international fame was a book of expressly educational tone, instructive to a high degree.

In *The Swiss family Robinson* (1812) the formation of character of the ship-wrecked children is just as strongly stressed as their general instruction in matters of agriculture, botany, zoology, and handicraft. The excitements of the plot are a kind of funnel through which all these important matters are poured—a thing which was of course the aim of Campe's *Robinson* (1779), but which Wyss takes a stage further. His subject is catastrophe, suffered and overcome by communal strength. The life of the community was to remain for democratic Switzerland a ruling principle down to the present day, so that Swiss literature for young people is less familiar with the complications of the unusual and the fantastic. Even *The Swiss family Robinson*, which, despite all the realism of its details, is based on a quite fantastic adventure, has remained in this respect an unrepeated experiment.

There is one book which brings together in itself all the positive factors in Swiss idealism, containing the historical, the educational, and the narrative in one pair of covers. It is a book by Jeremias Gotthelf (1797–1854), written because he felt about the textbooks of his day much the same as Hoffmann felt about the unctuous, boring 'Biedermeier' picture-books which drove him to write *Struwwelpeter*. When Gotthelf, a vigorous pastor from the Emmental, came across such titles as *The happiness of a virtuous upbringing*, or *The power of love*, or *Salvation for the children of Christ*, or any of those books which concealed much pious instruction behind seductive titles, then he felt very sorry for the children who had to read them. For their sake, therefore, he wrote the hero saga *Der Knabe des Tells* (1846). I often think that the spread of this wonderful book for young people was greatly impeded by the fact that ever since Schiller the story of Wilhelm Tell has only been conceived in terms of the stage. Gotthelf, however, made a warm-hearted family story out of it within the context of contemporary European history. The relationship of father to son, the boy's upbringing, the life on a farm in the mountains, everything is told with such naturalness and humanity that the past comes alive for us in a way which it had seldom previously done. The myth of Tell, whose famous shot at the apple has always been for children one of the great basic thrills, is now transferred to his son, whose story is followed up to the famous battle at Morgarten. So successfully was this done that the book became more than just a tale for children; it became a *Volksbuch* in the best sense of the word, a category into which most of Gotthelf's books can be fitted, together with Pestalozzi's *Lienhard und Gertrud* and the *Kalendergeschichten* which were so popular at this time.

Only in the eighties, when Johanna Spyri began to write her children's books, did this literature which was so typical of its region penetrate beyond the borders of Switzerland. Johanna Spyri was a friend of C. F. Meyer (1825–98) and other Zürich intellectuals and she was anxious to write good books without consciously talking down to her child readers. It is for this reason that her books, too, are *Volksbücher* rather than books expressly for children—with the exception, of course, of *Heidi* which became an attraction for children all over the world through the portrayal of its young heroine, its sensitive treatment of homesickness and its superb descriptions of Swiss scenery.

SPYRI, Johanna. *Heidis Lehr- und Wanderjahre. Eine Geschichte für Kinder und auch für solche, welch die Kinder lieb haben.* Gotha, 1881.
An engraving by Wilhelm Pfeiffer from the third edition.

Johanna Spyri's success soon became a clear danger for the future of children's literature, for it provided a fixed recipe for children's writers to copy in the same way that *The Swiss family Robinson* had done earlier in the century with its curious mixture of adventure, precept, and instruction (Robinsonnades, like history, geography, and travel books, have always had a big attraction for the Swiss). These new tales created their effects from real life, a thing which few German books were doing at that time. Above all, religious and social questions figured in these tales and they were based on the actual experience of Johanna Spyri, who was the daughter of a country doctor. Almost everything she describes could actually have taken place. Even the rural elements played a bigger part here than in the corresponding German publications. The result was that the Swiss writers pounced on the salient features and would not let go of them. What in Johanna Spyri had been new and unique now became a general Swiss style, only a little modified or changed.

From the middle of the nineteenth century onwards, Switzerland, like Germany, has possessed an abundant choice of anthologies and fairy-tale collections. But the only book of this kind which has survived to our own day, which is still to be found in many households and which can even still be bought, is *Staubs Kinderbüchlein*. From 1842 on, the schoolteacher Johannes Staub published at his own expense a series of little volumes containing verses and poems by the best poets of the day and by himself as well. Each was illustrated with little woodcuts and all were later brought together into a single volume intended for use in the family circle. Before long the idea linked to the same kind of contents and format had spread to many other little publications for children, the best known of which was the *Pestalozzikalender*, a bountiful collection which found its way into all parts of the globe.

In tune with the times, which demanded pictures, there appeared at the end of the century a series of large and splendidly produced oleographs under the title *J. Staubs Bilderbücher*. These were designed to show the universe in pictures, beginning with simple household objects and things from the child's immediate environment and progressing to such out-of-the-way matters as 'A desert railway', 'Travel by airship', 'Javanese actors', 'The Taj Mahal', and other prodigies. There were six volumes of such pictures and, following the tradition of the little anthologies, each volume had a supplement of four large pages containing some thirty rhymes and sayings, fairy tales and stories, to ensure that the mind had its sustenance as well as the eye. These Staub picturebooks seem to be a last attempt to capture the world for children between the two boards of a book. In 1923 they were reprinted for the last time, but they should be remembered for their appeal to all sections of society and for their efforts to present the manifold riches of the world. They were a delightful addition to the children's bookshelves, and in translation they spread to many countries of the world.

From the multitude of books of past times I have selected here a few that seemed to me to be typical, but I should also mention fairy tales which have naturally flourished in a country which is geographically so divided. It is also in the nature of the people to conserve such things and many research workers and writers have devoted themselves to this storehouse in exemplary fashion. Here are only a few titles of books which are still worth noticing today, some of them even being still available in modern editions.

The oldest collection known to me is the volume *Kinder und Hausmärchen aus der Schweiz* (1873) by Otto Sutermeister, a book which also contains many fairy stories in dialect. In 1941 the anthropologist C. Englert Faye published a magnificent book of Swiss fairy tales told in a language appropriate to the child of today. Soon afterwards this was followed by a volume called *Alpensagen und Sennengeschichten aus der Schweiz* and both books (which are still obtainable today) were illustrated by Berta Tappolet. A special collection of legends and tales from the Canton of Wallis was made by Johannes Jegerlehner and this was reissued in 1959.

As a reader the Swiss child, like children the world over, tends to prefer the stories of Hans Andersen and the Brothers Grimm to home-produced goods, but he has a greater inclination to sagas, with their historical associations, rather than to fairy tales. Of the former the most famous are Meinrad Lienert's *Schweizer Sagen und Heldengeschichten* but one should also mention again *Die Märchen des Barba Plasch*, the stories by a contemporary story-teller, a travelling cobbler from the Engadine, which were issued in a German language edition in Zürich in 1956.

In this chapter I have not covered a number of matters where Swiss and German developments have been identical. But from the roots which I have laid bare much of the special character of Swiss children's books as we know them today has sprung. The things that have given this character to Swiss literature for children in the past are the preponderance of stories closely modelled on reality and the treatment of historical subjects based on Switzerland's past. These two tendencies are at the back of twentieth-century books as well. After Johanna Spyri, Ida Bindschedler has had the greatest success with her story from real life, *Turnachkindern* (1906). And in Niklaus Bolt's *Peterli am Lift* (1907) we meet a straightforward but charming account of the brave doings of a boy who leaves his mountain home to work as a hotel lift-boy and who might well be a brother to Heidi. Similarly Swiss in its realistic descriptions of technical and some associated social problems is *Svizzero* (1912) by the same author. In this book are recounted the adventures of a little Swiss boy among the Italian nationals working on the Jungfrau railway.

Among the writers who are continuing these traditions today are Elisabeth Müller, Olga Meyer, and Elsa Muschg, who have won a great deal of popularity for their stories which give natural and often moving accounts of Swiss children in their own surroundings. Fritz Brunner, René Gardi, Max Vögeli, Adolf Haller, and Elsa Steinmann are authors who have cast their nets farther afield, either into the past or into other lands, but their work, too, is distinguished by the features which we have noted as typically Swiss.

In this way the ideals of freedom and political thought have been constantly formulated in a fine tradition of children's literature, a tradition which is of the highest importance in a country whose citizens take such an uncommonly active part in the direction of the state.

COMMENT

Of all Switzerland's literature in the nineteenth century, *Heidi* is the export that has lasted the best, but her appeal and influence have been greater in

America than in Britain. This cannot be assigned entirely to the backwash of the enthusiasm for Shirley Temple, for right from the start it was in America rather than in Britain that translations proliferated.

The first translation appeared anonymously in London in 1884. It was published by Low in two volumes: *Heidi's early experiences* and *Heidi's further experiences*. These correspond with a translation by Louise Brooks published in Boston in the same year in one volume: *Heidi, her years of wandering and learning*. From 1884 onwards many more editions appeared in America and it is worth noting that an edition published in Britain by Nelson in 1952 was still relying on the original translation by Louise Brooks.

Of translations currently available, that by Eileen Hall is the most natural piece of English, but the other editions noted here have the virtue of a cloth binding.

SPYRI, Johanna: *Heidi*, translated by Eileen Hall, illustrated by Cecil Leslie (Puffin Books, 1956); also: an anonymous translation illustrated by Vincent O. Cohen (Dutton, 1950); and a Rainbow Classics edition illustrated by Leonard Weisgard (World, 1946).

Also available:

SPYRI, J.: *The pet lamb and other Swiss stories*, translated by M. E. Calthrop and E. M. Popper, illustrated by Michael Ross. Dutton, 1958.

SPYRI, J.: *All alone in the world*, illustrated by Michael Ross. Dutton, 1959.

18 MEN OF LETTERS WRITE FOR CHILDREN

In the foregoing pages we have frequently come across writers who have devoted all their talents to writing for children. Now, to close with, I should like to pay tribute to those people, often formally referred to as 'men of letters', who usually write their books for adults but who have persuaded their muse to spare some time for children. It is these writers who put a bit of spice into children's literature, which is all too often inclined to be somewhat stodgy. They provide an artistic standard against which the professional writer for children can measure himself; in short, they are a most necessary influence and we cannot have enough of them.

Naturally a subject like this really requires a book to itself. Many writers, from Goethe to T. S. Eliot, have occasionally produced a poem or a story for children, but since I do not want simply to draw up a list I should like to pick out one or two from the multitude, limiting myself to the last sixty years or so. Nor is my courage heightened by finding among such writers the names of Selma Lagerlöf, Robert Louis Stevenson, Walter de la Mare, Christian Morgenstern, Mark Twain, Hugo von Hofmannsthal, Frank Wedekind, Erich Kästner, and Graham Greene.

To begin with, I should like to go back to the last century, to Robert Louis Stevenson. Of all the people I have just mentioned, he, along with Mark Twain and Erich Kästner, is the man whose influence on subsequent children's literature has been greatest—and that, of course, is not surprising.

Stevenson was born in Edinburgh in 1850, the son of a lighthouse engineer, and he died in Samoa in 1894, in search of the peace and restitution that so long eluded him. He was a man who had seen many lands and sailed many seas, sometimes on boats of his own chartering, but he remained through and through a Scotsman. And it was to his native land that he raised a memorial in *Kidnapped* (1886). As in *Treasure Island* the hero of the book is a boy, but the scene is this time set among the lochs and islands, the misty forests and the windy plateaux of Scotland's wild coast. It was Stevenson's favourite book and he wrote it while living at Bournemouth, recovering from one of his periodic bouts of illness. Through it he was carried back to his own childhood and although, like many of his books, it was originally written in serial form (for the magazine *Young Folks*) and from an urgent need to pay his bills, it is nevertheless pervaded by a rich sense of poetry. At the same time it is an adventure story with a powerful appeal to young people everywhere, not just to the inhabitants of 'the Balfour country'. All Stevenson's admirers have rated the book very highly and Henry James suggested that the author was behaving with perverse diffidence in directing such a literary masterpiece at the immaturity of youth.

Four years earlier Stevenson had published *Treasure Island*, first as a serial and immediately afterwards, in 1883, as a book. This, of course, was to triumph over half the world and, with *Kidnapped*, was to lead to Stevenson's years of success, even though he was never entirely freed from financial worries because of the many wanderings that he had to make for the sake of his health.

Treasure Island is boys' adventure *par excellence* and, moreover, a story written with concentrated speed. Stevenson produced it for his stepson Lloyd Osbourne, but would scarcely have been able to do so had not his own father filled him up with 'bedtime tales of blood and thunder' when he was a child. His nurse, too, had impressed upon him in his childhood all sorts of strange and grisly tales of ghosts, body-snatchers, martyrs, and similar extraordinary characters. All this was by no means the rule in Victorian times and *Treasure Island* must have surprised as many parents as it delighted their children.

Call to mind for a moment the opening of this marvellous tale of treasure and treachery: the inn in the lonely cove, the comings and goings of the old pirates, the ominous hints of the fearful events which are to come. It is a superb overture, reaching its climax with the appearance of John Silver, stumping in on his wooden leg, as sympathetic a ship's cook as you could ever wish to meet.

John Silver and Jim Hawkins are the two heroes of the action which follows and had it not been written by a true artist this must surely have turned into a ferocious essay in horror. Thanks to the quality of its writing, however, it has become the epitome of all pirate yarns, all tales of buried treasure, and it shows no sign of losing its hold today. As with *Kidnapped* the central character is a boy—but what a boy. Left on his own he achieves the most difficult feats, never failing in courage even when the hardened reader has quite lost his own. Nor is the necessary helping of morality entirely absent, but the whole book is written with such directness, the landscapes, the atmosphere, the description of individual characters are all so perfectly attuned, that one can truly talk of it as a work of art for young people. It has a narrative mastery which is comparable to that in the best adult literature, but which is rarely to be found in a book entirely written for children.

KIPLING, Rudyard. *Skazki*. Moscow, 1936.
A line drawing by V. Kurdov from a Russian edition of *The just so stories*, translated by K. Chukovsky and S. Marshak.

Another man of letters who stands in the top rank of those who gave of their best for children and at the same time achieved fame among adults is Rudyard Kipling (1865–1936). Born in India, he spent his early childhood there and returned as a young man to become editor of a newspaper in Allahabad. All his experiences from that time on cannot disguise how much his work draws its sustenance from these early influences.

Everyone who has read the two *Jungle Books* (1894 and 1895) should beware of ever visiting the Indian jungle, for the reality will never come up to his experience of it as he found it in the books. There the primeval forest takes on a life of its own. It hums with it; there are wild cries in the night; but there are also animals who, when they meet in the forest clearing to decide the fate of a human foundling, turn into fabulous beings with powers of speech and their actions take on an affinity with those of humans. But nature is never entirely submerged in all this literary anthropomorphism.

When in 1901 Kipling wrote his great novel *Kim* his audience of young people was by no means accustomed to such writing, nor even to tales which took their material from political affairs and the invisible network of the Secret Service. And yet this is through and through a book for the young. The hero is a fearless boy who leads a life of adventure between the Indian natives and their white rulers. Through his close familiarity with the customs of the country we get an experience of India which is so real that we might ourselves be wandering the highways of that protean sub-continent. One of the most attractive characters in the book is the Tibetan lama whose 'chela' Kim becomes and who can teach us all that love and goodness are not the privileges solely of Christian white men.

Next to the *Jungle Books* and *Kim*, Kipling's chief books for children were *Stalky and Co.* (1899), *The just so stories* (1902), *Puck of Pook's Hill* (1906), and *Rewards and fairies* (1910), while in 1907 he was awarded the Nobel Prize for literature. Today, all his work is considered the common possession of young and old alike and, although in his time he was regarded as a thoroughgoing imperialist, there can be no better way to a love and understanding of the remarkable land that is India than through his books.

Contemporary with Stevenson and Kipling is 'Mark Twain' (1835–1910). Hailing from the Southern state of Missouri he became first an itinerant printer, then for quite a while a river-pilot on the Mississippi and, later still, a journalist, a writer of novels and travel books, a publisher and a traveller across many lands and oceans. His books have immortalized the life on the Mississippi of his times, and in *Tom Sawyer* (1876) and *Huckleberry Finn* (1884) he created two of the foundation-stones of modern children's literature. He tells these tales with a directness which is only perhaps possible in America and he uses one of the vastest inhabited landscapes of the world for the backcloth against which his children have their exciting adventures. The flight of the three boys, their life on the island, the thunderstorm there, Tom's nocturnal visit home when he hears the conversation of the grown-ups despairing over their presumed death, their final return home during their own funeral celebrations— it is all a magnificently conceived account of the experiences of youth, the like of which is hardly possible any longer on this continent of ours. Between the lines, however, there is a delicious humour and a profound sadness. Also, for perhaps the first time in a modern children's book, we meet with the horror of crime in the churchyard murder which the two boys accidentally witness. This provides the book with an atmosphere of the macabre and at the same time ensures that the qualities and possibilities inherent in mankind are fully presented, something which was unique in a children's book at that time. Completely new ground is broken with figures like Injun Joe and Huckleberry Finn, whose very name summarizes a whole world of experience.

Emil und die Detektive (1929) by Erich Kästner (born 1899) is scarcely conceivable without these American predecessors. As with Mark Twain, Kästner's places and people are taken from his own childhood experiences, thereby gaining that tremendous power of conviction which is the property of only a few children's books. This has become very clear since Erich Kästner has recorded for us his recollections of childhood and youth in *Als ich ein kleiner Junge war* (1957). This book belongs among the finest and most revealing of modern memoirs and, in spite of its occasional rather questionable sections, it is a good book for the more mature adolescent to tackle. As with all important

259

writers in the field of literature for young people, Kästner does not lack his moments of sadness, which serve as an effective matt background to his rampant sense of humour, just as they do in the books of Mark Twain and Astrid Lindgren (who, incidentally, singles out Twain as her favourite writer for children). As a matter of interest, Kästner himself does not consider Twain the ideal writer of his youth but refers to Dickens, *Leatherstocking*, *Robinson*, and a number of German authors of second rank.

The universal and timeless classics among children's books do not lie thick on the ground. Twenty years after *Treasure Island* and *Huckleberry Finn* there appeared in Sweden a book produced for the educational authorities which could hold its own with these other two in fame and in the pleasure which it has given. This was *Nils Holgerssons underbara resa genom Sverige* (*Nils Holgersson's wonderful travels round Sweden*: two volumes, Stockholm, 1906–7).

The writer of this beautiful book was Selma Lagerlöf who was born in 1858 on an estate in central Sweden. Both the place and the country of her birth were important in this case for rarely has a writer looked at his homeland with so much affection and so much curiosity. Next to her most famous novel, *Gösta Berling's saga*, which is set deep in her home country, *Nils Holgersson* is the biggest and best example of a truly creative patriotism.

The story of Nils grew out of a geography book about Sweden. The boy, who is a little ne'er-do-well, is turned into a Tom Thumb creature and, on the back of a runaway gander, he makes a series of adventurous journeys into the Sweden of the past and of the present along with the rest of the flock of wild geese. Running to five hundred pages, the work is exceptionally long for a children's book but its main elements are brought together most successfully in a way that keeps the reader constantly amused. Information becomes part of the story and the exciting events also serve to show how a life in the wild can be a great moulder of character. Above all, there is the superb creation of Mother Akka, the leader of the wild geese, who, with her great wisdom, is one of the unforgettable characters of children's literature. The book's departures into history or legend or natural descriptions are the sort of thing which children normally skip or reject altogether, but here they are built into the story in so masterly a fashion that the reader's patience with them is never extended. Admittedly there is some doubt as to how far a modern city child will put up with them and it is quite likely that he would have to be encouraged by a sympathetic mother or teacher who would read and explain the less easily understandable passages of the story.

Such a remarkable book has naturally had its successors and I should like to mention two of them here, both by women writers of considerable standing. The first is *Martins Reise* (1949) by Luise Rinser, who was born in 1911. Originally planned as a book in several volumes, it again tells the story of a good-for-nothing young fellow, who this time goes off with a wandering shepherd through the provinces of Southern Germany. The wisdom of the shepherd and the hard life among the animals have a reforming and instructive influence upon the young Martin and his own enjoyment of his experiences is transmitted to the reader.

The second is *Das Land deiner Mutter* by the Swiss authoress Cécile Lauber. Without doubt she makes even greater demands upon the patience of her readers, for the four volumes (all published at Zürich between 1946 and 1957) finally totalled 1,450 pages, and although he does not fly around on the backs of geese, her robust hero Nicco has a great deal in common with the little Swedish Nils. He does not start off as quite such a sluggard, being instead a tough orphan lad from an Italian travelling circus. In a two-year journey through Switzerland he gets on the trail of, and ultimately finds, his grandfather. Like Nils, however, he understands the language of animals and this adds a new dimension to his life and, through it, gives the book notable moments of excitement and enjoyment. Once again, though, it is an example of a story-book journey which uses adventures and fabulous happenings to put across factual information about a country's geography and history.

Any consideration of the role which children play in the work of the great novelists of the present and of the immediate past leads to many splendid examples; one has only to think, for instance, of Thomas Mann. But hardly any of these important people were prepared to take the quite different course of actually writing books for children. One must, therefore, feel particularly grateful to the exceptions to this rule, many of whom are English writers and only very few Continental. On the whole, poetry and short stories predominate in the work of these moderns and they have often been so successful that I cannot forbear mentioning a few of them here.

First of all, though, I should briefly refer to the few full-length stories that have come from these men of letters: such as the entertaining tale *Zwieselchen* (Stuttgart, 1938) by the sober Werner Bergengruen, whom one would scarcely have believed capable of a joviality so suited to young people. Then there are the many stories for girls by the Danish authoress Karin Michaelis, and the superb story for boys *Die Spiegelklöpfler* (Zürich, 1937) by the serious-minded writer Traugott Vogel, a book which can be compared with those of Erich Kästner in its romantic understanding of 'the boys of the back streets'. Nor must one forget Scotland in the person of Eric Linklater whose *The wind on the moon* (1944) and *The pirates in the deep green sea* (1949) are among the most delightful stories in all modern literature for children. *The wind on the moon*, honoured by the Carnegie Medal for 1944, is one of the few examples of a writer making use of time-hallowed English nonsense not only to triumph in the dream world of the nursery, like *Winnie-the-Pooh* and *Mary Poppins*, but also to make an entry into modern life, where there are such things as court-room scenes, disappearing fathers, and modern tyrants. The two perverse little heroines of the book, Dinah and Dorinda, are worthy to be included in any catalogue of immortal characters from children's story-books.

·   ·   ·   ·   ·   ·   ·   ·   ·   ·

·

Up till now the works I have mentioned have been almost without exception great books directed more or less successfully at a wide youthful public. But just as there are volumes of poems or essays for adults which are only familiar to a small section of them, so there are similar books for children in which the writer has presupposed a certain measure of sophistication in the child's early background.

Here also England is to the fore, especially in her enormous wealth of poetry. In this it could be said that William Blake had a pioneering influence through his *Songs of innocence* (1789) in which can be found some of the most moving poems that he ever produced. A new edition of the book was published by Faber and Faber as recently as 1958 with beautifully sympathetic illustrations by Harold Jones. Another book, dating from 1885, of which several newly illustrated editions have appeared recently, is Stevenson's *A child's garden of verses*. The poems were written at roughly the same time as *Treasure Island* and their dedication expresses a little of the gratitude which Stevenson felt towards his old nurse for the affection she had shown him in his own childhood.

A tradition with such precursors in it lessens our surprise at finding one of the best-known of England's modern lyricists, Walter de la Mare (1873–1956) devoting a considerable part of his output to children. His marvellous animal allegory *The three royal monkeys* (first published in 1910 as *The three Mullamulgars*) has delighted many children who are prepared to accept his sensitive and poetic handling of the English language. This was followed by many other stories, including his famous *Stories from the Bible* (1929) and by some outstanding collections of poetry. *Peacock Pie* is perhaps the most famous of these and since its first publication in 1913 it has appeared in editions illustrated by artists of no less distinction than W. Heath Robinson, Lovat Fraser, Roland Emett, and (most successfully of all) Edward Ardizzone. It would seem that wherever in England children are brought into touch with this elevated lyricism it brings with it a deeper understanding of literary experience, although even here a change seems to be taking place today.

Two more of England's foremost writers have also produced books for children: T. S. Eliot's *Old Possum's book of practical cats* (1939) splendidly illustrated by Nicolas Bentley but not perhaps entirely within the compass of young Continental readers; and Graham Greene, who provided amusing and rumbustious texts for a group of books illustrated by Dorothy Craigie: *The little train* (1946), *The little fire-engine* (1950), *The little horse-bus* (1952), and *The little steam-roller* (1953).

Against such modern writers as these, Germany has produced only one who has turned out comparable work for children. This is Christian Morgenstern (1871–1914), whose children's book *Klein Irmchen* was first published in 1921 with illustrations which were its equal by Josua L. Gampp. (The book has also been illustrated by Elsa Eisgruber.) In its pathos, its delicacy, and its humour this is one of the loveliest of children's poetry-books and with it Morgenstern brought a new accent into children's literature, something capable of enriching the child's imaginative world and at the same time heightening his feeling for language. The actual poetry is quite inimitable, but it has borne indirect fruit in such admirable verse as Susan Ehmcke's *Vogelbart* or her *Lieder aus dem Schneckenhaus* (*Songs from under the snail's shell*).

From the beginning of the century up to the twenties, Richard Dehmel and his wife Paula attempted to make contact with children through poetry. Both of them produced some splendid pieces, but it seems to me that in their experiments using the actual way children talk they are no longer in accord with contemporary taste (e.g. *Fitzebutze*, Munich, 1900). At the beginning of the century Paula Dehmel produced her *Rumpumpel*, a lyrical collection somewhat reminiscent of Morgenstern which found in Karl Hofer an outstanding illustrator. From a little later there also came a book which is remembered by few today: a splendid picture-book in the vanished idiom of art-nouveau telling the story of the great Austrian general *Prinz Eugen* and illustrating it with stately pictures by Franz Wacik. The text came from the pen of Hugo von Hofmannsthal and was first published in Vienna in 1915, which date may account for the author's now somewhat alien patriotic and anti-French sentiments. For all this, however, the rich and eloquent text is clearly the work of a writer who knew what he was about.

One other piece of writing which until recently had disappeared from human ken deserves mention here, for it belongs among the most delightful productions in this particular field. It is one of the first literary works of the young Frank Wedekind, written at the age of seventeen while he was still at school. Entitled *Hänseken*, a children's saga, it was decorated with amusing illustrations by Frank's brother Arnim and dedicated by the two of them to their little sister Emilie, who is still alive today. Later on when Frank Wedekind had made a name for himself it was published (Munich, 1897) only to disappear until a new edition was issued in Zürich in 1961. Like so many little children in stories Hänseken has run away from home, but this time on a moonbeam, and like all such children he comes back the next day. Since, however, he has fallen into a lake of ink his mother does not recognize him and he must make his way to the land of the blackamoors:

Nun zieht man die Moral daraus,	Now here's the moral of this tale
weil sich das stets der Mühe lohnt!	(an apt reward for my travail):
So lang es Nacht ist, bleib zu Haus!	while it's dark, just stay at home
Auch reite niemals auf den Mond!	and don't go riding on the moon.
Doch wenn die Weissen dich miss-	If folk are cross because you do
handeln,	You'll have to go to Timbuctoo.
Dann kannst du zu den Mohren	
wandeln.	

Thus Wedekind at seventeen! But there was yet another German comic writer who wrote similarly perplexing stuff for children and grown-ups alike.

His name was Joachim Ringelnatz, but it is unlikely that many children got hold of his *Kinder-Verwirr-Buch* (Berlin, 1931) since a number of its verses were scarcely suitable for them. Nevertheless, it is a pity that they should have lost the best ones just on this account.

Eine Wiese singt.	Brooks sing,
Dein Ohr klingt.	Ears ring,
Eine Telephonstange rauscht.	Telephone wires hum;
Ob du im Bettchen liegst	Lying in bed,
oder über Frankfurt fliegst	Flying overhead,
Du bist überall gesehen und belauscht.	You're seen or heard by someone.
Was du verschweigst,	Things concealed,
Was du den andern nicht zeigst,	Things never revealed,
was dein Mund spricht	Words uttered,
und deine Hand tut,	Deeds done,
Es kommt alles ans Licht.	All is sooner or later uncovered—
Sei ohnedies gut.	But why not just be good for fun.

A number of German poets have from time to time felt the need to turn out something for children, but on the whole these have been exceptions. Among others, Hans Magnus Enzensberger has tried it in his one book of children's verse, *Zupp* (1959), but this is little more than a joke, though at least one where the poet is trying to see things through the child's eyes and to speak with the child's own jargon. The attractiveness of the book is not greatly helped by Gisela Andersch's heavily stylized illustrations.

Enzensberger's urge to give children writing of true quality found expression in a quite different fashion when in 1961 he published an anthology of children's verse under the significant fairy-tale title of *Allerleirauh*,[1] the book being decorated with English woodcuts from the eighteenth century. By the preference which it gave to the wealth of traditional verse before the year 1800 this anthology mirrors clearly an attitude prevalent among contemporary writers. It rigidly avoids the sensuousness of much nineteenth-century verse with its softer tones and rhythms, and by insisting on the earlier work this now famous collection has achieved a character all its own.

Brief mention should also be made of Bertolt Brecht—a man who possessed a plainness of speech and a sufficiency of pictorial imagination to be able to tell children incomparable stories. But, with the exception of a few poems he has not done so. It is true, however, that, thanks to their simplicity of language, his didactic poems and ballads have been accepted by young and

[1] 'Allerleirauh' means literally 'all kinds of fur' and the significance lies in its reference to the traditional tale found under that title in Grimm. Versions of it have cropped up in all parts of Europe and a brief discussion of these may be found in the introduction to *Peau d'âne* in Geoffrey Brereton's Penguin edition of *The fairy tales of Charles Perrault* (1957). (B.A.)

old alike in at least one part of the world. I can visualize the children of the next decade no longer reciting the old party-pieces but turning perhaps to a ballad like Bert Brecht's *Kinderkreuzzug* (*Children's crusade*)—a poem with the simplicity of a folk-song, the language of everyday speech stripped of all its unnecessary encumbrances:

In Polen, im Jahr Neununddreissig	In 'thirty nine in Poland
War eine blutige Schlacht	There was a bloody fight
Die hatte viele Städte und Dörfer	And many a town and village
Zu einer Wildnis gemacht . . .	Turned to waste land over night . . .
Schnee fiel als man sich's erzählte	Snow fell, as they related
in einer östlichen Stadt	In a certain eastern town
von einem Kinderkreuzzug	How a new crusade of children
der in Polen begonnen hat,	In Poland had begun.
Da trippelten Kinder hungernd	For all along the highways
In Trüpplein hinab die Chausseen	Troops of hungry children roamed
Und nahmen mit sich andere, die	And gathered to them others
In zerschossenen Dörfern stehn . . .	Who stood by ruined homes . . .
Ein kleiner Jude marschierte im Trupp	In a coat with a velvet collar A little Jew was dressed
Mit einem samtenen Kragen	He had been reared on white bread
Der war das weisseste Brot gewohnt	But he marched on with the rest . . .
Und hat sich gut geschlagen . . .	
Da war auch ein Begräbnis	They had a funeral besides
Eines Jungen mit samtenem Kragen	Two Poles and two Germans carried
Der wurde von zwei Deutschen	The boy with the velvet collar
Und zwei Polen zu Grabe getragen.	To the place where he was buried.

(Translated from Bertolt Brecht: *Selected Poems*, translated by H. R. Hays. London, Calder, 1959)[1]

The fate of the children of Eastern Europe is here conjured up in a poem of thirty-five stanzas cast in the language of today. How can it fail to grip the young people of our time? The same is true of Brecht's other songs: *Der Pflaumenbaum* (*The plum tree*) or *Vom Kind, das sich nicht waschen wollte* (*The boy who wouldn't wash*). These short poems have brought all the sorrows of the world down to their simplest common linguistic denominator.

Should writers for adults write for children? Are they capable of doing so? These are open questions and it behoves us to take what has been written with

[1] A full translation by Michael Hamburger can also be found in the anthology for young people *Rising early* (Brockhampton, 1964).

gratitude and to hope that future men of letters will not put the needs of children entirely out of mind.

BOOK LIST

KÄSTNER, Erich: *Emil and the detectives*, translated by Eileen Hall, illustrated by Walter Trier and with an introduction by Walter de la Mare. Doubleday, 1959.

An earlier translation by Cyrus Brooks appeared in 1931. Other children's books by Kästner published in London by Cape are: *Emil and the three twins* (1935); *The 35th May* (1933); *Annaluise and Anton* (1932); *The flying classroom* (1934) and *Lottie and Lisa* (1950). The latter was published in America as *Lisa and Lottie*. Little, Brown, 1951.

KÄSTNER, E.: *When I was a little boy*, translated by Isabel and Florence McHugh, illustrated by Horst Lemke. Watts, 1961.

The Little Man, illustrated by Rick Schreiter, Knopf, 1966.

LAGERLÖF, S.: *The wonderful adventures of Nils*, an adapted version, translated by Velma Swanston Howard, illustrated by Hans Baumhauer. Pantheon, 1950.

The further adventures of Nils, with the same translator and illustrator, was published in London by Dent in 1953.

LIFE WITH CHILDREN'S BOOKS
Instead of a conclusion

There are many grown-ups who, as either teachers or librarians or publishers, have a serious and sympathetic concern for children's books and each of them must still be to some extent conscious of the child that he or she once was. But it is impossible even for these privileged adults to experience the reading of children's books as children do.

It is true that there are rare moments of illumination when the fifty-year-old can hear the fir-trees soughing over his head just as they did for Heidi when she first climbed up to the pasture. It is true that an adult can weep at the loneliness of Huck or the destitution of David Copperfield, or that he can feel the same apprehension that a twelve-year-old will feel when he glides in Leatherstocking's canoe up uncharted rivers, but this is only possible in retrospect. And even then there is something wonderful about such an ability to recall the happiest hours of childhood. In reading we learned for the first time to grow beyond ourselves, to forget ourselves completely, and what can be finer than that!

In these concluding pages I should like to say a little bit about what it is like to live constantly with children's books. It is something which has never bored me. It has led me into many fields of thought and to many human encounters which I would otherwise never have experienced and, more than the literature of adults, it has taught me to distinguish the genuine from the false and to recognize the language writers use in its simplest and at the same time most poetic manifestations. Years of professional work in this field have given me the chance of experiencing much that is remarkable, much that is beautiful and occasionally much that is truly wonderful. I should now like to describe a little of all this experience.

Ever since children's books were thought of, fathers and mothers, grandfathers and grandmothers, aunts and uncles, all sorts of people with a kindly inclination towards children, have set pens and paint-brushes to work to put

267

down and illustrate stories for them. Direct personal action like that has led to the production of books like *Der Struwwelpeter* and *Alice in Wonderland*; but hardly any have shared with these two the good fortune of having been read by literally millions of children.

Books which never get into print

As a publisher I often come by original manuscripts which for some reason or other cannot be printed. This can often be painful. I remember, for instance, a lady with a romantic-sounding Spanish name who visited me in Zürich during the Second World War. She was learning fashion drawing, but some current of fate had sent her along to us; she had with her two beautiful children and in her bag she had two children's books which she had prepared herself. One of them was about a doll who led a troubled life in a children's nursery until, greatly put upon, worn out from too much cuddling and rough usage, she was granted a face of her own and began actually to live. The whole thing was a little psychological masterpiece, illustrated in delicate water-colours, but impossible to print at that time. The other book was even more beautiful. A group of white children are wrecked on an island inhabited only by coloured people. They are well received, remain there, marry, and give birth to children who are striped and grandchildren who are chequered, while the whole community turn the island into a veritable paradise. From the graphic and from the human point of view this was one of the most original picture-books that I have ever seen, but because of its ironic treatment of racial questions (then as now) it was difficult to see how it could be done. I have often asked myself what finally became of these two little books which I have never been able to forget.

When my own daughter was fifteen she brought me for my birthday a picture-book which she had made herself about a little mermaid who came into the world with two feet instead of a tail and on this account was rejected by her fellows. This, too, has affected me more profoundly than many books that I have seen in print.

There are, of course, vast numbers of books which are made up by a particular family and which never get near a publisher's catalogue. Many have passed through my hands and have often delighted me with their freshness. One in particular struck me as being in its own way true to life, witty and moving. A foreign worker from Greece comes to a Swiss village as labourer for one of the farmers. On arrival he proves to be a Centaur and thus pulls the plough like a horse, takes part in the yodelling competition as a man, builds a bed corresponding with his curious shape and is altogether the delight of the village boys. He looks his best with his horse's limbs spread out all over the floor while he milks the cows. This book is the work of an eighteen-year-old Swiss girl and I fancy she will get herself into print before very long.[1]

[1] This prophecy has now been fulfilled. Bettina Trunninger's *Nastja und das ABC* was published in Zürich in 1964. (B.A.)

Lovers of children's books all over the world

Those people who, although they have reached the years of discretion, continue to concern themselves seriously and with pleasure in collecting and enjoying children's books sooner or later all get to know each other. I myself have had, and still have, connexions with many of them all over the world and among them are important people to whom I owe much gratitude.

In Berlin in the thirties there was Karl Hobrecker, who over a long period got together a wonderful collection of children's books. He was responsible for a book on early and forgotten volumes which is still among the best of its kind: *Alte vergessene Kinderbücher* (1924). He is now dead and his books, which he presented to the Third Reich, have vanished from the face of the earth along with the régime itself.

A similarly charming and knowledgeable man who died only recently in Munich was Arthur Rümann whose book on early German children's books (*Alte deutsche Kinderbücher*, Vienna, 1937) is one of those definitive compilations which are used as standard references by antiquarian booksellers.

Moving on to New York I must recall the name of Frederic Melcher, the late editor of *Publishers' Weekly* and a book-man whose reputation was world-wide. He was among the first to take children's books really seriously and in order to encourage the best he was instrumental in establishing in 1921 the Newbery Medal for the best American children's book of the year. (This was to be followed by the Caldecott Medal in 1937, awarded specifically for picture-books.) It is such variously gifted men as these who have been in the forefront of the struggle for better children's books and, at the same time, by their knowledge and their activity as collectors they have performed a great service to future investigators.

Among them, of course, there also belongs that learned man of literature, Paul Hazard, who has written the most sparkling book about children's books: *Les livres, les enfants et les hommes* (1932). Among other books which can be most useful in this subject are the catalogues of those private collections which have grown up during past decades, especially in the U.S.A., and which have passed into institutional libraries as rare material for the use of students. Chief among these catalogues is perhaps that of *The Osborne collection of early children's books at Toronto* (1958). There is also Percy Muir's book on *English children's books 1600 to 1900* (1954) which arose out of an exhibition which he prepared for the National Book League.

Gradually, however, the passion for children's books, which at one time was shared by only a few individuals, is moving into wider waters. Studies of the subject are sprouting like mushrooms and among the organizers of children's services in public libraries in many countries there are specialists of high reputation. The founder and for a long time director of the International Youth Library in Munich was Jella Lepman who, after the Second World War, established children's books as a means for reconciliation and the betterment of

ISHII, Momoko. *The Dolls' Day for Yoshiko*, London, O.U.P., 1965.
Line drawing by Gaynor Chapman. A sign of the complete internationalization of children's books. A Japanese story, illustrated in Japanese style, by an English artist.

international understanding. It was through her that the lives of many children were enriched by gifts from all over the world (an operation which proved highly beneficial to children's book production which was recovering only slowly in post-war conditions). She also founded the International Board on Books for Young People which every two years awards the Hans Christian Andersen Medal to an author of world renown in the field of children's literature.[1]

Children's books can also lead to some memorable encounters in foreign places. For example, I was staying in Tokyo, and, as I always do when visiting other countries, I spent my first day looking for good, home-produced children's books. To my delight I found in a subterranean bookshop a couple of extraordinarily well-produced picture-books, but nobody could tell me

[1] The Board's periodical publication *Bookbird* (issued from Vienna jointly with the International Institute for Children's, Juvenile and Popular Literature) performs a special service in recommending books which it considers most suitable for translation into other languages. (B.A.)

where they came from, nor did I see them anywhere else. On the day before my departure I received a visit from Momoko Ishii, a wonderful story-teller and collector of fairy tales who lives in Tokyo and every Saturday holds open house for countless children and tells them stories or shows them books from other parts of the world. She was accompanied by a young man in spectacles who, as is the custom in those parts, carried a package in a knotted cloth over his arm in the manner of a handbag. Apparently he knew of the first edition of this book of mine and he now wanted to get to know the author. He carefully laid his wrapped-up package on the low table in front of me, undid the knots, and, lo and behold! produced a large bundle of books, among which were the two which I had admired and sought for with so much trouble. And he was their editor and publisher. His name is Tadasho Matsui and he is one of the pioneers of the modern Japanese children's book, a man who, from our point of view, is achieving magnificent success.

It is perhaps appropriate for me to end my book with this momentary visit to Japan, for children's books can no longer be confined to a single country or even a single continent. The lovers of children's books recognize each other all round the world and the books themselves have become a powerful factor in international publishing. Whatever the dangers that may be inherent in such a widespread market, it is greatly to be hoped that the final arbiters will always be those adults who have so much sympathy for children and who have so curiously retained their dedication to children's literature.

PETRIDES, Heidrun. *Der Xaver und der Wastl.* Zürich, 1962.
Line drawing by the fifteen-year-old author reproduced by lithography.

BIBLIOGRAPHY

This bibliography is based upon Mrs. Hürlimann's two lists of subject material and biography. Most of the books used by her have been included and these are marked with an asterisk (*).

My expansion of the two sections has been made in an attempt to provide some additional guidance on sources for further reference. The first section is devoted to books which deal with the development of children's literature in Europe as a whole and in various individual countries; the biographical section shows a few of the books about the main foreign authors mentioned in Mrs. Hürlimann's text. I have given preference to biographies in English where possible.

Only a few books on illustrators or illustration have been included. An immediate resort to further reference may be made in the books by Bertha Mahony and Marcus Crouch listed in the General Section below.

I am very grateful to Miss Anne Pellowski for looking over the bibliography and for making many helpful suggestions. She has drawn my attention to the intensive work that is being done in the field of children's literature in Eastern Europe and mentions that Russia alone has produced over two hundred books on the subject. Necessarily, therefore, this section of the bibliography is random rather than selective.

Since the English edition of this book appeared, the Library of Congress has published *Children's literature: a guide to reference sources* under the direction of Virginia Haviland. This is the most valuable general bibliography on the subject available and includes a substantial International section.

B. W. A.

Books About Children's Literature

GENERAL

BAMBERGER, Richard. *Jugendlektüre; Jugendschriftenkunde, Leseunterricht, Literaturerziehung*. Vienna, Verlag für Jugend und Volk, 1965.

Includes a bibliography of 1369 references to books, articles, and journals.

BERLIN. Deutsche Staatsbibliothek. *Internationale Kinderbuchausstellung 1956–1957*. Berlin, 1957.

Exhibition catalogue with a section on early books.

BESTERMAN, Theodore. *A world bibliography of bibliographies*. Fourth edition. Lausanne, Societas Bibliographica, 1965–6.

Vol I, under 'Children', contains an international list of bibliographies with many references to exhibition catalogues.

GAVAULT, Paul. *Les livres de l'enfance du XVe au XIXe siècle.* 2 volumes. Paris, Gumuchian, 1930.*

A one-volume reissue of the whole text with selected plates is to be published by Holland Press, London, 1967.

GENEVA. International Bureau of Education. *Children's books and international goodwill; book list and report of an enquiry.* Second edition. Geneva, 1932.

Reports from 36 countries with the catalogue of a permanent exhibition.

GREAT BRITAIN. Library Association, Youth Libraries Group. *Books about children's literature, a book list edited by Marcus Crouch.* London, 1963.

Includes references to foreign books and authors.

HAZARD, Paul. *Les livres, les enfants et les hommes.* Paris, Flammarion, 1932.*

Translated by Marguerite Mitchell as *Books, children and men.* Boston, The Horn Book, 1944. Includes references to periodical articles. Also available in German, Spanish, Swedish, Polish, and Japanese editions.

HILL, Ruth and DE BONDELI, Elsa, compilers. *Children's books from foreign languages: English translations from published and unpublished sources.* Compiled in co-operation with the International Committee of the Children's Section of the American Library Association. New York, H. W. Wilson Co., 1937.

HOELDER, Anneliese. *Jugendbuch in aller Welt, Ergebnisse einer Umfrage bei 24 Nationen über den Stand des Jugendbuches.* Vienna, Verlag für Jugend und Volk, Munich, Juventa, 1956.

LÜTHI, Max. *Das europäische Volksmärchen; Form und Wesen.* Second edition. Bern, Francke, 1960.*

MAHONY, Bertha E. and others. Illustrators of children's books 1744–1945. Boston, The Horn Book, 1947.*

Contains bibliographies of books illustrated by artists and of sources. A supplementary volume covering the years 1945–56 was issued in 1958, edited by Ruth Viguers.

MUNICH, International youth library. *History and theory of youth literature, with an introduction by Metka Simončič.* Munich, [1964].

479 books from 22 countries exhibited at the Library.

PLISCHKE, Hans. *Von Cooper bis Karl May, eine Geschichte des völkerkundlichen Reise- und Abenteuerromans.* Düsseldorf, Droste, 1951.*

ULLRICH, Hermann. *Robinson und Robinsonaden; Bibliographie, Geschichte, Kritik. Ein Beitrag zur vergleichenden Literaturgeschichte . . .* Weimar, Emil Felber, 1898.

VAN DER MEULEN, A. J. M., compiler. *Professional literature on library work with children.* The Hague, Bureau Boek en Jeugd, for the International Federation of Library Associations. 1966.

Includes sections arranged by country on literature, the creating of books, and children's reading.

AUSTRIA

MOISSL, Konrad and KRAUTSTENGEL, Ferdinand. *Die deutsch-österreichische Jugendliteratur.* 2 volumes. Aussig, Grohmann, 1900–1.

SCHWAB, E. *Beiträge zur Geschichte der Kinder- und Jugendschrifttums in Österreich.* Vienna, 1949.

A dissertation.

CZECHOSLOVAKIA

ČERVENKA, Jan and others. *Literatura pro mládez.* Prague, Státní nakladatelstvi, 1961.

HOLEŠOVSKÝ, František. *Naše ilustrace pro děti a její vychorné půshobení.* Prague, Státní nakladatelstvi, 1960.

MAJEROVA, Marie. *O dětské literatuře.* Prague. Státní nakladatelství, 1956.

POSPÍŠIL, O. and SUK, V. F. *Dětská literatura česká. Příručka dějin literárních pro školu, knihovny i širsi verejnost.* Prague, Státní nakladatelstvi, 1924. A supplement by Suk: *Dobré knihy dětem* was added in 1929.

STEJSKAL, Václav. *Moderní česká literatura pro děti.* Prague, Státní nakladatelstvi, 1962.

DENMARK

SIMONSEN, Inger. *Den Danske børnebog i det 19. aarhundrede.* Copenhagen, Nyt Nordisk Forlag, Arnold Busck, 1942.

Includes bibliography of German, English, and Danish sources.

STYBE, Vibeke. *Fra Askepot til Anders And; Børnebogen i kulturhistorisk perspectiv.* Copenhagen, Munksgaard, 1962.

ENGLAND, THE U.S.A. AND CANADA

ARBUTHNOT, May Hill. *Children and books.* Third edition. Chicago, Scott, Foresman, 1964.*

CROUCH, Marcus. *Treasure seekers and borrowers; children's books in Britain. 1900–1960.* London, The Library Association, 1962.*

DARTON, F. J. Harvey. *Children's books in England, five centuries of social life.* Second edition. Cambridge University Press, 1958.*

The first edition appeared in 1932. The book is linked to bibliographies now published in the *Cambridge bibliography of English literature.* 4 volumes. Cambridge, 1940, and Supplement, Cambridge, 1957.

ERNEST, Edward E., editor. *A Kate Greenaway Treasury.* World, 1967.

GREEN, Roger Lancelyn. *Tellers of tales; children's books and their authors from 1800 to 1964.* Third edition. London, Ward, 1965.

Includes a chronological list and a group of author bibliographies.

JAMES, Philip. *Children's books of yesterday.* London, Studio, 1933.*

KIEFER, Monica. *American children through their books, 1700–1835.* Philadelphia, University of Pennsylvania Press, 1948.*

MEIGS, Cornelia and others. *A critical history of children's literature.* New York, Macmillan, 1953.

MUIR, Percy. *English children's books 1600–1900.* London, Batsford, 1954.*

The bibliographical notes and checklists form 'the anatomy of this book'.

OPIE, Iona and Peter, editors. *The Oxford dictionary of nursery rhymes.* Oxford, Clarendon Press, 1951.

Contains much valuable comparative information.

PICKARD, P. M. *I could a tale unfold: violence, horror and sensationalism in stories for children.* London, Tavistock, 1961.*

ST. JOHN, Judith, compiler. *The Osborne collection of early children's books 1566–1910; a catalogue.* Toronto Public Library, 1958.*

A select list of additions was issued in 1964.

SLOANE, William. *Children's books in England and America in the seventeenth century; a history and checklist.* New York, King's Crown Press of Columbia University, 1955.

SMITH, Elva. *The history of children's literature, a syllabus with selected bibliographies.* Chicago, American Library Association, 1937.

SMITH, Janet Adam. *Children's illustrated books.* London, Collins, 1948.*

SPEAIGHT, George. *Juvenile drama.* London. Macdonald, 1946.

THWAITE, M. F. *From primer to pleasure, an introduction to the history of children's books in England from the invention of printing to 1900.* London, The Library Association, 1963.

Contains a chapter on children's books abroad, and a bibliography which includes references to periodical articles.

275

TOWNSEND, John Rowe. *Written for children, an outline of English children's literature.* London, Garnet Miller, 1965.

VRIES, Leonard de. *Little Wide-Awake, an anthology of Victorian children's books and periodicals.* World, 1967.

FRANCE

DELARUE, Paul. *Le conte populaire français: catalogue raisonné.* Paris, Editions Érasme, 1957.*

A second volume by P. D. and M-L. Tenèze was published in Paris by Eds. G-P Maisonneuve et Larose, 1964.

LATZARUS, Marie-Thérèse. *La littérature enfantine en France dans la seconde moitié du XIXe siècle.* Paris, Les Presses Universitaires de France, 1923.

MISTLER, Jean and others. *Épinal et l'imagerie populaire.* Paris, Hachette, 1961.

ROYER, Anne Marie. *Le livre pour les enfants. L'édition enfantine d'hier et d'aujourd'hui.* Aurillac, Bibliotheque municipale, 1960.

An exhibition catalogue.

SORIANO, Marc. *Guide de la littérature enfantine.* Paris, Flammarion, 1959.

STORER, Mary-Elizabeth. *La mode des contes de fées, 1685–1700; un épisode littéraire de la fin du XVII siècle.* Paris, Champion, 1928.

Includes a full bibliography of 'contes' by various authors.

TRIGON, Jean de. *Histoire de la littérature enfantine de Ma Mère l'Oye au Roi Babar.* Paris, Hachette, 1950.*

GERMANY

DODERER, Klaus. *Jugendliteratur heute.* Frankfurt a. M., Institut für Jugendbuch-forschung, 1965.

DYHRENFURTH-GRAEBSCH, Irene. *Geschichte des deutschen Jugendbuches.* Second edition. Hamburg, Stichnote, 1951.*

Includes a bibliography.

FRAENGER, Wilhelm. *Materialien zur Frühgeschichte der Neuruppiner Bilderbogen.* Berlin, Jahrbuch für historische Volkskunde, 1925.*

GÖHRING, Ludwig. *Die Anfänge der deutschen Jugendliteratur im 18 Jahrhundert.* Nuremberg, Korn, 1904.

HAMANN, Herman. *Die literarischen Vorlagen der Kinder- und Hausmärchen und ihre Bearbeitung durch die Brüder Grimm.* [Palaestra, vol. XLVII]. Berlin, Mayer u. Müller, 1906.

HOBRECKER, Karl. *Alte vergessene Kinderbücher.* Berlin, Mauritius, 1924.*

KÖSTER, Herman L. *Geschichte der deutschen Jugendliteratur.* Fourth edition. Hamburg, Westermann, 1927.

KUNZE, Horst. *Schatzbehalter vom besten aus der älteren deutschen Kinderliteratur.* Second edition. Berlin, Kinderbuchverlag, 1965.

LICHTENBERGER, Franz. *Der neue Weg der deutschen Jugendschrift.* Halle, Marhold, 1930.

NUREMBERG, Stadtbibliothek. *Bibliographie der Nürnberger Kinder- und Jugendbücher 1522–1914.* Bamberg, Meisenbach, 1961.

RÜMANN, Arthur. *Alte deutsche Kinderbücher.* Vienna, Herbert Reichner, 1937.*

SCHNEIDER, Harriet. *Münchner Bilderbogen in ihrer Wirkung auf Kinder.* Leipzig, 1924. A dissertation.

WOLGAST, Heinrich. *Das Elend unserer Jugendliteratur. Ein Beitrag zur künstlerischen Erziehung der Jugend.* Hamburg, Selbstverlag, 1896.*
A new edition was published at Worms by Wunderlich in 1950.

WOLGAST, Heinrich. *Vom Kinderbuch. Gesammelte Aufsätze.* Leipzig, Teubner, 1906.*

HUNGARY
DRESCHER, Pál. *Régi magyar gyermekkönyvek, 1538–1875.* Budapest, Magyar bibliophil társaság, 1934.

LAKITS, Pál. *Közepisholásaiak és ar irodalomi.* Budapest, Tankönyvkiado, 1962.

ITALY
BATTISTELLI, Vincenzina. *Il libro del fanciullo.* Second revised edition. Florence, La nuova Italia, 1962.

BONAFIN, Ottavia. *Le letteratura per l'infanzia.* Eleventh edition. Brescia, La Scuola, 1962.

FANCIULLI, Giuseppe and PUCCI, Mario. *Scrittori e libri per l'infanzia.* Revised edition. Turin, Societa editrice internazionele, 1960. First published 1949.

HAWKES, Louise R. *Before and after Pinocchio; a study of Italian children's books.* Paris, The Puppet Press, 1933.

LUGLI, Antonio. *Storia della letteratura per l'infanzia.* Florence, Sansoni, 1963.

MICHIELI, Armando. *Della letteratura per l'infanzia e la fanciullezza.* Fourth edition, revised. Padua, Cedam, 1948.

277

SACCHETTI, Lina. *Storia della letteratura per ragazzi.* Second edition. Florence, Le Monnier, 1962.

SANTUCCI, Luigi. *La letteratura infantile.* Milan, Fabbri. 1958.*

LOW COUNTRIES

AMSTERDAM. Stadelijk museum. *Kinderen lazen kinderen lezen.* Amsterdam, 1958.
   An exhibition catalogue.

CAPPE, Jeanne. *Contes bleus, livres roses.* Brussels, Ed. des Artistes, 1940.

DAALDER, D. L. *Wormcruyt met suycker; historisch-critisch overzicht van de Nederlandse kinderliteratuur.* Amsterdam, Arbeiderspers, 1950.
   Includes information on regional and denominational literature. Bibliography.

GEBHARD, Annie C. *Kinderboeken als vitamines, een ABC over kinderen en elzen.* Amsterdam, Ploegsma, 1963.

KNUTTEL-FABIUS, E. *Oude kinderboeken; paedagogie en moraal in oude Nederlandsche kinderboeken.* The Hague, Nijhoff, 1906.

NOESEN, Paul. *Geschichte der Luxemburger Jugendliteratur.* Luxemburg, L.K.A., 1951.

RIEMENS-REURSLAG, J. *Het jeugdboek in de loop der euwen.* The Hague, Van Stockum, 1949.

SCHMOOK, Gerard. *Het oude en het nieuwe kinderboek.* Antwerp, De Sikkel, 1934.

TICHELEN, Hendrik van. *Over boeken van kindsheit en jeugd.* Antwerp, Ontwikkeling, 1952.

TIERIE-HOGERZEIL, E. *Hoe men het ABC begeerde en leerde.* Amsterdam, Spectrum, 1946.

VRIES, Leonard de. *Bloempjes der vreugd voor de lieve jeugd.* Amsterdam, De Bezige Bij, 1958.
   This volume set the pattern for an English version based upon the Osborne Collection: *Flowers of delight.* Pantheon, 1965.

NORWAY

HAGEMANN, Sonja. *Barnelitteratur i Norge inntil 1850.* Oslo, Aschehoug, 1965.
   Part I of what is to be a two-volume history.

TENFJORD, J. *Barn og lesning.* Oslo, Aschehoug, 1947.

POLAND

KANIOWSKI-LEWAŃSKA, Izabela. *Literatura dla dzieci i młodzieży od poczatków do roku 1964.* Warsaw, Państwowe zakł ady wydawnictw szkolnych, 1960.

KRZEMIŃSKA, Wanda. *Literatura dla dzieci i młodzieży.* Warsaw, Stowarzyszenie bibliotekarzy polskich, 1963.

KULICZKOWSKA, Krystyna. *Literatura dla dzieci i młodzieży w latach, 1864–1914.* Warsaw, Państwowe zakłady wydawnictw szkolnych, 1959.

KULICZKOWSKA, Krystyna and SLÓNSKA, Irena. *Mały słownik literatury dla dzieci i młodziezy.* Warsaw, Wieda Powszechna, 1964.

SZUMAN, Stefan. *Ilustracja w ksiazkach dla dzieci i młodzieży,* Cracow, Zapior, 1951.

SPAIN

BRAVO-VILLASANTE, Carmen. *Historia de la literatura infantil española.* Madrid, Doncel, 1963.*

   A two-volume *Antologiá de la literatura infantil en lengua española* by the same author is also published by Doncel.

TORAL, Carolina. *Literatura infantil española.* Two volumes. Madrid, Editorial Coculsa, 1957.*

SWEDEN

KLINGBERG, Göte. *Svensk barn- och ungdomslitteratur 1591–1839; en pedagogikhistorisk och bibliografisk översikt.* Stockholm, Natur och Kultur, 1964.

   Includes an eighteen-page summary of chapters in English. A bibliographical catalogue is planned as a supplement.

LARSON, Lorentz and ØRVIG, Mary. *Barnböcker i Sverige, 1945-1965.* Stockholm, Svenska Sektionen av Internationella Ungdomsboksrådet, 1966.

   An exhibition catalogue.

LINDER, Gurli. *Våre barns fria läsning.* Stockholm, Norstedt, 1916.

LINDER, Gurli. *Våre barns nöjesläsning.* Stockholm, Bonnier, 1902.

WILLKE, Ingeborg. *ABC-Bücher in Schweden. Ihre Entwicklung bis Ende des 19 Jahrhunderts und ihre Beziehungen zu Deutschland.* Lund, 1965.

ZWEIGBERGK, Eva von. *Barnboken i Sverige 1750–1950.* Stockholm, Rabén & Sjögren, 1965.

   Includes a seven-page summary in English and a bibliography of sources.

SWITZERLAND

ANGST, Anny. *Die religions- und moralpädagogische Jugendschrift in der deutschen Schweiz von der Reformation bis zur Mitte des 19. Jahrhunderts.* Zürich, 1947.
A dissertation.

KRAUT, Dora. *Die Jugendbücher in der deutschen Schweiz bis 1850.* Bern, Schweizer Bibliophilengesellschaft, 1945.*

SEEBASS, Adolf. *Alte Kinderbücher und Jugendschriften.* Basel, Haus der Bücher, 1955.
A catalogue.

ZÜRICH, Stadtbibliothek. *Geschichte der schweizerischen Neujahrsblätter.* Zürich, Orell Füssli, 1856–8.*

U.S.S.R.

ALEKSEEVA, O. V. *Detskaia literatura.* Moscow, State Publishing House, 1957.

BABUSHKINA, A. P. *Istoria russkoi detskoi literatury.* Moscow, 1948.

BELINSKY, V. G. and others. *O detskoi literature.* Moscow, State Publishing House, 1954.

HURVYCH, Fenia K. *Ukrainska dytiacha literatura.* Kiev, Radianska School, 1962.

IVICH, Aleksandr. *Vospitanie pokoleny.* Moscow, The Soviet Writer, 1960.

KON, Lidya F. *Detskaia literatura v gody grazhdanskoi voiny.* Moscow, State Publishing House, 1953.

KON, Lidya F. *Sovietskaia detskaia literatura.* Moscow, State Publishing House, 1960.

KRUPSKAYA, N. K. *Krupskaia o detskoi literature i detskom chteny.* Moscow, State Publishing House. 1954.

Biographies

AMICIS

GIGLI, Lorenzo. *Edmondo de Amicis.* Turin, Unione Tipografico, 1962.
Includes an annotated bibliography of sources.

VALERI, Mario. *Edmondo de Amicis.* Florence, Le Monnier, 1954.

ANDERSEN

GODDEN, Rumer. *Hans Christian Andersen.* London, Hutchinson, 1955.

STERLING, Monica. *The wild swan; the life and times of Hans Christian Andersen.* London, Collins, 1965.

   Includes a bibliography of sources. See also p. 52.

AYMÉ

CATHELIN, Jean. *Marcel Aymé, ou le paysan de Paris.* Paris, Debresse, 1958.

   Includes a bibliography.

BERTUCH

HEINEMANN, Albrecht von. *Ein Kaufmann der Goethezeit; Friedrich Johann Justin Bertuchs Leben und Werk.* Weimar, Böhlans, 1955.

   Includes a bibliography of sources.

BESKOW

BESKOW, Natanael and others. *Natanael och Elsa Beskow, studier och minnesbilder.* Stockholm, Norstedt, 1954.

   Includes a list of books illustrated by Elsa Beskow.

BUSCH

BOHNE, Friedrich. *Wilhelm Busch, Leben, Werk und Schicksal.* Zürich, 1958.*

DANGERS, Robert. *Wilhelm Busch.* Berlin, Klemm, 1930.

NOVOTNY, Fritz. *Wilhelm Busch als Zeichner und Maler.* Vienna, 1949.*

COLLODI

BERTACCHINI, Renato. *Collodi educatore.* Florence, La nuova Italia, 1964.

   Includes a bibliography of sources.

MARCHETTI, Italiano. *Carlo Collodi.* Florence, Le Monnier, 1959.

   Includes a bio-bibliography of works and sources.

SANTUCCHI, Luigi. *Collodi,* Brescia, La scuola, 1961.

COMENIUS

ECKSTEIN, Friedrich. *Comenius und die Böhmischen Brüder.* Leipzig, Insel. (n.d.)*

SADLER, John Edward. *Comenius and the concept of universal education.* London, Allen and Unwin, 1966.

SPINKA, Matthew. *John Amos Comenius; that incomparable Moravian.* Chicago, University Press, 1943.

GENLIS

KERBY, William M. *The educational ideas and activities of Madame la Comtesse de Genlis, with special reference to her work 'Adèle et Théodore'*. Paris, Les Presses Universitaires de France, 1926.

The bibliography includes a list of all Madame de Genlis' works in the Bibliothèque Nationale.

WYNDHAM, Violet. *Madame de Genlis, a biography*. London, Deutsch, 1958.

GRIMM

BERLIN. Deutsche Staatsbibliothek. *150 Jahre 'Kinder- und Hausmärchen' der Brüder Grimm. Bibliographie und Materialien zu einer Ausstellung*. Berlin, 1964.

GRIMM, Ludwig Emil. *Lebenserinnerungen*, hsg. Adolf Stoll. Leipzig, 1911.

QUIRIN, Gerstl. *Die Brüder Grimm als Erzieher*. Munich, 1964.

HELD

TETZNER, Lisa. *Das war Kurt Held; 40 Jahre Leben mit ihm*. Aarau, Sauerländer, 1961.

HOFFMANN

BOGENG, Gustav. *Der Struwwelpeter und sein Vater; Geschichte eines Bilderbuchs*. Potsdam, Rütten u. Loening, 1939.

HOFFMANN, Heinrich. *Struwwelpeter-Hoffman, Lebenserinnerungen*. Frankfurt, Englert, 1926.*

HOSEMANN

BRIEGER, Lothar. *Theodor Hosemann, ein Altmeister Berliner Malerei; mit einem Katalog der graphischen Werke des Künstlers von Karl Hobrecker*. Munich, Delphin, 1920.

KÄSTNER

ENDERLE, Liselotte. *Kästner, eine Bildbiographie*. Munich, Kindler, 1960.

See also p. 266.

KREIDOLF

FRAENGER, Wilhelm. *Ernst Kreidolf ein schweizer Maler und Dichter*. Zürich, Rascher, 1917.*

KEHRLI, Jacob Otto. *Ernst Kreidolf, Lebenserinnerungen*. Zürich, Rotapfel, 1957.*

LADA

LADA, Josef. *Ein Schusterbub wird Maler*. Berlin, Kinderbuchverlag, (n.d.).*

LADOVÁ, Alena. *Muj táta Josef Lada.* Prague, Mladá fronta, 1963.

LAGERLÖF

AFZELIUS, J. A. *Nils Holgerssons underbara resa.* Stockholm, 1956.
  Catalogue of an exhibition which included versions of the book in 29 different languages.

BERENDSOHN, W. A. *Selma Lagerlöf, her life and work; adapted from the German by George F. Timpson.* London, Nicholson and Watson, 1931.
  Contains a list of English translations of her works to 1930.

MAY

DWORCZAK, K. H. *Karl May, das Leben Old Shatterhands.* Salzburg. Pfad, 1950.
  An appreciation worthy of the old romancer himself.

SCHMIDT, Arno. *Sitara und der Weg dorthin; eine Studie über Wesen, Werk und Wirkung Karl May's.* Karlsruhe, Stahlberg, 1963.
  A study remarkable for its irony, wit, and literary perception.

MOE

HAGEMANN, Sonja. *Jørgen Moe; Barnas Dikter.* Oslo, Aschehoug, 1963.

POCCI

DREYER, *Aloys. Franz Pocci; Dichter, Künstler und Kinderfreund.* Munich, Müller, 1907.*

LUCAS, Anna. *Franz Pocci und das Kinderbuch.* Münster, Regensberg, 1929.

RICHTER

HOFF, J. F. *Adrian Ludwig Richter, Maler und Radierer. Verzeichnis seines gesamten graphischen Werkes.* Second edition. Freiburg, Ragoczy, 1922.

ST. EXUPÉRY

RUMBOLD, Richard and STEWART, Lady Margaret. *The winged life, a portrait of Antoine de Saint-Exupéry.* London, Weidenfeld, 1953.

SCHMID

SCHMID, Christoph von. *Erinnerungen aus meinem Leben.* Augsburg, Wolf, 1853–55.

SEALSFIELD

CASTLE, Eduard. *Der grosse Unbekannte; das Leben von Charles Sealsfield (Karl Postl)* Volume I. Vienna, Manutius, 1952. Volume 2. *Briefe und Aktenstücke.* Vienna, Werner, 1955.

SÉGUR

KILLIP, E. H. *The stories of the Comtesse de Ségur and her contribution to children's literature.* 1956.

A dissertation with full bibliographies.

SPYRI

PAUR-ULRICH, Marguerite. *Johanna Spyri.* Zürich, Waldmann, (n.d.).*

TRNKA

BOČEK, Jaroslav. *Jiří Trnka, artist and puppet master.* London, Hamlyn, 1965.

INDEX

Accumulative rhymes 14–17
Achterhuis, Het (Frank) 192, 194
Ackerhielm, G. 230
Adèle et Théodore (Genlis) xii
Aimard, Gustave 120
Albums du Père Castor 136–40, 150, 225, 231
Alice's adventures in Wonderland (Carroll) 64–72
  illus. 67, 69, 70
Alice's adventures underground (Carroll) 65–66
  plate ix
All alone in the world (Spyri) 255
Allerleirauh (Enzensberger) 264
Als ich ein kleiner Junge war (Kästner) 259, 266
Alte deutsche Kinderbücher (Rümann) 269, 277
Alte vergessene Kinderbücher (Hobrecker) 269, 276
Alti Versli und Liedli 214
Ambrose, Kenneth 180 *n*
America
  children's books xvii–xviii
  comics 160–1, 168–70
  and picture-books 232–3
  and Twain 259
  bibliog. 274–6
Amicis, Edmondo de 178
  biog. 280
  plate xvi
Anderson, E. (trans.) xv *n*
Andersen, H. Hans *père* 43–46
Andersen, Hans Christian 28, 42–52
  and Arabian nights 26, 48
  and Lewis Carroll 68
  bibliog. 51–52

Andersen, Hans Christian (*cont.*):
  biog. 280–1
  illus. 47, 50
  plate iii
Andersen, Marie 43–45
Andres, Stefan 244
Animal's conference, The (Kästner) 194
Ano lebt in der Tundra (Dobrinskaja) 223, 245
Anti-Semitism and children's books 183, 192–3
Apoutsiak (Castor) 137
Arabian nights' entertainments 21, 25–26, 31, 38
  and Andersen 26, 48, 50
  bibliog. 39
  illus. 25
Ardizzone, E. 230, 262
Armancour, P. d' 30
Arnim, A. von xv, 6, 31
Asbjörnsen, P. C. 36, 40
Atala (Chateaubriand) 119
Atlantis Kinderbücher 140
Austria
  bibliog. 274
Autojagd, Die (Witzleben) 149
Aymé, Marcel 87–89
  bibliog. 92
  biog. 281

Babar 195–200, 236
  and *Le petit prince* 96
  and politics 181, 196
  plate xviii
Babar books (in English) 200
Babar books (in French) 195–200
Baby's opera (Crane) 202–3

285

Bakule, František 138
Baldner, Gaby 244
Balon rouge, Le (Lamorisse) 147, 151
Barker, Cicely 207 n
Barnes, Malcolm (trans.) 151
Baroque, The—and fairy stories 28
Barrie, J. M. 76, 77n
Basedow, J. B. B. xiii, 132–4, 135
    illus. 133
Basile, G. 21–22, 26–28, 30, 35, 38–39
    illus. 27
Basket of flowers, The (Schmid) xv n
Bastian der Faulpelz (Hoffmann) 59
Baumberger O. and H. (illus.) 214
Bäumer, E. and V. (illus.) 140 n, 220–1
    plate xx
Baumhauer, H. (illus.) 52, 266
Baynes, P. (illus.) 39
Beattie, Janet 230, 245
Bechstein, Ludwig 32, 35
Belgium
    bibliog. 278
Bell, Anthea (trans.) 244, 245
Bell for Ursli, A. (Chönz) 237, 239, 243
Berg, Leila (trans.) 91, 228, 243, 245
Berg hinauf, Den (Bäumer) 140 n, 221
Bergengruen, Werner 261
Bergman, Astrid 147, 151
    plate xv
Bergmann, W. 140, 221
Berkenkamp, Lou Scheper- (illus.) 221
    plate xxi
Berle, Reidar (illus.) 230
Bertuch, F. J. J. xiii, 134, 135
    biog. 281, plate xi
Beskow, Elsa 207–8, 243
    biog. 281
Besuch bei Frau Sonne (Hoffmann) 59
Bewick, Thomas 202
Bilderakademie für die Jugend (Stoy) 135
Bilderbogen 152–9
    illus. 153, 154, 157, 163
Bilderbuch für Kinder, Das (Bertuch) xiii, 134,
    135, 202 plate ii
Bilderpossen, Die (Busch) 162
Bim (Lamorisse) 147, 151
Bindschedler, Ida 254
Birthday, The (Fischer) 244
Bischoff, Helmut (illus.) 141
Blake, William 176–7, 262
Blumenmärchen, Die (Kreidolf) 203–5, 207
Blyton, Enid 200
Bock, V. (illus.) 39
Bodmer, J. J. 250
Böer, Friedrich 140, 148–9, 159
    bibliog. 144
    plate xiv
Bohemia—Unity of Brethren 127
Bolt, Niklaus 254

Bon voyage, M. Dumollet (Samivel) 231
    plate xxvii
Boner, C. (trans.) 51
Book of nonsense, A (Lear) 73
Bookbird (I.B.B.Y.P.) 270 n
Borg, Inga 230
    bibliog. 243
Borrowers, The (Norton) 80
Bothmer, G. (trans.) 91
Braun & Schneider (publishers) 158, 162
    illus. 154
Braun-Fock, Beatrice (illus.) 220
    bibliog. 243
Brecht, Bertolt 264–5
Bremer Stadtmusikanten, Die (Grimm) 240–2
Brentano, C. xv, 6, 31, 36
Brereton, G. (trans.) 35 n, 39, 264 n
Brick, A. Riwkin- 149, 151
Brinkmann, D. 58
Britten, Benjamin 177
Britton, A. (trans.) 92
Brookes, C. T. (trans.) 172
Brookes, Louise (trans.) 255
Brooks, Cyrus (trans.) 266
Bruckner, Karl 193, 194
Brunhoff, Jean de 195–200
    and Le petit prince 96
    and social problems 181
    bibliog. 200
    plate xviii
Brunhoff, Laurent de 197, 199, biog. 200
Brunhoff, Michel de 197
Bruno books, The (Munari) 244
Brzechwa, Jan 143
Bullock, Michael (trans.) 244
Burrita non, La (Sanchez-Silva) 87
Burton, Sir R. (trans.) 39
Busch, W. xvi, 19, 161–6, 169
    and Lear 74
    and illustration 205
    bibliog. 172
    biog. 281
    illus. 161, 163
Butterfly's ball, The (Roscoe) xvi

Caldecott, Randolph (illus.) 203
Calthrop, M. E. (trans.) 255
Campe, J. H. xiii, 103–6
    and Basedow 134
    bibliog. 111
    illus. 101
Capp, A. (illus.) 165–6
Caricature 164
Carigiet, Alois (illus.) 236–9
    bibliog. 243
    illus. 238
Carrington, Noel 139 n, 140
Carroll, Lewis xvi, 64–72
    and Busch 162

Carroll, Lewis (*cont.*):
  as illustrator 71
  and Lear 73
  and *Le petit prince* 95
  illus. 67, 69, 70
  plates VIII, IX
Caspari, G. (illus.) 212
Castor, Père 80, 136–40, 143, 216, 231
  and photographic books 139, 146, 150
  bibliog. 144
Century of the child, The (Key) xii, 203
Chamisso, A. von 86 *n*
Chanticleer and Partlet (Fischer) 244
Chapbooks xv
  and Robinson Crusoe 104
  illus. xiv
Chapman, Gaynor (illus.) 270
Chateaubriand, F. 119
Chawerim (de Vries) 193
Chekhov, A. 231
Chendru and the tiger (Sucksdorff) 150, 151
Children everywhere series 151
Child's garden of verses, A (Stevenson) 262
Chimney-sweep 176–7
Chodowiecki, Daniel xiii, 132–3
  illus. 133
Chönz, Selina 236–9
Christmas in the stable (Lindgren) 245
Chukovsky, Kornei 258
  plate XXII
Cinderella (Basile) 21–22, 28, 35
Cinema 147–8, 166
Cipollino, Il romanzo di (Rodari) 190
Clark, Audrey (trans.) 112
Classics for children xvii, 81
Claudius, Matthias xv, 8, 105
Cohen, V. O. (illus.) 255
Collection le montreur d'images (Castor) 150
Collier, Peter (trans.) 244
Collin, Hedvig (illus.) 40
Collin, Jonas 46
Collodi, C. 49, 77–78
  bibliog. 91
  biog. 281
Colour fairy books (Lang) 41
Colour printing, 62, 202, 205
Colour prints 152–9
Comenius, Jan Amos xii, 127–43, 246
  biog. 281
  illus. 128, 130
Comics 78, 93, 156, 160–72
  illus. 167, 168, 169
Contes du chat perché, Les (Aymé) 87
  bibliog. 92
Cook, Olive (trans.) 144
Cooper, J. Fenimore xvii, 113–19, 176
  in France 119–20
  in Germany 119–22
  and May 124

Coureur des bois, Le (Ferry) 119
Cowboys and Indians 113–26, 171
Craigie, Dorothy (illus.) 262
Crin-blanc (Lamorisse) 147, 151
Croce, B. 28, 39
Crozier, Eric 177
Cruikshank, G. (illus.) 38
  illus. 27, 33
Cunto de li cunti, Lo (Basile) 26
Cuore (Amicis) 178
  plate XVI
Czechoslovakia
  and Père Castor 138
  and educational books 142
  and picture-books 226–7, plate XXIV
  bibliog. 274

da Silva, Viera (illus.) 232
Daiken, L. 20
Danish fairy-legends and tales (Andersen) 51
Danish story-book, A. (Andersen) 51
d'Armancour, P. 30
Dasent, Sir G. W. (trans.) 36, 40
Day of the bomb (Bruckner) 194
Day, Thomas
  Swedish illus. xvii
Deerslayer, The (Cooper) 116–18
Defoe, Daniel 99–111
  illus. 100
Dehmel, P. and R. 206, 215–16, 263
  plate XIX
De Jong, Meindert 193
De la Mare, W. 11, 73, 262
Denmark 43, 51
  and photographic books 147, 149
  plates XV, XXVI
  bibliog. 274
Dent, A. A. (trans.) 40
Derby, Earl of 72
Deutsche Märchen vor Grimm (Wesselsky) 35
De Vries, Leonard 193, 194, 278
Dichtung als Spiel (Liede) 75
Dichtung und Wahrheit (Goethe) xiii, 103
Dickens, Charles 43, 177–8
Diederichs, Inge 140 *n*
Dimson, T. (illus.) 41
Discovery of America, The (Campe) 111
Disney, Walt 72, 78 *n*, 165–6, 170
Divine songs (Watts) xvi
Dixon, Charlotte 39
Dixon, E. 39
Dobrinskaja, Anna 223, 245
Doctor Dolittle, The story of (Lofting) 78
Dodd, M. (illus.) 92
Dodgson, C. L. *see* Carroll, L.
Dole, H. B. (trans.) 255
Doremi (Brzechwa) 143, 228
Doyle, Richard (illus.) 207 *n*
Drei Jungen erforschen eine Stadt (Böer) 149

Drummers of dreams (Zimnik) 245
Druon, M. 89
  bibliog. 92
  illus. 89
du Faur, Faber, *see* Faber du Faur, I. von
Duhème, J. (illus.) 89, 92
Duvoisin, Roger (illus.) 171, 232–3
  illus. 233

East Europe
  and educational books 142–3
  and picture-books 224–9
East of the sun and west of the moon 36, 40
Eastman, C. A. 113, 126
Edgeworth, Maria
  plate IV
Education
  and comics 170
  and picture-books 127–44, 203–4, 216, 243
  and Reformation 129
  Gorky on 186–8
Edwards, J. R. (trans.) 40
Egner, T. 84
  bibliog. 91
  illus. 84
Ehmcke, Susanne (illus.) 159, 218–19, 263
  bibliog. 243
Eia Popeia 214
  illus. 3, 8, 18
Eichendorff, J. von 118
Eisgruber, Elsa (illus.) 220, 243, 262
Eldest in the class, The (Hallqvist) 84
Elementarwerk, Das (Basedow) xiii, 132–4, 135
  illus. 133
Elend unserer Jugendliteratur, Das (Wolgast) 203, 277
Eliot, T. S. 262
Elle Kari (Brick) 149, 151
Ellis, A. Williams- 39, 40
Emett, Roland (illus.) 262
Emil und die Detektive (Kästner) 179
  bibliog. 266
Émile (Rousseau) 102–3
Encyclopaedias 135–6, 143
Ende, Michael 86
  bibliog. 92
England
  and comics 160, 166–7, 169
  and *Des Knaben Wunderhorn* 20
  and educational books 139, 142
  and fairy stories 36, 64
  and nursery rhymes 8–9
  and picture-books 228, 230–1, plate xxv
  and poetry for children xv–xvi, 261, 262
  and toy theatres 155, 158
  and umbrellas 110–11
  bibliog. 274–6

English fairy tales (ed. Macleod) 244
English Struwwelpeter, The (Hoffmann) 62
Enzensberger, H. M. 264
Epinal 152, 156, 161
Erdkühlein, Das 35
Ett hem (Larsson) 197, 211–12
  illus. 212
Etwas von denWurzelkindern (Olfers) 207
Evans, Edmund (engraver) 202–3, 207 *n*, 210
Eventyr fortalte for børn (Andersen) 47
Exupéry, Antoine de Saint- *see* Saint-Exupéry

Faber book of nursery verse 20
Faber du Faur, I. von 5, 15–16, 20
Fairchild Family (Sherwood) xiii
Fairy stories xii, xv, 21–41
  in England 36, 64, 244
  in France 29–31
  in Germany 31–36
  in Italy 26–28
  in Switzerland 253–4
  and Andersen 48–51
  and the Baroque 28
  and *The borrowers* 80
  and Busch 164
  and children 29–30, 33–34
  and illustrations 235
  and *Le petit prince* 93
  and *Mary Poppins* 79
  and nonsense 76
  and Romanticism 22, 31, 34
  bibliog. 39–41
Fairy tale of my life (Andersen) 44, 45
Fairy tales (Perrault) 35
Family Robinson Crusoe, The (Wyss) 111
Fatio, Louise 232–3
Faur, Faber du, I. von 5, 15–16, 20
Favourite fairy tales (Haviland) 41
Fénelon, F. 104
Ferdinand (Leaf) 171, 180–1, 228
  illus. 182
Ferry, Gabriel 119
Figge (Mall) 229
Fischer, Hans 239–43
  bibliog. 244
  illus. 241
  plate xxviii
Fitzebutze (Dehmel) 206, 215, 263
  plate xix
Flight to Arras (Saint-Exupéry) 98
Flower fairy books (Barker) 207 *n*
Flurina und das Wildvöglein (Chönz) 237–8, 243
Flusspiraten des Mississippi (Gerstäcker) 121
Fock, Beatrice Braun- (illus.) 220
  bibliog. 243

Folk-songs, Essays in the study of (Martinengo-Cesaresco) 20
Folkard, C. (illus.) 40
  bibliog. 91, 112
Football's revolt, The (Lewitt-Him) 228
  plate XXV
Forster, Georg 103
France
  and Babar 198
  and cowboys 119–20
  and fairy stories 29–31
  and picture-books 213, 225, 231–2, plate XXVII
  and political stories 178
  and popular literature 152
  and Saint-Exupéry 96
  bibliog. 276
France, Anatole 213
Frank, Anne 192, 194
Fraser, Lovat (illus.) 262
Freud, T. Seidmann- 140, 216
  illus. 217
Freyhold, K. F. von (illus.) 216
Frith, H. (trans.) 112
Fröbel, J. 250
Frølich, L. (illus.) 52
Fromm, Lilo (illus.) 222
  bibliog. 244
Fyleman, R. 20, 144

Gág, W. (trans.) 40
Gailer, Magister 135
Galantiére, Lewis (trans.) 98
Galgenlieder (Morgenstern) 75
Galland, A. (trans.) 25
Gampp, Josua L. (illus.) 159, 216, 262
Gavarni 58
  plate VI
Geburtstag, Der (Fischer) 242
Geburtstagsreise, Die (Grieder) 142
Geist H. F. (publisher) 159
Genlis, Madame de xii
  biog. 282
German popular stories (Grimm) xvi, 38
  illus. 33
Germany
  and cowboys 119–22
  and nonsense 85–6
  and photographic books 148–9
  and picture-books 215–24, illus. 217, 218, 223, plates XIX, XXI
  and political stories 178–80, 181, 183, 190–3
  popular literature 152–4, 156–9
  bibliog. 276–7
Gerstäcker, Friedrich 121
Geschichte vom Fluss, Die (Bäumer) 220–1
  plate XX
Gestiefelte Kater, Der (Fischer) 242

Giuseppe und Maria (Held) 180, 194
Globo de colores (Aguilar) 142
Godkin G. S. (trans.) plate XVI
Godwin, W. (trans.) 111
Goethe, J. W. von
  and Andersen 43
  and Cooper 119
  and fairy stories 6, 31
  and Orbis pictus 132
  and Robinson Crusoe 103, 104, 106
  and Volksbücher xiii, 31
Golden books 141
Goni (illus.) 92
Gorky, Maxim, views on children's literature, 184–9
Gösta Berlings saga (Lagerlöf) 260
Gotha, Fritz Koch- 208
Gotthelf, Jeremias 251
Grabianski, J. (illus.) 39, 40, 52
Grahame, K. 78
Green, R. L. 41, 275
Greenaway, Kate (illus.) 202–3
Greene, Grahame 73, 262
Grieder, Walter 142
Grimm, Jakob and Wilhelm xv, xvi, 6, 24, 28, 30, 31–38
  and Andersen 42–43, 48, 49
  and Felix Hoffmann 235, 244
  and Hans Fischer 240–2, 244
  bibliog. 40
  biog. 282
  illus. 33, 241
  plates I, II
Grimm, Ludwig E. plate II
Grimmelshausen, J. J. von 106
  bibliog. 111
Gueguen, Pierre 232

Halas, František 227
Hale, Kathleen 230
Hall, Eileen (trans.) 255, 266
Hallqvist, Britt 84, 230
Hänseken (Wedekind) 263
Hänsel and Gretel 24, 35
Happy lion, The (Fatio) 232–3
  illus. 233
Hare, H. (trans.) 92
Harris, J. Chandler xviii
Häschenschule, Die (Koch-Gotha) 208
Hauff, W. 26, 36, 40, 119
Haviland, V. 41
Hawthorne, N. xviii
Hazard, Paul 30, 32, 138, 269, 273
Heart (Amicis) plate XVI
Hebel, J. P. xv
Heidi (Spyri) 22, 76, 236, 251–2
  bibliog. 255
  illus. 252
Heimeran, Ernst 220, 243

Held, Kurt 180, 194
  biog. 282
Hellsing, Lennart 230
  bibliog. 244
Henning-Jensen, A. and B. 149
Herder, J. G. 6, 32
Hergé 170–1
Hiawatha (Longfellow) 115
  and Winnetou 124
  plate XIII
Hill, Oliver 140
Him, George (illus.) 228
Hirtz, Lise 232
Histoires ou contes du temps passé (Perrault)
  29–31
Hobrecker, Karl 269, 276
Hochwald (Stifter) 118, 119
Hodges, C. Walter (illus.) 112
Hofer, Karl (illus.) 215–16, 221, 263
Hoffmann, E. T. A. 40
Hoffmann, Felix 235
  bibliog. 244
Hoffmann, Heinrich xi, 19, 53–63
  and Carroll 69
  and Busch 162
  and illustration 205
  bibliog. 62–63
  biog. 282
  illus. 57
  plates V, VI, VII
Hofmannsthal, H. von 263
Holland
  and political stories 182
  bibliog. 278
Hoole, Charles 131
Hosch-Wackernagel, Esther 234–5, illus.
  234
Hosemann, Theodor (illus.) 158
  biog. 282
House of sixty fathers, The (de Jong) 193
Howard, Alan 231
Howard, V. S. (trans.) 266
Howitt, M. (trans.) 51
Hrubin, František 226
  bibliog. 245, plate XXIV
Huckleberry Finn (Twain) 259
Hughes, Shirley (illus.) 52
Humboldt, A. and W. 103–4, 121
Hündchen Benjamin (Roser) 222
Hungary
  Revolution 173, illus. 191
  bibliog. 277
Hunt, M. (trans.) 40
Hurup, E. (trans.) 91

I never saw another butterfly 194
  plate XVII
Igloos and totem poles (Böer) 144
Il était une petite pie (Hirtz) 232

Im Himmel wie auf Erden (Hoffmann) 59
Imagerie populaire 152
In fairyland (Allingham) 207 *n*, plate XXIII
Indian life, Tales of (Aimard) 120
Insel Felsenburg, Die (Schnabel) 106
Instructional tales xii
International Board on Books for Young
  People 270
International Youth Library, Munich 269
  catalogue 273
Internationalism 269–271
  in children's books xviii
  and fairy stories 24
  and picture-books 213
Irving, Washington 115
Ishii, Momoko 271
  illus. 270
Italy
  and comics 167
  and cowboys 126
  and fairy stories 26–28
  and picture-books 232
  and political stories 178
  popular literature 232
  bibliog. 277–8
Iversen, P. S. (trans.) 40

Jackdaw Series 151 *n*
Jacobs, Joseph 36
Jacques, R. (illus.) 52
James, M. R. (trans.) 52
Jan und Jon (Scheper-Berkenkamp) 221
  plate XXI
Janeček, Ota (illus.) 227
  bibliog. 244
Janosch (illus.) 223
  bibliog. 244
Jansson, T. 80–81, 83
  bibliog. 91
  illus. 81
Jensen, A. and B. Henning- 149
Jim Button and Luke the engine driver (Ende) 92
Johnson, A. E. (trans.) 40
Jones, Harold (illus.) 4, 262
  illus. 4
Jugga jagga (Ackerhielm) 230
Jungle books (Kipling) 258
Just so stories, The (Kipling) 259
  illus. 258

Kalinin, V. 188
Karina with love (Linklater) 150
Kashtanka (Chekhov) 231
Kästner, Erich 179, 194, 196, 259–60
  bibliog. 194, 266
  biog. 282
Kater Mikesch, Der (Lada) 226
Keigwin, R. P. (trans.) 52

Kennedy, R. (illus.) 91
 illus. 83
Key, Ellen xii, 203
Kiddell-Monroe, J. (illus.) 39, 41
Kidnapped (Stevenson) 256-7
Kiepenheuer, Bettina 140
Kilian, Adam (illus.) 229
Kim (Kipling) 258-9
Kinder aus Nr. 67, Die (Tetzner) 179
Kinderbuchbrücke, Die (Lepman) 181
Kinder-Duden 219, 243
Kinder-und Hausmärchen (Grimm) 32-34
 plate II
Kinder-Verwirr-Buch (Ringelnatz) 264
Kinder Wunderhorn, Der 6
Kinderreime der Welt (Faber du Faur) 5, 20
King Nut-cracker (Hoffmann) 63
Kingsley, Charles 43, 177
Kingsland, L. W. (trans.) 52
Kingston, W. H. G. (trans.) 112
Kipling R. 258-9
 illus. 258
Kirkup, J. (trans.) 91
Kittelsen, T. (illus.) 40
Klaus der Herr der Eisenbahnen (Böer) 148
 plate XIV
Klein, H. A. and M. C. (trans.) 172
Klein Irmchen (Morgenstern) 60, 216, 262
 quoted 3
Klemke, Werner (illus.) 223
 bibliog. 244
Knabe des Tells, Der (Gotthelf) 251
Knaben Wunderhorn, Des (Brentano and
 Arnim) 6, 20, 74
 quoted 1, 3, 4, 5, 7, 17
 illus. 12-13
Knight, M. (trans.) 75
Ko et Ko (da Silva) 232
Koch-Gotha, Fritz 208
Komensky, Jan Amos, *see* Comenius, Jan
 Amos
Konashsvicha, V. (illus.) plate XX
Könferenz der Tiere, Die (Kästner) 194, 196
König Nussknacker, Der (Hoffmann) 58-59,
 63
Kredel, F. (illus.) 35, 214
 illus. 3, 8, 18
Kreidolf, Ernst 203-8, 212
 biog. 282
 plate XIX
Krüss, J. 85-86
 bibliog. 91
Kühn, Gustav (publisher) 152
Kurdov, V. (illus.) 258

Lada, Josef (illus.) 226
 bibliog. 244
 biog. 282-3
Lagerlöf, Selma 150, 260

Lagerlöf, Selma (*cont.*):
 bibliog. 266
 biog. 283
Lamorisse, Albert 147, 151
Land deiner Mutter, Das (Lauber) 261
Land is bright, The (de Vries) 194
Länder and Völker (With) 140-1
Lang, Andrew 38, 39, 41
Larsson, Carl 197, 211-12, 243
 illus. 212
Last of the Mohicans, The (Cooper) 116-18
Lauber, Cécile 261
Lauckhard C. F. 136
Lavater, J. K. 110, 110 *n*
Lavender's blue illus. 4
Lawson, Robert (illus.) 181, 182
Leaf, Munro 171, 180-1
 illus. 182
Leander, R. von Volkmann- 36
Lear, Edward xvi, 9, 72-74
 as illustrator 74
Leatherstocking Saga, The (Cooper) 116 *n*
Lebedev, V. (illus.) 225
Lemke, Horst (illus.) 266
Lenica, Jan (illus.) 228
Lepman, Jella 179, 181, 194, 196, 269-70
Leslie, Cecil (illus.) 255
Let's make an opera (Crozier) 177
Leuchtturm, Der (Schnitter) 235
 plate XX
Leupin, H. 235
Lewitt-Him (illus.) 228, 230
 bibliog. 244
 plate XXV
Librairie bleue xv
Lichtenstein (Hauff) 119
Lida 137
Liddell, Alice 64-66
Liede, A. 75
Life of a queen, The (Portal) 141
Lillegg, E. 85
Lind, Jenny 48
Lindgren, Astrid 81-83, 149, 151, 260
 bibliog. 91, 245
 illus. 83
Linklater, Eric 73, 150, 261
Literacy 170
Lithography 54, 62, 202, 204-5
Little lion, The (Ylla) 146, 151
Little pretty pocket-book, A (Newbery)
 247
Little prince, The (Saint-Exupéry) 87, 93-98
 bibliog. 98
 illus. 94
Little Red Engine, The (Ross) 228, 230
Little Red Riding Hood 30-31
Little woman who forgot everything (Beattie)
 230, 245
Little white bird, The (Barrie) 76

Livres, les enfants et les hommes, Les (Hazard) 138, 269, 273
Lobb, Frances (trans.) 194
Lofting, H. 78
Lokomotywa (Tuwim) 227–8, 244
Longfellow, H. W. 115, 176
  plate XIII
Löning, Dr. 54
Lorenzini, C. *see* Collodi, C.
Lorimer, E. O. 39
Louis XIV 29
Low countries
  and political stories 182
  bibliog. 278
Lubbock, Roger (trans.) 151
Lullabies 2, 20
Lullaby book, The (Daiken) 20
Lumpengesindel, Das (Fischer) 242
Lustige Männlein, Das (Hosch-Wacker-nagel) 234
Luxembourg
  bibliog. 278

McHugh, I. and F. (trans.) 144, 266
McNeill, J. 41
Mahlau, Alfred (illus.) 159
Mahler, G. 20
Maier, Otto (publisher) 141
Malheurs de Sophie, Les (Ségur) xvi
Malheurs d'Ysengrin, Les (Samivel) 231
Mall, Victor 229
Männchen, Das (Meissen) 217–18
Marcelino, Pan y Vino (Sanchez-Silva) 86
  bibliog. 92
Marryat, F. xvii, 110
Marsh, Gwen (trans.) 151
Martinengo-Cesaresco, Countess 20
Martins Reise (Rinser) 260
Mary Poppins (Travers), 79, 261
Masterman Ready (Marryat) 110
Mathiesen, Egon (illus.) 230
  bibliog. 244
Matsui, Tadasho 271
Maurois, André 150, 151
Max und Moritz (Busch) 161–5
May, Karl 113–14, 117, 121, 122–6
  biog. 283
Mayo, Eileen 140
Meggendorfer, L. (illus.) 158
Mein Urgrossvater und ich (Krüss) 85
Meissen, Conny 217–18
Melcher, Frederic 269
Menzel, Adolf (illus.) 158
Meyer, Conrad 247
Meyer, Johannes 247
Michaelis, Karin 261
Mickey Mouse 165–6, 168–9
Micky the fox-cub (*Micki Rävungen*) (Berg-man) 147, 149, 151

Micky the fox-cub (cont.):
  plate XV
Mikisoq (Henning-Jensen) 149
Milne, A. A. 78
Miró, Joan (illus.) 232
Mischmash (Carroll) 68
Mrs. Tiggy-Winkle (Potter) 210
Moe, J. E. 36, 40
  biog. 283
Möllhausen, Balduin 121
Monroe, J. Kiddell- 39, 41
Montolieu, Baroness de (trans.) 112
Monvel, M. Boutet de (illus.) 213, 243
Mool, was der Maulwurf erlebt (Winter) 141
Moomin stories (Jansson) 80–81
  bibliog. 91
Mooyaart-Doubleday, B. M. (trans.) 194
Moral tales xii–xiii, xvi, 86
  and *Robinson Crusoe* 105, 110
  and *Struwwelpeter* 55
  and *Tistou* 90
  illus. xiii
  plate IV
Morgenstern, C. 3, 19, 60, 216, 262–3
  and Lear 74
Morris, Rev. Marcus 160
  illus. 169
Mother Goose (Greenaway) 203
Mother Goose's tales (Perrault) 38
  illus. 29
Muir, Percy 30, 51 *n*, 269, 275
Muller fairy-tale books 41
Munari, Bruno (illus.) 232
Münchener Bilderbogen 154, 156, 158, 159, 162–4
  illus. 154
Musäus, I. K. A. xv, 31–32
My great-grandfather and I (Krüss) 91
My mother is the most beautiful woman (Reyher) 225

Nardi, Marcia (trans.) 141
Netherlands
  and political stories 182
  bibliog. 278
Neuer Orbis pictus (Gailer) 135
Neujahrsblätter, Zürich 246–50
  illus. 248
New Robinson Crusoe, The (Campe) 111
Newbery, John xv, 247
Nico (Maurois) 150, 151
Nils, The adventures of (Lagerlöf) 150, 260
  bibliog. 266 283
Noack, H. G. 192
Nonsense 64–75
  and fairy stories 76
  and Heinrich Hoffmann 61
  and nursery rhymes 9
Noriko-San (Lindgren) 149

Norman, C. (trans.) 40
Norton, M. 80
Norway
   and folk-tales 36, bibliog. 40
   and picture-books 84, 230
   bibliog. 278
Norwegian folk tales (Asbjörnsen) 40
Nursery rhymes 1–20
   and England 8–9
   and picture-books 2, 201
   and Romanticism 6
   oral transmission 6
   sequence (accumulative) 14–17
   chapbook illus. xiv
Nyman, Ingrid van (illus.) 230

Oberländer, Gerhard (illus.) 141, 222
   bibliog. 244–5
Ockenden, Ray (trans.) 194
Ohijesa (Eastman) 113, 126
Old Possum's book of practical cats (Eliot) 262
Olfers, Sibylle von 207, 243
Olsen, I. S. (illus.) 230
   plate XXVI
Openshaw, Olive (illus.) 200
Opie, I. *and* P. 15 *n*, 19, 275
   See also *Oxford dictionary of nursery rhymes*
   Oxford nursery rhyme book
Oral transmission
   and fairy stories 28, 31–32
   and nursery rhymes 6
Orbis sensualium pictus (Comenius) xii, 127–
    32, 143, 246, 249
   and encyclopaedias 135–6
   imitations 132, 135
   illus. 128, 130
Original poems for infant minds (Taylor) xvi
Orlowska, Maria (illus.) 181, 228
Osborne collection 269, 275
Over the tree-tops (Fyleman) 20
Oxford dictionary of nursery rhymes (Opie) 20,
   275
   illus. xiv
Oxford myths and legends 41
Oxford nursery rhyme book, The (Opie) 19
   quoted 5, 9, 11
   illus. 9

Paint a black horse (Heimeran) 243
Palle alene i verden (Sigsgaard) 229, 245
Palmblätter, Die (Herder) 32
Paradies, Das (Stefula) 222
Parain, N. (illus.) 89, 139, 225
Parrak (Borg) 230, 243
Parrish colour books (Neurath) 142
Pathfinder, The (Cooper) 116–18
Paul et Virginie (Saint-Pierre) 106, 156
   bibliog. 111

Paull, H. B. (trans.) 112
Paur-Ulrich, M. 235
Peachey, C. (trans.) 51, 52
Peacock pie (de la Mare) 262
Peau d'âne (Perrault) 29
Pedersen, V. (illus.) 52, illus. 47, 50
Penny plain (Stevenson) 155
Pentamerone, The (Basile) 38
   illus. 27
Penzer, N. M. 39
Perrault, Charles xii, 22, 24, 28, 29–31, 32, 38
   and Hans Fischer 242
   bibliog. 39–40
   illus. 29
Pestalozzi, J. H. 130, 134, 250, 251, 253
Pet lamb, The (Spyri) 255
Peter and the wolf (Prokofiev) 245
Peter Pan (Barrie) 71, 76–77, 78, 80, 83, 87
Peter Rabbit (Potter) 208–11
   illus. 209
Peter Schlemihl (Chamisso) 86
Peterli am Lift (Bolt) 254
Petit prince, Le (Saint-Exupéry) 87, 93–98
   bibliog. 98
   illus. 94
Petrides, Heidrun (illus.) 271
Phillipps, W. F. (illus.) 40
Photography 142, 145–51
   plates XIV, XV
Piacevoli Notti (Straparola) 26
Picture-book of knowledge 144
Picture-book without pictures (Andersen) 26,
   48, 50
Picture-books 201–43
   in America 232–3
   in Czechoslovakia 226–7
   in Denmark 229–30
   in East Europe 224–9
   in England 228, 230–1
   in France 213, 225, 231–2
   in Germany 215–24
   in Italy 232
   in Norway 230
   in Poland 227–9
   in Russia 224–5
   in Sweden 207–8, 229–30
   in Switzerland 204, 233–43
   and children's experience 201–2, 213–15,
    224, 236
   and comics 161, 167
   and education 127–44, 203–4, 216, 243
   and fairy stories 235, 240–2
   and graphic techniques 202–3, 224–5
   and nursery rhymes 2, 201
   and personified nature 207–11
   and photography 145–51
   and politics 180–3
   internationalism and 213
   bibliog. 243–5

Picture-sheets 152–9
Pierre, Bernardin de Saint- 106
Pilote de guerre (Saint-Exupéry) 97
    bibliog. 98
Pimpelmaus, Die (Roser) 222
Pinkhoff, Clara A. 193, 194
Pinocchio (Collodi) 49, 77
    bibliog. 91
Pioneers, The (Cooper) 116–19
Pippi Longstocking (Lindgren) 81–83
    and Russia 189–90
    bibliog. 91
    illus. 83
Pirates in the deep green sea (Linklater) 150,
    261
Pitschi (Fischer) 242, 244
Planché, J. R. 63
Plasch, Barba 37, 254
    illus. 38
Pleiades Books 140
Plischke, Hans 118, 273
Plouf, canard sauvage (Lida) 137
Pocci, Franz xvi, 19, 51, 158, 164
    biog. 283
    illus. 154
Poetry for children xv, 9–11, 262–5
Poland
    and educational books 143
    and picture-books 227–9
    bibliog. 279
Politics and children's books 173–94, 263,
    265
    illus. 175, 191
    plates XVI, XVII
Portal, Colette 141
Portch, E. (trans.) 91
Postl, K. *see* Sealsfield, C.
Potter, Beatrix 208–11
    illus. 209
Prairie, The (Cooper) 116–18
Prinz Eugen (Hofmannsthal) 263
Prinz Grünewald und Perlenfein (Hoffmann)
    59
Prokofiev, Serge 245
Puffin Picture Books 139, 205 *n*
Puppetry 226
Purrkin (Lada) 226, 244
Puss-in-boots (Fischer) 242, 244
Putte i blåbärsskogen (Beskow) 207–8

Rackham, A. (illus.) 19, 71, 220
    illus. 19
Ramsden, E. (trans.) 91
Rapp, Rita (illus.) 230
    bibliog. 245
Rapunzel (Grimm) 244
Rasmus and the tramp (Lindgren) 91
Realism
    and cowboys 120–2

Realism (*cont.*):
    and photography 145–51
    in fiction 22
Red balloon, The (Lamorisse) 151
Red Indians 113–26, 174–6
*Red Riding Hood, see Little Red Riding
    Hood*
Reformation, and education 129
Reidel, Marlene (illus.) 222
    bibliog. 245
Reineke Fuchs 31
Reschofsky, Jean (illus.) 151
Reyher, Becky 225
Richter, Ludwig (illus.) 23, 162
    biog. 283, illus. 23
Ridge, Antonia (trans.) 144
Rikejte si se mnou (Hrubin) 226
Ringelnatz, Joachim 263–4
Rinser, Luise 140 *n*, 260
Riwkin-Brick, Anna 149, 151
Robinson, W. Heath (illus.) 40, 262
Robinson Crusoe (Defoe) xii, 99–111
    and Cooper 114, 116
    illus. 100
Robinson der Jüngere (Campe) xiii, 103–6
    bibliog. 111
    illus. 101
Robinsonnades 31, 99, 105, 252
    bibliog. 111, 273
Rodari, Gianni 190
Rojankovsky, F. (illus.) 137, 139, 225
Rolland, R. 184
Romanticism
    and cowboys 115, 116–22
    and fairy stories 22, 32
    and nursery rhymes 6
    and Robinson Crusoe 110
Roome, W. (trans.) 172
Roscoe, William xvi
Rose, Gerald 231
Roser, Wiltrud 222
Ross, Diana 230
Ross, Michael (trans.) 255
Rote Zora, Die (Held) 180
Roth-Streiff, Lili (illus.) 235
Rousseau, Jean-Jacques xii, 118, 174
    and Robinson Crusoe 102–4
Routledge, George (publisher) 62, 203
Rum-pum-pum (Fischer) 244
Rümann, Arthur 269, 277
Rumpumpel (Dehmel) 215–16, 263
Russia 183–90
    and picture-books 224–5
    children's book production 183–4
    children's literature 184–90
    bibliog. 280
    plates XIII, XXII

Sadako will leben (Bruckner) 193

Saint-Exupéry, Antoine de 93–98
  bibliog. 98
  biog. 283
  illus. 94
Saint-Pierre, Bernardin de 106
Salgari, Emilio 126
Samivel 231, 243
  plate XXVII
Sanchez-Silva, J. M. 86–87
  bibliog. 92
Sandford and Merton (Day)
  Swedish illus. xvii
Sandman, The 2, 10
Scancer, Jan Marcin 143, 228
Scharl, J. (illus.) 40
Schauensee, Zita de (trans.) 194
Scheel, Marianne 140 *n*, 220
  bibliog. 245
  illus. 11
Schellen-Ursli (Chönz) 236–9
  illus. 238
Scheper-Berkenkamp, Lou (illus.) 221
  plate XXI
Schmid, Christoph von xv
  biog. 283
Schnabel, Gottfried 106
Schnitter, Rosie 235
  plate XX
Schönsten Märchen der Welt, Die (Tetzner)
  37
Schramm, U. (illus.) 40
Schwab, G. xv, 32
Schwarze Schimmel, Der (Heimeran) 220
Schwarzen Brüder, Die (Tetzner) 177
Schweizerische Robinson, Der (Wyss) 106–11
  bibliog. 111–12
  plate XII
Sealsfield, Charles 120–22
  and May 124
  biog. 283
Séchan, Edmond 150
Sechs Geschichten für Nichten und Neffen
  (Busch) 164
Ségur, Comtesse de xvi
  biog. 284
Seidmann-Freud, Tom 140, 216
  illus. 217
Selkirk, Alexander 102
Sequence rhymes 14–17
Serraillier, Ian 180 *n*, 243
Seven ravens, The (Grimm) 244
Sharp, William (illus.) 255
Shepard, E. H. (illus.) 52
Sheppard, Katya (trans.) 244
Sherwood, M. M. xiii
Siemaszko, Olga (illus.) 229
Sigismund Rüstig (Marryat) 110
Sigsgaard, Jens 229, 245
Silva, J. M. Sanchez-, *see* Sanchez-Silva

Simrock, K. xv, 32
Singing town, The (Egner) 84
  bibliog. 91
Sketch-Book of Geoffrey Crayon, Gent.
  (Irving) 115
Sladek, Josef 227
  plate XXII
Slavery 174
Sleeping Beauty, The (Basile) 21–22, 28
Sleeping beauty, The (Grimm) 244
Slevogt, M. (illus.) 116
Smith, Audrey (illus.) 194
Snowstorm, The (Chönz) 243
So lebt man anderswo (Böer) 144
Sonne im alten Kinderlied, Die 213–14
Songs of innocence (Blake) 262
Soviet Union *see* Russia
Spain
  and educational books 142
  popular literature 155
  illus. (comic) 168
  bibliog. 279
Speaight, George 155, 275
Speckter, Otto (illus.) 158
Spiegelklöpfler, Die (vogel) 261
Spier, Peter (illus.) 194
Spink, R. (trans.) 52
Spy, The (Cooper) 116
Spyri, Johanna 251–3, 254, illus. 252
  bibliog. 255
  biog. 284
Stefula, Georgy 222
Steinbeck, John 166
Steinrisser, C. (illus.) 38
Stern über der Mauer (Noack) 192
Sterrekinderen (Pinkhoff) 193
Steuben, Fritz 126
Stevenson, R. L. 155, 256–7, 262
Stifter, Adalbert 116, 118, 119
Stimmen der Völker (Herder) 6, 32
Stobbs, W. (illus.) 40, 231
Story of a puppet, The (Collodi) 78 *n*
Story-telling 25, 32, 37–38
  and Andersen 48
  and Carroll 68
  in Japan 271
  illus. 23
  plates 2, 3
Stowe, H. Beecher xvii, 173–4
  illus. 175
Stoys Bilderakademie 135
Straparola, G. F. 26
Streicher, Julius 183
Streiff, L. Roth- (illus.) 235
Strøyer, Poul (illus.) 230
  bibliog. 244, 245
Struwwelpeter (Hoffmann) xvi, 53–63, 71, 73,
  161–2, 205
  bibliog. 62–63

Struwwelpeter (cont.):
  illus. 57
  plate VI
  see also *English Struwwelpeter*
Stuffer, Herbert (publisher) 140, 148 *n*, 149,
  159, 216
Sucksdorff, A. B. 150, 151
Svizzero (Bolt) 254
Sweden
  and children's books 260
  and photographic books 149, 151
  and picture-books 207, 229–30
  bibliog. 279
Swiss family Robinson, The (Wyss) 106–11,
  250–1, 252
  bibliog. 111–12
  illus. 108–9
  plate XII
Switzerland
  and picture-books 204, 233–43, illus. 238,
    plate XX
  children's literature in 246–54
  popular literature 155, 158
  bibliog. 254–5, 280
Symonds, R. (trans.) 92, 244

Tappolet, Berta (illus.) 235, 254
  plate XX
Taylor, Ann and Jane xvi
Taylor, J. E. (trans.) 38
Télémaque (Fénelon) 104
Television 148 *n*, 170
Tenniel, J. (illus.) 71
Terre des hommes (Saint-Exupéry) 98
Tetzner, L. 37, 179–80, 194
Theresienstadt 1942–4 192, 194
  plate XVII
Thienhaus, Peter 140 *n*
Thom, Andreas 214–15
*Thousand and one nights, The, see Arabian
  nights*
Three royal monkeys, The (de la Mare) 262
Through the looking-glass (Carroll) 68–69
Thun, Roderich 141
Timm Thaler (Krüss) 85
Tintin (Hergé) 170–1
Tirtsa (Pinkhoff) 193
Tisdall, Hans 140
Tistou, les pouces verts (Druon) 89–91
Tistou of the green fingers (Druon) 92
Tokeah (Sealsfield) 120
Tolkien, J. R. R. 1 *n*
Tolstoy, L. 37
Tom Sawyer (Twain) 259
Tomten, The (Lindgren) 230, 245
Toy-books 155, 216–7
Träumereien am Französischen Kamin (Volk-
  mann-Leander) 36
Travelling musicians, The (Grimm) 244

Travers, P. L. 79
Treasure Island (Stevenson) 256–7
Trier, Walter (illus.) 194, 266
Trnka, Jiří (illus.) 40, 226–7, 228
  bibliog. 245
  biog. 284
Turner, M. (trans.) 91
Tuwim, Juljan 227–8
  bibliog. 244
Twain, Mark xviii, 56, 259, 260

U.S.S.R. *see* Russia
Uffer, L. 37, 254
  illus. 38
Ullrich, Hermann 111, 273
Ulrich, M. Paur- (illus.) 235
Uncle Remus (Harris) xviii
Uncle Tom's cabin (Stowe) 114, 173–4
  illus. 175
Under the window (Greenaway) 203
Ungermann, Arne 229
  bibliog. 245

Vasnetsov, X. A. (illus.) 225
Vegetabull (le Witt) 228
Vevi (Lillegg) 85
Viehmännin, Die 32
  plate II
Vietor, Else Wenz- 219–20
Vogelbart (Ehmcke) 219
Volkmann-Leander, R. von 36
Volksbücher xiii, 31, 155, 251
  and Robinson Crusoe 104, 106
Volksmärchen der Deutschen, Die (Musäus)
  xv, 31
Von Cooper bis Karl May (Plischke) 118, 273
Vries, Leonard de 193, 194, 278

Wacik, F. (illus.) 263
Wackernagel, E. Hosch- 234–5
Waldröschen (May) 123
Warne, Frederick (publisher) 203, 210–11
Water babies, The (Kingsley) 43, 177
Watts, I. xvi
Wedekind, Frank 263
Weise, Gustav (publisher) 152, 158
Wells, H. G. 184
Wendlandt, Kurth (illus.) 223
  bibliog. 245
Wenz-Vietor, Else (illus.) 219–20
Werenskiold, E. (illus.) 40
Wesselsky, A. 35
Whistler, R. (illus.) 52
Wiberg, Harald (illus.) 230
  bibliog. 245
Widdy-Widdy-Wurkey (Fyleman) 20
Wiesenzwerge, Die (Kreidolf) 204, 206–7
Wild white stallion, The (Guillot) 151
Wildsmith, Brian (illus.) 39, 231

Wilhelm, Charles 207 *n*
Williams-Ellis, A. 39, 40
Wimmer, Hed 150
Wind in the willows, The (Grahame) 78
Wind on the moon (Linklater) 150, 261
Wind, sand and stars (Saint-Exupéry) 98
Winnetou (May) 117, 123–6
Winnie-the-Pooh (Milne) 78, 261
Winona (Eastman) 126
Winter, Klaus (illus.) 141
With, Claire 140–1
Witzleben, Uta von 149
Wolf and the seven little kids (Grimm) 235, 244
Wolfe, Lawrence (trans.) 194
Wolgast, Heinrich 203, 277
Wonderful farm, The (Aymé) 92
Wonderful stories for children (Anderson) 51
Wood, Leslie 230
Woods, Katherine (trans.) 98
World we live in, The 143

Wunderhaus, Das (Seidmann-Freud) 216
Wyss, J. D. (and sons) 106–12, 250–1
    illus. 108–9 plate XII
    bibliog 111–12

Ylla (photog.) 146–7
    bibliog. 151

Zábransky, Adolf (illus.) 227
    bibliog. 245
    plate XXII
Zauberboot, Das (Seidmann-Freud) 216
    illus. 217
Zimmern, H. 39
Zimnik, Reiner (illus.) 222, 224
    bibliog. 245
    illus. 223
Zschokke, Heinrich 120
Zürich, *Neujahrsblätter* 246–50
    illus. 248
Zwieselchen (Bergengruen) 261